The Complete
Keto Air Fryer
Cookbook For Beginners

1200+ Mouth-watering and Healthy Recipes
to lose weight and Get Great Look

Teresa McCall

CONTENTS

Chapter 4 Beef, Pork, And Lamb Recipes 46

Chapter 5 Fish And Seafood Recipes 64

Chapter 6 Poultry Recipes 79

Chapter 7 Side Dishes Recipes 97

Chapter 8 Main, Sides And Vegetarian Recipes 112

Chapter 9 Desserts Recipes 129

APPENDIX : Recipes Index 145

INTRODUCTION

Welcome!I am thrilled and grateful you make the purchase this The Complete Keto Air Fryer Cookbook. Weather you are new or a pro to Keto diet, I will help you level up your Keto diet game by this cookbook.

Hi, My name is Teresa McCall. I am a fitness trainer, a cookbook author and a nutritionist. I've spent hundreds of hours cooking and testing recipes. And I've had about the same number of students, acquaintances, and sceptics ask me, "Will your Keto Air Fryer recipes help me lose weight easier and faster?" I look them right in the eye and say, "YES!"

I'll show you that delicious meals can be prepared quickly and easily without a long list of ingredients or complicated steps. I've combined my decades of experience writing cookbooks, teaching home-made Keto diet classes, and doing extensive work developing recipes for the Keto Air Fryer to come up with five hundred recipes featuring just for Keto diet.

In this book you will find out 500 delicious, simple, easy recipes with categorizes: breakfast, Snacks & appetizer, fish & seafood, poultry, side dishes, main course, vegetarian, dessert recipes etc. And it will make sure you stick to your Keto diet 365 days for every occasion. From everyday meal, New Years dinner, Christmas dinner, birthday party, wedding party, Thanksgiving dinner to family get-together party.

In this book you will find a selection of keto friendly recipes that are both simple to prepare and cook using an air fryer. My aim is to offer a wide variety of healthful keto recipes that help you stay on track, are stress free and suitable for the whole family to enjoy.

The ingredients I use are super common that you can easily get from most grocery stores. I noted down which brands I find work best in the book. So you can avoid lot of trouble to find out which fit the Keto diet most.

I know that your time is limited and you're probably coming to the kitchen at "hungry o'clock."That's why I include information at the head of every recipe that will tell you exactly how much active time (chopping, sautéing) and how much total time you'll need for each recipe.

Speaking of time, look for tasty tips notes for ideas on making the recipe faster, choosing the best ingredients, or changing up the recipe with additional ideas so you can make the recipe your own and make the most of whatever ingredients you happen to have on hand.

Armed with this complete Keto Air Fryer cookbook and your trusty Air Fryer, I hope you'll discover familiar favorites made easy and exciting new dishes to add to your regular dinner rotation, this book is definitely worth having to get the most out of your Air Fryer, and they're inexpensive.

I hope you become more confident with Keto diet and believe if you stick with long enough, you will witness your wonderful body and health change. Good luck and bon appétit!

KETO DIET
FOOD PYRAMID

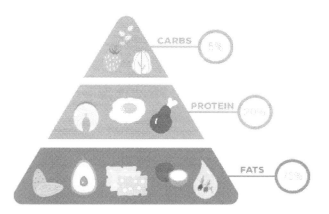

Chapter 1 Keto Diet

What is Ketogenic Diet?

A ketogenic diet is essentially a very strict high-fat, moderate-protein and low-carb diet. When you cut down on your carbohydrate intake, your body eventually enters a state known as ketosis.

When you reach ketosis, your body burns fat instead of carbohydrates from food, and produces ketones, which are acids your body can use as fuel. This is very much an individualised process, however, and some people will need a more restricted diet than others to begin producing sufficient ketones.

The keto diet involves cutting out foods like bread, pasta, rice and sugar, so you take in less than 50g of carbohydrates per day. The standard keto diet is usually made up of 55 – 60% fat, 30 – 35% protein and 5 – 10% carbohydrates.

How Does the Ketogenic Diet Work?

Macronutrient counting is the base of the ketogenic diet.

Tracking how many grams of fat, protein, and carbohydrates you eat tells you if you are on track to be in ketosis, which we'll explain below. The important part of macro tracking is to monitor the ratio of fat to protein plus carbs.

The goal in the ketogenic diet is a ratio of three grams of fat for every one gram of protein and carbs you have. Controlling this ratio affects your metabolism, forcing your

body to burn fat for the primary energy source.

Typically, this is done by drastically decreasing your total carbohydrate intake to less than 50 grams per day, shifting your body from using carbs for energy to ketosis.

The Health benefits of the keto diet

Researchers and keto diet enthusiasts attribute several health benefits to the keto lifestyle, including:

Blood glucose control

Carbs are the main contributors of blood sugars. The consumption of very low amounts of carbs eliminates large rises in blood sugar levels. Studies have shown that keto diets are effective at reducing HbA1c, which is the long-term measure of blood glucose control.

Improved blood pressure levels

Reduction of blood pressure have been observed in people who are overweight or with type 2 diabetes on keto diets.

Induces satiety

Keto diets are effective at reducing appetite and cravings, promoting feelings of fullness, and reducing preference for sugary foods. In a state of ketosis, the body gets used to obtaining energy from breaking down body fat.

Helps treat epilepsy among children

The keto diet has been used long ago for the treatment of epilepsy among children because both ketones and decanoic acid, another chemical produced by this diet, help to prevent seizures.

Helps manage other medical conditions

As ketones are a brain-healthy fuel source because of its neuroprotective effects, researchers are also conducting ongoing research to look into the possible benefits of the keto diet for conditions including brain disorders such as Alzheimer's disease and Parkinson›s disease.

Keto-Friendly Foods to Eat

When you are sticking to the ketogenic diet scheme, there are some foods should constitute your diet and some that you should avoid.

Examples of keto-centric foods are:

Eggs: Organic and pastured eggs.

Poultry: Turkey and chicken.

Fatty fish: Mackerel, herring, and wild-caught salmon.

Meat: Pork, venison, grass-fed beef, bison, and organ meats.

Full-fat dairy: Cream, butter, and yogurt.

Full-fat cheese: Brie, mozzarella, cheddar, cream cheese, and goat cheese.

Seeds and nuts: Almonds, macadamia nuts, pumpkin seeds, walnuts, flaxseeds, and peanuts.

Nut butter: Cashew butter, almond, and natural peanut.

Healthy fats: Avocado oil, olive oil, coconut oil, sesame oil, and coconut butter.

Avocados: You can add whole avocados to almost any snack or meal.

Non-starchy vegetables: Tomatoes, broccoli, greens, peppers, and mushrooms.

Condiments: Vinegar, pepper, salt, spices, fresh herbs, and lemon juice.

Foods to Stay Away From

When you are observing the ketogenic diet, there are some foods that you need to stay away from. These are generally foods that are rich in carbohydrates. Below are some of the foods that you should avoid to get the most in your ketogenic diet commitments.

Baked Foods and Bread: Whole-wheat bread, white bread, cookies, crackers, rolls, and doughnuts.

Sugary and Sweets Foods: Ice cream, sugar, maple syrup, candy, coconut sugar, and agave syrup.

Sweetened Beverages: Juice, soda, sports drinks, and sweetened teas.

Pasta: Noodles and spaghetti.

Grain products and Grains: Rice, wheat, tortillas, breakfast cereals, and oats.

Starchy vegetables: Sweet potatoes, potatoes, corn, butternut squash, pumpkin, and peas.

Legumes and Beans: Chickpeas, black beans, kidney beans, and lentils.

Fruit: Grapes, citrus, pineapples, and bananas.

High-carb Sauces: Dipping sauces, sugar-rich salad dressings, and Barbecue sauce.

Some Alcoholic Beverages: Sugar-rich mixed beverages and beer.

Even though it is not advisable to consume carbohydrate-rich foods when you are on the ketogenic diet scheme, fruits with low-glycemic values like berries may be taken in restricted amounts if you are sticking to a keto-centric macronutrient range.

Have Your Air Fryer Preheated

If you bring an air fryer that does not come with preheat settings, then set it to your preferred temperature and let it work for some three minutes before putting your food inside.

Utilize Oil on Certain Foods

There are some types of foods that you can make crisp using oil. Some others do not require oil to achieve the same results.

Lubricate the Air Fryer Basket

Take a little time and lubricate the basket of your air fryer. Get this done even the food you are preparing does not need oil. This helps prevent the food from becoming non-sticky.

Use Aerosol Spray Cans

Using an aerosol spray can can keep food from sticking on the air fryer basket, and thus reduce the burden of cleaning it.

Do Not Choke the Air Fryer Basket

If you desire that your fried meals become crispy, then you must keep the basket relatively free. Don't stuff it with too many things. If you do, you risk preventing whatever you are preparing from browning and crisping. If you don't want this to occur, then prepare your meal in different batches or buy a larger air fryer.

Shake the Basket

When you are preparing smaller food like French fries, chicken wings, it makes sense that you frequently shake the air fryer basket for some minutes to make sure the cooking is even.

Spray Midway While Cooking

Foods that are coated need to be sprayed. And, don't forget to spray dry flour patches that will occur midway while air frying your foods.

Put Water at the Bottom

If you are preparing a greasy meal with your air fryer, do not be astonished if you discover that some white smoke is coming out of the apparatus. All you need to do to address this is to put a small amount of water at the bottom of your device's basket.

Be Cautious of Petite-Sized Items

All air fryers feature a very effective fan fixed atop them. This fan makes some items with lighter weight to be swept up by the fan and this can be very dangerous.

Regulate the Temperature for Particular Foods

Sometimes, it can be appealing to crank the temperature of your air fryer to its maximum so that it can work faster, but you need to take great care because certain foods can quickly dry out.

One great rule that works the magic is to regulate the time and heat to the time required for the preparation of the meal you are preparing. If you regulate the temperature below 350°F for twenty minutes in your oven, but for your air fryer, you can decrease the temperature to about 320°F and cook the meal for sixteen minutes.

Buy a Good Thermometer

You must acquire a quick-read thermometer for your air fryer particularly in the preparation of certain kinds of meats, such as pork, chicken, and steak.

BASIC KITCHEN CONVERSIONS & EQUIVALENTS

DRY MEASUREMENTS CONVERSION CHART

3 TEASPOONS = 1 TABLESPOON = 1/16 CUP

6 TEASPOONS = 2 TABLESPOONS = 1/8 CUP

12 TEASPOONS = 4 TABLESPOONS = 1/4 CUP

24 TEASPOONS = 8 TABLESPOONS = 1/2 CUP

36 TEASPOONS = 12 TABLESPOONS = 3/4 CUP

48 TEASPOONS = 16 TABLESPOONS = 1 CUP

METRIC TO US COOKING CONVERSIONS

OVEN TEMPERATURES

120 °C = 250 °F

160 °C = 320 °F

180° C = 350 °F

205 °C = 400 °F

220 °C = 425 °F

LIQUID MEASUREMENTS CONVERSION CHART

8 FLUID OUNCES = 1 CUP = 1/2 PINT = 1/4 QUART

16 FLUID OUNCES = 2 CUPS = 1 PINT = 1/2 QUART

32 FLUID OUNCES = 4 CUPS = 2 PINTS = 1 QUART = 1/4 GALLON

128 FLUID OUNCES = 16 CUPS = 8 PINTS = 4 QUARTS = 1 GALLON

BAKING IN GRAMS

1 CUP FLOUR = 140 GRAMS

1 CUP SUGAR = 150 GRAMS

1 CUP POWDERED SUGAR = 160 GRAMS

1 CUP HEAVY CREAM = 235 GRAMS

VOLUME

1 MILLILITER = 1/5 TEASPOON

5 ML = 1 TEASPOON

15 ML = 1 TABLESPOON

240 ML = 1 CUP OR 8 FLUID OUNCES

1 LITER = 34 FL. OUNCES

WEIGHT

1 GRAM = .035 OUNCES

100 GRAMS = 3.5 OUNCES

500 GRAMS = 1.1 POUNDS

1 KILOGRAM = 35 OUNCES

US TO METRIC COOKING CONVERSIONS

1/5 TSP = 1 ML

1 TSP = 5 ML

1 TBSP = 15 ML

1 FL OUNCE = 30 ML

1 CUP = 237 ML

1 PINT (2 CUPS) = 473 ML

1 QUART (4 CUPS) = .95 LITER

1 GALLON (16 CUPS) = 3.8 LITERS

1 OZ = 28 GRAMS

1 POUND = 454 GRAMS

BUTTER

1 CUP BUTTER = 2 STICKS = 8 OUNCES = 230 GRAMS = 8 TABLESPOONS

WHAT DOES 1 CUP EQUAL

1 CUP = 8 FLUID OUNCES

1 CUP = 16 TABLESPOONS

1 CUP = 48 TEASPOONS

1 CUP = 1/2 PINT

1 CUP = 1/4 QUART

1 CUP = 1/16 GALLON

1 CUP = 240 ML

BAKING PAN CONVERSIONS

1 CUP ALL-PURPOSE FLOUR = 4.5 OZ

1 CUP ROLLED OATS = 3 OZ 1 LARGE EGG = 1.7 OZ

1 CUP BUTTER = 8 OZ 1 CUP MILK = 8 OZ

1 CUP HEAVY CREAM = 8.4 OZ

1 CUP GRANULATED SUGAR = 7.1 OZ

1 CUP PACKED BROWN SUGAR = 7.75 OZ

1 CUP VEGETABLE OIL = 7.7 OZ

1 CUP UNSIFTED POWDERED SUGAR = 4.4 OZ

BAKING PAN CONVERSIONS

9-INCH ROUND CAKE PAN = 12 CUPS

10-INCH TUBE PAN =16 CUPS

11-INCH BUNDT PAN = 12 CUPS

9-INCH SPRINGFORM PAN = 10 CUPS

9 X 5 INCH LOAF PAN = 8 CUPS

9-INCH SQUARE PAN = 8 CUPS

Chapter 2 Breakfast Recipes

Chapter 2 Breakfast Recipes

Lemony Cake

Servings: 6 | Cooking Time: 14 Minutes

Ingredients:
- 1 cup blanched finely ground almond flour
- ½ cup powdered erythritol
- ½ teaspoon baking powder
- ¼ cup unsalted butter, melted
- ¼ cup unsweetened almond milk
- 2 large eggs
- 1 teaspoon vanilla extract
- 1 medium lemon
- 1 teaspoon poppy seeds

Directions:
1. In a large bowl, mix almond flour, erythritol, baking powder, butter, almond milk, eggs, and vanilla.
2. Slice the lemon in half and squeeze the juice into a small bowl, then add to the batter.
3. Using a fine grater, zest the lemon and add 1 tablespoon of zest to the batter and stir. Add poppy seeds to batter.
4. Pour batter into nonstick 6-inch round cake pan. Place pan into the air fryer basket.
5. Adjust the temperature to 300°F (150°C) and set the timer for 14 minutes.
6. When fully cooked, a toothpick inserted in center will come out mostly clean. The cake will finish cooking and firm up as it cools. Serve at room temperature.

Nutrition:
- (per serving) calories 204 | fat 18 | protein 6 | total carbs 17 | fiber 15

Bacon Scrambled Eggs

Servings: 4 | Cooking Time: 10 Minutes

Ingredients:
- 6 oz. bacon
- 4 eggs
- 5 tablespoon heavy cream
- 1 tablespoon butter
- 1 teaspoon paprika
- ½ teaspoon nutmeg
- 1 teaspoon salt
- 1 teaspoon ground black pepper

Directions:
1. Chop the bacon into small pieces and sprinkle it with salt.
2. Mix to combine and put in the air fryer basket.
3. Preheat the air fryer to 360 F and cook the bacon for 5 minutes.
4. Meanwhile, crack the eggs in a bowl and whisk them using a hand whisker.
5. Sprinkle the egg mixture with paprika, nutmeg, and ground black pepper.
6. Whisk egg mixture gently.
7. Toss the butter into the bacon and pour the egg mixture.
8. Add the heavy cream and cook for 2 minutes.
9. Stir the mixture with a spatula until you get scrambled eggs and cook for 3 minutes more.

10. Transfer onto serving plates.

Nutrition:
- (per serving) calories 387 | fat 32.1 | protein 21.9 | total carbs 2.3 | fiber 0.4

Crunchy Canadian Bacon

Servings: 4 | Cooking Time: 10 Minutes

Ingredients:
- ½ teaspoon ground thyme
- ½ teaspoon ground coriander
- ¼ teaspoon ground black pepper
- ½ teaspoon salt
- 1 teaspoon cream
- 10 oz. Canadian bacon

Directions:
1. Slice Canadian bacon.
2. Combine the ground thyme, ground coriander, ground black pepper, and salt in the shallow bowl. Shake gently.
3. Then sprinkle the sliced bacon with the spices.
4. Preheat the air fryer to 360 F.
5. Put the prepared sliced bacon in the air fryer and cook it for 5 minutes.
6. Turn the bacon over and cook it for 5 minutes more.
7. When the bacon is cooked and slightly crunchy remove from the air fryer and serve it with the cream.

Nutrition:
- (per serving) calories 150 | fat 6.7 | protein 19.6 | total carbs 1.9 | fiber 0.1

Eggs In Zucchini Nests

Servings: 4 | Cooking Time: 7 Minutes

Ingredients:
- 8 oz. zucchini
- 4 eggs
- 4 oz. Cheddar cheese, shredded
- ¼ teaspoon salt
- ½ teaspoon ground black pepper
- ½ teaspoon paprika
- 4 teaspoon butter

Directions:
1. Grate the zucchini.
2. Grease 4 ramekins with butter.
3. Add the grated zucchini to make the shape of the nests.
4. Sprinkle the zucchini nests with the salt, ground black pepper, and paprika.
5. Crack the eggs into the zucchini nests and sprinkle each one with the shredded cheese.
6. Preheat the air fryer to 360 F.
7. Put the ramekins in the air fryer basket and cook for 7 minutes.
8. When the zucchini nests are cooked – let them chill for 2-3 minutes.

Nutrition:
- (per serving) calories 221 | fat 17.7 | protein 13.4 | total carbs 2.9 | fiber 0.8

Cauliflower Hash Browns

Servings: 4 | Cooking Time: 12 Minutes

Ingredients:
- 1 (12-ounce / 340-g) steamer bag cauliflower
- 1 large egg
- 1 cup shredded sharp Cheddar cheese

Directions:
1. Place the bag in microwave and cook according to package instructions. Allow it to cool completely and put cauliflower into a cheesecloth or kitchen towel and squeeze to remove excess moisture.
2. Mash cauliflower with a fork and add egg and cheese.
3. Cut a piece of parchment to fit your air fryer basket. Take ¼ of the mixture and form it into a hash brown patty shape. Place it onto the parchment and into the air fryer basket, working in batches if necessary.
4. Adjust the temperature to 400°F (205°C) and set the timer for 12 minutes.
5. Flip the hash browns halfway through the cooking time. When completely cooked, they will be golden brown. Serve immediately.

Nutrition:
- (per serving) calories 153 | fat 9 | protein 10 | total carbs 5 | fiber 3

Sausage Eggs With Smoky Mustard Sauce

Servings: 8 | Cooking Time: 12 Minutes

Ingredients:
- 1 pound (454 g) pork sausage
- 8 soft-boiled or hard-boiled eggs, peeled
- 1 large egg
- 2 tablespoons milk
- 1 cup crushed pork rinds
- Smoky Mustard Sauce:
- ¼ cup mayonnaise
- 2 tablespoons sour cream
- 1 tablespoon Dijon mustard
- 1 teaspoon chipotle hot sauce

Directions:
1. Preheat the air fryer to 390°F (199°C).
2. Divide the sausage into 8 portions. Take each portion of sausage, pat it down into a patty, and place 1 egg in the middle, gently wrapping the sausage around the egg until the egg is completely covered. (Wet your hands slightly if you find the sausage to be too sticky.) Repeat with the remaining eggs and sausage.
3. In a small shallow bowl, whisk the egg and milk until frothy. In another shallow bowl, place the crushed pork rinds. Working one at a time, dip a sausage-wrapped egg into the beaten egg and then into the pork rinds, gently rolling to coat evenly. Repeat with the remaining sausage-wrapped eggs.
4. Arrange the eggs in a single layer in the air fryer basket, and lightly spray with olive oil. Air fry for 10 to 12 minutes, pausing halfway through the baking time to turn the eggs, until the eggs are hot and the sausage is cooked through.
5. To make the sauce: In a small bowl, combine the mayonnaise, sour cream, Dijon, and hot sauce. Whisk until thoroughly combined. Serve with the Scotch eggs.

Nutrition:
- (per serving) calories 340 | fat 28 | protein 22 | total carbs 1 | fiber 1

Pecan And Almond Granola

Servings: 6 | Cooking Time: 5 Minutes

Ingredients:
- 2 cups pecans, chopped
- 1 cup unsweetened coconut flakes
- 1 cup almond slivers
- ⅓ cup sunflower seeds
- ¼ cup golden flaxseed
- ¼ cup low-carb, sugar-free chocolate chips
- ¼ cup granular erythritol
- 2 tablespoons unsalted butter
- 1 teaspoon ground cinnamon

Directions:
1. In a large bowl, mix all ingredients.
2. Place the mixture into a 4-cup round baking dish. Place dish into the air fryer basket.
3. Adjust the temperature to 320°F (160°C) and set the timer for 5 minutes.
4. Allow it to cool completely before serving.

Nutrition:
- (per serving) calories 617 | fat 55 | protein 11 | total carbs 32 | fiber 21

Flax Meal Porridge

Servings: 7 | Cooking Time: 8 Minutes

Ingredients:
- 2 tablespoon sesame seeds
- 4 tablespoon chia seeds
- 1 cup almond milk
- 3 tablespoon flax meal
- 1 teaspoon stevia
- 1 tablespoon butter
- ½ teaspoon vanilla extract

Directions:
1. Preheat the air fryer to 375 F.
2. Put the sesame seeds, chia seeds, almond milk, flax meal, stevia, and butter in the air fryer basket tray.
3. Add the vanilla extract and cook the porridge for 8 minutes.
4. Stir the porridge carefully and leave it for 5 minutes to rest.
5. Transfer to serving bowls or ramekins.

Nutrition:
- (per serving) calories 198 | fat 21.7 | protein 4.8 | total carbs 8.3 | fiber 6.4

Breakfast Blackberry Muffins

Servings: 5 | Cooking Time: 10 Minutes

Ingredients:
- 1 teaspoon apple cider vinegar
- 1 cup almond flour
- 4 tablespoon butter
- 6 tablespoon almond milk
- 1 teaspoon baking soda
- 3 oz. blackberry
- ½ teaspoon salt
- 3 teaspoon stevia
- 1 teaspoon vanilla extract

Directions:
1. Put the almond flour in a mixing bowl.
2. Add baking soda, salt, stevia, and vanilla extract.

3. Add butter, almond milk, and apple cider vinegar.
4. Crush the blackberries gently and add into the almond flour mixture.
5. Stir carefully with a fork until well combined.
6. Leave the mixture to one side for 5 minutes.
7. Meanwhile, preheat the air fryer to 400 F.
8. Prepare the muffin molds.
9. Pour the dough in the muffin molds filling half way.
10. Put the muffing molds in the air fryer basket. Close the air fryer.
11. Cook the muffins for 10 minutes.
12. Remove the muffins from the air fryer basket.
13. Chill them until warm.
14. Serve.

Nutrition:
• (per serving) calories 165 | fat 16.4 | protein 2 | total carbs 4 | fiber 1.9

Breakfast Pizza

Servings:1 | Cooking Time: 8 Minutes

Ingredients:
• 2 large eggs
• ¼ cup unsweetened, unflavored almond milk (or unflavored hemp milk for nut-free)
• ¼ teaspoon fine sea salt
• ⅛ teaspoon ground black pepper
• ¼ cup diced onions
• ¼ cup shredded Parmesan cheese (omit for dairy-free)
• 6 pepperoni slices (omit for vegetarian)
• ¼ teaspoon dried oregano leaves
• ¼ cup pizza sauce, warmed, for serving

Directions:
1. Preheat the air fryer to 350°F. Grease a 6 by 3-inch cake pan.
2. In a small bowl, use a fork to whisk together the eggs, almond milk, salt, and pepper. Add the onions and stir to mix. Pour the mixture into the greased pan. Top with the cheese (if using), pepperoni slices (if using), and oregano.
3. Place the pan in the air fryer and cook for 8 minutes, or until the eggs are cooked to your liking.
4. Loosen the eggs from the sides of the pan with a spatula and place them on a serving plate. Drizzle the pizza sauce on top. Best served fresh.

Nutrition:
• (per serving)   calories 357 | fat 25g | protein 24g | total carbs 9g | fiber 2g

Bacon Lettuce Wraps

Servings: 4 | Cooking Time: 13 Minutes

Ingredients:
• 8 ounces (227 g) (about 12 slices) reduced-sodium bacon
• 8 tablespoons mayonnaise
• 8 large romaine lettuce leaves
• 4 Roma tomatoes, sliced
• Salt and freshly ground black pepper

Directions:
1. Arrange the bacon in a single layer in the air fryer basket. (It's OK if the bacon sits a bit on the sides.) Set the air fryer to 350°F (180ºC) and cook for 10 minutes. Check for crispiness and cook for 2 to 3 minutes longer if needed. Cook in batches, if necessary, and drain the grease in between batches.

2. Spread 1 tablespoon of mayonnaise on each of the lettuce leaves and top with the tomatoes and cooked bacon. Season to taste with salt and freshly ground black pepper. Roll the lettuce leaves as you would a burrito, securing with a toothpick if desired.

Nutrition:
• (per serving) calories 370 | fat 34 | protein 11 | total carbs 7 | fiber 4

Easy Bacon

Servings:2 | Cooking Time: 6 Minutes

Ingredients:
• 4 slices thin-cut bacon or beef bacon

Directions:
1. Spray the air fryer basket with avocado oil. Preheat the air fryer to 360°F.
2. Place the bacon in the air fryer basket in a single layer, spaced about ¼ inch apart. (I made mine into heart shapes and placed a small baking sheet on top to keep the shape.) Cook for 4 to 6 minutes (thicker bacon will take longer). Check the bacon after 4 minutes to make sure it is not overcooking.
3. Best served fresh. Store extras in an airtight container in the fridge for up to 4 days. Reheat in a preheated 360°F air fryer for 2 minutes, or until heated through.

Nutrition:
• (per serving)   calories 140 | fat 12g | protein 8g | total carbs 0g | fiber 0g

Herbed Eggs

Servings: 2 | Cooking Time: 17 Minutes

Ingredients:
• 4 eggs
• 1 teaspoon paprika
• 1 tablespoon cream
• 1 tablespoon chives
• ½ teaspoon salt
• 1 teaspoon dried parsley
• 1 teaspoon oregano

Directions:
1. Put the eggs in the air fryer basket and cook them for 17 minutes at 320 F.
2. Meanwhile, combine the cream, salt, dried parsley, and oregano in a shallow bowl.
3. Chop the chives and add to the cream mixture.
4. When the eggs are cooked – place them in the cold water and let them cool.
5. Once cooled, peel the eggs and cut them into halves.
6. Remove the egg yolks and add them to the cream mixture.
7. Mash well with a fork.
8. Then fill the egg whites with the cream-egg yolk mixture.
9. Serve immediately.

Nutrition:
• (per serving) calories 136 | fat 9.3 | protein 11.4 | total carbs 2.1 | fiber 0.8

Breakfast Cookies

Servings: 12 | Cooking Time: 15 Minutes

Ingredients:
- ½ cup coconut flour
- ½ cup almond flour
- 1/3 teaspoon salt
- 1 teaspoon baking powder
- 1 teaspoon apple cider vinegar
- 4 oz. bacon, cooked, chopped
- 3 tablespoon butter
- 1 tablespoon cream
- 1 egg

Directions:
1. Crack the egg in a bowl and whisk it.
2. Add the baking powder, apple cider vinegar, and cream.
3. Stir it gently and add butter.
4. Add salt, almond flour, and coconut flour.
5. Sprinkle the mixture with the chopped bacon and knead the dough until smooth, soft, and slightly sticky.
6. Preheat the air fryer to 360 F.
7. Cover the air fryer tray with foil.
8. Make 6 medium balls from the prepared dough and place the balls in the air fryer basket.
9. Cook the cookies for 15 minutes.
10. Allow to cool before serving.

Nutrition:
- (per serving) calories 182 | fat 13.1 | protein 8.1 | total carbs 6.7 | fiber 3.3

Cloud Eggs

Servings: 2 | Cooking Time: 4 Minutes

Ingredients:
- 2 eggs
- 1 teaspoon butter

Directions:
1. Separate the egg whites and egg yolks into separate bowls.
2. Whisk the egg whites with a hand mixer until you get strong white peaks.
3. Grease the Air Fryer basket tray with butter.
4. Preheat the Air Fryer to 300 F.
5. Make the medium clouds from the egg white peaks in the prepared Air Fryer basket tray.
6. Place the basket tray in the Air Fryer and cook the cloud eggs for 2 minutes.
7. Remove the basket from the Air Fryer, place the egg yolks in the center of every egg cloud, and return the basket back in the Air Fryer.
8. Cook the dish for 2 minutes.
9. Remove the cooked dish from the basket and serve.

Nutrition:
- (per serving) calories 80 | fat 6.3 | protein 5.6 | total carbs 0.3 | fiber 0

Mushroom Omelet

Servings: 9 | Cooking Time: 12 Minutes

Ingredients:
- 1 tablespoon flax seeds
- 7 eggs
- ½ cup cream cheese
- 4 oz. white mushrooms
- 1 teaspoon olive oil
- 1 teaspoon ground black pepper
- ½ teaspoon paprika
- ¼ teaspoon salt

Directions:
1. Slice the mushrooms and sprinkle them with the salt, paprika, and ground black pepper.
2. Preheat the air fryer to 400 F.
3. Grease the air fryer basket tray with olive oil and place the sliced mushrooms inside.
4. Cook the mushrooms for 3 minutes.
5. Stir them carefully after 2 minutes of cooking.
6. Meanwhile, crack the eggs in a bowl.
7. Add the cream cheese and flax seeds.
8. Mix carefully until you get a smooth texture.
9. Pour the omelet mixture into the air fryer basket tray over the mushrooms.
10. Stir the omelet gently and cook it for 7 minutes more.
11. Remove the cooked omelet from the air fryer basket tray using a wooden spatula.
12. Slice it into servings.

Nutrition:
- (per serving) calories 106 | fat 8.7 | protein 5.9 | total carbs 1.5 | fiber 0.4

Keto Spinach Quiche

Servings: 6 | Cooking Time: 21 Minutes

Ingredients:
- ½ cup almond flour
- 4 tablespoon water, boiled
- 1 teaspoon salt
- 1 cup spinach
- ¼ cup cream cheese
- 3 oz chive stems
- 1 teaspoon ground black pepper
- 3 eggs
- 6 oz. Cheddar cheese, shredded
- 1 teaspoon olive oil

Directions:
1. Combine the water with the almond flour and add salt.
2. Mix well and knead into a non-sticky soft dough.
3. Then grease the air fryer basket tray with the olive oil.
4. Preheat the air fryer to 375 F.
5. Roll the dough and place it in the air fryer basket tray in the shape of a crust.
6. Put the basket tray in the air fryer and cook for 5 minutes.
7. Meanwhile, chop the spinach and combine it with the cream cheese and ground black pepper.
8. Dice the chives and add it to the spinach mixture. Stir carefully.
9. Crack the eggs in the bowl and whisk them.
10. When the quiche crust is cooked – transfer the spinach filling in it.

11. Sprinkle the filling with the shredded cheese and pour the whisked eggs.
12. Set the air fryer to 350 F and cook the quiche for 7 minutes.
13. Then reduce the heat to 300 F and cook the quiche for 9 minutes more.
14. Let the cooked quiche chill well and cut it into pieces.

Nutrition:
- (per serving) calories 248 | fat 20.2 | protein 12.8 | total carbs 4.1 | fiber 1.4

Pound Cake

Servings: 8 | Cooking Time: 30 Minutes

Ingredients:
- 1 stick butter, at room temperature
- 1 cup Swerve
- 4 eggs
- 1½ cups coconut flour
- ½ teaspoon baking powder
- ½ teaspoon baking soda
- ¼ teaspoon salt
- A pinch of freshly grated nutmeg
- A pinch of ground star anise
- ½ cup buttermilk
- 1 teaspoon vanilla essence

Directions:
1. Begin by preheating your Air Fryer to 320ºF. Spritz the bottom and sides of a baking pan with cooking spray.
2. Beat the butter and swerve with a hand mixer until creamy. Then, fold in the eggs, one at a time, and mix well until fluffy.
3. Stir in the flour along with the remaining ingredients. Mix to combine well. Scrape the batter into the prepared baking pan.
4. Bake for 15 minutes, rotate the pan and bake an additional 15 minutes, until the top of the cake springs back when gently pressed with your fingers. Bon appétit!

Nutrition:
- (per serving) calories 193 | fat 19 | protein 4 | total carbs 3 | fiber 2

Everything Bagels

Servings:6 | Cooking Time: 14 Minutes

Ingredients:
- 1¾ cups shredded mozzarella cheese or goat cheese mozzarella
- 2 tablespoons unsalted butter or coconut oil
- 1 large egg, beaten
- 1 tablespoon apple cider vinegar
- 1 cup blanched almond flour
- 1 tablespoon baking powder
- ⅛ teaspoon fine sea salt
- 1½ teaspoons everything bagel seasoning

Directions:
1. Make the dough: Put the mozzarella and butter in a large microwave-safe bowl and microwave for 1 to 2 minutes, until the cheese is entirely melted. Stir well. Add the egg and vinegar. Using a hand mixer on medium, combine well. Add the almond flour, baking powder, and salt and, using the mixer, combine well.
2. Lay a piece of parchment paper on the countertop and place the dough on it. Knead it for about 3 minutes. The dough should be a little sticky but pliable. (If the dough is too sticky, chill it in the refrigerator for an hour or overnight.)
3. Preheat the air fryer to 350°F. Spray a baking sheet or pie pan that will fit into your air fryer with avocado oil.
4. Divide the dough into 6 equal portions. Roll 1 portion into a log that is 6 inches long and about ½ inch thick. Form the log into a circle and seal the edges together, making a bagel shape. Repeat with the remaining portions of dough, making 6 bagels.
5. Place the bagels on the greased baking sheet. Spray the bagels with avocado oil and top with everything bagel seasoning, pressing the seasoning into the dough with your hands.
6. Place the bagels in the air fryer and cook for 14 minutes, or until cooked through and golden brown, flipping after 6 minutes.
7. Remove the bagels from the air fryer and allow them to cool slightly before slicing them in half and serving. Store leftovers in an airtight container in the fridge for up to 4 days or in the freezer for up to a month.

Nutrition:
- (per serving) calories 224 | fat 19g | protein 12g | total carbs 4g | fiber 2g

Breakfast Sausages

Servings: 6 | Cooking Time: 12 Minutes

Ingredients:
- 7 oz. ground chicken
- 7 oz. ground pork
- 1 teaspoon minced garlic
- 1 teaspoon salt
- ½ teaspoon nutmeg
- 1 teaspoon olive oil
- 1 tablespoon almond flour
- 1 egg
- 1 teaspoon chili flakes
- 1 teaspoon ground coriander

Directions:
1. Combine the ground chicken and ground pork together in a bowl.
2. Crack the egg into the mixture.
3. Mix well with a spoon.
4. Sprinkle the mixture with minced garlic, salt, nutmeg, almond flour, chili flakes, and ground coriander.
5. Combine well.
6. Preheat the air fryer to 360 F.
7. Make medium sausages from the mixture.
8. Spray the air fryer basket tray with olive oil.
9. Put the sausages in the air fryer basket and place in the air fryer.
10. Cook for 6 minutes.
11. Turn the sausages over and cook for 6 minutes more.
12. Allow the sausages to cool a little.
13. Serve.

Nutrition:
- (per serving) calories 156 | fat 7.5 | protein 20.2 | total carbs 1.3 | fiber 0.6

Blueberry Muffin

Servings: 6 | Cooking Time: 15 Minutes

Ingredients:
- 1½ cups blanched finely ground almond flour
- ½ cup granular erythritol
- 4 tablespoons salted butter, melted
- 2 large eggs, whisked
- 2 teaspoons baking powder
- ⅓ cup fresh blueberries, chopped

Directions:
1. In a large bowl, combine all ingredients. Evenly pour batter into six silicone muffin cups greased with cooking spray.
2. Place muffin cups into air fryer basket. Adjust the temperature to 320°F (160°C) and set the timer for 15 minutes. Muffins should be golden brown when done.
3. Let the muffins cool in cups 15 minutes to avoid crumbling. Serve warm.

Nutrition:
- (per serving) calories 269 | fat 24 | protein 8 | total carbs 23 | fiber 20

Chicken Strips

Servings: 4 | Cooking Time: 12 Minutes

Ingredients:
- 1 teaspoon paprika
- ½ teaspoon ground black pepper
- 1 tablespoon butter
- ½ teaspoon salt
- 1-pound chicken fillet
- 1 tablespoon cream

Directions:
1. Cut the chicken fillet into strips.
2. Sprinkle the chicken with the ground black pepper and salt.
3. Preheat the air fryer to 365 F.
4. Put the butter in the air fryer basket tray and add the chicken strips.
5. Cook the chicken strips for 6 minutes.
6. Turn the chicken strips over and cook them for 5 minutes more.
7. After this, sprinkle the chicken strips with the cream and let them rest for 1 minute.
8. Transfer the cooked chicken strips to serving plates.

Nutrition:
- (per serving) calories 245 | fat 11.5 | protein 33 | total carbs 0.6 | fiber 0.3

Gold Muffin

Servings: 6 | Cooking Time: 15 Minutes

Ingredients:
- 1 cup blanched finely ground almond flour
- ¼ cup granular erythritol
- 2 tablespoons salted butter, melted
- 1 large egg, whisked
- 2 teaspoons baking powder
- 1 teaspoon ground allspice

Directions:
1. In a large bowl, combine all ingredients. Evenly pour batter into six silicone muffin cups greased with cooking spray.
2. Place muffin cups into air fryer basket. Adjust the temperature to 320°F (160°C) and set the timer for 15 minutes. Cooked muffins should be golden brown.
3. Let the muffins cool in cups 15 minutes to avoid crumbling. Serve warm.

Nutrition:
- (per serving) calories 160 | fat 14 | protein 5 | total carbs 20 | fiber 18

Fluffy Pancakes With Cream Cheese

Servings: 3 | Cooking Time: 5 Minutes

Ingredients:
- ½ cup coconut flour
- 1 teaspoon baking powder
- ¼ teaspoon salt
- 2 tablespoons erythritol
- ½ teaspoon cinnamon
- 1 teaspoon red paste food color
- 1 egg
- ½ cup milk
- 1 teaspoon vanilla
- Topping:
- 2 ounces (57 g) cream cheese, softened
- 2 tablespoons butter, softened
- ¾ cup powdered swerve

Directions:
1. Mix the coconut flour, baking powder, salt, erythritol, cinnamon, red paste food color in a large bowl.
2. Gradually add the egg, milk and vanilla, whisking continuously, until well combined. Let it stand for 20 minutes.
3. Spritz the Air Fryer baking pan with cooking spray. Pour the batter into the pan using a measuring cup.
4. Cook at 230°F for 4 to 5 minutes or until golden brown. Repeat with the remaining batter.
5. Meanwhile, make your topping by mixing the ingredients until creamy and fluffy. Decorate your pancakes with topping. Bon appétit!

Nutrition:
- (per serving) calories 315 | fat 31 | protein 6 | total carbs 5 | fiber 3

The Best Keto Quiche

Servings: 6 | Cooking Time: 1 Hour

Ingredients:
- CRUST:
- 1¼ cups blanched almond flour
- 1¼ cups grated Parmesan or Gouda cheese (about 3¾ ounces)
- ¼ teaspoon fine sea salt
- 1 large egg, beaten
- FILLING:
- ½ cup chicken or beef broth (or vegetable broth for vegetarian)
- 1 cup shredded Swiss cheese (about 4 ounces)
- 4 ounces cream cheese (½ cup)
- 1 tablespoon unsalted butter, melted
- 4 large eggs, beaten
- ⅓ cup minced leeks or sliced green onions
- ¾ teaspoon fine sea salt
- ⅛ teaspoon cayenne pepper
- Chopped green onions, for garnish

Directions:
1. Preheat the air fryer to 325°F. Grease a 6-inch pie pan. Spray

two large pieces of parchment paper with avocado oil and set them on the countertop.

2. Make the crust: In a medium-sized bowl, combine the flour, cheese, and salt and mix well. Add the egg and mix until the dough is well combined and stiff.

3. Place the dough in the center of one of the greased pieces of parchment. Top with the other piece of parchment. Using a rolling pin, roll out the dough into a circle about 1/16 inch thick.

4. Press the pie crust into the prepared pie pan. Place it in the air fryer and bake for 12 minutes, or until it starts to lightly brown.

5. While the crust bakes, make the filling: In a large bowl, combine the broth, Swiss cheese, cream cheese, and butter. Stir in the eggs, leeks, salt, and cayenne pepper. When the crust is ready, pour the mixture into the crust.

6. Place the quiche in the air fryer and bake for 15 minutes. Turn the heat down to 300°F and bake for an additional 30 minutes, or until a knife inserted 1 inch from the edge comes out clean. You may have to cover the edges of the crust with foil to prevent burning.

7. Allow the quiche to cool for 10 minutes before garnishing it with chopped green onions and cutting it into wedges.

8. Store leftovers in an airtight container in the refrigerator for up to 4 days or in the freezer for up to a month. Reheat in a preheated 350°F air fryer for a few minutes, until warmed through.

Nutrition:
• (per serving)   calories 333 | fat 26g | protein 20g | total carbs 6g | fiber 2g

Cheese And Bacon Quiche

Servings: 2 | Cooking Time: 12 Minutes

Ingredients:
• 3 large eggs
• 2 tablespoons heavy whipping cream
• ¼ teaspoon salt
• 4 slices cooked sugar-free bacon, crumbled
• ½ cup shredded mild Cheddar cheese

Directions:
1. In a large bowl, whisk eggs, cream, and salt together until combined. Mix the bacon and Cheddar.
2. Pour mixture evenly into two ungreased 4-inch ramekins. Place into air fryer basket. Adjust the temperature to 320°F (160ºC) and set the timer for 12 minutes. Quiche will be fluffy and set in the middle when done.
3. Let the quiche cool in ramekins 5 minutes. Serve warm.

Nutrition:
• (per serving) calories 380 | fat 28 | protein 24 | total carbs 2 | fiber 2

Egg In Avocado Boats

Servings: 2 | Cooking Time: 15 Minutes

Ingredients:
• 1 avocado, pitted
• ¼ teaspoon turmeric
• ¼ teaspoon ground black pepper
• ¼ teaspoon salt
• 2 eggs
• 1 teaspoon butter
• ¼ teaspoon flax seeds

Directions:
1. Take a shallow bowl and add the turmeric, ground black pep-

per, salt, and flax seeds together. Shake gently to combine.
2. Cut the avocado into 2 halves.
3. Crack the eggs in a separate bowl.
4. Sprinkle the eggs with the spice mixture.
5. Place the eggs in the avocado halves.
6. Put the avocado boats in the Air Fryer.
7. Set the Air Fryer to 355 F and close it.
8. Cook the dish for 15 minutes or until the eggs are cooked to preference.
9. Serve immediately.

Nutrition:
• (per serving) calories 288 | fat 26 | protein 7.6 | total carbs 9.4 | fiber 6.9

Gyro Breakfast Patties With Tzatziki

Servings:16 | Cooking Time: 20 Minutes Per Batch

Ingredients:
• PATTIES:
• 2 pounds ground lamb or beef
• ½ cup diced red onions
• ¼ cup sliced black olives
• 2 tablespoons tomato sauce
• 1 teaspoon dried oregano leaves
• 1 teaspoon Greek seasoning
• 2 cloves garlic, minced
• 1 teaspoon fine sea salt
• TZATZIKI:
• 1 cup full-fat sour cream
• 1 small cucumber, chopped
• ½ teaspoon fine sea salt
• ½ teaspoon garlic powder, or 1 clove garlic, minced
• ¼ teaspoon dried dill weed, or 1 teaspoon finely chopped fresh dill
• FOR GARNISH/SERVING:
• ½ cup crumbled feta cheese (about 2 ounces)
• Diced red onions
• Sliced black olives
• Sliced cucumbers

Directions:
1. Preheat the air fryer to 350°F.
2. Place the ground lamb, onions, olives, tomato sauce, oregano, Greek seasoning, garlic, and salt in a large bowl. Mix well to combine the ingredients.
3. Using your hands, form the mixture into sixteen 3-inch patties. Place about 5 of the patties in the air fryer and fry for 20 minutes, flipping halfway through. Remove the patties and place them on a serving platter. Repeat with the remaining patties.
4. While the patties cook, make the tzatziki: Place all the ingredients in a small bowl and stir well. Cover and store in the fridge until ready to serve. Garnish with ground black pepper before serving.
5. Serve the patties with a dollop of tzatziki, a sprinkle of crumbled feta cheese, diced red onions, sliced black olives, and sliced cucumbers.
6. Store leftovers in an airtight container in the refrigerator for up to 5 days or in the freezer for up to a month. Reheat the patties in a preheated 390°F air fryer for a few minutes, until warmed through.

Nutrition:
• (per serving)   calories 396 | fat 31g | protein 23g | total carbs 4g | fiber 0.4g

Liver Pate

Servings: 7 | Cooking Time: 10 Minutes

Ingredients:
- 1-pound chicken liver
- 1 teaspoon salt
- 4 tablespoon butter
- 1 cup water
- 1 teaspoon ground black pepper
- 5 oz chive stems
- ½ teaspoon dried cilantro

Directions:
1. Chop the chicken liver roughly and place it in the air fryer basket tray.
2. Dice the chives.
3. Pour the water in the air fryer basket tray and add the diced chives.
4. Preheat the air fryer to 360 F and cook the chicken liver for 10 minutes.
5. Once cooked, strain the chicken liver mixture to discard the liquid.
6. Transfer the chicken liver into a blender.
7. Add the butter, ground black pepper, and dried cilantro.
8. Blend the mixture till you get the pate texture.
9. Transfer the liver pate to a bowl and serve it immediately or keep in the fridge.

Nutrition:
- (per serving) calories 173 | fat 10.8 | protein 16.1 | total carbs 2.2 | fiber 0.4

Spaghetti Squash Patties

Servings: 4 | Cooking Time: 8 Minutes

Ingredients:
- 2 cups cooked spaghetti squash
- 2 tablespoons unsalted butter, softened
- 1 large egg
- ¼ cup blanched finely ground almond flour
- 2 stalks green onion, sliced
- ½ teaspoon garlic powder
- 1 teaspoon dried parsley

Directions:
1. Remove excess moisture from the squash using a cheesecloth or kitchen towel.
2. Mix all ingredients in a large bowl. Form into four patties.
3. Cut a piece of parchment to fit your air fryer basket. Place each patty on the parchment and place into the air fryer basket.
4. Adjust the temperature to 400°F (205ºC) and set the timer for 8 minutes.
5. Flip the patties halfway through the cooking time. Serve warm.

Nutrition:
- (per serving) calories 131 | fat 10 | protein 4 | total carbs 7 | fiber 5

Golden Biscuits

Servings: 8 | Cooking Time: 13 Minutes

Ingredients:
- 2 cups blanched almond flour
- ½ cup Swerve confectioners-style sweetener
- 1 teaspoon baking powder
- ½ teaspoon fine sea salt
- ¼ cup plus 2 tablespoons (¾ stick) very cold unsalted butter
- ¼ cup unsweetened, unflavored almond milk
- 1 large egg
- 1 teaspoon vanilla extract
- 3 teaspoons ground cinnamon
- Glaze:
- ½ cup Swerve confectioners-style sweetener
- ¼ cup heavy cream

Directions:
1. Preheat the air fryer to 350°F (180ºC). Line a pie pan that fits into your air fryer with parchment paper.
2. In a medium-sized bowl, mix together the almond flour, sweetener (if powdered, do not add liquid sweetener), baking powder, and salt. Cut the butter into ½-inch squares, and then use a hand mixer to work the butter into the dry ingredients. When you are done, the mixture should still have chunks of butter.
3. In a small bowl, whisk together the almond milk, egg, and vanilla extract (if using liquid sweetener, add it as well) until blended. Using a fork, stir the wet ingredients into the dry ingredients until large clumps form. Add the cinnamon and use your hands to swirl it into the dough.
4. Form the dough into sixteen 1-inch balls and place them on the prepared pan, spacing them about ½-inch apart. (If you're using a smaller air fryer, work in batches if necessary.) Bake in the air fryer until golden, for 10 to 13 minutes. Remove from the air fryer and let it cool on the pan for at least 5 minutes.
5. While the biscuits bake, make the glaze: Place the powdered sweetener in a small bowl and slowly stir in the heavy cream with a fork.
6. When the biscuits have cooled somewhat, dip the tops into the glaze, allow it to dry a bit, and then dip again for a thick glaze.
7. Serve warm or at room temperature. Store unglazed biscuits in an airtight container in the refrigerator for up to 3 days or in the freezer for up to a month. Reheat in a preheated 350°F (180ºC) air fryer for 5 minutes, or until warmed through, and dip in the glaze as instructed above.

Nutrition:
- (per serving) calories 546 | fat 51 | protein 14 | total carbs 13 | fiber 7

Sausage Balls

Servings: 5 | Cooking Time: 8 Minutes

Ingredients:
- 8 oz. ground chicken
- 1 egg white
- 1 tablespoon dried parsley
- ½ teaspoon salt
- ½ teaspoon ground black pepper
- 2 tablespoon almond flour
- 1 tablespoon olive oil
- 1 teaspoon paprika

Directions:
1. Whisk the egg white and combine it with the ground chicken.

2. Sprinkle the chicken mixture with the dried parsley and salt.
3. Add ground black pepper and paprika.
4. Stir carefully using a spoon.
5. Using wet hands, make small balls from the ground chicken mixture.
6. Sprinkle each sausage ball with the almond flour.
7. Preheat the air fryer to 380 F.
8. Grease the air fryer basket tray with olive oil and place the sausage balls inside.
9. Cook for 8 minutes.
10. Turn halfway to crisp each side.
11. Serve hot.

Nutrition:
• (per serving) calories 180 | fat 11.8 | protein 16.3 | total carbs 2.9 | fiber 1.5

Toast Pavlova

Servings: 4 | Cooking Time: 60 Minutes

Ingredients:
• 3 large egg whites
• ¼ teaspoon cream of tartar
• ¾ cup Swerve confectioners-style sweetener
• 1 teaspoon ground cinnamon
• 1 teaspoon maple extract
• Toppings:
• ½ cup heavy cream
• 3 tablespoons Swerve confectioners-style sweetener, plus more for garnish
• Fresh strawberries (optional)

Directions:
1. Preheat the air fryer to 275°F. Thoroughly grease a 7-inch pie pan with butter or coconut oil. Place a large bowl in the refrigerator to chill.
2. In a small bowl, combine the egg whites and cream of tartar. Using a hand mixer, beat until soft peaks form. Turn the mixer to low and slowly sprinkle in the sweetener while mixing until completely incorporated. Add the cinnamon and maple extract and beat on medium-high until the peaks become stiff.
3. Spoon the mixture into the greased pie pan, then smooth it across the bottom, up the sides, and onto the rim of the pie pan to form a shell. Cook in the air fryer for 1 hour, then turn off the air fryer and let the shell stand in the air fryer for another 20 minutes. Once the shell has set, transfer it to the refrigerator to chill for 20 minutes or the freezer to chill for 10 minutes.
4. While the shell sets and chills, make the topping: Remove the large bowl from the refrigerator and place the heavy cream in it. Whip with a hand mixer on high until soft peaks form. Add the sweetener and beat until medium peaks form. Taste and adjust the sweetness to your liking.
5. Place the chilled shell on a serving platter and spoon on the cream topping. Top with the strawberries, if desired, and garnish with powdered sweetener. Slice and serve.
6. If you won't be eating the pavlova right away, store the shell and topping in separate airtight containers in the refrigerator for up to 3 days.

Nutrition:
• (per serving) calories 115 | fat 11 | protein 3 | total carbs 2 | fiber 1.7

Cheese Tots

Servings: 5 | Cooking Time: 3 Minutes

Ingredients:
• 8 oz. mozzarella balls
• 1 egg
• ½ cup coconut flakes
• ½ cup almond flour
• 1 teaspoon thyme
• 1 teaspoon ground black pepper
• 1 teaspoon paprika

Directions:
1. Crack the egg in a bowl and whisk.
2. Combine the coconut flour with the thyme, ground black pepper, and paprika. Stir carefully.
3. Sprinkle Mozzarella balls with the coconut flakes.
4. Transfer the balls to the whisked egg mixture.
5. Coat in the almond flour mixture.
6. Put Mozzarella balls in the freezer for 5 minutes.
7. Meanwhile, preheat the air fryer to 400 F.
8. Put the frozen cheese balls in the preheated air fryer and cook them for 3 minutes.
9. Remove the cheese tots from the air fryer basket and chill them for 2 minutes.
10. Serve.

Nutrition:
• (per serving) calories 166 | fat 12.8 | protein 9.5 | total carbs 2.8 | fiber 1.4

Keto Breakfast Quiche

Servings: 8 | Cooking Time: 60 Minutes

Ingredients:
• Crust:
• Cooking spray
• 1¼ cups blanched almond flour
• 1¼ cups grated Parmesan or Gouda cheese
• ¼ teaspoon fine sea salt
• 1 large egg, beaten
• Filling:
• ½ cup chicken or beef broth (or vegetable broth for vegetarian)
• 1 cup shredded Swiss cheese
• 4 ounces cream cheese
• 1 tablespoon unsalted butter, melted
• 4 large eggs, beaten
• ⅓ cup minced leeks or sliced green onions
• ¾ teaspoon fine sea salt
• ⅛ teaspoon cayenne pepper
• Chopped green onions, for garnish

Directions:
1. Preheat the air fryer to 325°F. Grease a 6-inch pie pan. Spray two large pieces of parchment paper with avocado oil and set them on the countertop.
2. Make the crust: In a medium-sized bowl, combine the flour, cheese, and salt and mix well. Add the egg and mix until the dough is well combined and stiff.
3. Place the dough in the center of one of the greased pieces of parchment. Top with the other piece of parchment. Using a rolling pin, roll out the dough into a circle about 1/16 inch thick.
4. Press the pie crust into the prepared pie pan. Place it in the air fryer and bake for 12 minutes, or until it starts to lightly brown.
5. While the crust bakes, make the filling: In a large bowl, com-

bine the broth, Swiss cheese, cream cheese, and butter. Stir in the eggs, leeks, salt, and cayenne pepper. When the crust is ready, pour the mixture into the crust.

6. Place the quiche in the air fryer and bake for 15 minutes. Turn the heat down to 300°F and bake for an additional 30 minutes, or until a knife inserted 1 inch from the edge comes out clean. You may have to cover the edges of the crust with foil to prevent burning.

7. Allow the quiche to cool for 10 minutes before garnishing it with chopped green onions and cutting it into wedges.

8. Store leftovers in an airtight container in the refrigerator for up to 4 days or in the freezer for up to a month. Reheat in a preheated 350°F air fryer for a few minutes, until warmed through.

Nutrition:
• (per serving) calories 333 | fat 26 | protein 20 | total carbs 6 | fiber 4

Meatloaf Slices

Servings: 6 | Cooking Time: 20 Minutes

Ingredients:
• 8 oz. ground pork
• 7 oz. ground beef
• 6 oz chive stems
• 1 egg
• 1 tablespoon almond flour
• 1 tablespoon chives
• 1 teaspoon salt
• 1 teaspoon cayenne pepper
• 1 tablespoon dried oregano
• 1 teaspoon butter
• 1 teaspoon olive oil

Directions:
1. Crack the egg into a large bowl.
2. Add the ground beef and ground pork.
3. Add the almond flour, chives, salt, cayenne pepper, dried oregano, and butter.
4. Dice the chives.
5. Put the diced chives in the ground meat mixture.
6. Use your hands to combine the mixture.
7. Preheat the air fryer to 350 F.
8. Make the meatloaf form from the ground meat mixture.
9. Grease the air fryer basket with the olive oil and place the meatloaf inside.
10. Cook the meatloaf for 20 minutes.
11. Allow the meatloaf to rest for a few minutes.
12. Slice and serve.

Nutrition:
• (per serving) calories 176 | fat 2.2 | protein 22.2 | total carbs 3.4 | fiber 1.3

Egg Cups With Bacon

Servings: 4 | Cooking Time: 15 Minutes

Ingredients:
• 4 eggs
• 6 oz. bacon
• ¼ teaspoon salt
• ½ teaspoon dried dill
• ½ teaspoon paprika
• 1 tablespoon butter

Directions:

1. Crack the eggs in a mixer bowl.
2. Add salt, dried dill, and paprika. Mix the egg mixture carefully with a hand mixer.
3. Grease 4 ramekins with butter.
4. Slice the bacon and put it in the prepared ramekins in the shape of cups.
5. Pour the egg mixture in the middle of each bacon cup.
6. Set the Air Fryer to 360 F.
7. Put the ramekins in the Air Fryer and close it.
8. Cook the dish for 15 minutes.
9. Remove the egg cups from the Air Fryer and serve them.

Nutrition:
• (per serving) calories 319 | fat 25.1 | protein 21.4 | total carbs 1.2 | fiber 0.1

Breakfast Hash

Servings: 4 | Cooking Time: 8 Minutes

Ingredients:
• 1 zucchini
• 7 oz. bacon, cooked
• 4 oz. Cheddar cheese
• 2 tablespoon butter
• 1 teaspoon salt
• 1 teaspoon ground black pepper
• 1 teaspoon paprika
• 1 teaspoon cilantro
• 1 teaspoon ground thyme

Directions:
1. Chop the zucchini into the small cubes and sprinkle it with salt, ground black pepper, paprika, cilantro, and ground thyme.
2. Preheat the air fryer to 400 F and toss the butter into the air fryer basket tray.
3. Melt it and add the zucchini cubes.
4. Cook the zucchini for 5 minutes.
5. Meanwhile, shred Cheddar cheese.
6. Shake the zucchini cubes carefully and add the cooked bacon.
7. Sprinkle the zucchini mixture with the shredded cheese and cook it for 3 minutes more.
8. Transfer the breakfast hash in the serving bowls and stir.

Nutrition:
• (per serving) calories 445 | fat 36.1 | protein 26.3 | total carbs 3.5 | fiber 1

Chocolate Chip Muffin

Servings:6 | Cooking Time: 15 Minutes

Ingredients:
• 1½ cups blanched finely ground almond flour
• ⅓ cup granular brown erythritol
• 4 tablespoons salted butter, melted
• 2 large eggs, whisked
• 1 tablespoon baking powder
• ½ cup low-carb chocolate chips

Directions:
1. In a large bowl, combine all ingredients. Evenly pour batter into six silicone muffin cups greased with cooking spray.
2. Place muffin cups into air fryer basket. Adjust the temperature to 320°F (160ºC) and set the timer for 15 minutes. Muffins will be golden brown when done.
3. Let the muffins cool in cups for 15 minutes to avoid crumbling. Serve warm.

Nutrition:
- (per serving) calories 329 | fat 29 | protein 10 | total carbs 28 | fiber 20

Cheddar Soufflé With Herbs

Servings: 4 | Cooking Time: 8 Minutes

Ingredients:
- 5 oz. Cheddar cheese, shredded
- 3 eggs
- 4 tablespoon heavy cream
- 1 tablespoon chives
- 1 tablespoon dill
- 1 teaspoon parsley
- ½ teaspoon ground thyme

Directions:
1. Crack the eggs into a bowl and whisk them carefully.
2. Add the heavy cream and whisk it for 10 seconds more.
3. Add the chives, dill, parsley, and ground thyme.
4. Sprinkle the egg mixture with the shredded cheese and stir it.
5. Transfer the egg mixture into 4 ramekins and place the ramekins in the air fryer basket.
6. Preheat the air fryer to 390 F and cook the soufflé for 8 minutes.
7. Once cooked, chill well.

Nutrition:
- (per serving) calories 244 | fat 20.6 | protein 13.5 | total carbs 1.7 | fiber 0.2

Sausage Egg Cup

Servings: 6 | Cooking Time: 15 Minutes

Ingredients:
- 12 ounces (340 g) ground pork breakfast sausage
- 6 large eggs
- ½ teaspoon salt
- ¼ teaspoon ground black pepper
- ½ teaspoon crushed red pepper flakes

Directions:
1. Place sausage in six 4-inch ramekins (about 2 ounces, 57 g per ramekin) greased with cooking oil. Press sausage down to cover bottom and about ½-inch up the sides of ramekins. Crack one egg into each ramekin and sprinkle evenly with salt, black pepper, and red pepper flakes.
2. Place ramekins into air fryer basket. Adjust the temperature to 350°F (180°C) and set the timer for 15 minutes. Egg cups will be done when sausage is fully cooked to at least 145°F (63°C) and the egg is firm. Serve warm.

Nutrition:
- (per serving) calories 267 | fat 21 | protein 14 | total carbs 1 | fiber 1

Minced Beef Keto Sandwich

Servings: 2 | Cooking Time: 16 Minutes

Ingredients:
- 6 oz. minced beef
- ½ avocado pitted
- ½ tomato
- ½ teaspoon chili flakes
- 1/3 teaspoon salt
- ½ teaspoon ground black pepper
- 1 teaspoon olive oil
- 1 teaspoon flax seeds
- 4 lettuce leaves

Directions:
1. Combine the minced beef with the chili flakes and salt.
2. Add flax seeds and stir the meat mixture with a fork.
3. Preheat the air fryer to 370 F.
4. Pour the olive oil in the air fryer basket tray.
5. Make 2 burgers from the beef mixture and place them in the air fryer basket tray.
6. Cook the burgers for 8 minutes on each side.
7. Meanwhile, slice the tomato and avocado.
8. Separate the sliced ingredients into 2 servings.
9. Place the avocado and tomato on 2 lettuce leaves.
10. Then add the cooked minced beef burgers.
11. Serve the sandwiches hot.

Nutrition:
- (per serving) calories 292 | fat 17.9 | protein 27.2 | total carbs 5.9 | fiber 4.1

Pork Breakfast Sticks

Servings: 4 | Cooking Time: 10 Minutes

Ingredients:
- 1 teaspoon dried basil
- ¼ teaspoon ground ginger
- 1 teaspoon nutmeg
- 1 teaspoon oregano
- 1 teaspoon apple cider vinegar
- 1 teaspoon paprika
- 10 oz. pork fillet
- ½ teaspoon salt
- 1 tablespoon olive oil
- 5 oz. Parmesan, shredded

Directions:
1. Cut the pork fillet into thick strips.
2. Combine the ground ginger, nutmeg, oregano, paprika, and salt in a shallow bowl and stir.
3. Sprinkle the pork strips with the spice mixture.
4. Sprinkle the meat with the apple cider vinegar.
5. Preheat the air fryer to 380 F.
6. Grease the air fryer basket with the olive oil and place the pork strips inside.
7. Cook for 5 minutes.
8. Turn the pork strips over and cook for a further 4 minutes.
9. Cover the pork strips with the shredded Parmesan and cook for 1 minute more.
10. Remove the pork from the air fryer and serve immediately. The cheese should be soft.

Nutrition:
- (per serving) calories 315 | fat 20.4 | protein 31.3 | total carbs 2.2 | fiber 0.5

Kale Fritters

Servings: 8 | Cooking Time: 8 Minutes

Ingredients:
- 12 oz. kale
- 3 oz chive stems
- 1 tablespoon butter
- 1 egg
- 2 tablespoons almond flour
- ½ teaspoon salt
- 1 teaspoon paprika
- 1 tablespoon cream
- 1 teaspoon oil

Directions:
1. Wash the kale carefully and chop it roughly.
2. Place the chopped kale in a blender and blend it until smooth.
3. Dice the chives.
4. Crack the egg in a bowl and whisk it using a hand whisker.
5. Add almond flour, salt, paprika, and cream. Stir it.
6. Then add the diced chives and blended kale.
7. Mix it up until you get well combined fritter dough.
8. Preheat the air fryer to 360 F.
9. Grease the air fryer basket tray with the olive oil.
10. Make 8 medium fritters from the prepared dough and place them in the air fryer basket tray.
11. Cook the kale fritters for 4 minutes on each side.
12. When the kale fritters are cooked – remove them from the air fryer and chill.

Nutrition:
- (per serving) calories 86 | fat 5.6 | protein 3.6 | total carbs 6.8 | fiber 1.6

Broccoli Frittata

Servings: 4 | Cooking Time: 12 Minutes

Ingredients:
- 6 large eggs
- ¼ cup heavy whipping cream
- ½ cup chopped broccoli
- ¼ cup chopped yellow onion
- ¼ cup chopped green bell pepper

Directions:
1. In a large bowl, whisk eggs and heavy whipping cream. Mix in broccoli, onion, and bell pepper.
2. Pour into a 6-inch round oven-safe baking dish. Place baking dish into the air fryer basket.
3. Adjust the temperature to 350°F (180ºC) and set the timer for 12 minutes.
4. Eggs should be firm and cooked fully when the frittata is done. Serve warm.

Nutrition:
- (per serving) calories 168 | fat 11 | protein 10 | total carbs 3 | fiber 2

Egg Butter

Servings: 10 | Cooking Time: 17 Minutes

Ingredients:
- 5 eggs
- 5 tablespoon butter
- 1 teaspoon salt

Directions:
1. Cover the air fryer basket with foil and place the eggs inside.
2. Transfer the basket to the air fryer and cook the eggs for 17 minutes at 320 F.
3. Remove the cooked eggs from the air fryer basket and put them in cold water.
4. Peel the eggs and chop them finely.
5. Combine the chopped eggs with the butter and add salt.
6. Mix until you get a smooth texture.
7. Serve the egg butter with the keto almond bread.

Nutrition:
- (per serving) calories 82 | fat 4.2 | protein 1.5 | total carbs 9.2 | fiber 1.4

Hemp Seed Porridge

Servings: 3 | Cooking Time: 15 Minutes

Ingredients:
- 2 tablespoon flax seeds
- 4 tablespoon hemp seeds
- 1 tablespoon butter
- ¼ teaspoon salt
- 1 teaspoon stevia
- 7 tablespoon almond milk
- ½ teaspoon ground ginger

Directions:
1. Place the flax seeds and hemp seeds in the air fryer basket.
2. Sprinkle the seeds with salt and ground ginger.
3. Combine the almond milk and stevia together. Stir the liquid and pour it into the seed mixture.
4. Add butter.
5. Preheat the air fryer to 370 F and cook the hemp seed porridge for 15 minutes.
6. Stir carefully after 10 minutes of cooking.
7. Remove the hem porridge from the air fryer basket tray and chill it for 3 minutes.
8. Transfer the porridge into serving bowls.

Nutrition:
- (per serving) calories 196 | fat 18.2 | protein 5.1 | total carbs 4.2 | fiber 2.4

Keto Frittata

Servings: 6 | Cooking Time: 15 Minutes

Ingredients:
- 6 eggs
- 1/3 cup heavy cream
- 1 tomato
- 5 oz chive stems
- 1 tablespoon butter
- 1 teaspoon salt
- 1 tablespoon dried oregano
- 6 oz. Parmesan
- 1 teaspoon chili pepper

Directions:

1. Crack the eggs into the air fryer basket tray and whisk them with a hand whisker.
2. Chop the tomato and dice the chives.
3. Add the vegetables to the egg mixture.
4. Pour the heavy cream.
5. Sprinkle the liquid mixture with the butter, salt, dried oregano, and chili pepper.
6. Shred Parmesan cheese and add it to the mixture too.
7. Sprinkle the mixture with a silicone spatula.
8. Preheat the air fryer to 375 F and cook the frittata for 15 minutes.

Nutrition:
• (per serving) calories 202 | fat 15 | protein 15.1 | total carbs 3.4 | fiber 0.7

Cream Cauliflower With Cheese

Servings: 4 | Cooking Time: 20 Minutes

Ingredients:
• 6 large eggs
• ¼ cup heavy whipping cream
• 1½ cups chopped cauliflower
• 1 cup shredded medium Cheddar cheese
• 1 medium avocado, peeled and pitted
• 8 tablespoons full-fat sour cream
• 2 scallions, sliced on the bias
• 12 slices sugar-free bacon, cooked and crumbled

Directions:
1. In a medium bowl, whisk eggs and cream together. Pour into a 4-cup round baking dish.
2. Add cauliflower and mix, then top with Cheddar. Place dish into the air fryer basket.
3. Adjust the temperature to 320°F (160°C) and set the timer for 20 minutes.
4. When completely cooked, eggs will be firm and cheese will be browned. Slice into four pieces.
5. Slice avocado and divide evenly among pieces. Top each piece with 2 tablespoons sour cream, sliced scallions, and crumbled bacon.

Nutrition:
• (per serving) calories 512 | fat 38 | protein 27 | total carbs 8 | fiber 5

Tofu Scramble

Servings: 5 | Cooking Time: 20 Minutes

Ingredients:
• 10 oz tofu cheese
• 2 eggs
• 1 teaspoon chives
• 1 tablespoon apple cider vinegar
• ½ teaspoon salt
• 1 teaspoon ground white pepper
• ¼ teaspoon ground coriander

Directions:
1. Shred the tofu and sprinkle it with the apple cider vinegar, salt, ground white pepper, and ground coriander.
2. Mix and leave for 10 minutes to marinade.
3. Meanwhile, preheat the air fryer to 370 F.
4. Transfer the marinated tofu to the air fryer basket tray and cook for 13 minutes.
5. Meanwhile, crack the eggs in a bowl and whisk them.

6. When the tofu has cooked, pour the egg mixture in the shredded tofu cheese and stir with a spatula.
7. When the eggs start to firm place the air fryer basket tray in the air fryer and cook the dish for 7 minutes more.
8. Remove the cooked meal from the air fryer basket tray and serve.

Nutrition:
• (per serving) calories 109 | fat 6.7 | protein 11.2 | total carbs 2.9 | fiber 1.4

Bacon-and-eggs Avocado

Servings: 1 | Cooking Time: 17 Minutes

Ingredients:
• 1 large egg
• 1 avocado, halved, peeled, and pitted
• 2 slices bacon
• Fresh parsley, for serving (optional)
• Sea salt flakes, for garnish (optional)

Directions:
1. Spray the air fryer basket with avocado oil. Preheat the air fryer to 320°F (160°C). Fill a small bowl with cool water.
2. Soft-boil the egg: Place the egg in the air fryer basket. Cook for 6 minutes for a soft yolk or 7 minutes for a cooked yolk. Transfer the egg to the bowl of cool water and let it sit for 2 minutes. Peel and set aside.
3. Use a spoon to carve out extra space in the center of the avocado halves until the cavities are big enough to fit the soft-boiled egg. Place the soft-boiled egg in the center of one half of the avocado and replace the other half of the avocado on top, so the avocado appears whole on the outside.
4. Starting at one end of the avocado, wrap the bacon around the avocado to completely cover it. Use toothpicks to hold the bacon in place.
5. Place the bacon-wrapped avocado in the air fryer basket and cook for 5 minutes. Flip the avocado over and cook for another 5 minutes, or until the bacon is cooked to your liking. Serve on a bed of fresh parsley, if desired, and sprinkle with salt flakes, if desired.
6. Best served fresh. Store extras in an airtight container in the fridge for up to 4 days. Reheat in a preheated 320°F (160°C) air fryer for 4 minutes, or until heated through.

Nutrition:
• (per serving) calories 535 | fat 46 | protein 18 | total carbs 18 | fiber 4

Turkey Sausage With Tabasco Sauce

Servings: 8 | Cooking Time: 20 Minutes

Ingredients:
• 1½ pounds (680g) 85% lean ground turkey
• 3 cloves garlic, finely chopped
• ¼ onion, grated
• 1 teaspoon Tabasco sauce
• 1 teaspoon Creole seasoning
• 1 teaspoon dried thyme
• ½ teaspoon paprika
• ½ teaspoon cayenne

Directions:
1. Preheat the air fryer to 370°F (188°C).
2. In a large bowl, combine the turkey, garlic, onion, Tabasco, Creole seasoning, thyme, paprika, and cayenne. Mix with clean

hands until thoroughly combined. Shape into 16 patties, about ½-inch thick. (Wet your hands slightly if you find the sausage too sticky to handle.)

3. Working in batches if necessary, arrange the patties in a single layer in the air fryer basket. Pausing halfway through the cooking time to flip the patties, air fry for 15 to 20 minutes until a thermometer inserted into the thickest portion registers 165°F (74ºC).

Nutrition:
• (per serving) calories 170 | fat 11 | protein 16 | total carbs 1 | fiber 1

Morning Ham Hash

Servings: 6 | Cooking Time: 10 Minutes

Ingredients:
• 5 oz. Parmesan
• 10 oz. ham
• 1 tablespoon butter
• 3 oz chive stems
• 1 teaspoon ground black pepper
• 1 egg
• 1 teaspoon paprika

Directions:
1. Grate Parmesan cheese.
2. Cut the ham into small strips.
3. Dice the chive stems.
4. Crack the egg in a bowl and whisk with a hand whisker.
5. Add the ham strips, butter, diced chives, and butter.
6. Sprinkle the mixture with the ground black pepper and paprika.
7. Mix well.
8. Preheat Air Fryer to 350 F.
9. Transfer the ham mixture into 3 ramekins and sprinkle them with the grated Parmesan cheese.
10. Place the ramekins in the preheated Air Fryer and cook them for 10 minutes.
11. Remove the ramekins from the Air Fryer and mix the ham hash with a fork.
12. Serve the dish.

Nutrition:
• (per serving) calories 186 | fat 12 | protein 16.7 | total carbs 4 | fiber 1

Easy Mexican Shakshuka

Servings:1 | Cooking Time: 6 Minutes

Ingredients:
• ½ cup salsa
• 2 large eggs, room temperature
• ½ teaspoon fine sea salt
• ¼ teaspoon smoked paprika
• ⅛ teaspoon ground cumin
• FOR GARNISH:
• 2 tablespoons cilantro leaves

Directions:
1. Preheat the air fryer to 400°F.
2. Place the salsa in a 6-inch pie pan or a casserole dish that will fit into your air fryer. Crack the eggs into the salsa and sprinkle them with the salt, paprika, and cumin.
3. Place the pan in the air fryer and cook for 6 minutes, or until the egg whites are set and the yolks are cooked to your liking.
4. Remove from the air fryer and garnish with the cilantro before

serving.
5. Best served fresh.

Nutrition:
• (per serving) calories 258 | fat 17g | protein 14g | total carbs 11g | fiber 4g

Pepperoni Egg

Servings: 2 | Cooking Time: 10 Minutes

Ingredients:
• 1 cup shredded Mozzarella cheese
• 7 slices pepperoni, chopped
• 1 large egg, whisked
• ¼ teaspoon dried oregano
• ¼ teaspoon dried parsley
• ¼ teaspoon garlic powder
• ¼ teaspoon salt

Directions:
1. Place Mozzarella in a single layer on the bottom of an ungreased 6-inch round nonstick baking dish. Scatter pepperoni over cheese, then pour egg evenly around baking dish.
2. Sprinkle with the remaining ingredients and place into air fryer basket. Adjust the temperature to 330°F (166ºC) and set the timer for 10 minutes. When cheese is brown and egg is set, dish will be done.
3. Let it cool in dish 5 minutes before serving.

Nutrition:
• (per serving) calories 241 | fat 15 | protein 19 | total carbs 4 | fiber 4

Scrambled Pancake Hash

Servings: 9 | Cooking Time: 9 Minutes

Ingredients:
• 1 teaspoon baking soda
• 1 tablespoon apple cider vinegar
• 1 teaspoon salt
• 1 teaspoon ground ginger
• 1 cup coconut flour
• 5 tablespoon butter
• 1 egg
• ¼ cup heavy cream

Directions:
1. Combine the baking soda, salt, ground ginger, and flour in a bowl.
2. Take a separate bowl and crack in the egg.
3. Add butter and heavy cream.
4. Use a hand mixer and mix well.
5. Combine the dry and liquid mixture together and stir it until smooth.
6. Preheat the air fryer to 400 F.
7. Pour the pancake mixture into the air fryer basket tray.
8. Cook the pancake hash for 4 minutes.
9. Scramble the pancake hash well and keep cooking for 5 minutes more.
10. Transfer to serving plates and serve hot.

Nutrition:
• (per serving) calories 148 | fat 11.3 | protein 3.7 | total carbs 8.7 | fiber 5.3

No Bun Bacon Burger

Servings: 4 | Cooking Time: 8 Minutes

Ingredients:
- ½ tomato
- ½ cucumber
- 3 oz chive stems
- 8 oz. ground beef
- 4 oz. bacon, cooked
- 1 egg
- 1 teaspoon butter
- 2 oz. lettuce leaves
- 1 teaspoon ground black pepper
- ½ teaspoon salt
- 1 teaspoon olive oil
- ½ teaspoon minced garlic

Directions:
1. Crack the egg in a bowl and add the ground beef.
2. Chop the cooked bacon and add it to the ground beef mixture.
3. Add the butter, ground black pepper, salt, and minced garlic.
4. Mix carefully and make the burgers.
5. Preheat the oven to 370 F.
6. Grease the air fryer basket with olive oil and place the burgers inside.
7. Cook the burgers for 8 minutes on each side.
8. Meanwhile, slice the chives, cucumber, and tomato finely.
9. Place the tomato, cucumber, and chives on the lettuce leaves.
10. When the burgers are cooked let them chill to room temperature and place them over the vegetables.

Nutrition:
- (per serving) calories 495 | fat 33.4 | protein 59.4 | total carbs 6.5 | fiber 1.2

Western Omelet

Servings: 4 | Cooking Time: 10 Minutes

Ingredients:
- 1 green pepper
- 3 oz chive stems
- 5 eggs
- 3 tablespoon cream cheese
- 1 teaspoon olive oil
- 1 teaspoon dried cilantro
- 1 teaspoon dried oregano
- 1 teaspoon butter
- 3 oz. Parmesan, shredded

Directions:
1. Crack the eggs in a bowl and whisk them well.
2. Sprinkle the eggs with cream cheese, dried cilantro, and dried oregano.
3. Add shredded Parmesan and butter and mix well.
4. Preheat the air fryer to 360 F.
5. Pour the egg mixture into the air fryer basket tray and place it in the air fryer.
6. Cook the omelet for 10 minutes.
7. Meanwhile, chop the green pepper and dice the chives.
8. Pour the olive oil in a skillet and preheat to medium.
9. Add the chopped green pepper and roast for 3 minutes.
10. Add the diced chives and cook for 5 minutes more.
11. Stir the vegetables frequently.
12. Remove the cooked omelet from the air fryer basket tray and place it on a plate.

13. Add the roasted vegetables and serve.

Nutrition:
- (per serving) calories 204 | fat 14.9 | protein 14.8 | total carbs 4.3 | fiber 1

Green Eggs And Ham

Servings:2 | Cooking Time: 10 Minutes

Ingredients:
- 1 large Hass avocado, halved and pitted
- 2 thin slices ham
- 2 large eggs
- 2 tablespoons chopped green onions, plus more for garnish
- ½ teaspoon fine sea salt
- ¼ teaspoon ground black pepper
- ¼ cup shredded cheddar cheese (omit for dairy-free)

Directions:
1. Preheat the air fryer to 400°F.
2. Place a slice of ham into the cavity of each avocado half. Crack an egg on top of the ham, then sprinkle on the green onions, salt, and pepper.
3. Place the avocado halves in the air fryer cut side up and cook for 10 minutes, or until the egg is cooked to your desired doneness. Top with the cheese (if using) and cook for 30 seconds more, or until the cheese is melted. Garnish with chopped green onions.
4. Best served fresh. Store extras in an airtight container in the fridge for up to 4 days. Reheat in a preheated 350°F air fryer for a few minutes, until warmed through.

Nutrition:
- (per serving) calories 307 | fat 24g | protein 14g | total carbs 10g | fiber 7g

French Toast Pavlova

Servings:7 | Cooking Time: 1 Hour

Ingredients:
- 3 large egg whites
- ¼ teaspoon cream of tartar
- ¾ cup Swerve confectioners'-style sweetener or equivalent amount of powdered sweetener (see here)
- 1 teaspoon ground cinnamon
- 1 teaspoon maple extract
- TOPPINGS:
- ½ cup heavy cream
- 3 tablespoons Swerve confectioners'-style sweetener or equivalent amount of powdered sweetener (see here), plus more for garnish
- Fresh strawberries (optional)

Directions:
1. Preheat the air fryer to 275°F. Thoroughly grease a 7-inch pie pan with butter or coconut oil. Place a large bowl in the refrigerator to chill.
2. In a small bowl, combine the egg whites and cream of tartar. Using a hand mixer, beat until soft peaks form. Turn the mixer to low and slowly sprinkle in the sweetener while mixing until completely incorporated. Add the cinnamon and maple extract and beat on medium-high until the peaks become stiff.
3. Spoon the mixture into the greased pie pan, then smooth it across the bottom, up the sides, and onto the rim of the pie pan to form a shell. Cook in the air fryer for 1 hour, then turn off the air fryer and let the shell stand in the air fryer for another 20 minutes.

Once the shell has set, transfer it to the refrigerator to chill for 20 minutes or the freezer to chill for 10 minutes.

4. While the shell sets and chills, make the topping: Remove the large bowl from the refrigerator and place the heavy cream in it. Whip with a hand mixer on high until soft peaks form. Add the sweetener and beat until medium peaks form. Taste and adjust the sweetness to your liking.

5. Place the chilled shell on a serving platter and spoon on the cream topping. Top with the strawberries, if desired, and garnish with powdered sweetener. Slice and serve.

6. If you won't be eating the pavlova right away, store the shell and topping in separate airtight containers in the refrigerator for up to 3 days.

Nutrition:
• (per serving) calories 115 | fat 11g | protein 3g | total carbs 2g | fiber 0.3g

Breakfast Coconut Porridge

Servings: 7 | Cooking Time: 7 Minutes

Ingredients:
• 1 cup coconut milk
• 3 tablespoon blackberries
• ¼ teaspoon salt
• 3 tablespoon coconut flakes
• 5 tablespoon chia seeds
• 1 teaspoon ground cinnamon
• 1 teaspoon butter
• 2 tablespoon walnuts

Directions:
1. Pour the coconut milk in the air fryer basket tray.
2. Add the salt, coconut flakes, chia seeds, ground cinnamon, and butter.
3. Crush the walnuts and add them in the basket.
4. Sprinkle the mixture with salt.
5. Crush the blackberries with a fork and add them in the air fryer basket.
6. Cook the porridge at 375 F for 7 minutes.
7. Remove the air fryer basket from the air fryer and let sit for 5 minutes to rest.
8. Then stir the porridge carefully with a wooden spoon and serve.

Nutrition:
• (per serving) calories 219 | fat 17.6 | protein 3.8 | total carbs 8.3 | fiber 7.1

Bacon Cheese Pizza

Servings: 2 | Cooking Time: 10 Minutes

Ingredients:
• 1 cup shredded Mozzarella cheese
• 1 ounce (28 g) cream cheese, broken into small pieces
• 4 slices cooked sugar-free bacon, chopped
• ¼ cup chopped pickled jalapeños
• 1 large egg, whisked
• ¼ teaspoon salt

Directions:
1. Place Mozzarella in a single layer on the bottom of an ungreased 6-inch round nonstick baking dish. Scatter cream cheese pieces, bacon, and jalapeños over Mozzarella, then pour egg evenly around baking dish.
2. Sprinkle with salt and place into air fryer basket. Adjust the

temperature to 330°F (166ºC) and set the timer for 10 minutes. When cheese is brown and egg is set, pizza will be done.

3. Let it cool on a large plate 5 minutes before serving.

Nutrition:
• (per serving) calories 361 | fat 24 | protein 26 | total carbs 5 | fiber 5

Mozzarella Almond Bagels

Servings: 6 | Cooking Time: 14 Minutes

Ingredients:
• 1¾ cups shredded Mozzarella cheese or goat cheese
• 2 tablespoons unsalted butter or coconut oil
• 1 large egg, beaten
• 1 tablespoon apple cider vinegar
• 1 cup blanched almond flour
• 1 tablespoon baking powder
• ⅛ teaspoon fine sea salt
• 1½ teaspoons everything bagel seasoning

Directions:
1. Make the dough: Put the Mozzarella and butter in a large microwave-safe bowl and microwave for 1 to 2 minutes, until the cheese is entirely melted. Stir well. Add the egg and vinegar. Using a hand mixer on medium, combine well. Add the almond flour, baking powder, and salt and, using the mixer, combine well.
2. Lay a piece of parchment paper on the countertop and place the dough on it. Knead it for about 3 minutes. The dough should be a little sticky but pliable. (If the dough is too sticky, chill it in the refrigerator for an hour or overnight.)
3. Preheat the air fryer to 350°F (180ºC). Spray a baking sheet or pie pan that will fit into your air fryer with avocado oil.
4. Divide the dough into 6 equal portions. Roll 1 portion into a log that is 6 inches long and about ½ -inch thick. Form the log into a circle and seal the edges together, making a bagel shape. Repeat with the remaining portions of dough, making 6 bagels.
5. Place the bagels on the greased baking sheet. Spray the bagels with avocado oil and top with everything bagel seasoning, pressing the seasoning into the dough with your hands.
6. Place the bagels in the air fryer and cook for 14 minutes, or until cooked through and golden brown, flipping after 6 minutes.
7. Remove the bagels from the air fryer and allow them to cool slightly before slicing them in half and serving. Store leftovers in an airtight container in the fridge for up to 4 days or in the freezer for up to a month.

Nutrition:
• (per serving) calories 224 | fat 19 | protein 12 | total carbs 4 | fiber 2

Bell Pepper And Ham Omelet

Servings: 2 | Cooking Time: 15 Minutes

Ingredients:
• 3 large eggs
• 1 tablespoon salted butter, melted
• ¼ cup seeded and chopped green bell pepper
• 2 tablespoons peeled and chopped yellow onion
• ¼ cup chopped cooked no-sugar-added ham
• ¼ teaspoon salt
• ¼ teaspoon ground black pepper

Directions:
1. Crack eggs into an ungreased 6-inch round nonstick baking dish. Mix in butter, bell pepper, onion, ham, salt, and black pep-

per.

2. Place dish into air fryer basket. Adjust the temperature to 320°F (160ºC) and set the timer for 15 minutes. The eggs will be fully cooked and firm in the middle when done.

3. Slice in half and serve warm on two medium plates.

Nutrition:
• (per serving) calories 201 | fat 14 | protein 13 | total carbs 3 | fiber 2

Cheesy Danish

Servings: 6 | Cooking Time: 20 Minutes

Ingredients:
• Pastry:
• 3 large eggs
• ¼ teaspoon cream of tartar
• ¼ cup vanilla-flavored egg white protein powder
• ¼ cup Swerve confectioners-style sweetener
• 3 tablespoons full-fat sour cream
• 1 teaspoon vanilla extract
• Filling:
• 4 ounces (113 g) cream cheese, softened
• 2 large egg yolks (from above)
• ¼ cup Swerve confectioners-style sweetener
• 1 teaspoon vanilla extract
• ¼ teaspoon ground cinnamon
• Drizzle:
• 1 ounce (28 g) cream cheese, softened
• 1 tablespoon Swerve confectioners-style sweetener
• 1 tablespoon unsweetened, unflavored almond milk

Directions:
1. Preheat the air fryer to 300°F (150ºC). Spray a casserole dish that will fit in your air fryer with avocado oil.

2. Make the pastry: Separate the eggs, putting all the whites in a large bowl, one yolk in a medium-sized bowl, and two yolks in a small bowl. Beat all the egg yolks and set aside.

3. Add the cream of tartar to the egg whites. Whip the whites with a hand mixer until very stiff, then turn the hand mixer's setting to low and slowly add the protein powder while mixing. Mix until only just combined, if you mix too long, the whites will fall. Set aside.

4. To the egg yolk in the medium-sized bowl, add the sweetener, sour cream, and vanilla extract. Mix well. Slowly pour the yolk mixture into the egg whites and gently combine. Dollop 6 equal-sized mounds of batter into the casserole dish. Use the back of a large spoon to make an indentation on the top of each mound. Set aside.

5. Make the filling: Place the cream cheese in a small bowl and stir to break it up. Add the 2 remaining egg yolks, the sweetener, vanilla extract, and cinnamon and stir until well combined. Divide the filling among the mounds of batter, pouring it into the indentations on the tops.

6. Place the Danish in the air fryer and bake for about 20 minutes, or until golden brown.

7. While the Danish bake, make the drizzle: In a small bowl, stir the cream cheese to break it up. Stir in the sweetener and almond milk. Place the mixture in a piping bag or a small resealable plastic bag with one corner snipped off. After the Danish have cooled, pipe the drizzle over the Danish.

8. Store leftovers in airtight container in the fridge for up to 4 days.

Nutrition:
• (per serving) calories 160 | fat 12 | protein 8 | total carbs 2 | fiber 1

Turkey Sausage And Avocado Burger

Servings: 4 | Cooking Time: 15 Minutes

Ingredients:
• 1 pound (454 g) ground turkey breakfast sausage
• ½ teaspoon salt
• ¼ teaspoon ground black pepper
• ¼ cup seeded and chopped green bell pepper
• 2 tablespoons mayonnaise
• 1 medium avocado, peeled, pitted, and sliced

Directions:
1. In a large bowl, mix sausage with salt, black pepper, bell pepper, and mayonnaise. Form meat into four patties.

2. Place patties into ungreased air fryer basket. Adjust the temperature to 370°F and set the timer for 15 minutes, turning patties halfway through cooking. Burgers will be done when dark brown and they have an internal temperature of at least 165°F (74ºC).

3. Serve burgers topped with avocado slices on four medium plates.

Nutrition:
• (per serving) calories 276 | fat 17 | protein 22 | total carbs 4 | fiber 1

Chapter 3 Snacks And Appetizers Recipes

Air Fryer Meatballs

Servings: 7 | Cooking Time: 13 Minutes

Ingredients:
- 1 egg
- 1-pound ground beef
- 1 tablespoon tomato puree
- 1 teaspoon salt
- 1 teaspoon curry paste
- ½ teaspoon ground coriander
- 2 oz chive stems
- 1 tablespoon butter
- ¼ teaspoon chili flakes

Directions:
1. Crack the egg in a bowl.
2. Add salt, curry paste, ground coriander, diced chives, and chili flakes.
3. Mix well until the curry paste has dissolved.
4. Add the ground beef and stir well.
5. Preheat the air fryer to 360 F.
6. Make 7 small meatballs from the ground beef mixture.
7. Place the meatballs in the air fryer basket tray.
8. Add butter and tomato puree.
9. Cook the meatballs for 13 minutes, stirring halfway through.
10. Serve hot.

Nutrition:
- (per serving) calories 153 | fat 6.8 | protein 20.6 | total carbs 1.2 | fiber 0.2

Eggplants Circles

Servings: 9 | Cooking Time: 8 Minutes

Ingredients:
- 2 eggplants
- 1 tablespoon olive oil
- 1 teaspoon minced garlic
- ½ teaspoon salt
- 1 teaspoon ground turmeric
- 1 teaspoon dried rosemary

Directions:
1. Wash the eggplants carefully and slice into thick circles.
2. Combine the olive oil, minced garlic, salt, ground turmeric, and dried rosemary in a bowl.
3. Mix well.
4. Brush each eggplant circle with the oil mixture.
5. Preheat the air fryer to 400 F.
6. Place the eggplant in the air fryer rack and cook for 5 minutes.
7. Turn the eggplant and cook for 3 minutes more or until soft and golden brown.

Nutrition:
- (per serving) calories 49 | fat 1.5 | protein 1.1 | total carbs 7.5 | fiber 4.7

Keto Meat Bombs

Servings: 7 | Cooking Time: 14 Minutes

Ingredients:
- 6 oz. ground chicken
- 6 oz. ground beef
- 6 oz. ground pork
- 2 oz chive stems
- 3 garlic cloves, minced
- 1 tablespoon dried parsley
- ½ teaspoon salt
- ½ teaspoon chili flakes
- 1 egg
- 1 tablespoon butter

Directions:
1. Put the ground chicken, ground beef, and ground pork in a mixing bowl.
2. Add the diced chives, minced garlic, dried parsley, salt, and chili flakes.
3. Crack the egg into the bowl with the ground meat.
4. Stir the meat mixture using your hands.
5. Melt butter and add it to the ground meat mixture.
6. Stir.
7. Leave the ground meat mixture for 5 minutes to rest.
8. Preheat the air fryer to 370 F.
9. Make small meatballs from the meat mixture and put them in the air fryer.
10. Cook the meatballs for 14 minutes.
11. Cool before serving.

Nutrition:
- (per serving) calories 155 | fat 6.5 | protein 21.8 | total carbs 1.3 | fiber 0.2

Cheese Crisps

Servings: 2 | Cooking Time: 12 Minutes

Ingredients:
- ½ cup shredded Cheddar cheese
- 1 egg white

Directions:
1. Preheat the air fryer to 400°F (205ºC). Place a piece of parchment paper in the bottom of the air fryer basket.
2. In a medium bowl, combine the cheese and egg white, stirring with a fork until thoroughly combined.
3. Place small scoops of the cheese mixture in a single layer in the basket of the air fryer (about 1-inch apart). Use the fork to spread the mixture as thin as possible. Air fry for 10 to 12 minutes until the crisps are golden brown. Let it cool for a few minutes before transferring them to a plate. Store at room temperature in an airtight container for up to 3 days.

Nutrition:
- (per serving) calories 120 | fat 10 | protein 9 | total carbs 1 | fiber 1

Lamb Burgers

Servings: 6 | Cooking Time: 9 Minutes

Ingredients:
- 1-pound ground lamb
- 3 oz chive stems
- 1 teaspoon minced garlic
- 1 teaspoon salt
- ½ teaspoon chili pepper
- 1 teaspoon ground black pepper
- 1 large egg
- 2 tablespoon coconut flour
- 1 teaspoon olive oil

Directions:
1. Combine the ground lamb with the diced chives.
2. Stir carefully and sprinkle the mixture with minced garlic and salt.
3. Add chili pepper, ground black pepper, and coconut flour.
4. Crack the egg into the mixture and mix with your hands.
5. Place the mixture in the fridge for 10 minutes.
6. Meanwhile, preheat the air fryer to 400 F.
7. Make 6 large balls from the ground lamb mixture and flatten them to make the shape of a burger patty.
8. Place the burgers in the air fryer rack and drizzle them with olive oil.
9. Cook for 6 minutes.
10. Turn them using a spatula.
11. Cook the lamb burgers for 3 minutes.
12. Serve hot.

Nutrition:
- (per serving) calories 178 | fat 7.4 | protein 22.9 | total carbs 3.9 | fiber 1.5

Bacon Mozzarella Balls

Servings: 6 | Cooking Time: 10 Minutes

Ingredients:
- 5 oz. bacon, sliced
- 10 oz. mozzarella
- ¼ teaspoon ground black pepper
- ¼ teaspoon paprika

Directions:
1. Sprinkle the sliced bacon with ground black pepper and paprika.
2. Wrap the mozzarella balls in the bacon.
3. Secure the mozzarella balls with toothpicks.
4. Preheat the air fryer to 360 F.
5. Put the mozzarella balls in the air fryer rack and cook for 10 minutes.

Nutrition:
- (per serving) calories 262 | fat 18.2 | protein 22.1 | total carbs 2.1 | fiber 0.1

Spinach Chips

Servings: 3 | Cooking Time: 10 Minutes

Ingredients:
- 3 cups fresh spinach leaves
- 1 tablespoon extra-virgin olive oil
- 1 teaspoon sea salt
- ½ teaspoon cayenne pepper
- 1 teaspoon garlic powder
- Chili Yogurt Dip:
- ¼ cup yogurt
- 2 tablespoons mayonnaise
- ½ teaspoon chili powder

Directions:
1. Toss the spinach leaves with the olive oil and seasonings.
2. Bake in the preheated Air Fryer at 350°F (180°C) for 10 minutes, shaking the cooking basket occasionally.
3. Bake until the edges brown, working in batches.
4. In the meantime, make the sauce by whisking all ingredients in a mixing dish. Serve immediately.

Nutrition:
- (per serving) calories 128 | fat 12 | protein 2 | total carbs 3 | fiber 2

Calamari Rings

Servings: 4 | Cooking Time: 15 Minutes

Ingredients:
- 2 large egg yolks
- 1 cup powdered Parmesan cheese
- ¼ cup coconut flour
- 3 teaspoons dried oregano leaves
- ½ teaspoon garlic powder
- ½ teaspoon onion powder
- 1 pound (454 g) calamari, sliced into rings
- Fresh oregano leaves, for garnish (optional)
- 1 cup no-sugar-added marinara sauce, for serving (optional)
- Lemon slices, for serving (optional)

Directions:
1. Spray the air fryer basket with avocado oil. Preheat the air fryer to 400°F (205°C).
2. In a shallow dish, whisk the egg yolks. In a separate bowl, mix together the Parmesan, coconut flour, and spices.
3. Dip the calamari rings in the egg yolks, tap off any excess egg, then dip them into the cheese mixture and coat well. Use your hands to press the coating onto the calamari if necessary. Spray the coated rings with avocado oil.
4. Place the calamari rings in the air fryer, leaving space between them, and cook for 15 minutes, or until golden brown. Garnish with fresh oregano, if desired, and serve with marinara sauce for dipping and lemon slices, if desired.
5. Best served fresh. Store leftovers in an airtight container in the fridge for up to 5 days. Reheat in a preheated 400°F (205°C) air fryer for 3 minutes, or until heated through.

Nutrition:
- (per serving) calories 287 | fat 13 | protein 28 | total carbs 11 | fiber 8

Pork Egg

Servings:12 | Cooking Time: 25 Minutes

Ingredients:
- 7 large eggs, divided
- 1 ounce (28 g) plain pork rinds, finely crushed
- 2 tablespoons mayonnaise
- ¼ teaspoon salt
- ¼ teaspoon ground black pepper

Directions:
1. Place 6 whole eggs into ungreased air fryer basket. Adjust the temperature to 220°F (104°C) and set the timer for 20 minutes. When done, place eggs into a bowl of ice water to cool 5 minutes.
2. Peel cool eggs, then cut in half lengthwise. Remove yolks and place aside in a medium bowl.
3. In a separate small bowl, whisk remaining raw egg. Place pork rinds in a separate medium bowl. Dip each egg white into whisked egg, then gently coat with pork rinds. Spritz with cooking spray and place into ungreased air fryer basket. Adjust the temperature to 400°F (205°C) and set the timer for 5 minutes, turning eggs halfway through cooking. Eggs will be golden when done.
4. Mash yolks in bowl with mayonnaise until smooth. Sprinkle with salt and pepper and mix.
5. Spoon 2 tablespoons of yolk mixture into each fried egg white. Serve warm.

Nutrition:
- (per serving) calories 141 | fat 10 | protein 10 | total carbs 1 | fiber 1

Onion Circles

Servings: 10 | Cooking Time: 8 Minutes

Ingredients:
- 2 white onions
- ½ teaspoon salt
- ½ cup coconut flour
- ½ teaspoon paprika
- ½ teaspoon ground black pepper
- 1 egg
- 1/3 cup heavy cream
- 1/3 cup almond flour
- 1 tablespoon olive oil

Directions:
1. Peel the onions and slice them roughly.
2. Separate the sliced onions into circles.
3. Crack the egg into a bowl and whisk.
4. Sprinkle the whisked egg with the paprika, salt, ground black pepper, and heavy cream.
5. Whisk well until combined.
6. Preheat the air fryer to 360 F.
7. Coat the onion rings in the almond flour.
8. Dip the onion circles in the whisked egg mixture.
9. Coat the onion circles in the coconut flour.
10. Grease the air fryer basket tray with the olive oil and place the onion circles inside.
11. Cook the onion circles for 8 minutes.

Nutrition:
- (per serving) calories 88 | fat 5.7 | protein 2.5 | total carbs 7.1 | fiber 3.3

Bloomin' Onion

Servings:8 | Cooking Time: 35 Minutes

Ingredients:
- 1 extra-large onion (about 3 inches in diameter)
- 2 large eggs
- 1 tablespoon water
- ½ cup powdered Parmesan cheese (about 1½ ounces; see here) (or pork dust for dairy-free; see here)
- 2 teaspoons paprika
- 1 teaspoon garlic powder
- ¼ teaspoon cayenne pepper
- ¼ teaspoon fine sea salt
- ¼ teaspoon ground black pepper
- FOR GARNISH (OPTIONAL):
- Fresh parsley leaves
- Powdered Parmesan cheese (see here)
- FOR SERVING (OPTIONAL):
- Prepared yellow mustard
- Ranch Dressing (here)
- Reduced-sugar or sugar-free ketchup

Directions:
1. Spray the air fryer basket with avocado oil. Preheat the air fryer to 350°F.
2. Using a sharp knife, cut the top ½ inch off the onion and peel off the outer layer. Cut the onion into 8 equal sections, stopping 1 inch from the bottom—you want the onion to stay together at the base. Gently spread the sections, or "petals," apart.
3. Crack the eggs into a large bowl, add the water, and whisk well. Place the onion in the dish and coat it well in the egg. Use a spoon to coat the inside of the onion and all of the petals.
4. In a small bowl, combine the Parmesan, seasonings, salt, and pepper.
5. Place the onion in a 6-inch pie pan or casserole dish. Sprinkle the seasoning mixture all over the onion and use your fingers to press it into the petals. Spray the onion with avocado oil.
6. Loosely cover the onion with parchment paper and then foil. Place the dish in the air fryer. Cook for 30 minutes, then remove it from the air fryer and increase the air fryer temperature to 400°F.
7. Remove the foil and parchment and spray the onion with avocado oil again. Protecting your hands with oven-safe gloves or a tea towel, transfer the onion to the air fryer basket. Cook for an additional 3 to 5 minutes, until light brown and crispy.
8. Garnish with fresh parsley and powdered Parmesan, if desired. Serve with mustard, ranch dressing, and ketchup, if desired.
9. Store leftovers in an airtight container in the fridge for up to 4 days. Reheat in a preheated 400°F air fryer for 3 to 5 minutes, until warm and crispy.

Nutrition:
- (per serving)   calories 51 | fat 3g | protein 4g | total carbs 3g | fiber 0.4g

Cucumber Chips

Servings: 12 | Cooking Time: 11 Minutes

Ingredients:
- 1-pound cucumber
- 1 teaspoon salt
- 1 tablespoon smoked paprika
- ½ teaspoon garlic powder

Directions:
1. Wash the cucumbers carefully and slice them into chips.

2. Sprinkle the chips with salt, smoked paprika, and garlic powder.
3. Preheat the air fryer to 370 F.
4. Place the cucumber slices in the air fryer rack.
5. Cook the cucumber chips for 11 minutes.
6. Transfer the cucumber chips to a paper towel and allow to cool.
7. Serve the cucumber chips immediately or keep them in a paper bag.

Nutrition:
• (per serving) calories 8 | fat 0.1 | protein 0.4 | total carbs 1.8 | fiber 0.4

Zucchini Fries

Servings: 8 | Cooking Time: 10 Minutes

Ingredients:
• 2 medium zucchini, ends removed, quartered lengthwise, and sliced into 3-inch long fries
• ½ teaspoon salt
• ⅓ cup heavy whipping cream
• ½ cup blanched finely ground almond flour
• ¾ cup grated Parmesan cheese
• 1 teaspoon Italian seasoning

Directions:
1. Sprinkle zucchini with salt and wrap in a kitchen towel to draw out excess moisture. Let it sit 2 hours.
2. Pour cream into a medium bowl. In a separate medium bowl, whisk together flour, Parmesan, and Italian seasoning.
3. Place each zucchini fry into cream, then gently shake off excess. Press each fry into dry mixture, coating each side, then place into ungreased air fryer basket. Adjust the temperature to 400°F (205ºC) and set the timer for 10 minutes, turning fries halfway through cooking. Fries will be golden and crispy when done. Place on clean parchment sheet to cool for 5 minutes before serving.

Nutrition:
• (per serving) calories 124 | fat 10 | protein 5 | total carbs 4 | fiber 3

Broccoli Fries With Spicy Dip

Servings: 4 | Cooking Time: 6 Minutes

Ingredients:
• ¾ pound (340g) broccoli florets
• ½ teaspoon onion powder
• 1 teaspoon granulated garlic
• ½ teaspoon cayenne pepper
• Sea salt and ground black pepper, to taste
• 2 tablespoons sesame oil
• 4 tablespoons Parmesan cheese, preferably freshly grated
• Spicy Dip:
• ¼ cup mayonnaise
• ¼ cup Greek yogurt
• ¼ teaspoon Dijon mustard
• 1 teaspoon keto hot sauce

Directions:
1. Start by preheating the Air Fryer to 400ºF (205ºC).
2. Blanch the broccoli in salted boiling water until al dente, for about 3 to 4 minutes. Drain well and transfer to the lightly greased Air Fryer basket.
3. Add the onion powder, garlic, cayenne pepper, salt, black pepper, sesame oil, and Parmesan cheese.
4. Cook for 6 minutes, tossing halfway through the cooking time.
5. Meanwhile, mix all of the spicy dip ingredients. Serve broccoli fries with chilled dipping sauce. Bon appétit!

Nutrition:
• (per serving) calories 219 | fat 19 | protein 5 | total carbs 9 | fiber 6

Cauliflower And Prosciutto Pierogi

Servings:4 | Cooking Time: 20 Minutes

Ingredients:
• 1 cup chopped cauliflower
• 2 tablespoons diced onions
• 1 tablespoon unsalted butter (or lard or bacon fat for dairy-free), melted
• pinch of fine sea salt
• ½ cup shredded sharp Cheddar cheese (about 2 ounces / 57 g) (or Kite Hill brand cream cheese style spread, softened, for dairy-free)
• 8 slices prosciutto
• Fresh oregano leaves, for garnish (optional)

Directions:
1. Preheat the air fryer to 350°F (180ºC). Lightly grease a 7-inch pie pan or a casserole dish that will fit in your air fryer.
2. Make the filling: Place the cauliflower and onion in the pan. Drizzle with the melted butter and sprinkle with the salt. Using your hands, mix everything together, making sure the cauliflower is coated in the butter.
3. Place the cauliflower mixture in the air fryer and cook for 10 minutes, until fork-tender, stirring halfway through.
4. Transfer the cauliflower mixture to a food processor or high-powered blender. Spray the air fryer basket with avocado oil and increase the air fryer temperature to 400°F (205ºC).
5. Pulse the cauliflower mixture in the food processor until smooth. Stir in the cheese.
6. Assemble the pierogi: Lay 1 slice of prosciutto on a sheet of parchment paper with a short end toward you. Lay another slice of prosciutto on top of it at a right angle, forming a cross. Spoon about 2 heaping tablespoons of the filling into the center of the cross.
7. Fold each arm of the prosciutto cross over the filling to form a square, making sure that the filling is well covered. Using your fingers, press down around the filling to even out the square shape. Repeat with the rest of the prosciutto and filling.
8. Spray the pierogi with avocado oil and place them in the air fryer basket. Cook for 10 minutes, or until crispy.
9. Garnish with oregano before serving, if desired. Store leftovers in an airtight container in the fridge for up to 4 days. Reheat in a preheated 400°F (205ºC) air fryer for 3 minutes, or until heated through.

Nutrition:
• (per serving) calories 150 | fat 11 | protein 11 | total carbs 2 | fiber 1

Salt And Vinegar Pork Belly Chips

Servings:4 | Cooking Time: 12 Minutes

Ingredients:
- 1 pound slab pork belly (see Tip)
- ½ cup apple cider vinegar
- Fine sea salt
- FOR SERVING (OPTIONAL):
- Guacamole
- Pico de gallo

Directions:
1. Slice the pork belly into ⅛-inch-thick strips and place them in a shallow dish. Pour in the vinegar and stir to coat the pork belly. Place in the fridge to marinate for 30 minutes.
2. Spray the air fryer basket with avocado oil. Preheat the air fryer to 400°F.
3. Remove the pork belly from the vinegar and place the strips in the air fryer basket in a single layer, leaving space between them. Cook in the air fryer for 10 to 12 minutes, until crispy, flipping after 5 minutes. Remove from the air fryer and sprinkle with salt. Serve with guacamole and pico de gallo, if desired.
4. Best served fresh. Store leftovers in an airtight container in the fridge for up to 5 days. Reheat in a preheated 400°F air fryer for 5 minutes, or until heated through, flipping halfway through.

Nutrition:
- (per serving) calories 240 | fat 21g | protein 13g | total carbs 0g | fiber 0g

Scallops And Bacon Kabobs

Servings: 6 | Cooking Time: 6 Minutes

Ingredients:
- 1 pound (454 g) sea scallops
- ½ cup coconut milk
- 1 tablespoon vermouth
- Sea salt and ground black pepper, to taste
- ½ pound (227g) bacon, diced
- 1 shallot, diced
- 1 teaspoon garlic powder
- 1 teaspoon paprika

Directions:
1. In a ceramic bowl, place the sea scallops, coconut milk, vermouth, salt, and black pepper, let it marinate for 30 minutes.
2. Assemble the skewers alternating the scallops, bacon, and shallots. Sprinkle garlic powder and paprika all over the skewers.
3. Bake in the preheated air Fryer at 400°F (205ºC) for 6 minutes. Serve warm and enjoy!

Nutrition:
- (per serving) calories 228 | fat 15 | protein 15 | total carbs 5 | fiber 5

Flax Seeds Wraps

Servings: 2 | Cooking Time: 2 Minutes

Ingredients:
- 1 cucumber
- 1 egg
- 3 oz. flax seeds
- 3 oz. mozzarella, grated
- 1 tablespoon water
- ½ tablespoon butter
- ¼ teaspoon baking soda
- ¼ teaspoon salt

Directions:
1. Crack the egg into a bowl and whisk it.
2. Sprinkle the whisked egg with the flax seeds, grated mozzarella, water, baking soda, and salt.
3. Whisk the mixture.
4. Preheat the air fryer to 360 F.
5. Toss the butter in the air fryer basket and melt it.
6. Separate the egg liquid into 2 servings.
7. Pour the first part of the serving in the air fryer basket.
8. Cook it for 1 minute on one side.
9. Turn over and cook for another minute.
10. Repeat the same steps with the remaining egg mixture.
11. Cut the cucumber into cubes.
12. Separate the cubed cucumber into 2 parts.
13. Place the cucumber cubes in the center of each egg pancake.
14. Wrap the eggs.

Nutrition:
- (per serving) calories 143 | fat 8.4 | protein 8.6 | total carbs 7.3 | fiber 6.2

Mozzarella Sticks

Servings:24 | Cooking Time: 14 Minutes Per Batch

Ingredients:
- DOUGH:
- 1¾ cups shredded mozzarella cheese (about 7 ounces)
- 2 tablespoons unsalted butter
- 1 large egg, beaten
- ¾ cup blanched almond flour
- ⅛ teaspoon fine sea salt
- 24 pieces of string cheese
- SPICE MIX:
- ¼ cup grated Parmesan cheese
- 3 tablespoons garlic powder
- 1 tablespoon dried oregano leaves
- 1 tablespoon onion powder
- FOR SERVING (OPTIONAL):
- ½ cup marinara sauce
- ½ cup pesto (here)

Directions:
1. Make the dough: Place the mozzarella and butter in a large microwave-safe bowl and microwave for 1 to 2 minutes, until the cheese is entirely melted. Stir well.
2. Add the egg and, using a hand mixer on low, combine well. Add the almond flour and salt and combine well with the mixer.
3. Lay a piece of parchment paper on the countertop and place the dough on it. Knead it for about 3 minutes; the dough should be thick yet pliable. (Note: If the dough is too sticky, chill it in the refrigerator for an hour or overnight.)
4. Scoop up 3 tablespoons of the dough and flatten it into a very thin 3½ by 2-inch rectangle. Place one piece of string cheese in the center and use your hands to press the dough tightly around it. Repeat with the remaining string cheese and dough.
5. In a shallow dish, combine the spice mix ingredients. Place a wrapped piece of string cheese in the dish and roll while pressing down to form a nice crust. Repeat with the remaining pieces of string cheese. Place in the freezer for 2 hours.
6. Ten minutes before air frying, spray the air fryer basket with avocado oil and preheat the air fryer to 425°F.
7. Place the frozen mozzarella sticks in the air fryer basket, leaving space between them, and cook for 9 to 12 minutes, until

golden brown. Remove from the air fryer and serve with marinara sauce and pesto, if desired.

8. Store leftovers in an airtight container in the refrigerator for up to 3 days or in the freezer for up to a month. Reheat in a preheated 425°F air fryer for 4 minutes, or until warmed through.

Nutrition:
• (per serving)   calories 337 | fat 27g | protein 23g | total carbs 4g | fiber 1g

Guacamole Rings In Prosciutto

Servings: 8 | Cooking Time: 6 Minutes

Ingredients:
• Guacamole:
• 2 avocados, halved, pitted, and peeled
• 3 tablespoons lime juice, plus more to taste
• 2 small plum tomatoes, diced
• ½ cup finely diced onions
• 2 small cloves garlic, smashed to a paste
• 3 tablespoons chopped fresh cilantro leaves
• ½ scant teaspoon fine sea salt
• ½ scant teaspoon ground cumin
• 2 small onions (about 1½ inches in diameter), cut into ½-inch-thick slices
• 8 slices prosciutto

Directions:
1. Make the guacamole: Place the avocados and lime juice in a large bowl and mash with a fork until it reaches your desired consistency. Add the tomatoes, onions, garlic, cilantro, salt, and cumin and stir until well combined. Taste and add more lime juice if desired. Set aside half of the guacamole for serving. (Note: If you're making the guacamole ahead of time, place it in a large resealable plastic bag, squeeze out all the air, and seal it shut. It will keep in the refrigerator for up to 3 days when stored this way.)
2. Place a piece of parchment paper on a tray that fits in your freezer and place the onion slices on it, breaking the slices apart into 8 rings. Fill each ring with about 2 tablespoons of guacamole. Place the tray in the freezer for 2 hours.
3. Spray the air fryer basket with avocado oil. Preheat the air fryer to 400°F.
4. Remove the rings from the freezer and wrap each in a slice of prosciutto. Place them in the air fryer basket, leaving space between them (if you're using a smaller air fryer, work in batches if necessary), and cook for 6 minutes, flipping halfway through. Use a spatula to remove the rings from the air fryer. Serve with the reserved half of the guacamole.
5. Store leftovers in an airtight container in the refrigerator for up to 4 days. Reheat in a preheated 400°F air fryer for about 3 minutes, until heated through.

Nutrition:
• (per serving) calories 132 | fat 9 | protein 5 | total carbs 10 | fiber 4

Sausage And Bacon Cheese Pizza

Servings: 1 | Cooking Time: 5 Minutes

Ingredients:
• ½ cup shredded Mozzarella cheese
• 7 slices pepperoni
• ¼ cup cooked ground sausage
• 2 slices sugar-free bacon, cooked and crumbled
• 1 tablespoon grated Parmesan cheese
• 2 tablespoons low-carb, sugar-free pizza sauce, for dipping

Directions:
1. Cover the bottom of a 6-inch cake pan with Mozzarella. Place pepperoni, sausage, and bacon on top of cheese and sprinkle with Parmesan. Place pan into the air fryer basket.
2. Adjust the temperature to 400°F (205ºC) and set the timer for 5 minutes.
3. Remove when cheese is bubbling and golden. Serve warm with pizza sauce for dipping.

Nutrition:
• (per serving) calories 466 | fat 34 | protein 28 | total carbs 5 | fiber 4

Beef Cheese Burger

Servings: 4 | Cooking Time: 15 Minutes

Ingredients:
• 1 tablespoon Dijon mustard
• 2 tablespoons minced scallions
• 1 pound (454 g) ground beef
• 1½ teaspoons minced green garlic
• ½ teaspoon cumin
• Salt and ground black pepper, to taste
• 12 cherry tomatoes
• 12 cubes Cheddar cheese

Directions:
1. In a large-sized mixing dish, place the mustard, ground beef, cumin, scallions, garlic, salt, and pepper, mix with your hands or a spatula so that everything is evenly coated.
2. Form into 12 meatballs and cook them in the preheated Air Fryer for 15 minutes at 375°F (190ºC). Air-fry until they are cooked in the middle.
3. Thread cherry tomatoes, mini burgers and cheese on cocktail sticks. Bon appétit!

Nutrition:
• (per serving) calories 469 | fat 30 | protein 3 | total carbs 4 | fiber 3

Easy Cooked Chicken Wings

Servings: 5 | Cooking Time: 12 Minutes

Ingredients:
• 1 teaspoon stevia extract
• 1 teaspoon salt
• 1-pound chicken wings
• 1 teaspoon paprika
• 1 teaspoon dried oregano
• 1 tablespoon olive oil

Directions:
1. Combine the salt, paprika, and dried oregano in a bowl and stir.
2. Coat the chicken wings with the spices.
3. Sprinkle the chicken wings with the stevia extract.

4. Preheat the air fryer to 400 F.
5. Place the prepared chicken wings in the air fryer rack and drizzle them with olive oil.
6. Cook for 12 minutes.
7. Remove and place them on a paper towel to drain any excess grease.

Nutrition:
- (per serving) calories 199 | fat 9.6 | protein 26.3 | total carbs 0.4 | fiber 0.3

Bourbon Chicken Wings

Servings:8 | Cooking Time: 32 Minutes

Ingredients:
- 2 pounds chicken wings or drummies
- ½ teaspoon fine sea salt
- SAUCE:
- ½ cup chicken broth
- ⅓ cup Swerve confectioners'-style sweetener or equivalent amount of liquid or powdered sweetener (see here)
- ¼ cup tomato sauce
- ¼ cup wheat-free tamari
- 1 tablespoon apple cider vinegar
- ¾ teaspoon red pepper flakes
- ¼ teaspoon grated fresh ginger
- 1 clove garlic, smashed to a paste
- FOR GARNISH (OPTIONAL):
- Chopped green onions
- Sesame seeds

Directions:
1. Spray the air fryer basket with avocado oil. Preheat the air fryer to 380°F.
2. Season the chicken wings on all sides with the salt and place them in the air fryer. Cook for 25 minutes, flipping after 15 minutes. After 25 minutes, increase the temperature to 400°F and cook for 6 to 7 minutes more, until the skin is browned and crisp.
3. While the wings cook, make the sauce: Place all the sauce ingredients in a large sauté pan and whisk to combine. Simmer until reduced and thickened, about 10 minutes.
4. Brush the cooked chicken wings with the sauce. Garnish with green onions and sesame seeds, if desired. Serve with extra sauce on the side for dipping.
5. Store leftovers in an airtight container in the refrigerator for up to 4 days. Reheat in a preheated 350°F air fryer for 5 minutes, then increase the temperature to 400°F and cook for 3 to 5 more minutes, until warm and crispy.

Nutrition:
- (per serving) calories 545 | fat 30g | protein 42g | total carbs 3g | fiber 0.1g

Pork Rind Chicken With Guacamole

Servings: 2 | Cooking Time: 5 Minutes

Ingredients:
- 1 ounce (28 g) pork rinds
- 4 ounces (113 g) shredded cooked chicken
- ½ cup shredded Monterey jack cheese
- ¼ cup sliced pickled jalapeños
- ¼ cup guacamole
- ¼ cup full-fat sour cream

Directions:
1. Place pork rinds into 6-inch round baking pan. Cover with

shredded chicken and Monterey jack cheese. Place pan into the air fryer basket.
2. Adjust the temperature to 370°F (188°C) and set the timer for 5 minutes or until cheese is melted.
3. Top with jalapeños, guacamole, and sour cream. Serve immediately.

Nutrition:
- (per serving) calories 395 | fat 27 | protein 30 | total carbs 3 | fiber 2

Keto Sesame Cloud Buns

Servings: 10 | Cooking Time: 13 Minutes

Ingredients:
- 1 cup almond flour
- 5 tablespoon sesame seeds
- 1 tablespoon pumpkin seeds, crushed
- 1 teaspoon stevia extract
- ½ tablespoon baking powder
- 1 teaspoon apple cider vinegar
- ¼ teaspoon salt
- ½ cup water, hot
- 4 eggs

Directions:
1. Place the almond flour, sesame seeds, crushed pumpkin seeds, baking powder, and salt in a large mixing bowl.
2. Then crack the eggs in a separate bowl.
3. Whisk them and add stevia extract and apple cider vinegar.
4. Stir the egg mixture gently.
5. Pour the hot water into the almond flour mixture.
6. Stir and add the whisked egg mixture.
7. Knead the dough until well combined.
8. Preheat the air fryer to 350 F.
9. Cover the air fryer basket with some parchment paper.
10. Make 10 small buns from the dough and put them in the air fryer.
11. Cook the sesame cloud buns for 13 minutes.
12. Check if the buns are cooked. If they require a little more time – cook for 1 minute more.
13. Allow to cool before serving.

Nutrition:
- (per serving) calories 72 | fat 5.8 | protein 3.8 | total carbs 2.3 | fiber 0.9

Eggplant Chips

Servings: 10 | Cooking Time: 13 Minutes

Ingredients:
- 1 teaspoon onion powder
- 1 teaspoon salt
- 3 eggplants
- 1 teaspoon paprika
- ½ teaspoon ground black pepper
- 1 tablespoon olive oil

Directions:
1. Wash the eggplants and slice them into chips.
2. Sprinkle the eggplant slices with salt and let it absorb the eggplant juice and bitterness.
3. Dry the eggplant slices and sprinkle them with onion powder, paprika, and ground black pepper.
4. Stir the eggplant slices using your fingertips.
5. Then preheat the air fryer to 400 F.

6. Place the eggplant slices in the air fryer rack and cook them for 13 minutes. The temperature of cooking depends on the thickness of the eggplant slices.

Nutrition:
- (per serving) calories 46 | fat 1.4 | protein 1.1 | total carbs 8.2 | fiber 5.3

Chicken Nuggets

Servings: 6 | Cooking Time: 12 Minutes

Ingredients:
- 1 pound (454 g) chicken breasts, slice into tenders
- ½ teaspoon cayenne pepper
- Salt and black pepper, to taste
- ¼ cup almond meal
- 1 egg, whisked
- ½ cup Parmesan cheese, freshly grated
- ¼ cup mayo
- ¼ cup no-sugar-added barbecue sauce

Directions:
1. Pat the chicken tenders dry with a kitchen towel. Season with the cayenne pepper, salt, and black pepper.
2. Dip the chicken tenders into the almond meal, followed by the egg. Press the chicken tenders into the Parmesan cheese, coating evenly.
3. Place the chicken tenders in the lightly greased Air Fryer basket. Cook at 360°for 9 to 12 minutes, turning them over to cook evenly.
4. In a mixing bowl, thoroughly combine the mayonnaise with the barbecue sauce. Serve the chicken nuggets with the sauce for dipping. Bon appétit!

Nutrition:
- (per serving) calories 268 | fat 18 | protein 2 | total carbs 4 | fiber 3

Cauliflower With Buffalo Sauce

Servings: 6 | Cooking Time: 15 Minutes

Ingredients:
- 1 medium head cauliflower, leaves and core removed, cut into bite-sized pieces
- 4 tablespoons salted butter, melted
- ¼ cup dry ranch seasoning
- ⅓ cup sugar-free buffalo sauce

Directions:
1. Place cauliflower pieces into a large bowl. Pour butter over cauliflower and toss to coat. Sprinkle in ranch seasoning and toss to coat.
2. Place cauliflower into ungreased air fryer basket. Adjust the temperature to 350°F (180ºC) and set the timer for 12 minutes, shaking the basket three times during cooking.
3. When timer beeps, place cooked cauliflower in a clean large bowl. Toss with buffalo sauce, then return to air fryer basket to cook for another 3 minutes. Cauliflower bites will be darkened at the edges and tender when done. Serve warm.

Nutrition:
- (per serving) calories 112 | fat 7 | protein 2 | total carbs 9 | fiber 7

Kohlrabi Chips

Servings: 10 | Cooking Time: 20 Minutes

Ingredients:
- 1-pound kohlrabi
- 1 teaspoon salt
- 1 tablespoon sesame oil
- 1 teaspoon smoked paprika

Directions:
1. Peel the kohlrabi.
2. Slice it into thin pieces.
3. Sprinkle the kohlrabi slices with salt, smoked paprika, and sesame oil.
4. Shake the mixture.
5. Preheat the air fryer to 320 F.
6. Put the kohlrabi slices in the air fryer rack and cook for 20 minutes.
7. Stir during cooking.
8. Cool before serving.

Nutrition:
- (per serving) calories 25 | fat 1.4 | protein 0.8 | total carbs 2.9 | fiber 1.7

Pumpkin Fries

Servings: 7 | Cooking Time: 15 Minutes

Ingredients:
- 1-pound pumpkin
- 1 teaspoon ground cinnamon
- ½ teaspoon ground ginger
- ½ teaspoon salt
- 1 teaspoon olive oil
- 1 teaspoon turmeric

Directions:
1. Peel the pumpkin and cut it into thick strips.
2. Coat the pumpkin strips with the ground cinnamon, ground ginger, salt, and turmeric.
3. Stir the pumpkin carefully and leave for 5 minutes to marinade.
4. Preheat the air fryer to 360 F.
5. Drizzle the pumpkin with the olive oil and transfer it to the air fryer basket.
6. Cook the pumpkin fries for 15 minutes, stirring occasionally.
7. Place the cooked pumpkin fries on paper towel.
8. Chill them for 3-4 minutes before serving.

Nutrition:
- (per serving) calories 30 | fat 0.9 | protein 0.8 | total carbs 5.8 | fiber 2.2

Pepperoni Chips

Servings: 2 | Cooking Time: 8 Minutes

Ingredients:
- 14 slices pepperoni

Directions:
1. Place pepperoni slices into ungreased air fryer basket. Adjust the temperature to 350°F (180°C) and set the timer for 8 minutes. Pepperoni will be browned and crispy when done. Let it cool 5 minutes before serving. Store in airtight container at room temperature up to 3 days.

Nutrition:
- (per serving) calories 69 | fat 5 | protein 3 | total carbs 0 | fiber 0

Cheesy Mini Peppers With Bacon

Servings: 16 Halves | Cooking Time: 8 Minutes

Ingredients:
- 8 mini sweet peppers
- 4 ounces (113 g) full-fat cream cheese, softened
- 4 slices sugar-free bacon, cooked and crumbled
- ¼ cup shredded pepper jack cheese

Directions:
1. Remove the tops from the peppers and slice each one in half lengthwise. Use a small knife to remove seeds and membranes.
2. In a small bowl, mix cream cheese, bacon, and pepper jack.
3. Place 3 teaspoons of the mixture into each sweet pepper and press down smooth. Place into the fryer basket.
4. Adjust the temperature to 400°F (205°C) and set the timer for 8 minutes.
5. Serve warm.

Nutrition:
- (per serving) calories 176 | fat 13 | protein 7 | total carbs 4 | fiber 3

Turnip Slices

Servings: 8 | Cooking Time: 10 Minutes

Ingredients:
- 1 teaspoon garlic powder
- 1-pound turnip
- 1 teaspoon salt
- 3 oz. Parmesan, shredded
- 1 tablespoon olive oil

Directions:
1. Peel the turnip and slice it.
2. Sprinkle the sliced turnip with salt and garlic powder.
3. Drizzle the turnip slices with olive oil.
4. Preheat the air fryer to 360 F.
5. Put the turnip slices in the air fryer basket and cook them for 10 minutes.
6. Serve.

Nutrition:
- (per serving) calories 66 | fat 4.1 | protein 4 | total carbs 4.3 | fiber 1.1

Crackling Bites

Servings: 10 | Cooking Time: 16 Minutes

Ingredients:
- 1 pound (454 g) pork rind raw, scored by the butcher
- 1 tablespoon sea salt
- 2 tablespoons smoked paprika

Directions:
1. Sprinkle and rub salt on the skin side of the pork rind. Allow it to sit for 30 minutes.
2. Roast at 380°F for 8 minutes, turn them over and cook for a further 8 minutes or until blistered.
3. Sprinkle the smoked paprika all over the pork crackling and serve. Bon appétit!

Nutrition:
- (per serving) calories 245 | fat 14.1 | protein 2 | total carbs 2.6 | fiber 0

Bacon And Beef Cheese Dip

Servings: 6 | Cooking Time: 10 Minutes

Ingredients:
- 8 ounces (227 g) full-fat cream cheese
- ¼ cup full-fat mayonnaise
- ¼ cup full-fat sour cream
- ¼ cup chopped onion
- 1 teaspoon garlic powder
- 1 tablespoon Worcestershire sauce
- 1¼ cups shredded medium Cheddar cheese, divided
- ½ pound (227g) cooked 80/20 ground beef
- 6 slices sugar-free bacon, cooked and crumbled
- 2 large pickle spears, chopped

Directions:
1. Place cream cheese in a large microwave-safe bowl and microwave for 45 seconds. Stir in mayonnaise, sour cream, onion, garlic powder, Worcestershire sauce, and 1 cup of Cheddar. Add cooked ground beef and bacon. Sprinkle the remaining Cheddar on top.
2. Place in 6-inch bowl and put into the air fryer basket.
3. Adjust the temperature to 400°F (205°C) and set the timer for 10 minutes.
4. Dip is done when top is golden and bubbling. Sprinkle pickles over dish. Serve warm.

Nutrition:
- (per serving) calories 457 | fat 35 | protein 22 | total carbs 4 | fiber 3

Keto Crab Cakes

Servings: 6 | Cooking Time: 10 Minutes

Ingredients:
- 12 oz crabmeat
- ¼ teaspoon salt
- 1 teaspoon chili powder
- 1 teaspoon ground white pepper
- 1 egg
- 1 tablespoon almond flour
- 1 tablespoon butter
- 1 tablespoon chives

Directions:
1. Chop the crabmeat into small pieces and place in a bowl.
2. Sprinkle the crabmeat with salt, chili powder, ground white

pepper, and chives.
3. Stir the mixture gently with a spoon.
4. Then crack the egg into the crabmeat.
5. Add almond flour and stir carefully until you have a smooth texture.
6. Preheat the air fryer to 400 F.
7. Take 2 spoons and place a small amount of the crabmeat mixture in one of them.
8. Cover it with the second spoon and make the crab cake.
9. Toss the butter in the air fryer and melt it.
10. Transfer the crab cakes to the air fryer and cook them for 10 minutes turning halfway through.
11. Cool before serving.

Nutrition:
- (per serving) calories 107 | fat 6.1 | protein 9.1 | total carbs 2.6 | fiber 0.8

Kohlrabi French Fries

Servings: 8 | Cooking Time: 20 Minutes

Ingredients:
- 1 egg
- 2 tablespoon almond flour
- ½ teaspoon salt
- 1 teaspoon ground black pepper
- 1 teaspoon thyme
- 1 tablespoon olive oil
- 14 oz. kohlrabi

Directions:
1. Crack the egg into a bowl and whisk.
2. Sprinkle the whisked egg with the salt, ground black pepper, and thyme.
3. Whisk for 1 minute.
4. Peel the kohlrabi and cut it into French fries.
5. Put the kohlrabi pieces in the whisked egg mixture.
6. Coat the kohlrabi in the almond flour.
7. Preheat the air fryer to 360 F.
8. Coat the kohlrabi with olive oil and put in the air fryer.
9. Cook for 20 minutes.
10. Stir frequently.
11. Allow to cool before serving.

Nutrition:
- (per serving) calories 77 | fat 5.9 | protein 3.1 | total carbs 4.9 | fiber 2.7

Egg Rolls With Thousand Island Dipping Sauce

Servings: 10 | Cooking Time: 10 Minutes

Ingredients:
- 1 (8-ounce / 227-g) package cream cheese, softened
- ½ pound (227 g) cooked corned beef, chopped
- ½ cup drained and chopped sauerkraut
- ½ cup shredded Swiss cheese
- 20 slices prosciutto
- Thousand Island Dipping Sauce:
- ¾ cup mayonnaise
- ¼ cup chopped dill pickles
- ¼ cup tomato sauce
- 2 tablespoons Swerve confectioners-style sweetener
- ⅛ teaspoon fine sea salt
- Fresh thyme leaves, for garnish

- Ground black pepper, for garnish
- Sauerkraut, for serving (optional)

Directions:
1. Spray the air fryer basket with avocado oil. Preheat the air fryer to 400°F.
2. Make the filling: Place the cream cheese in a medium-sized bowl and stir to break it up. Add the corned beef, sauerkraut, and Swiss cheese and stir well to combine.
3. Assemble the egg rolls: Lay 1 slice of prosciutto on a sushi mat or a sheet of parchment paper with a short end toward you. Lay another slice of prosciutto on top of it at a right angle, forming a cross. Spoon 3 to 4 tablespoons of the filling into the center of the cross.
4. Fold the sides of the top slice up and over the filling to form the ends of the roll. Tightly roll up the long piece of prosciutto, starting at the edge closest to you, into a tight egg roll shape that overlaps by an inch or so. (Note: If the prosciutto rips, it's okay. It will seal when you fry it.) Repeat with the remaining prosciutto and filling.
5. Place the egg rolls in the air fryer seam side down, leaving space between them. (If you're using a smaller air fryer, cook in batches if necessary.) Cook for 10 minutes, or until the outside is crispy.
6. While the egg rolls are cooking, make the dipping sauce: In a small bowl, combine the mayo, pickles, tomato sauce, sweetener, and salt. Stir well and garnish with thyme and ground black pepper. (The dipping sauce can be made up to 3 days ahead.)
7. Serve the egg rolls with the dipping sauce and sauerkraut if desired. Best served fresh. Store leftovers in an airtight container in the refrigerator for up to 5 days or in the freezer for up to a month. Reheat in a preheated 400°F air fryer for 4 minutes, or until heated through and crispy.

Nutrition:
- (per serving) calories 321 | fat 29 | protein 13 | total carbs 1 | fiber 0.1

Brussels Sprouts Crisps

Servings: 4 | Cooking Time: 15 Minutes

Ingredients:
- 1 pound (454 g) Brussels sprouts, ends and yellow leaves removed and halved lengthwise
- Salt and black pepper, to taste
- 1 tablespoon toasted sesame oil
- 1 teaspoon fennel seeds
- Chopped fresh parsley, for garnish

Directions:
1. Place the Brussels sprouts, salt, pepper, sesame oil, and fennel seeds in a resealable plastic bag. Seal the bag and shake to coat.
2. Air-fry at 380°F for 15 minutes or until tender. Make sure to flip them over halfway through the cooking time.
3. Serve sprinkled with fresh parsley. Bon appétit!

Nutrition:
- (per serving) calories 174 | fat 3.8 | protein 8.8 | total carbs 3.4 | fiber 1

Chicken Bites

Servings: 8 | Cooking Time: 15 Minutes

Ingredients:
- 1-pound chicken fillet
- 1 teaspoon chili flakes
- 1 teaspoon turmeric
- 1 teaspoon paprika
- ½ teaspoon curry powder
- ½ cup heavy cream
- 2 tablespoons almond flour
- 1 teaspoon olive oil

Directions:
1. Chop the chicken fillet into 8 cubes.
2. Place the chicken cubes in a large bowl.
3. Sprinkle the meat with the chili flakes, turmeric, paprika, and curry powder.
4. Mix well using your hands.
5. Combine the heavy cream and almond flour in a separate bowl.
6. Whisk well.
7. Preheat the air fryer to 365 F.
8. Place the chicken cubes in the air fryer rack and drizzle them with olive oil.
9. Cook the chicken for 15 minutes.

Nutrition:
- (per serving) calories 151 | fat 8.5 | protein 17 | total carbs 1 | fiber 0.4

Crispy Cauliflower Florets

Servings: 2 | Cooking Time: 12 Minutes

Ingredients:
- 3 cups cauliflower florets
- 2 tablespoons sesame oil
- 1 teaspoon onion powder
- 1 teaspoon garlic powder
- 1 teaspoon thyme
- 1 teaspoon sage
- 1 teaspoon rosemary
- Sea salt and cracked black pepper, to taste
- 1 teaspoon paprika

Directions:
1. Start by preheating your Air Fryer to 400°F (205°C).
2. Toss the cauliflower with the remaining ingredients, toss to coat well.
3. Cook for 12 minutes, shaking the cooking basket halfway through the cooking time. They will crisp up as they cool. Bon appétit!

Nutrition:
- (per serving) calories 160 | fat 14 | protein 3 | total carbs 8 | fiber 5

Zucchini Fritters With Dill And Hard Cheese

Servings: 7 | Cooking Time: 8 Minutes

Ingredients:
- 4 oz. Mozzarella
- 3 oz. Cheddar cheese
- 1 zucchini, grated
- 2 tablespoon dried dill
- 1 tablespoon coconut flour
- 1 tablespoon almond flour
- ¼ teaspoon salt
- 1 teaspoon butter

Directions:
1. Shred the Cheddar and Mozzarella.
2. Combine the grated zucchini with the shredded cheese.
3. Add dried dill and coconut flour.
4. Add almond flour and salt.
5. Stir carefully with a fork.
6. Mix well to combine and leave to marinade for 3 minutes.
7. Preheat the air fryer to 400 F.
8. Melt the butter in the air fryer tray.
9. Make the fritters from the zucchini mixture and put them in the melted butter.
10. Cook the fritters for 5 minutes.
11. Turn the zucchini fritters over and cook for 3 minutes more.

Nutrition:
- (per serving) calories 133 | fat 9.6 | protein 9.1 | total carbs 3.7 | fiber 1.3

Cheese Tortillas With Pork Rinds

Servings:4 | Cooking Time: 5 Minutes

Ingredients:
- 1 ounce (28 g) pork rinds
- ¾ cup shredded Mozzarella cheese
- 2 tablespoons full-fat cream cheese
- 1 large egg

Directions:
1. Place pork rinds into food processor and pulse until finely ground.
2. Place Mozzarella into a large microwave-safe bowl. Break cream cheese into small pieces and add them to the bowl. Microwave for 30 seconds, or until both cheeses are melted and can easily be stirred together into a ball. Add ground pork rinds and egg to the cheese mixture.
3. Continue stirring until the mixture forms a ball. If it cools too much and cheese hardens, microwave for 10 more seconds.
4. Separate the dough into four small balls. Place each ball of dough between two sheets of parchment and roll into ¼-inch flat layer.
5. Place tortillas into the air fryer basket in single layer, working in batches if necessary.
6. Adjust the temperature to 400°F (205°C) and set the timer for 5 minutes.
7. Tortillas will be crispy and firm when fully cooked. Serve immediately.

Nutrition:
- (per serving) calories 145 | fat 10 | protein 11 | total carbs 1 | fiber 1

Three Cheese Dip

Servings: 8 | Cooking Time: 12 Minutes

Ingredients:
- 8 ounces (227 g) cream cheese, softened
- ½ cup mayonnaise
- ¼ cup sour cream
- ½ cup shredded sharp Cheddar cheese
- ¼ cup shredded Monterey jack cheese

Directions:
1. In a large bowl, combine all ingredients. Scoop mixture into

an ungreased 4-cup nonstick baking dish and place into air fryer basket.

2. Adjust the temperature to 375°F (190°C) and set the timer for 12 minutes. Dip will be browned on top and bubbling when done. Serve warm.

Nutrition:
- (per serving) calories 245 | fat 23 | protein 5 | total carbs 2 | fiber 2

Salami Roll-ups

Servings:16 | Cooking Time: 4 Minutes

Ingredients:
- 4 ounces (113 g) cream cheese, broken into 16 equal pieces
- 16 (0.5-ounce / 14-g) deli slices Genoa salami

Directions:
1. Place a piece of cream cheese at the edge of a slice of salami and roll to close. Secure with a toothpick. Repeat with remaining cream cheese pieces and salami.
2. Place roll-ups in an ungreased 6-inch round nonstick baking dish and place into air fryer basket. Adjust the temperature to 350°F (180°C) and set the timer for 4 minutes. Salami will be crispy and cream cheese will be warm when done. Let it cool 5 minutes before serving.

Nutrition:
- (per serving) calories 269 | fat 22 | protein 11 | total carbs 2 | fiber 2

Pecorino Toscano And Broccoli Fat Bombs

Servings: 6 | Cooking Time: 15 Minutes

Ingredients:
- 1 large-sized head of broccoli, broken into small florets
- ½ teaspoon sea salt
- ¼ teaspoon ground black pepper, or more to taste
- 1 tablespoon Shoyu sauce
- 1 teaspoon groundnut oil
- 1 cup bacon bits
- 1 cup Pecorino Toscano, freshly grated
- Paprika, to taste

Directions:
1. Add the broccoli florets to boiling water, boil for approximately 4 minutes, drain well.
2. Season with salt and pepper, drizzle with Shoyu sauce and groundnut oil. Mash with a potato masher.
3. Add the bacon and cheese to the mixture, shape the mixture into bite-sized balls.
4. Air-fry at 390°F for 10 minutes, shake the Air Fryer basket, push the power button again, and continue to cook for 5 minutes or more.
5. Toss the fried keto bombs with paprika. Bon appétit!

Nutrition:
- (per serving) calories 171 | fat 12.2 | protein 7.7 | total carbs 9.1 | fiber 1.5

Pickle Poppers Wrapped With Bacon

Servings: 6 | Cooking Time: 10 Minutes

Ingredients:
- 12 medium dill pickles
- 1 (8-ounce / 227-g) package cream cheese, softened
- 1 cup shredded sharp Cheddar cheese
- 12 slices bacon or beef bacon, sliced in half lengthwise
- Ranch Dressing or Blue Cheese Dressing, for serving (optional)

Directions:
1. Spray the air fryer basket with avocado oil. Preheat the air fryer to 400°F.
2. Slice the dill pickles in half lengthwise and use a spoon to scoop out the centers.
3. Place the cream cheese and Cheddar cheese in a small bowl and stir until well combined.
4. Divide the cream cheese mixture among the pickles, spooning equal amounts into the scooped-out centers. Wrap each filled pickle with a slice of bacon and secure the bacon with toothpicks.
5. Place the bacon-wrapped pickles in the air fryer basket with the bacon seam side down and cook for 8 to 10 minutes, until the bacon is crispy, flipping halfway through. Serve warm with ranch or blue cheese dressing, if desired.
6. Best served fresh. Store leftovers in an airtight container in the fridge for up to 5 days. Reheat in a preheated 400°F air fryer for 3 minutes, or until heated through.

Nutrition:
- (per serving) calories 87 | fat 8 | protein 4 | total carbs 1 | fiber 2

Zucchini Chips

Servings: 5 | Cooking Time: 13 Minutes

Ingredients:
- 2 zucchinis
- 1 teaspoon olive oil
- ½ teaspoon salt
- 1 teaspoon paprika

Directions:
1. Wash the zucchini carefully and slice into chips pieces.
2. Preheat the air fryer to 370 F.
3. Sprinkle the zucchini slices with salt and paprika.
4. Place the zucchini slices in the air fryer rack.
5. Drizzle the zucchini slices with olive oil.
6. Cook for 13 minutes.
7. Turn the zucchini over if required.
8. When the zucchini chips are cooked let them cool.
9. Serve or keep them in a paper bag.

Nutrition:
- (per serving) calories 22 | fat 1.1 | protein 1 | total carbs 2.9 | fiber 1

Pork Meatball With Romano Cheese

Servings: 8 | Cooking Time: 18 Minutes

Ingredients:
- ½ teaspoon fine sea salt
- 1 cup Romano cheese, grated
- 3 cloves garlic, minced
- 1½ pound (680g) ground pork
- ½ cup scallions, finely chopped
- 2 eggs, well whisked
- ⅓ teaspoon cumin powder

- ⅔ teaspoon ground black pepper, or more to taste
- 2 teaspoons basil

Directions:
1. Simply combine all the ingredients in a large-sized mixing bowl.
2. Shape into bite-sized balls, cook the meatballs in the air fryer for 18 minutes at 345ºF (174ºC). Serve with some tangy sauce such as marinara sauce if desired. Bon appétit!

Nutrition:
- (per serving) calories 350 | fat 25 | protein 28 | total carbs 2 | fiber 1

Keto French Fries

Servings: 6 | Cooking Time: 15 Minutes

Ingredients:
- 2 sweet dumpling squashes
- 1 teaspoon paprika
- ¼ teaspoon ground white pepper
- ¼ teaspoon salt
- 1 tablespoon olive oil

Directions:
1. Peel the sweet dumpling squash and cut it into the strips.
2. Cover the air fryer basket tray with the parchment and place the sweet dumpling squash strips there.
3. Then sprinkle the sweet dumpling squash strips with the ground white pepper, paprika, and salt.
4. Spray the sweet dumpling squash strips with the olive oil.
5. Preheat the air fryer to 365 F.
6. Cook the sweet dumpling squash fries for 15 minutes. The time can be less or more – depends on the size of the sweet dumpling squash strips.
7. Then transfer the fries to the serving plate and chill them.
8. Enjoy!

Nutrition:
- (per serving) calories 30 | fat 2.4 | protein 0.2 | total carbs 2.3 | fiber 0.7

Pork Cheese Sticks

Servings:12 | Cooking Time: 10 Minutes

Ingredients:
- 6 (1-ounce / 28-g) Mozzarella string cheese sticks
- ½ cup grated Parmesan cheese
- ½ ounce (14 g) pork rinds, finely ground
- 1 teaspoon dried parsley
- 2 large eggs

Directions:
1. Place Mozzarella sticks on a cutting board and cut in half. Freeze 45 minutes or until firm. If freezing overnight, remove frozen sticks after 1 hour and place into airtight zip-top storage bag and place back in freezer for future use.
2. In a large bowl, mix Parmesan, ground pork rinds, and parsley.
3. In a medium bowl, whisk eggs.
4. Dip a frozen Mozzarella stick into beaten eggs and then into Parmesan mixture to coat. Repeat with remaining sticks. Place Mozzarella sticks into the air fryer basket.
5. Adjust the temperature to 400°F (205ºC) and set the timer for 10 minutes or until golden.
6. Serve warm.

Nutrition:

- (per serving) calories 236 | fat 13 | protein 19 | total carbs 5 | fiber 5

Crispy Nacho Avocado Fries

Servings:6 | Cooking Time: 15 Minutes

Ingredients:
- 3 firm, barely ripe avocados, halved, peeled, and pitted (see Tip)
- 2 cups pork dust (see here) (or powdered Parmesan cheese for vegetarian; see here)
- 2 teaspoons fine sea salt
- 2 teaspoons ground black pepper
- 2 teaspoons ground cumin
- 1 teaspoon chili powder
- 1 teaspoon paprika
- ½ teaspoon garlic powder
- ½ teaspoon onion powder
- 2 large eggs
- Salsa, for serving (optional)
- Fresh chopped cilantro leaves, for garnish (optional)

Directions:
1. Spray the air fryer basket with avocado oil. Preheat the air fryer to 400°F.
2. Slice the avocados into thick-cut french fry shapes.
3. In a bowl, mix together the pork dust, salt, pepper, and seasonings.
4. In a separate shallow bowl, beat the eggs.
5. Dip the avocado fries into the beaten eggs and shake off any excess, then dip them into the pork dust mixture. Use your hands to press the breading into each fry.
6. Spray the fries with avocado oil and place them in the air fryer basket in a single layer, leaving space between them. If there are too many fries to fit in a single layer, work in batches. Cook in the air fryer for 13 to 15 minutes, until golden brown, flipping after 5 minutes.
7. Serve with salsa, if desired, and garnish with fresh chopped cilantro, if desired. Best served fresh.
8. Store leftovers in an airtight container in the fridge for up to 5 days. Reheat in a preheated 400°F air fryer for 3 minutes, or until heated through.

Nutrition:
- (per serving) calories 282 | fat 22g | protein 15g | total carbs 9g | fiber 7g

Prosciutto-wrapped Guacamole Rings

Servings:8 | Cooking Time: 6 Minutes

Ingredients:
- GUACAMOLE:
- 2 avocados, halved, pitted, and peeled
- 3 tablespoons lime juice, plus more to taste
- 2 small plum tomatoes, diced
- ½ cup finely diced onions
- 2 small cloves garlic, smashed to a paste
- 3 tablespoons chopped fresh cilantro leaves
- ½ scant teaspoon fine sea salt
- ½ scant teaspoon ground cumin
- 2 small onions (about 1½ inches in diameter), cut into ½-inch-thick slices
- 8 slices prosciutto

Directions:

1. Make the guacamole: Place the avocados and lime juice in a large bowl and mash with a fork until it reaches your desired consistency. Add the tomatoes, onions, garlic, cilantro, salt, and cumin and stir until well combined. Taste and add more lime juice if desired. Set aside half of the guacamole for serving. (Note: If you're making the guacamole ahead of time, place it in a large resealable plastic bag, squeeze out all the air, and seal it shut. It will keep in the refrigerator for up to 3 days when stored this way.)

2. Place a piece of parchment paper on a tray that fits in your freezer and place the onion slices on it, breaking the slices apart into 8 rings. Fill each ring with about 2 tablespoons of guacamole. Place the tray in the freezer for 2 hours.

3. Spray the air fryer basket with avocado oil. Preheat the air fryer to 400°F.

4. Remove the rings from the freezer and wrap each in a slice of prosciutto. Place them in the air fryer basket, leaving space between them (if you're using a smaller air fryer, work in batches if necessary), and cook for 6 minutes, flipping halfway through. Use a spatula to remove the rings from the air fryer. Serve with the reserved half of the guacamole.

5. Store leftovers in an airtight container in the refrigerator for up to 4 days. Reheat in a preheated 400°F air fryer for about 3 minutes, until heated through.

Nutrition:
- (per serving) calories 132 | fat 9g | protein 5g | total carbs 10g | fiber 4g

Chicken Wings With Parmesan Butter

Servings: 4 | Cooking Time: 25 Minutes

Ingredients:
- 2 pounds (907 g) raw chicken wings
- 1 teaspoon pink Himalayan salt
- ½ teaspoon garlic powder
- 1 tablespoon baking powder
- 4 tablespoons unsalted butter, melted
- ⅓ cup grated Parmesan cheese
- ¼ teaspoon dried parsley

Directions:
1. In a large bowl, place chicken wings, salt, ½ teaspoon garlic powder, and baking powder, then toss. Place wings into the air fryer basket.
2. Adjust the temperature to 400°F (205ºC) and set the timer for 25 minutes.
3. Toss the basket two or three times during the cooking time.
4. In a small bowl, combine butter, Parmesan, and parsley.
5. Remove wings from the fryer and place into a clean large bowl. Pour the butter mixture over the wings and toss until coated. Serve warm.

Nutrition:
- (per serving) calories 565 | fat 42 | protein 42 | total carbs 2 | fiber 2

Fried Leek

Servings: 4 | Cooking Time: 10 Minutes

Ingredients:
- 1 large-sized leek, cut into ½-inch wide rings
- Salt and pepper, to taste
- 1 teaspoon mustard
- 1 cup milk
- 1 egg
- ½ cup almond flour
- ½ teaspoon baking powder
- ½ cup pork rinds, crushed

Directions:
1. Toss your leeks with salt and pepper.
2. In a mixing bowl, whisk the mustard, milk and egg until frothy and pale.
3. Now, combine almond flour and baking powder in another mixing bowl. In the third bowl, place the pork rinds.
4. Coat the leek slices with the almond meal mixture. Dredge the floured leek slices into the milk/egg mixture, coating well. Finally, roll them over the pork rinds.
5. Air-fry for approximately 10 minutes at 370°F. Bon appétit!

Nutrition:
- (per serving) calories 187 | fat 13.8 | protein 2.8 | total carbs 7.7 | fiber 0.6

Daikon Chips

Servings: 7 | Cooking Time: 15 Minutes

Ingredients:
- 1 teaspoon ground red pepper
- 3 teaspoon olive oil
- ½ teaspoon ground black pepper
- 1 teaspoon salt
- 15 oz. daikon

Directions:
1. Combine the ground red pepper, olive oil, ground black pepper, and salt in a small bowl.
2. Whisk.
3. Slice the daikon into chips.
4. Preheat the air fryer to 375 F.
5. Brush daikon chips with the olive oil mixture.
6. Place the daikon chips in the air fryer rack.
7. Cook for 16 minutes.
8. Stir the daikon chips after 8 minutes of cooking.
9. Then chill the chips and serve.

Nutrition:
- (per serving) calories 30 | fat 2 | protein 1.3 | total carbs 2.7 | fiber 1.3

Bacon-wrapped Onion Rings

Servings: 8 | Cooking Time: 10 Minutes

Ingredients:
- 1 large white onion, peeled and cut into 16 (¼-inch-thick) slices
- 8 slices sugar-free bacon

Directions:
1. Stack 2 slices onion and wrap with 1 slice bacon. Secure with a toothpick. Repeat with remaining onion slices and bacon.
2. Place onion rings into ungreased air fryer basket. Adjust the temperature to 350°F (180ºC) and set the timer for 10 minutes, turning rings halfway through cooking. Bacon will be crispy when done. Serve warm.

Nutrition:
- (per serving) calories 84 | fat 4 | protein 5 | total carbs 8 | fiber 6

Bacon-wrapped Shrimp

Servings: 10 | Cooking Time: 8 Minutes

Ingredients:
- 1¼ pounds (567g) shrimp, peeled and deveined
- 1 teaspoon paprika
- ½ teaspoon ground black pepper
- ½ teaspoon red pepper flakes, crushed
- 1 tablespoon salt
- 1 teaspoon chili powder
- 1 tablespoon shallot powder
- ¼ teaspoon cumin powder
- 1¼ pounds (567g) thin bacon slices

Directions:
1. Toss the shrimps with all the seasoning until they are coated well.
2. Next, wrap a slice of bacon around the shrimps, securing with a toothpick, repeat with the remaining ingredients, chill for 30 minutes.
3. Air-fry them at 360°F (182°C) for 7 to 8 minutes, working in batches. Serve with cocktail sticks if desired. Enjoy!

Nutrition:
- (per serving) calories 282 | fat 22 | protein 19 | total carbs 2 | fiber 1

Spiced Almond

Servings: 4 | Cooking Time: 6 Minutes

Ingredients:
- 1 cup raw almonds
- 2 teaspoons coconut oil
- 1 teaspoon chili powder
- ¼ teaspoon cumin
- ¼ teaspoon smoked paprika
- ¼ teaspoon onion powder

Directions:
1. In a large bowl, toss all ingredients until almonds are evenly coated with oil and spices. Place almonds into the air fryer basket.
2. Adjust the temperature to 320°F (160°C) and set the timer for 6 minutes.
3. Toss the fryer basket halfway through the cooking time. Allow to cool completely.

Nutrition:
- (per serving) calories 182 | fat 16 | protein 6 | total carbs 7 | fiber 3

Hot Jalapeno Bites

Servings: 5 | Cooking Time: 11 Minutes

Ingredients:
- 6 oz. bacon, sliced
- 1 cup jalapeno pepper
- ½ teaspoon salt
- ½ teaspoon paprika
- 1 teaspoon olive oil

Directions:
1. Wash the jalapeno peppers carefully.
2. Combine the salt, paprika, and olive oil together.
3. Stir gently.
4. Brush the jalapeno peppers with the olive oil mixture generously.
5. Wrap each jalapeno pepper in the bacon slices.
6. Secure the jalapeno bites with toothpicks.
7. Preheat the air fryer to 360 F.
8. Put the jalapeno bites in the air fryer rack.
9. Cook for 11 minutes or until the bacon is crisp.
10. Transfer the cooked jalapeno pepper bites to a plate and cover them with paper towels to remove excess grease before serving.

Nutrition:
- (per serving) calories 198 | fat 15.3 | protein 12.9 | total carbs 1.7 | fiber 0.6

French Artichoke Dip

Servings: 7 | Cooking Time: 27 Minutes

Ingredients:
- 1 cup spinach
- 8 oz. artichoke, chopped
- ½ cup heavy cream
- 5 oz. Cheddar cheese
- ¼ teaspoon salt
- 1 teaspoon paprika
- ½ teaspoon ground coriander
- ½ cup cream cheese
- ½ teaspoon garlic powder
- 1 teaspoon olive oil

Directions:
1. Put the chopped artichoke in foil.
2. Sprinkle with the salt, paprika, garlic powder, and ground coriander.
3. Drizzle the artichokes with olive oil.
4. Wrap the artichoke in foil.
5. Preheat the air fryer to 360 F.
6. Place the wrapped artichoke in the air fryer and cook it for 25 minutes.
7. Meanwhile, chop the spinach roughly and place it in a blender.
8. Add the heavy cream, salt, paprika, ground coriander, and cream cheese.
9. Blend until well combined.
10. Remove the artichoke from the air fryer and add to the spinach mixture.
11. Blend for 2 minutes.
12. Pour the blended mixture into the air fryer.
13. Add heavy cream.
14. Shred Cheddar cheese and add it to the air fryer.
15. Stir and cook for 3 minutes at 360 F.
16. When the cheese is melted – the dip is cooked.
17. Serve warm.

Nutrition:
- (per serving) calories 192 | fat 16.4 | protein 7.7 | total carbs 4.8 | fiber 2

Chapter 4 Beef, Pork, And Lamb Recipes

Chapter 4 Beef, Pork, And Lamb Recipes

Roasted Pork Belly With Bell Peppers

Servings: 6 | Cooking Time: 30 Minutes

Ingredients:
- 1½ pounds (680g) pork belly
- 2 bell peppers, sliced
- 2 cloves garlic, finely minced
- 4 green onions, quartered, white and green parts
- ¼ cup cooking wine
- Kosher salt and ground black pepper, to taste
- 1 teaspoon cayenne pepper
- 1 tablespoon coriander
- 1 teaspoon celery seeds

Directions:
1. Blanch the pork belly in boiling water for approximately 15 minutes. Then, cut it into chunks.
2. Arrange the pork chunks, bell peppers, garlic, and green onions in the Air Fryer basket. Drizzle everything with cooking wine of your choice.
3. Sprinkle with salt, black pepper, cayenne pepper, fresh coriander, and celery seeds. Toss to coat well.
4. Roast in the preheated Air Fryer at 330º(166ºC) F for 30 minutes.
5. Serve on individual serving plates. Bon appétit!

Nutrition:
- (per serving) calories 589 | fat 60 | protein 12 | total carbs 3 | fiber 2

Monterey-jack Cheeseburgers

Servings: 4 | Cooking Time: 11 Minutes

Ingredients:
- 1½ pounds (680 g) ground chuck
- 1 envelope onion soup mix
- Kosher salt and freshly ground black pepper, to taste
- 1 teaspoon paprika
- 4 slices Monterey-Jack cheese

Directions:
1. In a mixing dish, thoroughly combine ground chuck, onion soup mix, salt, black pepper, and paprika.
2. Then, set your Air Fryer to cook at 385ºF. Shape the mixture into 4 patties. Air-fry them for 10 minutes.
3. Next step, place the slices of cheese on the top of the warm burgers. Air-fry for one minute more.
4. Serve with mustard and pickled salad of choice. Bon appétit!

Nutrition:
- (per serving) calories 271 | fat 13 | protein 15 | total carbs 22 | fiber 21

Crispy Pork Chop With Parmesan

Servings: 4 | Cooking Time: 9 To 14 Minutes

Ingredients:
- 2 large eggs
- ½ cup finely grated Parmesan cheese
- ½ cup finely ground blanched almond flour
- 1 teaspoon paprika
- ½ teaspoon dried oregano
- ½ teaspoon garlic powder
- Salt, Freshly ground black pepper, to taste
- 1¼ pounds (567g) (1-inch-thick) boneless pork chops
- Avocado oil spray

Directions:
1. Beat the eggs in a shallow bowl. In a separate bowl, combine the Parmesan cheese, almond flour, paprika, oregano, garlic powder, and salt and pepper to taste.
2. Dip the pork chops into the eggs, then coat them with the Parmesan mixture, gently pressing the coating onto the meat. Spray the breaded pork chops with oil.
3. Set the air fryer to 400ºF. Place the pork chops in the air fryer basket in a single layer, working in batches if necessary. Cook for 6 minutes. Flip the chops and spray them with more oil. Cook for another 3 to 8 minutes, until an instant-read thermometer reads 145ºF (63ºC).
4. Allow the pork chops to rest for at least 5 minutes, and then serve.

Nutrition:
- (per serving) calories 351 | fat 20 | protein 38 | total carbs 4 | fiber 2

Mojito Lamb Chops

Servings:2 | Cooking Time: 5 Minutes

Ingredients:
- MARINADE:
- 2 teaspoons grated lime zest
- ½ cup lime juice
- ¼ cup avocado oil
- ¼ cup chopped fresh mint leaves
- 4 cloves garlic, roughly chopped
- 2 teaspoons fine sea salt
- ½ teaspoon ground black pepper
- 4 (1-inch-thick) lamb chops
- Sprigs of fresh mint, for garnish (optional)
- Lime slices, for serving (optional)

Directions:
1. Make the marinade: Place all the ingredients for the marinade in a food processor or blender and puree until mostly smooth with a few small chunks. Transfer half of the marinade to a shallow dish and set the other half aside for serving. Add the lamb to the shallow dish, cover, and place in the refrigerator to marinate for at least 2 hours or overnight.
2. Spray the air fryer basket with avocado oil. Preheat the air fryer to 390ºF.
3. Remove the chops from the marinade and place them in the air fryer basket. Cook for 5 minutes, or until the internal temperature reaches 145ºF for medium doneness.
4. Allow the chops to rest for 10 minutes before serving with the rest of the marinade as a sauce. Garnish with fresh mint leaves and serve with lime slices, if desired. Best served fresh.

Nutrition:
- (per serving) calories 692 | fat 53g | protein 48g | total carbs 2g | fiber 0.4g

Chuck And Arugula Kebab

Servings: 4 | Cooking Time: 25 Minutes

Ingredients:
- ½ cup leeks, chopped
- 2 garlic cloves, smashed
- 2 pounds (907 g) ground chuck
- Salt, to taste
- ¼ teaspoon ground black pepper, or more to taste
- 1 teaspoon cayenne pepper
- ½ teaspoon ground sumac
- 3 saffron threads
- 2 tablespoons loosely packed fresh continental parsley leaves
- 4 tablespoons tahini sauce
- 4 ounces (113 g) baby arugula
- 1 tomato, cut into slices

Directions:
1. In a bowl, mix the chopped leeks, garlic, ground chuck, and spices, knead with your hands until everything is well incorporated.
2. Now, mound the beef mixture around a wooden skewer into a pointed-ended sausage.
3. Cook in the preheated Air Fryer at 360°F (182°C) for 25 minutes.
4. Serve your kebab with the tahini sauce baby arugula and tomato. Enjoy!

Nutrition:
- (per serving) calories 354 | fat 15 | protein 49 | total carbs 6 | fiber 4

Loin Steak With Mayo

Servings: 4 | Cooking Time: 15 Minutes

Ingredients:
- 1 cup mayonnaise
- 1 tablespoon fresh rosemary, finely chopped
- 2 tablespoons Worcestershire sauce
- Sea salt, to taste
- ½ teaspoon ground black pepper
- 1 teaspoon smoked paprika
- 1 teaspoon garlic, minced
- 1½ pounds (680g) short loin steak

Directions:
1. Combine the mayonnaise, rosemary, Worcestershire sauce, salt, pepper, paprika, and garlic, mix to combine well.
2. Now, brush the mayonnaise mixture over both sides of the steak. Lower the steak onto the grill pan.
3. Grill in the preheated Air Fryer at 390°F (199°C) for 8 minutes. Turn the steaks over and grill for an additional 7 minutes.
4. Check for doneness with a meat thermometer. Serve warm and enjoy!

Nutrition:
- (per serving) calories 620 | fat 50 | protein 40 | total carbs 3 | fiber 2

Herbed Lamb Chops With Parmesan

Servings: 2 | Cooking Time: 5 Minutes

Ingredients:
- 1 large egg
- 2 cloves garlic, minced
- ¼ cup pork dust
- ¼ cup powdered Parmesan cheese
- 1 tablespoon chopped fresh oregano leaves
- 1 tablespoon chopped fresh rosemary leaves
- 1 teaspoon chopped fresh thyme leaves
- ½ teaspoon ground black pepper
- 4 (1-inch-thick) lamb chops
- For Garnish/Serving (Optional):
- Sprigs of fresh oregano
- Sprigs of fresh rosemary
- Sprigs of fresh thyme
- Lavender flowers
- Lemon slices

Directions:
1. Spray the air fryer basket with avocado oil. Preheat the air fryer to 400°F.
2. Beat the egg in a shallow bowl, add the garlic, and stir well to combine. In another shallow bowl, mix together the pork dust, Parmesan, herbs, and pepper.
3. One at a time, dip the lamb chops into the egg mixture, shake off the excess egg, and then dredge them in the Parmesan mixture. Use your hands to coat the chops well in the Parmesan mixture and form a nice crust on all sides, if necessary, dip the chops again in both the egg and the Parmesan mixture.
4. Place the lamb chops in the air fryer basket, leaving space between them, and cook for 5 minutes, or until the internal temperature reaches 145°F for medium doneness. Allow them to rest for 10 minutes before serving.
5. Garnish with sprigs of oregano, rosemary, and thyme, and lavender flowers, if desired. Serve with lemon slices, if desired.
6. Best served fresh. Store leftovers in an airtight container in the fridge for up to 4 days. Serve chilled over a salad, or reheat in a 350°F air fryer for 3 minutes, or until heated through.

Nutrition:
- (per serving) calories 790 | fat 60 | protein 57 | total carbs 2 | fiber 1.6

Italian Pork Top Loin

Servings: 3 | Cooking Time: 16 Minutes

Ingredients:
- 1 teaspoon Celtic sea salt
- ½ teaspoon black pepper, freshly cracked
- ¼ cup red wine
- 2 tablespoons mustard
- 2 garlic cloves, minced
- 1 pound (454 g) pork top loin
- 1 tablespoon Italian herb seasoning blend

Directions:
1. In a ceramic bowl, mix the salt, black pepper, red wine, mustard, and garlic. Add the pork top loin and let it marinate for at least 30 minutes.
2. Spritz the sides and bottom of the cooking basket with a nonstick cooking spray.
3. Place the pork top loin in the basket, sprinkle with the Italian herb seasoning blend.
4. Cook the pork tenderloin at 370°F (188°C) for 10 minutes. Flip halfway through, spraying with cooking oil and cook for 5 to 6 minutes. Serve immediately.

Nutrition:
- (per serving) calories 300 | fat 9 | protein 34 | total carbs 2 | fiber 1

Miso Flank Steak

Servings: 4 | Cooking Time: 12 Minutes

Ingredients:
- 1¼ pounds (567 g) flank steak
- 1½ tablespoons sake
- 1 tablespoon brown miso paste
- 2 garlic cloves, pressed
- 1 tablespoon olive oil

Directions:
1. Place all the ingredients in a sealable food bag, shake until completely coated and place in your refrigerator for at least 1 hour.
2. Then, spritz the steak with a non-stick cooking spray, make sure to coat on all sides. Place the steak in the Air Fryer baking pan.
3. Set your Air Fryer to cook at 400ºF. Roast for 12 minutes, flipping twice. Serve immediately.

Nutrition:
- (per serving) calories 367 | fat 15 | protein 49 | total carbs 6 | fiber 5

Double-cheese Sausage Balls

Servings: 12 | Cooking Time: 10 Minutes

Ingredients:
- 1¾ cups finely ground blanched almond flour
- 1 tablespoon baking powder
- ½ teaspoon sea salt
- ¼ teaspoon freshly ground black pepper
- ¼ teaspoon cayenne pepper
- 1 pound (454 g) fresh pork sausage, casings removed, crumbled
- 8 ounces (227 g) Cheddar cheese, shredded
- 8 ounces (227 g) cream cheese, at room temperature, cut into chunks

Directions:
1. In a large mixing bowl, combine the almond flour, baking powder, salt, black pepper, and cayenne pepper.
2. Add the sausage, Cheddar cheese, and cream cheese. Stir to combine, and then, using clean hands, mix until all of the ingredients are well incorporated.
3. Form the mixture into 1½-inch balls.
4. Set the air fryer to 350°F (180°C). Arrange the sausage balls in a single layer in the air fryer basket, working in batches if necessary. Cook for 5 minutes. Flip the sausage balls and cook for 5 minutes or more.

Nutrition:
- (per serving) calories 386 | fat 27 | protein 16 | total carbs 5 | fiber 3

Red Wine Rib

Servings: 4 | Cooking Time: 10 Minutes

Ingredients:
- 1½ pounds (680g) short ribs
- 1 cup red wine
- 1 lemon, juiced
- 1 teaspoon fresh ginger, grated
- 1 teaspoon salt
- 1 teaspoon black pepper
- 1 teaspoon paprika
- 1 teaspoon chipotle chili powder
- 1 cup keto tomato paste
- 1 teaspoon garlic powder
- 1 teaspoon cumin

Directions:
1. In a ceramic bowl, place the beef ribs, wine, lemon juice, ginger, salt, black pepper, paprika, and chipotle chili powder. Cover and let it marinate for 3 hours in the refrigerator.
2. Discard the marinade and add the short ribs to the Air Fryer basket. Cook in the preheated Air fry at 380ºF (193ºC) for 10 minutes, turning them over halfway through the cooking time.
3. In the meantime, heat the saucepan over medium heat, add the reserved marinade and stir in the tomato paste, garlic powder, and cumin. Cook until the sauce has thickened slightly.
4. Pour the sauce over the warm ribs and serve immediately. Bon appétit!

Nutrition:
- (per serving) calories 397 | fat 15 | protein 35 | total carbs 5 | fiber 4

Buttery Strip Steak

Servings: 6 | Cooking Time: 12 Minutes

Ingredients:
- ½ cup (1 stick) unsalted butter, at room temperature
- 1 cup finely grated Parmesan cheese
- ¼ cup finely ground blanched almond flour
- 1½ pounds (680g) New York strip steak
- Sea salt, freshly ground black pepper, to taste

Directions:
1. Place the butter, Parmesan cheese, and almond flour in a food processor. Process until smooth. Transfer to a sheet of parchment paper and form into a log. Wrap tightly in plastic wrap. Freeze for 45 minutes or refrigerate for at least 4 hours.
2. While the butter is chilling, season the steak liberally with salt and pepper. Let the steak rest at room temperature for about 45 minutes.
3. Place the grill pan or basket in your air fryer, set it to 400°F (205°C), and let it preheat for 5 minutes.
4. Working in batches, if necessary, place the steak on the grill pan and cook for 4 minutes. Flip and cook for 3 minutes or more, until the steak is brown on both sides.
5. Remove the steak from the air fryer and arrange an equal amount of the Parmesan butter on top of each steak. Return the steak to the air fryer and continue cooking for another 5 minutes, until an instant-read thermometer reads 120°F (49°C) for medium-rare and the crust is golden brown (or to your desired doneness).
6. Transfer the cooked steak to a plate, let it rest for 10 minutes before serving.

Nutrition:
- (per serving) calories 463 | fat 37 | protein 33 | total carbs 2 | fiber 1

Pork Chops With Vermouth

Servings: 6 | Cooking Time: 18 Minutes

Ingredients:
- 2 tablespoons vermouth
- 6 center-cut loin pork chops
- ½ tablespoon fresh basil, minced
- ⅓ teaspoon freshly ground black pepper, or more to taste
- 2 tablespoons whole grain mustard

• 1 teaspoon fine kosher salt

Directions:

1. Toss pork chops with other ingredients until they are well coated on both sides.

2. Air-fry your chops for 18 minutes at 405ºF (207ºC), turning once or twice.

3. Mound your favorite salad on a serving plate, top with pork chops and enjoy.

Nutrition:

• (per serving) calories 393 | fat 15 | protein 56 | total carbs 3 | fiber 2

Pork Belly With Onion Sauce

Servings: 4 | Cooking Time: 17 Minutes

Ingredients:

• 1 pound (454 g) unsalted pork belly
• 2 teaspoons Chinese five-spice powder
• Sauce:
• 1 tablespoon coconut oil
• 1 (1-inch) piece fresh ginger, peeled and grated
• 2 cloves garlic, minced
• ½ cup beef or chicken broth
• ¼ to ½ cup Swerve confectioners-style sweetener
• 3 tablespoons wheat-free tamari, or ½ cup coconut aminos
• 1 green onion, sliced, plus more for garnish

Directions:

1. Spray the air fryer basket with avocado oil. Preheat the air fryer to 400ºF (205ºC).

2. Cut the pork belly into ½-inch-thick slices and season well on all sides with the five-spice powder. Place the slices in a single layer in the air fryer basket (if you're using a smaller air fryer, work in batches if necessary) and cook for 8 minutes, or until cooked to your liking, flipping halfway through.

3. While the pork belly cooks, make the sauce: Heat the coconut oil in a small saucepan over medium heat. Add the ginger and garlic and sauté for 1 minute, or until fragrant. Add the broth, sweetener, and tamari and simmer for 10 to 15 minutes, until thickened. Add the green onion and cook for another minute, until the green onion is softened. Taste and adjust the seasoning to your liking.

4. Transfer the pork belly to a large bowl. Pour the sauce over the pork belly and coat well. Place the pork belly slices on a serving platter and garnish with sliced green onions.

5. Best served fresh. Store leftovers in an airtight container in the fridge for up to 4 days. Reheat in a preheated 400ºF (205ºC) air fryer for 3 minutes, or until heated through.

Nutrition:

• (per serving) calories 365 | fat 32 | protein 19 | total carbs 2 | fiber 1

Reuben Fritters

Servings:1 | Cooking Time: 16 Minutes

Ingredients:

• 2 cups finely diced cooked corned beef
• 1 (8-ounce) package cream cheese, softened
• ½ cup finely shredded Swiss cheese (about 2 ounces)
• ¼ cup sauerkraut
• 1 cup pork dust (see here) or powdered Parmesan cheese (see here)
• Chopped fresh thyme, for garnish

• Thousand Island Dipping Sauce (here), for serving (optional; omit for egg-free)
• Cornichons, for serving (optional)

Directions:

1. Spray the air fryer basket with avocado oil. Preheat the air fryer to 390ºF.

2. In a large bowl, mix together the corned beef, cream cheese, Swiss cheese, and sauerkraut until well combined. Form the corned beef mixture into twelve 1½-inch balls.

3. Place the pork dust in a shallow bowl. Roll the corned beef balls in the pork dust and use your hands to form it into a thick crust around each ball.

4. Place 6 balls in the air fryer basket, spaced about ½ inch apart, and cook for 8 minutes, or until golden brown and crispy. Allow them to cool a bit before lifting them out of the air fryer (the fritters are very soft when the cheese is melted; they're easier to handle once the cheese has hardened a bit). Repeat with the remaining fritters.

5. Garnish with chopped fresh thyme and serve with the dipping sauce and cornichons, if desired. Store leftovers in an airtight container in the fridge for 3 days or in the freezer for up to a month. Reheat in a preheated 350ºF air fryer for 4 minutes, or until heated through.

Nutrition:

• (per serving)   calories 527 | fat 50g | protein 18g | total carbs 2g | fiber 0.1g

Greek Stuffed Tenderloin

Servings:4 | Cooking Time: 10 Minutes

Ingredients:

• 1½ pounds venison or beef tenderloin, pounded to ¼ inch thick
• 3 teaspoons fine sea salt
• 1 teaspoon ground black pepper
• 2 ounces creamy goat cheese
• ½ cup crumbled feta cheese (about 2 ounces)
• ¼ cup finely chopped onions
• 2 cloves garlic, minced
• FOR GARNISH/SERVING (OPTIONAL):
• Prepared yellow mustard
• Halved cherry tomatoes
• Extra-virgin olive oil
• Sprigs of fresh rosemary
• Lavender flowers

Directions:

1. Spray the air fryer basket with avocado oil. Preheat the air fryer to 400ºF.

2. Season the tenderloin on all sides with the salt and pepper.

3. In a medium-sized mixing bowl, combine the goat cheese, feta, onions, and garlic. Place the mixture in the center of the tenderloin. Starting at the end closest to you, tightly roll the tenderloin like a jelly roll. Tie the rolled tenderloin tightly with kitchen twine.

4. Place the meat in the air fryer basket and cook for 5 minutes. Flip the meat over and cook for another 5 minutes, or until the internal temperature reaches 135ºF for medium-rare.

5. To serve, smear a line of prepared yellow mustard on a platter, then place the meat next to it and add halved cherry tomatoes on the side, if desired. Drizzle with olive oil and garnish with rosemary sprigs and lavender flowers, if desired.

6. Best served fresh. Store leftovers in an airtight container in the fridge for 3 days. Reheat in a preheated 350ºF air fryer for 4 min-

utes, or until heated through.

Nutrition:
- (per serving) calories 415 | fat 16g | protein 62g | total carbs 4g | fiber 0.3g

Baked Sauerkraut With Sausage

Servings: 4 | Cooking Time: 16 Minutes

Ingredients:
- 4 pork sausages, smoked
- 2 tablespoons olive oil
- 2 garlic cloves, minced
- 1 pound (454 g) sauerkraut
- 1 teaspoon cayenne pepper
- ½ teaspoon black peppercorns
- 2 bay leaves

Directions:
1. Start by preheating your Air Fryer to 360°F (182°C).
2. Prick holes into the sausages using a fork and transfer them to the cooking basket. Cook approximately 14 minutes, shaking the basket a couple of times. Set aside.
3. Now, heat the olive oil in a baking pan at 380°F (193°C). Add the garlic and cook for 1 minute. Immediately stir in the sauerkraut, cayenne pepper, peppercorns, and bay leaves.
4. Let it cook for 15 minutes, stirring every 5 minutes. Serve in individual bowls with warm sausages on the side!

Nutrition:
- (per serving) calories 453 | fat 42 | protein 17 | total carbs 6 | fiber 3

Beef Burger

Servings: 4 | Cooking Time: 12 Minutes

Ingredients:
- 1¼ pounds (567g) lean ground beef
- 1 tablespoon coconut aminos
- 1 teaspoon Dijon mustard
- A few dashes of liquid smoke
- 1 teaspoon shallot powder
- 1 clove garlic, minced
- ½ teaspoon cumin powder
- ¼ cup scallions, minced
- ⅓ teaspoon sea salt flakes
- ⅓ teaspoon freshly cracked mixed peppercorns
- 1 teaspoon celery seeds
- 1 teaspoon parsley flakes

Directions:
1. Mix all of the above ingredients in a bowl, knead until everything is well incorporated.
2. Shape the mixture into four patties. Next, make a shallow dip in the center of each patty to prevent them puffing up during air-frying.
3. Spritz the patties on all sides using a non-stick cooking spray. Cook for approximately 12 minutes at 360°F (182°C).
4. Check for doneness – an instant read thermometer should read 160°F (71°C). Bon appétit!

Nutrition:
- (per serving) calories 425 | fat 25 | protein 38 | total carbs 10 | fiber 8

Bacon-wrapped Cheese Pork

Servings: 4 | Cooking Time: 20 Minutes

Ingredients:
- 4 (1-inch-thick) boneless pork chops
- 2 (5.2-ounce / 147 g) packages Boursin cheese
- 8 slices thin-cut bacon

Directions:
1. Spray the air fryer basket with avocado oil. Preheat the air fryer to 400°F (205°C).
2. Place one of the chops on a cutting board. With a sharp knife held parallel to the cutting board, make a 1-inch-wide incision on the top edge of the chop. Carefully cut into the chop to form a large pocket, leaving a ½-inch border along the sides and bottom. Repeat with the other 3 chops.
3. Snip the corner of a large resealable plastic bag to form a ¾-inch hole. Place the Boursin cheese in the bag and pipe the cheese into the pockets in the chops, dividing the cheese evenly among them.
4. Wrap 2 slices of bacon around each chop and secure the ends with toothpicks. Place the bacon-wrapped chops in the air fryer basket and cook for 10 minutes, then flip the chops and cook for another 8 to 10 minutes, until the bacon is crisp, the chops are cooked through, and the internal temperature reaches 145°F (63°C).
5. Store the leftovers in an airtight container in the refrigerator for up to 3 days. Reheat in a preheated 400°F (205°C) air fryer for 5 minutes, or until warmed through.

Nutrition:
- (per serving) calories 578 | fat 45 | protein 37 | total carbs 16 | fiber 15

Herbed Top Chuck

Servings: 3 | Cooking Time: 50 Minutes

Ingredients:
- 1½ pounds (680g) top chuck
- 2 teaspoons olive oil
- 1 tablespoon Dijon mustard
- Sea salt and ground black pepper, to taste
- 1 teaspoon dried marjoram
- 1 teaspoon dried thyme
- ½ teaspoon fennel seeds

Directions:
1. Start by preheating your Air Fryer to 380°F (193°C)
2. Add all ingredients in a Ziploc bag, shake to mix well. Next, spritz the bottom of the Air Fryer basket with cooking spray.
3. Place the beef in the cooking basket and cook for 50 minutes, turning every 10 to 15 minutes.
4. Let it rest for 5 to 7 minutes before slicing and serving. Enjoy!

Nutrition:
- (per serving) calories 406 | fat 24 | protein 44 | total carbs 2 | fiber 1

Pork With Lime Sauce

Servings: 4 | Cooking Time: 15 Minutes

Ingredients:
- Marinade:
- ½ cup lime juice
- Grated zest of 1 lime
- 2 teaspoons stevia glycerite
- 3 cloves garlic, minced
- 1½ teaspoons fine sea salt
- 1 teaspoon chili powder, or more for more heat
- 1 teaspoon smoked paprika
- 1 pound (454 g) pork tenderloin
- Avocado Lime Sauce:
- 1 medium-sized ripe avocado, roughly chopped
- ½ cup full-fat sour cream
- Grated zest of 1 lime
- Juice of 1 lime
- 2 cloves garlic, roughly chopped
- ½ teaspoon fine sea salt
- ¼ teaspoon ground black pepper
- Chopped fresh cilantro leaves, for garnish
- Lime slices, for serving
- Pico de gallo, for serving

Directions:
1. In a medium-sized casserole dish, stir together all the marinade ingredients until well combined. Add the tenderloin and coat it well in the marinade. Cover and place in the fridge to marinate for 2 hours or overnight.
2. Spray the air fryer basket with avocado oil. Preheat the air fryer to 400°F (205°C).
3. Remove the pork from the marinade and place it in the air fryer basket. Cook for 13 to 15 minutes, until the internal temperature of the pork is 145°F (63°C), flipping after 7 minutes. Remove the pork from the air fryer and place it on a cutting board. Allow it to rest for 8 to 10 minutes, then cut it into ½-inch-thick slices.
4. While the pork cooks, make the avocado lime sauce: Place all the sauce ingredients in a food processor and purée until smooth. Taste and adjust the seasoning to your liking.
5. Place the pork slices on a serving platter and spoon the avocado lime sauce on top. Garnish with cilantro leaves and serve with lime slices and pico de gallo.
6. Store leftovers in an airtight container in the fridge for up to 4 days. Reheat in a preheated 400°F (205°C) air fryer for 5 minutes, or until heated through.

Nutrition:
- (per serving) calories 326 | fat 19 | protein 26 | total carbs 15 | fiber 9

Skirt Steak With Rice Vinegar

Servings: 5 | Cooking Time: 12 Minutes

Ingredients:
- 2 pounds (907 g) skirt steak
- 2 tablespoons keto tomato paste
- 1 tablespoon olive oil
- 1 tablespoon coconut aminos
- ¼ cup rice vinegar
- 1 tablespoon fish sauce
- Sea salt, to taste
- ½ teaspoon dried dill
- ½ teaspoon dried rosemary

- ¼ teaspoon black pepper, freshly cracked

Directions:
1. Place all ingredients in a large ceramic dish, let it marinate for 3 hours in your refrigerator.
2. Coat the sides and bottom of the Air Fryer with cooking spray.
3. Add your steak to the cooking basket, reserve the marinade. Cook the skirt steak in the preheated Air Fryer at 400°F (205°C) for 12 minutes, turning over a couple of times, basting with the reserved marinade.
4. Bon appétit!

Nutrition:
- (per serving) calories 401 | fat 21 | protein 51 | total carbs 2 | fiber 1

Beef Sausage With Tomato Bowl

Servings: 4 | Cooking Time: 20 Minutes

Ingredients:
- 4 bell peppers
- 2 tablespoons olive oil
- 2 medium-sized tomatoes, halved
- 4 spring onions
- 4 beef sausages
- 1 tablespoon mustard

Directions:
1. Start by preheating your Air Fryer to 400°F (205°C).
2. Add the bell peppers to the cooking basket. Drizzle 1 tablespoon of olive oil all over the bell peppers.
3. Cook for 5 minutes. Turn the temperature down to 350°F (180°C). Add the tomatoes and spring onions to the cooking basket and cook for an additional 10 minutes.
4. Reserve your vegetables.
5. Then, add the sausages to the cooking basket. Drizzle with the remaining tablespoon of olive oil.
6. Cook in the preheated Air Fryer at 380°F (193°C) for 15 minutes, flipping them halfway through the cooking time.
7. Serve sausages with the air-fried vegetables and mustard, serve.

Nutrition:
- (per serving) calories 490 | fat 42 | protein 19 | total carbs 9 | fiber 7

Pork Kebab With Yogurt Sauce

Servings: 4 | Cooking Time: 12 Minutes

Ingredients:
- 2 teaspoons olive oil
- ½ pound (227g) ground pork
- ½ pound (227g) ground beef
- 1 egg, whisked
- Sea salt and ground black pepper, to taste
- 1 teaspoon paprika
- 2 garlic cloves, minced
- 1 teaspoon dried marjoram
- 1 teaspoon mustard seeds
- ½ teaspoon celery seeds
- Yogurt Sauce:
- 2 tablespoons olive oil
- 2 tablespoons fresh lemon juice
- Sea salt, to taste
- ¼ teaspoon red pepper flakes, crushed
- ½ cup full-fat yogurt

- 1 teaspoon dried dill weed

Directions:
1. Spritz the sides and bottom of the cooking basket with 2 teaspoons of olive oil.
2. In a mixing dish, thoroughly combine the ground pork, beef, egg, salt, black pepper, paprika, garlic, marjoram, mustard seeds, and celery seeds.
3. Form the mixture into kebabs and transfer them to the greased cooking basket. Cook at 365°F (185°C) for 11 to 12 minutes, turning them over once or twice.
4. In the meantime, mix all the sauce ingredients and place in the refrigerator until ready to serve. Serve the pork kebabs with the yogurt sauce on the side. Enjoy!

Nutrition:
- (per serving) calories 407 | fat 29 | protein 33 | total carbs 4 | fiber 3

Flank Steak With Baby Spinach

Servings: 6 | Cooking Time: 14 Minutes

Ingredients:
- 1 pound (454 g) flank steak
- 1 tablespoon avocado oil
- ½ teaspoon sea salt
- ½ teaspoon garlic powder
- ¼ teaspoon freshly ground black pepper
- 2 ounces (57 g) goat cheese, crumbled
- 1 cup baby spinach, chopped

Directions:
1. Place the steak in a large zip-top bag or between two pieces of plastic wrap. Using a meat mallet or heavy-bottomed skillet, pound the steak to an even ¼-inch thickness.
2. Brush both sides of the steak with the avocado oil.
3. Mix the salt, garlic powder, and pepper in a small dish. Sprinkle this mixture over both sides of the steak.
4. Sprinkle the goat cheese over top, and top that with the spinach.
5. Starting at one of the long sides, roll the steak up tightly. Tie the rolled steak with kitchen string at 3-inch intervals.
6. Set the air fryer to 400°F (205°C). Place the steak roll-up in the air fryer basket. Cook for 7 minutes. Flip the steak and cook for an additional 7 minutes, until an instant-read thermometer reads 120°F (49°C) for medium-rare (adjust the cooking time for your desired doneness).

Nutrition:
- (per serving) calories 165 | fat 9 | protein 18 | total carbs 1 | fiber 0

Air Fried Flank Steak

Servings: 6 | Cooking Time: 8 To 10 Minutes

Ingredients:
- ½ cup avocado oil
- ¼ cup coconut aminos
- 1 shallot, minced
- 1 tablespoon minced garlic
- 2 tablespoons chopped fresh oregano, or 2 teaspoons dried
- 1½ teaspoons sea salt
- 1 teaspoon freshly ground black pepper
- ¼ teaspoon red pepper flakes
- 2 pounds (907 g) flank steak

Directions:

1. In a blender, combine the avocado oil, coconut aminos, shallot, garlic, oregano, salt, black pepper, and red pepper flakes. Process until smooth.
2. Place the steak in a zip-top plastic bag or shallow dish with the marinade. Seal the bag or cover the dish and marinate in the refrigerator for at least 2 hours or overnight.
3. Remove the steak from the bag and discard the marinade.
4. Set the air fryer to 400°F (205°C). Place the steak in the air fryer basket (if needed, cut into sections and work in batches). Cook for 4 to 6 minutes, flip the steak, and cook for another 4 minutes or until the internal temperature reaches 120°F (49°C) in the thickest part for medium-rare (or as desired).

Nutrition:
- (per serving) calories 304 | fat 23 | protein 16 | total carbs 4 | fiber 3

Swiss Burgers With Mushroom

Servings: 2 | Cooking Time: 15 Minutes

Ingredients:
- 2 large portobello mushrooms
- 1 teaspoon fine sea salt, divided
- ¼ teaspoon garlic powder
- ¼ teaspoon ground black pepper
- ¼ teaspoon onion powder
- ¼ teaspoon smoked paprika
- 2 (¼-pound / 113-g) hamburger patties, ½ inch thick
- 2 slices Swiss cheese (omit for dairy-free)
- Condiments of choice, such as Ranch Dressing, prepared yellow mustard, for serving

Directions:
1. Preheat the air fryer to 360°F.
2. Clean the portobello mushrooms and remove the stems. Spray the mushrooms on all sides with avocado oil and season them with ½ teaspoon of the salt. Place the mushrooms in the air fryer basket and cook for 7 to 8 minutes, until fork-tender and soft to the touch.
3. While the mushrooms cook, in a small bowl mix together the remaining ½ teaspoon of salt, the garlic powder, pepper, onion powder, and paprika. Sprinkle the hamburger patties with the seasoning mixture.
4. When the mushrooms are done cooking, remove them from the air fryer and place them on a serving platter with the cap side down.
5. Place the hamburger patties in the air fryer and cook for 7 minutes, or until the internal temperature reaches 145°F for a medium-done burger. Place a slice of Swiss cheese on each patty and cook for another minute to melt the cheese.
6. Place the burgers on top of the mushrooms and drizzle with condiments of your choice. Best served fresh.

Nutrition:
- (per serving) calories 345 | fat 23 | protein 30 | total carbs 5 | fiber 4

Lush Spiced Ribeye Steak

Servings: 3 | Cooking Time: 15 Minutes

Ingredients:
- 1½ pounds (680g) ribeye, bone-in
- 1 tablespoon butter, room temperature
- Salt, to taste
- ½ teaspoon crushed black pepper
- ½ teaspoon dried dill
- ½ teaspoon cayenne pepper
- ½ teaspoon garlic powder
- ½ teaspoon onion powder
- 1 teaspoon ground coriander
- 3 tablespoons mayonnaise
- 1 teaspoon garlic, minced

Directions:
1. Start by preheating your Air Fryer to 400ºF (205ºC).
2. Pat dry the ribeye and rub it with softened butter on all sides. Sprinkle with seasonings and transfer to the cooking basket.
3. Cook in the preheated Air Fryer for 15 minutes, flipping them halfway through the cooking time.
4. In the meantime, simply mix the mayonnaise with garlic and place in the refrigerator until ready to serve. Bon appétit!

Nutrition:
- (per serving) calories 437 | fat 24 | protein 51 | total carbs 2 | fiber 1

Beef And Mushroom Burger

Servings: 4 | Cooking Time: 21 To 23 Minutes

Ingredients:
- 1 pound (454 g) ground beef, formed into 4 patties
- Sea salt, freshly ground black pepper, to taste
- 1 cup thinly sliced onion
- 8 ounces (227 g) mushrooms, sliced
- 1 tablespoon avocado oil
- 2 ounces (57 g) Gruyère cheese, shredded (about ½ cup)

Directions:
1. Season the patties on both sides with salt and pepper.
2. Set the air fryer to 375°F (190°C). Place the patties in the basket and cook for 3 minutes. Flip and cook for another 2 minutes. Remove the burgers and set aside.
3. Place the onion and mushrooms in a medium bowl. Add the avocado oil and salt and pepper to taste, toss well.
4. Place the onion and mushrooms in the air fryer basket. Cook for 15 minutes, stirring occasionally.
5. Spoon the onions and mushrooms over the patties. Top with the cheese. Place the patties back in the air fryer basket and cook for another 1 to 3 minutes, until the cheese melts and an instant-read thermometer reads 160°F (71°C). Remove and let them rest. The temperature will rise to 165°F (74°C), yielding a perfect medium-well burger.

Nutrition:
- (per serving) calories 470 | fat 38 | protein 25 | total carbs 5 | fiber 4

Pork Cutlets With Red Wine

Servings: 2 | Cooking Time: 15 Minutes

Ingredients:
- 1 cup water
- 1 cup red wine
- 1 tablespoon sea salt
- 2 pork cutlets
- ¼ cup almond meal
- ¼ cup flaxseed meal
- ½ teaspoon baking powder
- 1 teaspoon shallot powder
- ½ teaspoon porcini powder
- Sea salt and ground black pepper, to taste
- 1 egg
- ¼ cup yogurt
- 1 teaspoon brown mustard
- ⅓ cup Parmesan cheese, grated

Directions:
1. In a large ceramic dish, combine the water, wine and salt. Add the pork cutlets and put for 1 hour in the refrigerator.
2. In a shallow bowl, mix the almond meal, flaxseed meal, baking powder, shallot powder, porcini powder, salt, and ground pepper. In another bowl, whisk the eggs with yogurt and mustard.
3. In a third bowl, place the grated Parmesan cheese.
4. Dip the pork cutlets in the seasoned flour mixture and toss evenly, then, in the egg mixture. Finally, roll them over the grated Parmesan cheese.
5. Spritz the bottom of the cooking basket with cooking oil. Add the breaded pork cutlets and cook at 395ºF (202ºC) and for 10 minutes.
6. Flip and cook for 5 minutes or more on the other side. Serve warm.

Nutrition:
- (per serving) calories 450 | fat 26 | protein 41 | total carbs 9 | fiber 7

Stuffed Beef Tenderloin

Servings: 4 | Cooking Time: 10 Minutes

Ingredients:
- 1½ pounds (680 g) venison or beef tenderloin, pounded to ¼ inch thick
- 3 teaspoons fine sea salt
- 1 teaspoon ground black pepper
- 2 ounces (57 g) creamy goat cheese
- ½ cup crumbled feta cheese
- ¼ cup finely chopped onions
- 2 cloves garlic, minced
- For Garnish/Serving (Optional):
- Prepared yellow mustard
- Halved cherry tomatoes
- Extra-virgin olive oil
- Sprigs of fresh rosemary
- Lavender flowers

Directions:
1. Spray the air fryer basket with avocado oil. Preheat the air fryer to 400°F.
2. Season the tenderloin on all sides with the salt and pepper.
3. In a medium-sized mixing bowl, combine the goat cheese, feta, onions, and garlic. Place the mixture in the center of the tenderloin. Starting at the end closest to you, tightly roll the tender-

loin like a jelly roll. Tie the rolled tenderloin tightly with kitchen twine.

4. Place the meat in the air fryer basket and cook for 5 minutes. Flip the meat over and cook for another 5 minutes, or until the internal temperature reaches 135°F for medium-rare.

5. To serve, smear a line of prepared yellow mustard on a platter, then place the meat next to it and add halved cherry tomatoes on the side, if desired. Drizzle with olive oil and garnish with rosemary sprigs and lavender flowers, if desired.

6. Best served fresh. Store leftovers in an airtight container in the fridge for 3 days. Reheat in a preheated 350°F air fryer for 4 minutes, or until heated through.

Nutrition:
• (per serving) calories 415 | fat 16 | protein 62 | total carbs 4 | fiber 3.7

Air Fried Beef Steak

Servings: 4 | Cooking Time: 10 Minutes

Ingredients:
• ⅓ cup almond flour
• 2 eggs
• 2 teaspoons caraway seeds
• 4 beef steaks
• 2 teaspoons garlic powder
• 1 tablespoon melted butter
• Fine sea salt and cayenne pepper, to taste

Directions:
1. Generously coat steaks with garlic powder, caraway seeds, salt, and cayenne pepper.
2. In a mixing dish, thoroughly combine melted butter with seasoned crumbs. In another bowl, beat the eggs until they're well whisked.
3. First, coat steaks with the beaten egg, then, coat beef steaks with the buttered crumb mixture.
4. Place the steaks in the Air Fryer cooking basket, cook for 10 minutes at 355°F (181°C). Bon appétit!

Nutrition:
• (per serving) calories 474 | fat 22 | protein 55 | total carbs 9 | fiber 8

Steak With Mushroom Onion Gravy

Servings: 2 | Cooking Time: 33 Minutes

Ingredients:
• Mushroom Onion Gravy:
• ¾ cup sliced button mushrooms
• ¼ cup thinly sliced onions
• ¼ cup unsalted butter, melted
• ½ teaspoon fine sea salt
• ¼ cup beef broth
• Steaks:
• ½ pound (227 g) ground beef (85% lean)
• ¼ cup minced onions, or ½ teaspoon onion powder
• 2 tablespoons tomato paste
• 1 tablespoon dry mustard
• 1 clove garlic, minced, or ¼ teaspoon garlic powder
• ½ teaspoon fine sea salt
• ¼ teaspoon ground black pepper, plus more for garnish if desired
• Chopped fresh thyme leaves, for garnish (optional)

Directions:

1. Preheat the air fryer to 390°F.
2. Make the gravy: Place the mushrooms and onions in a casserole dish that will fit in your air fryer. Pour the melted butter over them and stir to coat, then season with the salt. Place the dish in the air fryer and cook for 5 minutes, stir, then cook for another 3 minutes, or until the onions are soft and the mushrooms are browning. Add the broth and cook for another 10 minutes.
3. While the gravy is cooking, prepare the steaks: In a large bowl, mix together the ground beef, onions, tomato paste, dry mustard, garlic, salt, and pepper until well combined. Form the mixture into 2 oval-shaped patties.
4. Place the patties on top of the mushroom gravy. Cook for 10 minutes, gently flip the patties, then cook for another 2 to 5 minutes, until the beef is cooked through and the internal temperature reaches 145°F.
5. Transfer the steaks to a serving platter and pour the gravy over them. Garnish with ground black pepper and chopped fresh thyme, if desired. Store leftovers in an airtight container in the fridge for 3 days or in the freezer for up to a month. Reheat in a preheated 350°F air fryer for 4 minutes, or until heated through.

Nutrition:
• (per serving) calories 588 | fat 44 | protein 33 | total carbs 11 | fiber 8

Herbed Beef Steaks

Servings: 4 | Cooking Time: 20 Minutes

Ingredients:
• 2 tablespoons coconut aminos
• 3 heaping tablespoons fresh chives
• 2 tablespoons olive oil
• 3 tablespoons dry white wine
• 4 small-sized beef steaks
• 2 teaspoons smoked cayenne pepper
• ½ teaspoon dried basil
• ½ teaspoon dried rosemary
• 1 teaspoon freshly ground black pepper
• 1 teaspoon sea salt, or more to taste

Directions:
1. Firstly, coat the steaks with the cayenne pepper, black pepper, salt, basil, and rosemary.
2. Drizzle the steaks with olive oil, white wine, and coconut aminos.
3. Finally, roast in an Air Fryer basket for 20 minutes at 335°F (168°C). Serve garnished with fresh chives. Bon appétit!

Nutrition:
• (per serving) calories 445 | fat 23 | protein 51 | total carbs 11 | fiber 10

Roast Beef With Jalapeño Peppers

Servings: 8 | Cooking Time: 45 Minutes

Ingredients:
• 2 pounds (907 g) roast beef, at room temperature
• 2 tablespoons extra-virgin olive oil
• 1 teaspoon sea salt flakes
• 1 teaspoon black pepper, preferably freshly ground
• 1 teaspoon smoked paprika
• A few dashes of liquid smoke
• 2 jalapeño peppers, thinly sliced

Directions:
1. Start by preheating the Air Fryer to 330°F (166°C).

2. Then, pat the roast dry using kitchen towels. Rub with extra-virgin olive oil and all seasonings along with liquid smoke.

3. Roast for 30 minutes in the preheated Air Fryer, then, pause the machine and turn the roast over, roast for additional 15 minutes.

4. Check for doneness using a meat thermometer and serve sprinkled with sliced jalapeños. Bon appétit!

Nutrition:

• (per serving) calories 167 | fat 5 | protein 26 | total carbs 2 | fiber 1

Bacon-wrapped Stuffed Pork Chops

Servings:4 | Cooking Time: 20 Minutes

Ingredients:

• 4 (1-inch-thick) boneless pork chops
• 2 (5.2-ounce) packages Boursin cheese (or Kite Hill brand chive cream cheese style spread, softened, for dairy-free) (see Notes)
• 8 slices thin-cut bacon

Directions:

1. Spray the air fryer basket with avocado oil. Preheat the air fryer to 400°F.

2. Place one of the chops on a cutting board. With a sharp knife held parallel to the cutting board, make a 1-inch-wide incision on the top edge of the chop. Carefully cut into the chop to form a large pocket, leaving a ½-inch border along the sides and bottom. Repeat with the other 3 chops.

3. Snip the corner of a large resealable plastic bag to form a ¾-inch hole. Place the Boursin cheese in the bag and pipe the cheese into the pockets in the chops, dividing the cheese evenly among them.

4. Wrap 2 slices of bacon around each chop and secure the ends with toothpicks. Place the bacon-wrapped chops in the air fryer basket and cook for 10 minutes, then flip the chops and cook for another 8 to 10 minutes, until the bacon is crisp, the chops are cooked through, and the internal temperature reaches 145°F.

5. Store leftovers in an airtight container in the refrigerator for up to 3 days. Reheat in a preheated 400°F air fryer for 5 minutes, or until warmed through.

Nutrition:

• (per serving)   calories 578 | fat 45g | protein 37g | total carbs 16g | fiber 1g

Ribs With Chimichurri Sauce

Servings: 4 | Cooking Time: 13 Minutes

Ingredients:

• 1 pound (454 g) boneless short ribs
• 1½ teaspoons sea salt, divided
• ½ teaspoon freshly ground black pepper, divided
• ½ cup fresh parsley leaves
• ½ cup fresh cilantro leaves
• 1 teaspoon minced garlic
• 1 tablespoon freshly squeezed lemon juice
• ½ teaspoon ground cumin
• ¼ teaspoon red pepper flakes
• 2 tablespoons extra-virgin olive oil
• Avocado oil spray

Directions:

1. Pat the short ribs dry with paper towels. Sprinkle the ribs all over with 1 teaspoon salt and ¼ teaspoon black pepper. Let it sit at room temperature for 45 minutes.

2. Meanwhile, place the parsley, cilantro, garlic, lemon juice, cumin, red pepper flakes, the remaining ½ teaspoon salt, and the remaining ¼ teaspoon black pepper in a blender or food processor. With the blender running, slowly drizzle in the olive oil. Blend for about 1 minute, until the mixture is smooth and well combined.

3. Set the air fryer to 400°F (205°C). Spray both sides of the ribs with oil. Place in the basket and cook for 8 minutes. Flip and cook for another 5 minutes, until an instant-read thermometer reads 125°F (52°C) for medium-rare (or to your desired doneness).

4. Allow the meat to rest for 5 to 10 minutes, then slice. Serve warm with the chimichurri sauce.

Nutrition:

• (per serving) calories 329 | fat 24 | protein 21 | total carbs 7 | fiber 6

Beef Sausage And Veg Mélange

Servings: 2 | Cooking Time: 40 Minutes

Ingredients:

• 1 tablespoon lard, melted
• 1 shallot, chopped
• 1 bell pepper, chopped
• 2 red chilies, finely chopped
• 1 teaspoon ginger-garlic paste
• Sea salt, to taste
• ¼ teaspoon ground black pepper
• 4 beef good quality sausages, thinly sliced
• 2 teaspoons smoked paprika
• 1 cup beef bone broth
• ½ cup tomato puree
• 2 handfuls spring greens, shredded

Directions:

1. Melt the lard in a Dutch oven over medium-high flame, sauté the shallots and peppers about 4 minutes or until fragrant.

2. Add the ginger-garlic paste and cook for an additional minute. Season with salt and black pepper and transfer to a lightly greased baking pan.

3. Then, brown the sausages, stirring occasionally, working in batches. Add to the baking pan.

4. Add the smoked paprika, broth, and tomato puree. Lower the pan onto the Air Fryer basket. Bake at 325°F for 30 minutes.

5. Stir in the spring greens and cook for 5 minutes or more or until they wilt. Serve over the hot rice if desired. Bon appétit!

Nutrition:

• (per serving) calories 565 | fat 47 | protein 21 | total carbs 14 | fiber 13

Sausage And Beef Meatloaf

Servings: 4 | Cooking Time: 25 Minutes

Ingredients:

• ¾ pound (340 g) ground chuck
• ¼ pound (113 g) ground pork sausage
• 1 cup shallot, finely chopped
• 2 eggs, well beaten
• 3 tablespoons plain milk
• 1 tablespoon oyster sauce
• 1 teaspoon porcini mushrooms
• ½ teaspoon cumin powder
• 1 teaspoon garlic paste

- 1 tablespoon fresh parsley
- Seasoned salt and crushed red pepper flakes, to taste
- 1 cup Parmesan cheese, grated

Directions:
1. Simply place all ingredients in a large-sized mixing dish, mix until everything is thoroughly combined.
2. Press the meatloaf mixture into the Air Fryer baking dish, set your Air Fryer to cook at 360°F for 25 minutes. Press the power button and cook until heated through.
3. Check for doneness and serve with your favorite wine!

Nutrition:
- (per serving) calories 206 | fat 8 | protein 18 | total carbs 16 | fiber 15

Steak With Bell Pepper

Servings: 6 | Cooking Time: 20 To 23 Minutes

Ingredients:
- ¼ cup avocado oil
- ¼ cup freshly squeezed lime juice
- 2 teaspoons minced garlic
- 1 tablespoon chili powder
- ½ teaspoon ground cumin
- Sea salt, Freshly ground black pepper, to taste
- 1 pound (454 g) top sirloin steak
- 1 red bell pepper, cored, seeded, and cut into ½-inch slices
- 1 green bell pepper, cored, seeded, and cut into ½-inch slices
- 1 large onion, sliced

Directions:
1. In a small bowl or blender, combine the avocado oil, lime juice, garlic, chili powder, cumin, and salt and pepper to taste.
2. Place the sliced steak in a zip-top bag or shallow dish. Place the bell peppers and onion in a separate zip-top bag or dish. Pour half the marinade over the steak and the other half over the vegetables. Seal both bags and let the steak and vegetables marinate in the refrigerator for at least 1 hour or up to 4 hours.
3. Line the air fryer basket with an air fryer liner or aluminum foil. Remove the vegetables from their bag or dish and shake off any excess marinade. Set the air fryer to 400°F (205°C). Place the vegetables in the air fryer basket and cook for 13 minutes.
4. Remove the steak from its bag or dish and shake off any excess marinade. Place the steak on top of the vegetables in the air fryer, and cook for 7 to 10 minutes or until an instant-read thermometer reads 120°F (49°C) for medium-rare (or cook to your desired doneness).
5. Serve with desired fixings, such as keto tortillas, lettuce, sour cream, avocado slices, shredded Cheddar cheese, and cilantro.

Nutrition:
- (per serving) calories 229 | fat 14 | protein 17 | total carbs 7 | fiber 5

Greek Pork With Tzatziki Sauce

Servings: 4 | Cooking Time: 50 Minutes

Ingredients:
- Greek Pork:
- 2 pounds (907 g) pork sirloin roast
- Salt and black pepper, to taste
- 1 teaspoon smoked paprika
- ½ teaspoon mustard seeds
- ½ teaspoon celery seeds
- 1 teaspoon fennel seeds
- 1 teaspoon Ancho chili powder
- 1 teaspoon turmeric powder
- ½ teaspoon ground ginger
- 2 tablespoons olive oil
- 2 cloves garlic, finely chopped
- Tzatziki:
- ½ cucumber, finely chopped and squeezed
- 1 cup full-fat Greek yogurt
- 1 garlic clove, minced
- 1 tablespoon extra virgin olive oil
- 1 teaspoon balsamic vinegar
- 1 teaspoon minced fresh dill
- A pinch of salt

Directions:
1. Toss all ingredients for Greek pork in a large mixing bowl. Toss until the meat is well coated.
2. Cook in the preheated Air Fryer at 360°F (182°C) for 30 minutes, turn over and cook for another 20 minutes.
3. Meanwhile, prepare the tzatziki by mixing all the tzatziki ingredients. Place in your refrigerator until ready to use.
4. Serve the pork sirloin roast with the chilled tzatziki on the side. Enjoy!

Nutrition:
- (per serving) calories 560 | fat 30 | protein 64 | total carbs 5 | fiber 3

Blue Cheese Sirloin Steak With Spinach

Servings: 4 | Cooking Time: 22 Minutes

Ingredients:
- 2 tablespoons balsamic vinegar
- 2 tablespoons red wine vinegar
- 1 tablespoon Dijon mustard
- 1 tablespoon Swerve
- 1 teaspoon minced garlic
- Sea salt and freshly ground black pepper, to taste
- ¾ cup extra-virgin olive oil
- 1 pound (454 g) boneless sirloin steak
- Avocado oil spray
- 1 small red onion, cut into ¼-inch-thick rounds
- 6 ounces (170 g) baby spinach
- ½ cup cherry tomatoes, halved
- 3 ounces (85 g) blue cheese, crumbled

Directions:
1. In a blender, combine the balsamic vinegar, red wine vinegar, Dijon mustard, Swerve, and garlic. Season with salt and pepper and process until smooth. With the blender running, drizzle in the olive oil. Process until well combined. Transfer to a jar with a tight-fitting lid, and refrigerate until ready to serve (it will keep for up to 2 weeks).
2. Season the steak with salt and pepper and let sit at room temperature for at least 45 minutes, time permitting.
3. Set the air fryer to 400°F (205°C). Spray the steak with oil and place it in the air fryer basket. Cook for 6 minutes. Flip the steak and spray it with more oil. Cook for 6 minutes or more for medium-rare or until the steak is done to your liking.
4. Transfer the steak to a plate, tent with a piece of aluminum foil, and allow it to rest.
5. Spray the onion slices with oil and place them in the air fryer basket. Cook at 400°F (205°C) for 5 minutes. Flip the onion slices and spray them with more oil. Cook for 5 minutes or more.
6. Slice the steak diagonally into thin strips. Place the spinach,

cherry tomatoes, onion slices, and steak in a large bowl. Toss with the desired amount of dressing. Sprinkle with crumbled blue cheese and serve.

Nutrition:
- (per serving) calories 670 | fat 53 | protein 41 | total carbs 9 | fiber 7

Zucchini And Ham Casserole

Servings: 4 | Cooking Time: 26 Minutes

Ingredients:
- 2 tablespoons butter, melted
- 1 zucchini, diced
- 1 bell pepper, seeded and sliced
- 1 red chili pepper, seeded and minced
- 1 medium-sized leek, sliced
- ¾ pound (340 g) ham, cooked and diced
- 5 eggs
- 1 teaspoon cayenne pepper
- Sea salt, to taste
- ½ teaspoon ground black pepper
- 1 tablespoon fresh cilantro, chopped

Directions:
1. Start by preheating the Air Fryer to 380°F. Grease the sides and bottom of a baking pan with the melted butter.
2. Place the zucchini, peppers, leeks and ham in the baking pan. Bake in the preheated Air Fryer for 6 minutes.
3. Crack the eggs on top of ham and vegetables, season with the cayenne pepper, salt, and black pepper. Bake for a further 20 minutes or until the whites are completely set.
4. Garnish with fresh cilantro and serve. Bon appétit!

Nutrition:
- (per serving) calories 325 | fat 21 | protein 7 | total carbs 28 | fiber 26

Five-spice Pork Belly

Servings:4 | Cooking Time: 17 Minutes

Ingredients:
- 1 pound unsalted pork belly
- 2 teaspoons Chinese five-spice powder
- SAUCE:
- 1 tablespoon coconut oil
- 1 (1-inch) piece fresh ginger, peeled and grated
- 2 cloves garlic, minced
- ½ cup beef or chicken broth
- ¼ to ½ cup Swerve confectioners'-style sweetener or equivalent amount of liquid or powdered sweetener (see here)
- 3 tablespoons wheat-free tamari, or ½ cup coconut aminos
- 1 green onion, sliced, plus more for garnish
- 1 drop orange oil, or ½ teaspoon orange extract (optional)

Directions:
1. Spray the air fryer basket with avocado oil. Preheat the air fryer to 400°F.
2. Cut the pork belly into ½-inch-thick slices and season well on all sides with the five-spice powder. Place the slices in a single layer in the air fryer basket (if you're using a smaller air fryer, work in batches if necessary) and cook for 8 minutes, or until cooked to your liking, flipping halfway through.
3. While the pork belly cooks, make the sauce: Heat the coconut oil in a small saucepan over medium heat. Add the ginger and garlic and sauté for 1 minute, or until fragrant. Add the broth,

sweetener, and tamari and simmer for 10 to 15 minutes, until thickened. Add the green onion and cook for another minute, until the green onion is softened. Add the orange oil (if using). Taste and adjust the seasoning to your liking.
4. Transfer the pork belly to a large bowl. Pour the sauce over the pork belly and coat well. Place the pork belly slices on a serving platter and garnish with sliced green onions.
5. Best served fresh. Store leftovers in an airtight container in the fridge for up to 4 days. Reheat in a preheated 400°F air fryer for 3 minutes, or until heated through.

Nutrition:
- (per serving) calories 365 | fat 32g | protein 19g | total carbs 2g | fiber 0.3g

Mushroom And Swiss Burgers

Servings:2 | Cooking Time: 15 Minutes

Ingredients:
- 2 large portobello mushrooms
- 1 teaspoon fine sea salt, divided
- ¼ teaspoon garlic powder
- ¼ teaspoon ground black pepper
- ¼ teaspoon onion powder
- ¼ teaspoon smoked paprika
- 2 (¼-pound) hamburger patties, ½ inch thick
- 2 slices Swiss cheese (omit for dairy-free)
- Condiments of choice, such as Ranch Dressing (here; use dairy-free if needed), prepared yellow mustard, or mayonnaise, for serving

Directions:
1. Preheat the air fryer to 360°F.
2. Clean the portobello mushrooms and remove the stems. Spray the mushrooms on all sides with avocado oil and season them with ½ teaspoon of the salt. Place the mushrooms in the air fryer basket and cook for 7 to 8 minutes, until fork-tender and soft to the touch.
3. While the mushrooms cook, in a small bowl mix together the remaining ½ teaspoon of salt, the garlic powder, pepper, onion powder, and paprika. Sprinkle the hamburger patties with the seasoning mixture.
4. When the mushrooms are done cooking, remove them from the air fryer and place them on a serving platter with the cap side down.
5. Place the hamburger patties in the air fryer and cook for 7 minutes, or until the internal temperature reaches 145°F for a medium-done burger. Place a slice of Swiss cheese on each patty and cook for another minute to melt the cheese.
6. Place the burgers on top of the mushrooms and drizzle with condiments of your choice. Best served fresh.

Nutrition:
- (per serving) calories 345 | fat 23g | protein 30g | total carbs 5g | fiber 1g

Scotch Eggs

Servings:8 | Cooking Time: 15 Minutes

Ingredients:
- 2 pounds ground pork or ground beef
- 2 teaspoons fine sea salt
- ½ teaspoon ground black pepper, plus more for garnish
- 8 large hard-boiled eggs, peeled
- 2 cups pork dust (see here)
- Dijon mustard, for serving (optional)

Directions:
1. Spray the air fryer basket with avocado oil. Preheat the air fryer to 400°F.
2. Place the ground pork in a large bowl, add the salt and pepper, and use your hands to mix until seasoned throughout. Flatten about ¼ pound of ground pork in the palm of your hand and place a peeled egg in the center. Fold the pork completely around the egg. Repeat with the remaining eggs.
3. Place the pork dust in a medium-sized bowl. One at a time, roll the ground pork–covered eggs in the pork dust and use your hands to press it into the eggs to form a nice crust. Place the eggs in the air fryer basket and spray them with avocado oil.
4. Cook the eggs for 15 minutes, or until the internal temperature of the pork reaches 145°F and the outside is golden brown. Garnish with ground black pepper and serve with Dijon mustard, if desired.
5. Store leftovers in an airtight container in the fridge for up to 7 days or in the freezer for up to a month. Reheat in a preheated 400°F air fryer for 3 minutes, or until heated through.

Nutrition:
- (per serving) calories 447 | fat 34g | protein 43g | total carbs 0.5g | fiber 0g

Lime Marinated Lamb Chop

Servings: 2 | Cooking Time: 5 Minutes

Ingredients:
- 4 (1-inch-thick) lamb chops
- Sprigs of fresh mint, for garnish (optional)
- Lime slices, for serving (optional)
- Marinade:
- 2 teaspoons grated lime zest
- ½ cup lime juice
- ¼ cup avocado oil
- ¼ cup chopped fresh mint leaves
- 4 cloves garlic, roughly chopped
- 2 teaspoons fine sea salt
- ½ teaspoon ground black pepper

Directions:
1. Make the marinade: Place all the ingredients for the marinade in a food processor or blender and purée until mostly smooth with a few small chunks. Transfer half of the marinade to a shallow dish and set the other half aside for serving. Add the lamb to the shallow dish, cover, and place in the refrigerator to marinate for at least 2 hours or overnight.
2. Spray the air fryer basket with avocado oil. Preheat the air fryer to 390°F (199°C).
3. Remove the chops from the marinade and place them in the air fryer basket. Cook for 5 minutes, or until the internal temperature reaches 145°F for medium doneness.
4. Allow the chops to rest for 10 minutes before serving with the rest of the marinade as a sauce. Garnish with fresh mint leaves

and serve with lime slices, if desired. Best served fresh.

Nutrition:
- (per serving) calories 692 | fat 53 | protein 48 | total carbs 2 | fiber 1

Pork Tenderloin With Avocado Lime Sauce

Servings:4 | Cooking Time: 15 Minutes

Ingredients:
- MARINADE:
- ½ cup lime juice
- Grated zest of 1 lime
- 2 teaspoons stevia glycerite, or ¼ teaspoon liquid stevia
- 3 cloves garlic, minced
- 1½ teaspoons fine sea salt
- 1 teaspoon chili powder, or more for more heat
- 1 teaspoon smoked paprika
- 1 pound pork tenderloin
- AVOCADO LIME SAUCE:
- 1 medium-sized ripe avocado, roughly chopped
- ½ cup full-fat sour cream (or coconut cream for dairy-free)
- Grated zest of 1 lime
- Juice of 1 lime
- 2 cloves garlic, roughly chopped
- ½ teaspoon fine sea salt
- ¼ teaspoon ground black pepper
- Chopped fresh cilantro leaves, for garnish
- Lime slices, for serving
- Pico de gallo, for serving

Directions:
1. In a medium-sized casserole dish, stir together all the marinade ingredients until well combined. Add the tenderloin and coat it well in the marinade. Cover and place in the fridge to marinate for 2 hours or overnight.
2. Spray the air fryer basket with avocado oil. Preheat the air fryer to 400°F.
3. Remove the pork from the marinade and place it in the air fryer basket. Cook for 13 to 15 minutes, until the internal temperature of the pork is 145°F, flipping after 7 minutes. Remove the pork from the air fryer and place it on a cutting board. Allow it to rest for 8 to 10 minutes, then cut it into ½-inch-thick slices.
4. While the pork cooks, make the avocado lime sauce: Place all the sauce ingredients in a food processor and puree until smooth. Taste and adjust the seasoning to your liking.
5. Place the pork slices on a serving platter and spoon the avocado lime sauce on top. Garnish with cilantro leaves and serve with lime slices and pico de gallo.
6. Store leftovers in an airtight container in the fridge for up to 4 days. Reheat in a preheated 400°F air fryer for 5 minutes, or until heated through.

Nutrition:
- (per serving) calories 326 | fat 19g | protein 26g | total carbs 15g | fiber 6g

Herbed Filet Mignon

Servings: 4 | Cooking Time: 13 Minutes

Ingredients:
- 1 pound (454 g) filet mignon
- Sea salt and ground black pepper, to taste
- ½ teaspoon cayenne pepper
- 1 teaspoon dried basil
- 1 teaspoon dried rosemary
- 1 teaspoon dried thyme
- 1 tablespoon sesame oil
- 1 small-sized egg, well-whisked
- ½ cup Parmesan cheese, grated

Directions:
1. Season the filet mignon with salt, black pepper, cayenne pepper, basil, rosemary, and thyme. Brush with sesame oil.
2. Put the egg in a shallow plate. Now, place the Parmesan cheese in another plate.
3. Coat the filet mignon with the egg, then, lay it into the Parmesan cheese. Set your Air Fryer to cook at 360ºF (182ºC).
4. Cook for 10 to 13 minutes or until golden. Serve with mixed salad leaves and enjoy!

Nutrition:
- (per serving) calories 315 | fat 20 | protein 30 | total carbs 4 | fiber 3

Beef Poppers

Servings: 4 | Cooking Time: 15 Minutes

Ingredients:
- 8 medium jalapeño peppers, stemmed, halved, and seeded
- 1 (8-ounce / 227-g) package cream cheese, softened
- 2 pounds (907 g) ground beef (85% lean)
- 1 teaspoon fine sea salt
- ½ teaspoon ground black pepper
- 8 slices thin-cut bacon
- Fresh cilantro leaves, for garnish

Directions:
1. Spray the air fryer basket with avocado oil. Preheat the air fryer to 400°F.
2. Stuff each jalapeño half with a few tablespoons of cream cheese. Place the halves back together again to form 8 jalapeños.
3. Season the ground beef with the salt and pepper and mix with your hands to incorporate. Flatten about ¼ pound of ground beef in the palm of your hand and place a stuffed jalapeño in the center. Fold the beef around the jalapeño, forming an egg shape. Wrap the beef-covered jalapeño with a slice of bacon and secure it with a toothpick.
4. Place the jalapeños in the air fryer basket, leaving space between them (if you're using a smaller air fryer, work in batches if necessary), and cook for 15 minutes, or until the beef is cooked through and the bacon is crispy. Garnish with cilantro before serving.
5. Store leftovers in an airtight container in the fridge for 3 days or in the freezer for up to a month. Reheat in a preheated 350°F air fryer for 4 minutes, or until heated through and the bacon is crispy.

Nutrition:
- (per serving) calories 679 | fat 53 | protein 42 | total carbs 3 | fiber 2

Swedish Meatloaf

Servings:8 | Cooking Time: 35 Minutes

Ingredients:
- 1½ pounds ground beef (85% lean)
- ¼ pound ground pork or ground beef
- 1 large egg (omit for egg-free)
- ½ cup minced onions
- ¼ cup tomato sauce
- 2 tablespoons dry mustard
- 2 cloves garlic, minced
- 2 teaspoons fine sea salt
- 1 teaspoon ground black pepper, plus more for garnish
- SAUCE:
- ½ cup (1 stick) unsalted butter
- ½ cup shredded Swiss or mild cheddar cheese (about 2 ounces)
- 2 ounces cream cheese (¼ cup), softened
- ⅓ cup beef broth
- ⅛ teaspoon ground nutmeg
- Halved cherry tomatoes, for serving (optional)

Directions:
1. Preheat the air fryer to 390°F.
2. In a large bowl, combine the ground beef, ground pork, egg, onions, tomato sauce, dry mustard, garlic, salt, and pepper. Using your hands, mix until well combined.
3. Place the meatloaf mixture in a 9 by 5-inch loaf pan and place it in the air fryer. Cook for 35 minutes, or until cooked through and the internal temperature reaches 145°F. Check the meatloaf after 25 minutes; if it's getting too brown on the top, cover it loosely with foil to prevent burning.
4. While the meatloaf cooks, make the sauce: Heat the butter in a saucepan over medium-high heat until it sizzles and brown flecks appear, stirring constantly to keep the butter from burning. Turn the heat down to low and whisk in the Swiss cheese, cream cheese, broth, and nutmeg. Simmer for at least 10 minutes. The longer it simmers, the more the flavors open up.
5. When the meatloaf is done, transfer it to a serving tray and pour the sauce over it. Garnish with ground black pepper and serve with cherry tomatoes, if desired. Allow the meatloaf to rest for 10 minutes before slicing so it doesn't crumble apart.
6. Store leftovers in an airtight container in the fridge for 3 days or in the freezer for up to a month. Reheat in a preheated 350°F air fryer for 4 minutes, or until heated through.

Nutrition:
- (per serving) calories 395 | fat 32g | protein 23g | total carbs 3g | fiber 1g

Italian Sausages With Peppers And Onions

Servings:3 | Cooking Time: 28 Minutes

Ingredients:
- 1 medium onion, thinly sliced
- 1 yellow or orange bell pepper, thinly sliced
- 1 red bell pepper, thinly sliced
- ¼ cup avocado oil or melted coconut oil
- 1 teaspoon fine sea salt
- 6 Italian sausages
- Dijon mustard, for serving (optional)

Directions:
1. Preheat the air fryer to 400°F.
2. Place the onion and peppers in a large bowl. Drizzle with the oil and toss well to coat the veggies. Season with the salt.

3. Place the onion and peppers in a 6-inch pie pan and cook in the air fryer for 8 minutes, stirring halfway through. Remove from the air fryer and set aside.

4. Spray the air fryer basket with avocado oil. Place the sausages in the air fryer basket and cook for 20 minutes, or until crispy and golden brown. During the last minute or two of cooking, add the onion and peppers to the basket with the sausages to warm them through.

5. Place the onion and peppers on a serving platter and arrange the sausages on top. Serve Dijon mustard on the side, if desired.

6. Store leftovers in an airtight container in the fridge for up to 7 days or in the freezer for up to a month. Reheat in a preheated 390°F air fryer for 3 minutes, or until heated through.

Nutrition:
- (per serving) calories 576 | fat 49g | protein 25g | total carbs 8g | fiber 2g

Zucchini Noodle With Beef Meatball

Servings: 6 | Cooking Time: 11 To 13 Minutes

Ingredients:
- 1 pound (454 g) ground beef
- 1½ teaspoons sea salt, plus more for seasoning
- 1 large egg, beaten
- 1 teaspoon gelatin
- ¾ cup Parmesan cheese
- 2 teaspoons minced garlic
- 1 teaspoon Italian seasoning
- Freshly ground black pepper, to taste
- Avocado oil spray
- Keto-friendly marinara sauce, for serving
- 6 ounces (170 g) zucchini noodles, made using a spiralizer or store-bought

Directions:
1. Place the ground beef in a large bowl, and season with the salt.
2. Place the egg in a separate bowl and sprinkle with the gelatin. Allow it to sit for 5 minutes.
3. Stir the gelatin mixture, then pour it over the ground beef. Add the Parmesan, garlic, and Italian seasoning. Season with salt and pepper.
4. Form the mixture into 1½-inch meatballs and place them on a plate, cover with plastic wrap and refrigerate for at least 1 hour or overnight.
5. Spray the meatballs with oil. Set the air fryer to 400°F (205°C) and arrange the meatballs in a single layer in the air fryer basket. Cook for 4 minutes. Flip the meatballs and spray them with more oil. Cook for 4 minutes or more, until an instant-read thermometer reads 160°F (71°C). Transfer the meatballs to a plate and allow them to rest.
6. While the meatballs are resting, heat the marinara in a saucepan on the stove over medium heat.
7. Place the zucchini noodles in the air fryer, and cook at 400°F (205°C) for 3 to 5 minutes.
8. To serve, place the zucchini noodles in serving bowls. Top with meatballs and warm marinara.

Nutrition:
- (per serving) calories 312 | fat 25 | protein 20 | total carbs 2 | fiber 1

Balsamic London Broil

Servings: 8 | Cooking Time: 8 To 10 Minutes

Ingredients:
- 2 pounds (907 g) London broil
- 3 large garlic cloves, minced
- 3 tablespoons balsamic vinegar
- 3 tablespoons whole-grain mustard
- 2 tablespoons olive oil
- Sea salt and ground black pepper, to taste
- ½ teaspoon dried hot red pepper flakes

Directions:
1. Score both sides of the cleaned London broil.
2. Thoroughly combine the remaining ingredients, massage this mixture into the meat to coat it on all sides. Let it marinate for at least 3 hours.
3. Set the Air Fryer to cook at 400°F (205°C), Then cook the London broil for 15 minutes. Flip it over and cook another 10 to 12 minutes. Bon appétit!

Nutrition:
- (per serving) calories 257 | fat 9 | protein 41 | total carbs 1 | fiber 0

Pork And Beef Casserole

Servings: 4 | Cooking Time: 10 Minutes

Ingredients:
- 1 pound (454 g) lean ground pork
- ½ pound (227g) ground beef
- ¼ cup tomato purée
- Sea salt and ground black pepper, to taste
- 1 teaspoon smoked paprika
- ½ teaspoon dried oregano
- 1 teaspoon dried basil
- 1 teaspoon dried rosemary
- 2 eggs
- 1 cup Cottage cheese, crumbled, at room temperature
- ½ cup Cotija cheese, shredded

Directions:
1. Lightly grease a casserole dish with a nonstick cooking oil. Add the ground meat to the bottom of your casserole dish.
2. Add the tomato purée. Sprinkle with salt, black pepper, paprika, oregano, basil, and rosemary.
3. In a mixing bowl, whisk the egg with cheese. Place on top of the ground meat mixture. Place a piece of foil on top.
4. Bake in the preheated Air Fryer at 350°F (180°C) for 10 minutes, remove the foil and cook for an additional 6 minutes. Bon appétit!

Nutrition:
- (per serving) calories 449 | fat 23 | protein 54 | total carbs 5 | fiber 4

Pork Cheese Casserole

Servings: 4 | Cooking Time: 30 Minutes

Ingredients:
- 2 chili peppers
- 1 red bell pepper
- 2 tablespoons olive oil
- 1 large-sized shallot, chopped
- 1 pound (454 g) ground pork
- 2 garlic cloves, minced

- 2 ripe tomatoes, puréed
- 1 teaspoon dried marjoram
- ½ teaspoon mustard seeds
- ½ teaspoon celery seeds
- 1 teaspoon Mexican oregano
- 1 tablespoon fish sauce
- 2 tablespoons fresh coriander, chopped
- Salt and ground black pepper, to taste
- 2 cups water
- 1 tablespoon chicken bouillon granules
- 2 tablespoons sherry wine
- 1 cup Mexican cheese blend

Directions:
1. Roast the peppers in the preheated Air Fryer at 395ºF (202ºC) for 10 minutes, flipping them halfway through cook time.
2. Let them steam for 10 minutes, then, peel the skin and discard the stems and seeds. Slice the peppers into halves.
3. Heat the olive oil in a baking pan at 380ºF (193ºC) for 2 minutes, add the shallots and cook for 4 minutes. Add the ground pork and garlic, cook for a further 4 to 5 minutes.
4. After that, stir in the tomatoes, marjoram, mustard seeds, celery seeds, oregano, fish sauce, coriander, salt, and pepper. Add a layer of sliced peppers to the baking pan.
5. Mix the water with the chicken bouillon granules and sherry wine. Add the mixture to the baking pan.
6. Cook in the preheated Air Fryer at 395ºF (202ºC) for 10 minutes. Top with cheese and bake an additional 5 minutes until the cheese has melted. Serve immediately.

Nutrition:
- (per serving) calories 505 | fat 39 | protein 28 | total carbs 10 | fiber 8

Fajita Meatball Lettuce Wraps

Servings:4 | Cooking Time: 10 Minutes

Ingredients:
- 1 pound ground beef (85% lean)
- ½ cup salsa, plus more for serving if desired
- ¼ cup chopped onions
- ¼ cup diced green or red bell peppers
- 1 large egg, beaten
- 1 teaspoon fine sea salt
- ½ teaspoon chili powder
- ½ teaspoon ground cumin
- 1 clove garlic, minced
- FOR SERVING (OPTIONAL):
- 8 leaves Boston lettuce
- Pico de gallo or salsa
- Lime slices

Directions:
1. Spray the air fryer basket with avocado oil. Preheat the air fryer to 350°F.
2. In a large bowl, mix together all the ingredients until well combined.
3. Shape the meat mixture into eight 1-inch balls. Place the meatballs in the air fryer basket, leaving a little space between them. Cook for 10 minutes, or until cooked through and no longer pink inside and the internal temperature reaches 145°F.
4. Serve each meatball on a lettuce leaf, topped with pico de gallo or salsa, if desired. Serve with lime slices if desired.
5. Store leftovers in an airtight container in the fridge for 3 days or in the freezer for up to a month. Reheat in a preheated 350°F

air fryer for 4 minutes, or until heated through.

Nutrition:
- (per serving) calories 272 | fat 18g | protein 23g | total carbs 3g | fiber 0.5g

Blue Cheese Hamburgers

Servings: 2 | Cooking Time: 10 Minutes

Ingredients:
- ½ teaspoon fine sea salt
- ¼ teaspoon ground black pepper
- ¼ teaspoon garlic powder
- ¼ teaspoon onion powder
- ¼ teaspoon smoked paprika
- 2 (¼-pound / 113-g) hamburger patties, ½ inch thick
- ½ cup crumbled blue cheese (omit for dairy-free)
- 2 Hamburger Buns
- 2 tablespoons mayonnaise
- 6 red onion slices
- 2 Boston lettuce leaves

Directions:
1. Spray the air fryer basket with avocado oil. Preheat the air fryer to 360°F.
2. In a small bowl, combine the salt, pepper, and seasonings. Season the patties well on both sides with the seasoning mixture.
3. Place the patties in the air fryer basket and cook for 7 minutes, or until the internal temperature reaches 145°F for a medium-done burger. Place the blue cheese on top of the patties and cook for another minute to melt the cheese. Remove the burgers from the air fryer and allow them to rest for 5 minutes.
4. Slice the buns in half and smear 2 halves with a tablespoon of mayo each. Increase the heat to 400°F and place the buns in the air fryer basket cut side up. Toast the buns for 1 to 2 minutes, until golden brown.
5. Remove the buns from the air fryer and place them on a serving plate. Place the burgers on the buns and top each burger with 3 red onion slices and a lettuce leaf.
6. Best served fresh. Store leftover patties in an airtight container in the fridge for 3 days or in the freezer for up to a month. Reheat in a preheated 350°F air fryer for 4 minutes, or until heated through.

Nutrition:
- (per serving) calories 237 | fat 20 | protein 11 | total carbs 3 | fiber 2

Mixed Greens With Bacon

Servings: 2 | Cooking Time: 7 Minutes

Ingredients:
- 7 ounces (198 g) mixed greens
- 8 thick slices pork bacon
- 2 shallots, peeled and diced
- Nonstick cooking spray

Directions:
1. Begin by preheating the air fryer to 345°F (174°C).
2. Now, add the shallot and bacon to the Air Fryer cooking basket, set the timer for 2 minutes. Spritz with a nonstick cooking spray.
3. After that, pause the Air Fryer, throw in the mixed greens, give it a good stir and cook for an additional 5 minutes. Serve warm.

Nutrition:
- (per serving) calories 259 | fat 16 | protein 19 | total carbs 10 |

fiber 5

Italian Sausage And Pepper Casserole

Servings: 4 | Cooking Time: 15 Minutes

Ingredients:
- 1 pound (454 g) Italian sausage
- 2 Italian peppers, seeded and sliced
- 1 cup mushrooms, sliced
- 1 shallot, sliced
- 4 cloves garlic
- 1 teaspoon dried basil
- 1 teaspoon dried oregano
- ¼ teaspoon black pepper
- ¼ teaspoon cayenne pepper
- Sea salt, to taste
- 2 tablespoons Dijon mustard
- 1 cup chicken broth

Directions:
1. Toss all ingredients in a lightly greased baking pan. Make sure the sausages and vegetables are coated with the oil and seasonings.
2. Bake in the preheated Air Fryer at 380°F for 15 minutes.
3. Divide between individual bowls and serve warm. Bon appétit!

Nutrition:
- (per serving) calories 508 | fat 40 | protein 3 | total carbs 35 | fiber 31

Pork Twist With Bolognese Sauce

Servings: 4 | Cooking Time: 15 Minutes

Ingredients:
- 1 teaspoon kosher salt
- ⅓ teaspoon cayenne pepper
- 1½ pounds (680 g) ground pork
- ⅓ cup tomato paste
- 3 cloves garlic, minced
- ½ medium-sized white onion, peeled and chopped
- ⅓ tablespoon fresh cilantro, chopped
- ½ tablespoon extra-virgin olive oil
- ⅓ teaspoon freshly cracked black pepper
- ½ teaspoon grated fresh ginger

Directions:
1. Begin by preheating your Air Fryer to 395°F.
2. Then, thoroughly combine all the ingredients until the mixture is uniform.
3. Transfer the meat mixture to the Air Fryer baking dish and cook for about 14 minutes. Serve with zucchini noodles and enjoy.

Nutrition:
- (per serving) calories 490 | fat 37 | protein 29 | total carbs 6 | fiber 5

Salisbury Steak With Mushroom Onion Gravy

Servings:2 | Cooking Time: 33 Minutes

Ingredients:
- MUSHROOM ONION GRAVY:
- ¾ cup sliced button mushrooms
- ¼ cup thinly sliced onions
- ¼ cup unsalted butter, melted (or bacon fat for dairy-free)
- ½ teaspoon fine sea salt
- ¼ cup beef broth
- STEAKS:
- ½ pound ground beef (85% lean)
- ¼ cup minced onions, or ½ teaspoon onion powder
- 2 tablespoons tomato paste
- 1 tablespoon dry mustard
- 1 clove garlic, minced, or ¼ teaspoon garlic powder
- ½ teaspoon fine sea salt
- ¼ teaspoon ground black pepper, plus more for garnish if desired
- Chopped fresh thyme leaves, for garnish (optional)

Directions:
1. Preheat the air fryer to 390°F.
2. Make the gravy: Place the mushrooms and onions in a casserole dish that will fit in your air fryer. Pour the melted butter over them and stir to coat, then season with the salt. Place the dish in the air fryer and cook for 5 minutes, stir, then cook for another 3 minutes, or until the onions are soft and the mushrooms are browning. Add the broth and cook for another 10 minutes.
3. While the gravy is cooking, prepare the steaks: In a large bowl, mix together the ground beef, onions, tomato paste, dry mustard, garlic, salt, and pepper until well combined. Form the mixture into 2 oval-shaped patties.
4. Place the patties on top of the mushroom gravy. Cook for 10 minutes, gently flip the patties, then cook for another 2 to 5 minutes, until the beef is cooked through and the internal temperature reaches 145°F.
5. Transfer the steaks to a serving platter and pour the gravy over them. Garnish with ground black pepper and chopped fresh thyme, if desired. Store leftovers in an airtight container in the fridge for 3 days or in the freezer for up to a month. Reheat in a preheated 350°F air fryer for 4 minutes, or until heated through.

Nutrition:
- (per serving)   calories 588 | fat 44g | protein 33g | total carbs 11g | fiber 3g

Chapter 5 Fish And Seafood Recipes

Lemony Snapper

Servings: 4 | Cooking Time: 7 Minutes

Ingredients:
- 1 pound (454 g) snapper, grouper, or salmon fillets
- Sea salt, freshly ground black pepper, to taste
- 1 tablespoon avocado oil
- ¼ cup sour cream
- ¼ cup sugar-free mayonnaise (homemade, here, or store-bought)
- 2 tablespoons fresh dill, chopped, plus more for garnish
- 1 tablespoon freshly squeezed lemon juice
- ½ teaspoon grated lemon zest

Directions:
1. Pat the fish dry with paper towels and season well with salt and pepper. Brush with the avocado oil.
2. Set the air fryer to 400°F (205°C). Place the fillets in the air fryer basket and cook for 1 minute.
3. Lower the air fryer temperature to 325°F and continue cooking for 5 minutes. Flip the fish and cook for 1 minute more or until an instant-read thermometer reads 145°F (63°C). (If using salmon, cook it to 125°F (52°C) for medium-rare.)
4. While the fish is cooking, make the sauce by combining the sour cream, mayonnaise, dill, lemon juice, and lemon zest in a medium bowl. Season with salt and pepper and stir until combined. Refrigerate until ready to serve.
5. Serve the fish with the sauce, garnished with the remaining dill.

Nutrition:
- (per serving) calories 304 | fat 19 | protein 30 | total carbs 2 | fiber 2

Baked Monkfish With Olives

Servings: 2 | Cooking Time: 12 Minutes

Ingredients:
- 2 teaspoons olive oil
- 1 cup celery, sliced
- 2 bell peppers, sliced
- 1 teaspoon dried thyme
- ½ teaspoon dried marjoram
- ½ teaspoon dried rosemary
- 2 monkfish fillets
- 1 tablespoon coconut aminos
- 2 tablespoons lime juice
- Coarse salt and ground black pepper, to taste
- 1 teaspoon cayenne pepper
- ½ cup Kalamata olives, pitted and sliced

Directions:
1. In a nonstick skillet, heat the olive oil for 1 minute. Once hot, sauté the celery and peppers until tender, for about 4 minutes. Sprinkle with thyme, marjoram, and rosemary and set aside.
2. Toss the fish fillets with the coconut aminos, lime juice, salt, black pepper, and cayenne pepper. Place the fish fillets in a lightly greased cooking basket and bake at 390°F (199°C) for 8 minutes.
3. Turn them over, add the olives, and cook for an additional 4 minutes. Serve with the sautéed vegetables on the side. Bon appétit!

Nutrition:
- (per serving) calories 292 | fat 19 | protein 22 | total carbs 9 | fiber 6

Tilapia And Parmesan Bake

Servings: 6 | Cooking Time: 10 Minutes

Ingredients:
- 1 cup Parmesan cheese, grated
- 1 teaspoon paprika
- 1 teaspoon dried dill weed
- 2 pounds (907 g) tilapia fillets
- ⅓ cup mayonnaise
- ½ tablespoon lime juice
- Salt and ground black pepper, to taste

Directions:
1. Mix the mayonnaise, Parmesan, paprika, salt, black pepper, and dill weed until everything is thoroughly combined.
2. Then, drizzle tilapia fillets with the lime juice.
3. Cover each fish fillet with Parmesan/mayo mixture, roll them in Parmesan/paprika mixture. Bake at 335°F for about 10 minutes. Eat warm and enjoy!

Nutrition:
- (per serving) calories 294 | fat 16 | protein 36 | total carbs 3 | fiber 2

Creamy Haddock

Servings: 4 | Cooking Time: 8 Minutes

Ingredients:
- 1-pound (454-g) haddock fillet
- 1 teaspoon cayenne pepper
- 1 teaspoon salt
- 1 teaspoon coconut oil
- ½ cup heavy cream

Directions:
1. Grease the baking pan with coconut oil.
2. Then put haddock fillet inside and sprinkle it with cayenne pepper, salt, and heavy cream.
3. Put the baking pan in the air fryer basket and cook at 375F (190°C) for 8 minutes.

Nutrition:
- (per serving) calories 190 | fat 7 | protein 28 | total carbs 2 | fiber 1

Whitefish Fillet With Green Bean

Servings: 4 | Cooking Time: 15 Minutes

Ingredients:
- 1 pound (454 g) whitefish fillets, minced
- ½ pound (227g) green beans, finely chopped
- ½ cup scallions, chopped
- 1 chili pepper, seeded and minced
- 1 tablespoon red curry paste
- 1 tablespoon fish sauce
- 2 tablespoons apple cider vinegar

- 1 teaspoon water
- Sea salt flakes, to taste
- ½ teaspoon cracked black peppercorns
- 2 tablespoons butter, at room temperature
- ½ teaspoon lemon

Directions:
1. Add all ingredients in the order listed above to the mixing dish. Mix to combine well using a spatula or your hands.
2. Form into small cakes and chill for 1 hour. Place a piece of aluminum foil over the cooking basket. Place the cakes on foil.
3. Cook at 390ºF (199ºC) for 10 minutes, pause the machine, flip each fish cake over and air-fry for additional 5 minutes. Mound a cucumber relish onto the plates, add the fish cakes and serve warm.

Nutrition:
- (per serving) calories 231 | fat 12 | protein 23 | total carbs 6 | fiber 4

Lemony Shrimp Skewers With Vermouth

Servings: 4 | Cooking Time: 5 Minutes

Ingredients:
- 1½ pounds (680 g) shrimp
- ¼ cup vermouth
- 2 cloves garlic, crushed
- Kosher salt, to taste
- ¼ teaspoon black pepper, freshly ground
- 2 tablespoons olive oil
- 8 skewers, soaked in water for 30 minutes
- 1 lemon, cut into wedges

Directions:
1. Add the shrimp, vermouth, garlic, salt, black pepper, and olive oil in a ceramic bowl, let it sit for 1 hour in your refrigerator.
2. Discard the marinade and toss the shrimp with flour. Thread on to skewers and transfer to the lightly greased cooking basket.
3. Cook at 400ºF for 5 minutes, tossing halfway through. Serve with lemon wedges. Bon appétit!

Nutrition:
- (per serving) calories 228 | fat 7 | protein 26 | total carbs 5 | fiber 4

Creamy Mackerel

Servings: 4 | Cooking Time: 6 Minutes

Ingredients:
- 2-pound (907-g) mackerel fillet
- 1 cup coconut cream
- 1 teaspoon ground coriander
- 1 teaspoon cumin seeds
- 1 garlic clove, peeled, chopped

Directions:
1. Chop the mackerel roughly and sprinkle it with coconut cream, ground coriander, cumin seeds, and garlic.
2. Then put the fish in the air fryer and cook at 400F (205ºC) for 6 minutes.

Nutrition:
- (per serving) calories 735 | fat 54 | protein 55 | total carbs 4 | fiber 2

Japanese Flounder Fillets

Servings: 4 | Cooking Time: 12 Minutes

Ingredients:
- 4 flounder fillets
- Sea salt and freshly cracked mixed peppercorns, to taste
- 1½ tablespoons dark sesame oil
- 2 tablespoons sake
- ¼ cup soy sauce
- 1 tablespoon grated lemon rind
- 2 garlic cloves, minced
- 2 tablespoons chopped chives, to serve

Directions:
1. Place all the ingredients, without the chives, in a large-sized mixing dish. Cover and allow it to marinate for about 2 hours in your fridge.
2. Remove the fish from the marinade and cook in the Air Fryer cooking basket at 360ºF for 10 to 12 minutes, flip once during cooking.
3. Pour the remaining marinade into a pan that is preheated over a medium-low heat, let it simmer, stirring continuously, until it has thickened.
4. Pour the prepared glaze over flounder and serve garnished with fresh chives.

Nutrition:
- (per serving) calories 288 | fat 18.3 | protein 5.1 | total carbs 193.8 | fiber 0.2

Cod Fillets With Avocado And Cabbage

Servings: 2 | Cooking Time: 10 Minutes

Ingredients:
- 1 cup shredded cabbage
- ¼ cup full-fat sour cream
- 2 tablespoons full-fat mayonnaise
- ¼ cup chopped pickled jalapeños
- 2 (3-ounce / (85-g)) cod fillets
- 1 teaspoon chili powder
- 1 teaspoon cumin
- ½ teaspoon paprika
- ¼ teaspoon garlic powder
- 1 medium avocado, peeled, pitted, and sliced
- ½ medium lime

Directions:
1. In a large bowl, place cabbage, sour cream, mayonnaise, and jalapeños. Mix until fully coated. Let it sit for 20 minutes in the refrigerator.
2. Sprinkle cod fillets with chili powder, cumin, paprika, and garlic powder. Place each fillet into the air fryer basket.
3. Adjust the temperature to 370°F (188ºC) and set the timer for 10 minutes.
4. Flip the fillets halfway through the cooking time. When fully cooked, fish should have an internal temperature of at least 145°F (63ºC).
5. To serve, divide slaw mixture into two serving bowls, break cod fillets into pieces and spread over the bowls, and top with avocado. Squeeze lime juice over each bowl. Serve immediately.

Nutrition:
- (per serving) calories 342 | fat 25 | protein 16 | total carbs 12 | fiber 6

Fijan Coconut Tilapia

Servings: 2 | Cooking Time: 12 Minutes

Ingredients:
- 1 cup coconut milk
- 2 tablespoons lime juice
- 2 tablespoons Shoyu sauce
- Salt and white pepper, to taste
- 1 teaspoon turmeric powder
- ½ teaspoon ginger powder
- ½ Thai Bird's Eye chili, seeded and finely chopped
- 1 pound (454 g) tilapia
- 2 tablespoons olive oil

Directions:
1. In a mixing bowl, thoroughly combine the coconut milk with the lime juice, Shoyu sauce, salt, pepper, turmeric, ginger, and chili pepper. Add tilapia and let it marinate for 1 hour.
2. Brush the Air Fryer basket with olive oil. Discard the marinade and place the tilapia fillets in the Air Fryer basket.
3. Cook the tilapia in the preheated Air Fryer at 400°F for 6 minutes, turn them over and cook for 6 minutes or more. Work in batches.
4. Serve with some extra lime wedges if desired. Enjoy!

Nutrition:
- (per serving) calories 426 | fat 22 | protein 50 | total carbs 9 | fiber 6

Shrimp Scampi

Servings:4 | Cooking Time: 8 Minutes

Ingredients:
- ¼ cup unsalted butter (or butter-flavored coconut oil for dairy-free)
- 2 tablespoons fish stock or chicken broth
- 1 tablespoon lemon juice
- 2 cloves garlic, minced
- 2 tablespoons chopped fresh basil leaves
- 1 tablespoon chopped fresh parsley, plus more for garnish
- 1 teaspoon red pepper flakes
- 1 pound large shrimp, peeled and deveined, tails removed
- Fresh basil sprigs, for garnish

Directions:
1. Preheat the air fryer to 350° F.
2. Place the butter, fish stock, lemon juice, garlic, basil, parsley, and red pepper flakes in a 6 by 3-inch pan, stir to combine, and place in the air fryer. Cook for 3 minutes, or until fragrant and the garlic has softened.
3. Add the shrimp and stir to coat the shrimp in the sauce. Cook for 5 minutes, or until the shrimp are pink, stirring after 3 minutes. Garnish with fresh basil sprigs and chopped parsley before serving.
4. Store leftovers in an airtight container in the refrigerator for up to 4 days. Reheat in a preheated 400°F air fryer for about 3 minutes, until heated through.

Nutrition:
- (per serving) calories 175 | fat 11g | protein 18g | total carbs 1g | fiber 0.2g

Beer Marinated Scallops

Servings: 4 | Cooking Time: 7 Minutes

Ingredients:
- 2 pounds (907 g) sea scallops
- ½ cup beer
- 4 tablespoons butter
- 2 sprigs rosemary, only leaves
- Sea salt and freshly cracked black pepper, to taste

Directions:
1. In a ceramic dish, mix the sea scallops with beer, let it marinate for 1 hour.
2. Meanwhile, preheat your Air Fryer to 400°F. Melt the butter and add the rosemary leaves. Stir for a few minutes.
3. Discard the marinade and transfer the sea scallops to the Air Fryer basket. Season with salt and black pepper.
4. Cook the scallops in the preheated Air Fryer for 7 minutes, shaking the basket halfway through the cooking time. Work in batches.
5. Bon appétit!

Nutrition:
- (per serving) calories 471 | fat 27 | protein 54 | total carbs 2 | fiber 1.9

Cauliflower And Shrimp Casserole

Servings: 4 | Cooking Time: 22 Minutes

Ingredients:
- 1 pound (454 g) shrimp cleaned and deveined
- 2 cups cauliflower, cut into florets
- 2 bell peppers, sliced
- 1 shallot, sliced
- 2 tablespoons sesame oil
- 1 cup tomato paste

Directions:
1. Start by preheating your Air Fryer to 360°F. Spritz the baking pan with cooking spray.
2. Now, arrange the shrimp and vegetables in the baking pan. Then, drizzle the sesame oil over the vegetables. Pour the tomato paste over the vegetables.
3. Cook for 10 minutes in the preheated Air Fryer. Stir with a large spoon and cook for a further 12 minutes. Serve warm.

Nutrition:
- (per serving) calories 209 | fat 7 | protein 3 | total carbs 16 | fiber 14

Tuna Steak

Servings: 4 | Cooking Time: 12 Minutes

Ingredients:
- 1-pound (454-g) tuna steaks, boneless and cubed
- 1 tablespoon mustard
- 1 tablespoon avocado oil
- 1 tablespoon apple cider vinegar

Directions:
1. Mix avocado oil with mustard and apple cider vinegar.
2. Then brush tuna steaks with mustard mixture and put in the air fryer basket.
3. Cook the fish at 360F (182°C) for 6 minutes per side.

Nutrition:
- (per serving) calories 227 | fat 8 | protein 34 | total carbs 2 | fiber 1

Fried Haddock

Servings: 2 | Cooking Time: 13 Minutes

Ingredients:
- 2 haddock fillets
- ½ cup Parmesan cheese, freshly grated
- 1 teaspoon dried parsley flakes
- 1 egg, beaten
- ½ teaspoon coarse sea salt
- ¼ teaspoon ground black pepper
- ¼ teaspoon cayenne pepper
- 2 tablespoons olive oil

Directions:
1. Start by preheating your Air Fryer to 360°F. Pat dry the haddock fillets and set aside.
2. In a shallow bowl, thoroughly combine the Parmesan and parsley flakes. Mix until everything is well incorporated.
3. In a separate shallow bowl, whisk the egg with salt, black pepper, and cayenne pepper.
4. Dip the haddock fillets into the egg. Then, dip the fillets into the Parmesan mixture until well coated on all sides.
5. Drizzle the olive oil all over the fish fillets. Lower the coated fillets into the lightly greased Air Fryer basket. Cook for 11 to 13 minutes. Bon appétit!

Nutrition:
- (per serving) calories 434 | fat 26 | protein 43 | total carbs 4 | fiber 3

Tuna Avocado Bites

Servings:12 | Cooking Time: 7 Minutes

Ingredients:
- 1 (10-ounce / 283-g) can tuna, drained
- ¼ cup full-fat mayonnaise
- 1 stalk celery, chopped
- 1 medium avocado, peeled, pitted, and mashed
- ½ cup blanched finely ground almond flour, divided
- 2 teaspoons coconut oil

Directions:
1. In a large bowl, mix tuna, mayonnaise, celery, and mashed avocado. Form the mixture into balls.
2. Roll balls in almond flour and spritz with coconut oil. Place balls into the air fryer basket.
3. Adjust the temperature to 400°F (205°C) and set the timer for 7 minutes.
4. Gently turn tuna bites after 5 minutes. Serve warm.

Nutrition:
- (per serving) calories 323 | fat 25 | protein 17 | total carbs 6 | fiber 2

Breaded Shrimp Tacos

Servings:8 | Cooking Time: 9 Minutes

Ingredients:
- 2 large eggs
- 1 teaspoon prepared yellow mustard
- 1 pound small shrimp, peeled, deveined, and tails removed
- ½ cup finely shredded Gouda or Parmesan cheese (see Note, here)
- ½ cup pork dust (see here)
- FOR SERVING:
- 8 large Boston lettuce leaves
- ¼ cup pico de gallo
- ¼ cup shredded purple cabbage
- 1 lemon, sliced
- Guacamole (optional)

Directions:
1. Preheat the air fryer to 400°F.
2. Crack the eggs into a large bowl, add the mustard, and whisk until well combined. Add the shrimp and stir well to coat.
3. In a medium-sized bowl, mix together the cheese and pork dust until well combined.
4. One at a time, roll the coated shrimp in the pork dust mixture and use your hands to press it onto each shrimp. Spray the coated shrimp with avocado oil and place them in the air fryer basket, leaving space between them.
5. Cook the shrimp for 9 minutes, or until cooked through and no longer translucent, flipping after 4 minutes.
6. To serve, place a lettuce leaf on a serving plate, place several shrimp on top, and top with 1½ teaspoons each of pico de gallo and purple cabbage. Squeeze some lemon juice on top and serve with guacamole, if desired.
7. Store leftover shrimp in an airtight container in the refrigerator for up to 3 days. Reheat in a preheated 400°F air fryer for 5 minutes, or until warmed through.

Nutrition:
- (per serving) calories 194 | fat 8g | protein 28g | total carbs 3g | fiber 0.5g

Salmon Burgers With Asian Sauce

Servings: 4 | Cooking Time: 10 Minutes

Ingredients:
- 1 pound (454 g) salmon
- 1 egg
- 1 garlic clove, minced
- 2 green onions, minced
- 1 cup Parmesan cheese
- Sauce:
- 1 teaspoon rice wine
- 1½ tablespoons soy sauce
- A pinch of salt
- 1 teaspoon gochugaru (Korean red chili pepper flakes)

Directions:
1. Start by preheating your Air Fryer to 380°F. Spritz the Air Fryer basket with cooking oil.
2. Mix the salmon, egg, garlic, green onions, and Parmesan cheese in a bowl, knead with your hands until everything is well incorporated.
3. Shape the mixture into equally sized patties. Transfer your patties to the Air Fryer basket.
4. Cook the fish patties for 10 minutes, turning them over halfway through.
5. Meanwhile, make the sauce by whisking all ingredients. Serve the warm fish patties with the sauce on the side.

Nutrition:
- (per serving) calories 301 | fat 15 | protein 33 | total carbs 6 | fiber 5.8

Salmon With Coconut

Servings: 4 | Cooking Time: 8 Minutes

Ingredients:
- 2 pounds (907 g) salmon fillet
- ¼ cup coconut shred
- 2 eggs, beaten
- 1 teaspoon coconut oil
- 1 teaspoon Italian seasonings

Directions:
1. Cut the salmon fillet into servings.
2. Then sprinkle the fish with Italian seasonings and dip in the eggs.
3. After this, coat every salmon fillet in coconut shred and put it in the air fryer.
4. Cook the fish at 375F (190ºC) for 4 minutes per side.

Nutrition:
- (per serving) calories 395 | fat 22 | protein 47 | total carbs 2 | fiber 1

Almond Salmon Fillets With Pesto

Servings: 2 | Cooking Time: 12 Minutes

Ingredients:
- ¼ cup pesto
- ¼ cup sliced almonds, roughly chopped
- 2 (1½ -inch-thick) salmon fillets (about 4 ounces each/ 113 g)
- 2 tablespoons unsalted butter, melted

Directions:
1. In a small bowl, mix pesto and almonds. Set aside.
2. Place fillets into a 6 -inch round baking dish.
3. Brush each fillet with butter and place half of the pesto mixture on the top of each fillet. Place dish into the air fryer basket.
4. Adjust the temperature to 390°F (199°C) and set the timer for 12 minutes.
5. Salmon will easily flake when fully cooked and reach an internal temperature of at least 145°F (63°C). Serve warm.

Nutrition:
- (per serving) calories 433 | fat 34 | protein 23 | total carbs 6 | fiber 4

Friday Night Fish Fry

Servings:4 | Cooking Time: 10 Minutes

Ingredients:
- 1 large egg
- ½ cup powdered Parmesan cheese (about 1½ ounces; see here) (or pork dust for dairy-free; see here)
- 1 teaspoon smoked paprika
- ¼ teaspoon celery salt
- ¼ teaspoon ground black pepper
- 4 (4-ounce) cod fillets
- Chopped fresh oregano or parsley, for garnish (optional)
- Lemon slices, for serving (optional)

Directions:
1. Spray the air fryer basket with avocado oil. Preheat the air fryer to 400°F.
2. Crack the egg in a shallow bowl and beat it lightly with a fork. Combine the Parmesan cheese, paprika, celery salt, and pepper in a separate shallow bowl.
3. One at a time, dip the fillets into the egg, then dredge them in the Parmesan mixture. Using your hands, press the Parmesan onto the fillets to form a nice crust. As you finish, place the fish in the air fryer basket.
4. Cook the fish in the air fryer for 10 minutes, or until it is cooked through and flakes easily with a fork. Garnish with fresh oregano or parsley and serve with lemon slices, if desired.
5. Store leftovers in an airtight container in the refrigerator for up to 3 days. Reheat in a preheated 400°F air fryer for 5 minutes, or until warmed through.

Nutrition:
- (per serving) calories 164 | fat 5g | protein 26g | total carbs 1g | fiber 0.2g

Cod With Tomatillos

Servings: 4 | Cooking Time: 15 Minutes

Ingredients:
- 2 ounces (57 g) tomatillos, chopped
- 1-pound (454-g) cod fillet, roughly chopped
- 1 tablespoon avocado oil
- 1 tablespoon lemon juice
- 1 teaspoon keto tomato paste

Directions:
1. Mix avocado oil with lemon juice and tomato paste.
2. Then mix cod fillet with tomato mixture and put in the air fryer.
3. Add lemon juice and tomatillos.
4. Cook the cod at 370F (188ºC) for 15 minutes.

Nutrition:
- (per serving) calories 102 | fat 2 | protein 20 | total carbs 2 | fiber 1

Flounder Cutlets

Servings: 2 | Cooking Time: 10 Minutes

Ingredients:
- 1 egg
- 1 cup Pecorino Romano cheese, grated
- Sea salt and white pepper, to taste
- ½ teaspoon cayenne pepper
- 1 teaspoon dried parsley flakes
- 2 flounder fillets

Directions:
1. To make a breading station, whisk the egg until frothy.
2. In another bowl, mix Pecorino Romano cheese, and spices.
3. Dip the fish in the egg mixture and turn to coat evenly, then, dredge in the cracker crumb mixture, turning a couple of times to coat evenly.
4. Cook in the preheated Air Fryer at 390ºF (199ºC) for 5 minutes, turn them over and cook for another 5 minutes. Enjoy!

Nutrition:
- (per serving) calories 425 | fat 26 | protein 37 | total carbs 7 | fiber 7

Curried Halibut

Servings: 4 | Cooking Time: 10 Minutes

Ingredients:
- 2 medium-sized halibut fillets
- 1 teaspoon curry powder
- ½ teaspoon ground coriander
- Kosher salt and freshly cracked mixed peppercorns, to taste
- 1½ tablespoons olive oil

- ½ cup Parmesan cheese, grated
- 2 eggs
- ½ teaspoon hot paprika
- A few drizzles of tabasco sauce

Directions:

1. Set your Air Fryer to cook at 365ºF.
2. Then, grab two mixing bowls. In the first bowl, combine the Parmesan cheese with olive oil.
3. In another shallow bowl, thoroughly whisk the egg. Next step, evenly drizzle the halibut fillets with Tabasco sauce, add hot paprika, curry, coriander, salt, and cracked mixed peppercorns.
4. Dip each fish fillet into the whisked egg, now, roll it over the Parmesan mix.
5. Place in a single layer in the Air Fryer cooking basket. Cook for 10 minutes, working in batches. Serve over creamed salad if desired. Bon appétit!

Nutrition:

- (per serving) calories 237 | fat 18 | protein 14 | total carbs 5 | fiber 4

Tilapia With Pecan

Servings: 5 | Cooking Time: 16 Minutes

Ingredients:

- 2 tablespoons ground flaxseeds
- 1 teaspoon paprika
- Sea salt and white pepper, to taste
- 1 teaspoon garlic paste
- 2 tablespoons extra-virgin olive oil
- ½ cup pecans, ground
- 5 tilapia fillets, slice into halves

Directions:

1. Combine the ground flaxseeds, paprika, salt, white pepper, garlic paste, olive oil, and ground pecans in a Ziploc bag. Add the fish fillets and shake to coat well.
2. Spritz the Air Fryer basket with cooking spray. Cook in the preheated Air Fryer at 400ºF (205ºC) for 10 minutes, turn them over and cook for 6 minutes or more. Work in batches.
3. Serve with lemon wedges, if desired. Enjoy!

Nutrition:

- (per serving) calories 264 | fat 17 | protein 6 | total carbs 4 | fiber 2

Lobster Tails With Green Olives

Servings: 5 | Cooking Time: 7 Minutes

Ingredients:

- 2 pounds (907 g) fresh lobster tails, cleaned and halved, in shells
- 2 tablespoons butter, melted
- 1 teaspoon onion powder
- 1 teaspoon cayenne pepper
- Salt and ground black pepper, to taste
- 2 garlic cloves, minced
- 1 cup green olives

Directions:

1. In a plastic closeable bag, thoroughly combine all ingredients, shake to combine well.
2. Transfer the coated lobster tails to the greased cooking basket.
3. Cook in the preheated Air Fryer at 390ºfor 6 to 7 minutes, shaking the basket halfway through. Work in batches.
4. Serve with green olives and enjoy!

Nutrition:

- (per serving) calories 189 | fat 7 | protein 30 | total carbs 2 | fiber 1

Creamed And Smoked White Fish

Servings: 4 | Cooking Time: 13 Minutes

Ingredients:

- ½ tablespoon yogurt
- ⅓ cup spring garlic, finely chopped
- Fresh chopped chives, for garnish
- 3 eggs, beaten
- ½ teaspoon dried dill weed
- 1 teaspoon dried rosemary
- ⅓ cup scallions, chopped
- ⅓ cup smoked white fish, chopped
- 1½ tablespoons crème fraîche
- 1 teaspoon kosher salt
- 1 teaspoon dried marjoram
- ⅓ teaspoon ground black pepper, or more to taste
- Cooking spray

Directions:

1. Firstly, spritz four oven safe ramekins with cooking spray. Then, divide smoked whitefish, spring garlic, and scallions among greased ramekins.
2. Crack an egg into each ramekin, add the crème, yogurt and all seasonings.
3. Now, air-fry approximately 13 minutes at 355ºF. Taste for doneness and eat warm garnished with fresh chives. Bon appétit!

Nutrition:

- (per serving) calories 249 | fat 22 | protein 5 | total carbs 8 | fiber 7

Coconut Shrimp With Spicy Mayo

Servings:4 | Cooking Time: 6 Minutes

Ingredients:

- 1 pound large shrimp (about 2 dozen), peeled and deveined, tails on
- Fine sea salt and ground black pepper
- 2 large eggs
- 1 tablespoon water
- ½ cup unsweetened coconut flakes
- ½ cup pork dust (see here)
- SPICY MAYO:
- ½ cup mayonnaise
- 2 tablespoons beef or chicken broth
- ½ teaspoon hot sauce
- ½ teaspoon cayenne pepper
- FOR SERVING (OPTIONAL):
- Microgreens
- Thinly sliced radishes

Directions:

1. Spray the air fryer basket with avocado oil. Preheat the air fryer to 400ºF.
2. Season the shrimp well on all sides with salt and pepper.
3. Crack the eggs into a shallow baking dish, add the water and a pinch each of salt and pepper, and whisk to combine. In another shallow baking dish, stir together the coconut flakes and pork dust until well combined.
4. Dip one shrimp in the eggs and let any excess egg drip off, then dredge both sides of the shrimp in the coconut mixture.

Spray the shrimp with avocado oil and place it in the air fryer basket. Repeat with the remaining shrimp, leaving space between them in the air fryer basket.

5. Cook the shrimp in the air fryer for 6 minutes, or until cooked through and no longer translucent, flipping halfway through.

6. While the shrimp cook, make the spicy mayo: In a medium-sized bowl, stir together all the spicy mayo ingredients until well combined.

7. Serve the shrimp on a bed of microgreens and thinly sliced radishes, if desired. Serve the spicy mayo on the side for dipping.

8. Store leftovers in an airtight container in the refrigerator for up to 4 days. Reheat in a preheated 400°F air fryer for about 3 minutes, until heated through.

Nutrition:
- (per serving)   calories 360 | fat 28g | protein 25g | total carbs 2g | fiber 1g

Herbed Tuna With Parmesan

Servings: 4 | Cooking Time: 17 Minutes

Ingredients:
- 1 tablespoon butter, melted
- 1 medium-sized leek, thinly sliced
- 1 tablespoon chicken stock
- 1 tablespoon dry white wine
- 1 pound (454 g) tuna
- ½ teaspoon red pepper flakes, crushed
- Sea salt and ground black pepper, to taste
- ½ teaspoon dried rosemary
- ½ teaspoon dried basil
- ½ teaspoon dried thyme
- 2 small ripe tomatoes, puréed
- 1 cup Parmesan cheese, grated

Directions:
1. Melt ½ tablespoon of butter in a sauté pan over medium-high heat. Now, cook the leek and garlic until tender and aromatic. Add the stock and wine to deglaze the pan.

2. Preheat your Air Fryer to 370°F (188°C).

3. Grease a casserole dish with the remaining ½ tablespoon of melted butter. Place the fish in the casserole dish. Add the seasonings. Top with the sautéed leek mixture.

4. Add the tomato purée. Cook for 10 minutes in the preheated Air Fryer. Top with grated Parmesan cheese, cook for an additional 7 minutes until the crumbs are golden. Bon appétit!

Nutrition:
- (per serving) calories 313 | fat 15 | protein 34 | total carbs 8 | fiber 7

Crispy Crab Rangoon Patties With Sweet 'n' Sour Sauce

Servings:8 | Cooking Time: 12 Minutes Per Batch

Ingredients:
- PATTIES:
- 1 pound canned lump crabmeat, drained
- 1 (8-ounce) package cream cheese, softened
- 1 tablespoon chopped fresh chives
- 1 large egg
- 1 teaspoon grated fresh ginger
- 1 clove garlic, smashed to a paste or minced
- COATING:
- 1½ cups pork dust (see here)

- DIPPING SAUCE:
- ½ cup chicken broth
- ⅓ cup coconut aminos or wheat-free tamari
- ⅓ cup Swerve confectioners'-style sweetener or equivalent amount of liquid or powdered sweetener (see here)
- ¼ cup tomato sauce
- 1 tablespoon coconut vinegar or apple cider vinegar
- ¼ teaspoon grated fresh ginger
- 1 clove garlic, smashed to a paste
- Sliced green onions, for garnish (optional)
- Fried Cauliflower Rice (here), for serving (optional)

Directions:
1. Preheat the air fryer to 400°F.

2. In a medium-sized bowl, gently mix all the ingredients for the patties, without breaking up the crabmeat.

3. Form the crab mixture into 8 patties that are 2½ inches in diameter and ¾ inch thick.

4. Place the pork dust in a shallow dish. Place each patty in the pork dust and use your hands to press the pork dust into the patties to form a crust. Place the patties in a single layer in the air fryer, leaving space between them. (If you're using a smaller air fryer, work in batches if necessary.) Cook for 12 minutes, or until the crust is golden and crispy.

5. While the patties cook, make the dipping sauce: In a large saucepan, whisk together all the sauce ingredients. Bring to a simmer over medium-high heat, then turn the heat down to medium until the sauce has reduced and thickened, about 5 minutes. Taste and adjust the seasonings as desired.

6. Place the patties on a serving platter, drizzle with the dipping sauce, and garnish with sliced green onions, if desired. Serve the remaining dipping sauce on the side. Serve with fried cauliflower rice, if desired.

7. Store leftovers in an airtight container in the refrigerator for up to 3 days. Reheat the patties in a preheated 400°F air fryer for 4 minutes, or until crispy on the outside and heated through.

Nutrition:
- (per serving)   calories 411 | fat 30g | protein 35g | total carbs 4g | fiber 3g

Rosemary Shrimp Skewers

Servings: 5 | Cooking Time: 5 Minutes

Ingredients:
- 4-pounds (1.8-kg) shrimps, peeled
- 1 tablespoon dried rosemary
- 1 tablespoon avocado oil
- 1 teaspoon apple cider vinegar

Directions:
1. Mix the shrimps with dried rosemary, avocado oil, and apple cider vinegar.

2. Then sting the shrimps into skewers and put in the air fryer.

3. Cook the shrimps at 400F (205°C) for 5 minutes.

Nutrition:
- (per serving) calories 437 | fat 6 | protein 83 | total carbs 6 | fiber 5

Creamy Tuna Pork Casserole

Servings: 4 | Cooking Time: 15 Minutes

Ingredients:
- 2 tablespoons salted butter
- ¼ cup diced white onion
- ¼ cup chopped white mushrooms
- 2 stalks celery, finely chopped
- ½ cup heavy cream
- ½ cup vegetable broth
- 2 tablespoons full-fat mayonnaise
- ¼ teaspoon xanthan gum
- ½ teaspoon red pepper flakes
- 2 medium zucchini, spiralized
- 2 cans (5-ounce / (142-g)) albacore tuna
- 1 ounce (28 g) pork rinds, finely ground

Directions:
1. In a large saucepan over medium heat, melt butter. Add onion, mushrooms, and celery and sauté until fragrant, about 3 to 5 minutes.
2. Pour in heavy cream, vegetable broth, mayonnaise, and xanthan gum. Reduce heat and continue cooking for an additional 3 minutes, until the mixture begins to thicken.
3. Add red pepper flakes, zucchini, and tuna. Turn off heat and stir until zucchini noodles are coated.
4. Pour into 4-cup round baking dish. Top with ground pork rinds and cover the top of the dish with foil. Place into the air fryer basket.
5. Adjust the temperature to 370°F (188°C) and set the timer for 15 minutes.
6. When there is 3 minutes remaining, remove the foil to brown the top of the casserole. Serve warm.

Nutrition:
- (per serving) calories 339 | fat 25 | protein 20 | total carbs 6 | fiber 4

Blt Crab Cakes

Servings:4 | Cooking Time: 19 Minutes

Ingredients:
- 4 slices bacon
- CRAB CAKES:
- 1 pound canned lump crabmeat, drained well
- ¼ cup plus 1 tablespoon powdered Parmesan cheese (see here) (or pork dust for dairy-free; see here)
- 3 tablespoons mayonnaise
- 1 large egg
- ½ teaspoon dried chives
- ½ teaspoon dried parsley
- ½ teaspoon dried dill weed
- ¼ teaspoon garlic powder
- ¼ teaspoon onion powder
- ⅛ teaspoon ground black pepper
- 1 cup pork dust (see here)
- FOR SERVING:
- Leaves from 1 small head Boston lettuce
- 4 slices tomato
- ¼ cup mayonnaise

Directions:
1. Spray the air fryer basket with avocado oil. Preheat the air fryer to 350°F.
2. Place the bacon slices in the air fryer, leaving space between

them, and cook for 7 to 9 minutes, until crispy. Remove the bacon and increase the heat to 400°F. Set the bacon aside.
3. Make the crab cakes: Place all the crab cake ingredients except the pork dust in a large bowl and mix together with your hands until well blended. Divide the mixture into 4 equal-sized crab cakes (they should each be about 1 inch thick).
4. Place the pork dust in a small bowl. Dredge the crab cakes in the pork dust to coat them well and use your hands to press the pork dust into the cakes.
5. Place the crab cakes in the air fryer basket, leaving space between them, and cook for 10 minutes, or until crispy on the outside.
6. To serve, place 4 lettuce leaves on a serving platter and top each leaf with a slice of tomato, then a crab cake, then a dollop of mayo, and finally a slice of bacon.
7. Store leftovers in an airtight container in the refrigerator for up to 3 days. Reheat in a preheated 350°F air fryer for 6 minutes, or until heated through.

Nutrition:
- (per serving) calories 341 | fat 28g | protein 22g | total carbs 3g | fiber 1g

Snapper With Almond Sauce

Servings: 4 | Cooking Time: 15 Minutes

Ingredients:
- 4 skin-on snapper fillets
- Sea salt and ground pepper, to taste
- ½ cup Parmesan cheese, grated
- 2 tablespoons fresh cilantro, chopped
- ½ cup coconut flour
- 2 tablespoons flaxseed meal
- 2 medium-sized eggs
- For the Almond sauce:
- ¼ cup almonds
- 2 garlic cloves, pressed
- 1 cup tomato paste
- 1 teaspoon dried dill weed
- ½ teaspoon salt
- ¼ teaspoon freshly ground mixed peppercorns
- ¼ cup olive oil

Directions:
1. Season fish fillets with sea salt and pepper.
2. In a shallow plate, thoroughly combine the Parmesan cheese and fresh chopped cilantro.
3. In another shallow plate, whisk the eggs until frothy. Place the coconut flour and flaxseed meal in a third plate.
4. Dip the fish fillets in the flour, then in the egg, afterward, coat them with the Parmesan mixture. Set the Air Fryer to cook at 390°F, air fry for 14 to 16 minutes or until crisp.
5. To make the sauce, chop the almonds in a food processor. Add the remaining sauce ingredients, but not the olive oil.
6. Blitz for 30 seconds, then, slowly and gradually pour in the oil, process until smooth and even. Serve the sauce with the prepared snapper fillets. Bon appétit!

Nutrition:
- (per serving) calories 491 | fat 38 | protein 29 | total carbs 8 | fiber 5

Tuna With Red Onions And Herbs

Servings: 4 | Cooking Time: 10 Minutes

Ingredients:
- 4 tuna steaks
- ½ pound (227 g) red onions
- 4 teaspoons olive oil
- 1 teaspoon dried rosemary
- 1 teaspoon dried marjoram
- 1 tablespoon cayenne pepper
- ½ teaspoon sea salt
- ½ teaspoon black pepper, preferably freshly cracked
- 1 lemon, sliced

Directions:
1. Place the tuna steaks in the lightly greased cooking basket. Top with the pearl onions, add the olive oil, rosemary, marjoram, cayenne pepper, salt, and black pepper.
2. Bake in the preheated Air Fryer at 400°F for 9 to 10 minutes. Work in two batches.
3. Serve warm with lemon slices and enjoy!

Nutrition:
- (per serving) calories 487 | fat 19 | protein 68 | total carbs 7 | fiber 6

Salmon With Endives

Servings: 4 | Cooking Time: 20 Minutes

Ingredients:
- 2 endives, shredded
- 1 pound (454 g) salmon fillet, chopped
- 1 tablespoon ghee
- 1 teaspoon ground coriander
- ¼ cup coconut cream

Directions:
1. Put all ingredients in the air fryer and shake gently.
2. Close the lid and cook the meal ay 360F (182°C) for 20 minutes. Shake the fish every 5 minutes.

Nutrition:
- (per serving) calories 223 | fat 13 | protein 23 | total carbs 3 | fiber 1

Basil Salmon Fillet

Servings: 2 | Cooking Time: 8 Minutes

Ingredients:
- 10 ounces (283 g) salmon fillet
- ½ teaspoon ground coriander
- 1 teaspoon ground cumin
- 1 teaspoon dried basil
- 1 tablespoon avocado oil

Directions:
1. In the shallow bowl, mix ground coriander, ground cumin, and dried basil.
2. Then coat the salmon fillet in the spices and sprinkle with avocado oil.
3. Put the fish in the air fryer basket and cook at 395F (202°C) for 4 minutes per side.

Nutrition:
- (per serving) calories 201 | fat 9 | protein 28 | total carbs 1 | fiber 0

Shrimp With Swiss Chard

Servings: 4 | Cooking Time: 10 Minutes

Ingredients:
- 1-pound (454-g) shrimp, peeled and deveined
- ½ teaspoon smoked paprika
- ½ cup Swiss chard, chopped
- 2 tablespoons apple cider vinegar
- 1 tablespoon coconut oil
- ¼ cup heavy cream

Directions:
1. Mix shrimps with smoked paprika and apple cider vinegar.
2. Put the shrimps in the air fryer and add coconut oil.
3. Cook the shrimps at 350F (180°C) for 10 minutes.
4. Then mix cooked shrimps with remaining ingredients and carefully mix.

Nutrition:
- (per serving) calories 193 | fat 8 | protein 26 | total carbs 2 | fiber 1

Swordfish Skewers With Cherry Tomato

Servings: 4 | Cooking Time: 6 To 8 Minutes

Ingredients:
- 1 pound (454 g) filleted swordfish
- ¼ cup avocado oil
- 2 tablespoons freshly squeezed lemon juice
- 1 tablespoon minced fresh parsley
- 2 teaspoons Dijon mustard
- Sea salt, freshly ground black pepper, to taste
- 3 ounces (85 g) cherry tomatoes

Directions:
1. Cut the fish into 1½-inch chunks, picking out any remaining bones.
2. In a large bowl, whisk together the oil, lemon juice, parsley, and Dijon mustard. Season to taste with salt and pepper. Add the fish and toss to coat the pieces. Cover and marinate the fish chunks in the refrigerator for 30 minutes.
3. Remove the fish from the marinade. Thread the fish and cherry tomatoes on 4 skewers, alternating as you go.
4. Set the air fryer to 400°F (205°C). Place the skewers in the air fryer basket and cook for 3 minutes. Flip the skewers and cook for 3 to 5 minutes longer, until the fish is cooked through and an instant-read thermometer reads 140°F (60°C).

Nutrition:
- (per serving) calories 315 | fat 20 | protein 29 | total carbs 2 | fiber 1

Grilled Tuna Cake

Servings: 4 | Cooking Time: 8 Minutes

Ingredients:
- 2 cans canned tuna fish
- 2 celery stalks, trimmed and finely chopped
- 1 egg, whisked
- ½ cup Parmesan cheese, grated
- 1 teaspoon whole-grain mustard
- ½ teaspoon sea salt
- ¼ teaspoon freshly cracked black peppercorns
- 1 teaspoon paprika

Directions:
1. Mix all of the above ingredients in the order listed above, mix

to combine well and shape into four cakes, chill for 50 minutes.
2. Place on an Air Fryer grill pan. Spritz each cake with a non-stick cooking spray, covering all sides.
3. Grill at 360°F (182°C) for 5 minutes, then, pause the machine, flip the cakes over and set the timer for another 3 minutes. Serve.

Nutrition:
- (per serving) calories 241 | fat 11 | protein 30 | total carbs 2 | fiber 1

Tilapia Fingers

Servings: 4 | Cooking Time: 9 Minutes

Ingredients:
- 1 pound (454 g) tilapia fillet
- ½ cup coconut flour
- 2 eggs, beaten
- ½ teaspoon ground paprika
- 1 teaspoon dried oregano
- 1 teaspoon avocado oil

Directions:
1. Cut the tilapia fillets into fingers and sprinkle with ground paprika and dried oregano.
2. Then dip the tilapia fingers in eggs and coat in the coconut flour.
3. Sprinkle fish fingers with avocado oil and cook in the air fryer at 370F (188°C) for 9 minutes.

Nutrition:
- (per serving) calories 188 | fat 5 | protein 26 | total carbs 9 | fiber 4

Salmon With Lemon

Servings: 4 | Cooking Time: 10 Minutes

Ingredients:
- 1½ pounds (680g) salmon steak
- ½ teaspoon grated lemon zest
- Freshly cracked mixed peppercorns, to taste
- ⅓ cup lemon juice
- Fresh chopped chives, for garnish
- ½ cup dry white wine
- ½ teaspoon fresh cilantro, chopped
- Fine sea salt, to taste

Directions:
1. To prepare the marinade, place all ingredients, except for salmon steak and chives, in a deep pan. Bring to a boil over medium-high flame until it has reduced by half. Allow it to cool down.
2. After that, allow salmon steak to marinate in the refrigerator for approximately 40 minutes. Discard the marinade and transfer the fish steak to the preheated Air Fryer.
3. Air-fry at 400°F (205°C) for 9 to10 minutes. To finish, brush hot fish steaks with the reserved marinade, garnish with fresh chopped chives, and serve right away!

Nutrition:
- (per serving) calories 304 | fat 15 | protein 38 | total carbs 2 | fiber 1

Chipotle Salmon Cakes

Servings: 4 | Cooking Time: 13 Minutes

Ingredients:
- ½ teaspoon chipotle powder
- ½ teaspoon butter, at room temperature
- ⅓ teaspoon smoked cayenne pepper
- ½ teaspoon dried parsley flakes
- ⅓ teaspoon ground black pepper
- 1 pound (454 g) salmon, chopped into ½ inch pieces
- 1½ tablespoons milk
- ½ white onion, peeled and finely chopped
- 1 teaspoon fine sea salt
- 2 tablespoons coconut flour
- 2 tablespoons Parmesan cheese, grated

Directions:
1. Place all ingredients in a large-sized mixing dish.
2. Shape into cakes and roll each cake over seasoned breadcrumbs. After that, refrigerate for about 2 hours.
3. Then, set your Air Fryer to cook at 395°F for 13 minutes.
4. Serve warm with a dollop of sour cream if desired. Bon appétit!

Nutrition:
- (per serving) calories 401 | fat 19 | protein 53 | total carbs 2 | fiber 1

Snapper With Thai Sauce

Servings: 2 | Cooking Time: 27 Minutes

Ingredients:
- ½ cup full-fat coconut milk
- 2 tablespoons lemon juice
- 1 teaspoon fresh ginger, grated
- 2 snapper fillets
- 1 tablespoon olive oil
- Salt and white pepper, to taste

Directions:
1. Place the milk, lemon juice, and ginger in a glass bowl, add fish and let it marinate for 1 hour.
2. Removed the fish from the milk mixture and place in the Air Fryer basket. Drizzle olive oil all over the fish fillets.
3. Cook in the preheated Air Fryer at 390°F for 15 minutes.
4. Meanwhile, heat the milk mixture over medium-high heat, bring to a rapid boil, stirring continuously. Reduce to simmer and add the salt, and pepper, continue to cook 12 minutes or more.
5. Spoon the sauce over the warm snapper fillets and serve immediately. Bon appétit!

Nutrition:
- (per serving) calories 420 | fat 24 | protein 48 | total carbs 5 | fiber 4

Parmesan Mackerel

Servings: 2 | Cooking Time: 7 Minutes

Ingredients:
- 12 ounces (340 g) mackerel fillet
- 2 ounces (57 g) Parmesan, grated
- 1 teaspoon ground coriander
- 1 tablespoon olive oil

Directions:
1. Sprinkle the mackerel fillet with olive oil and put it in the air fryer basket.

2. Top the fish with ground coriander and Parmesan.
3. Cook the fish at 390F (199°C) for 7 minutes.

Nutrition:
• (per serving) calories 597 | fat 43 | protein 50 | total carbs 1 | fiber 1

Air Fried Sardines

Servings: 5 | Cooking Time: 10 Minutes

Ingredients:
• 12 ounces (340 g) sardines, trimmed, cleaned
• 1 cup coconut flour
• 1 tablespoon coconut oil
• 1 teaspoon salt

Directions:
1. Sprinkle the sardines with salt and coat in the coconut flour.
2. Then grease the air fryer basket with coconut oil and put the sardines inside.
3. Cook them at 385F (196°C) for 10 minutes.

Nutrition:
• (per serving) calories 165 | fat 10 | protein 17 | total carbs 1 | fiber 1

Parmesan-crusted Shrimp Over Pesto Zoodles

Servings:4 | Cooking Time: 7 Minutes Per Batch

Ingredients:
• 2 large eggs
• 3 cloves garlic, minced
• 2 teaspoons dried basil, divided
• ½ teaspoon fine sea salt
• ½ teaspoon ground black pepper
• ½ cup powdered Parmesan cheese (about 1½ ounces) (see here)
• 1 pound jumbo shrimp, peeled, deveined, butterflied, tails removed
• PESTO:
• 1 packed cup fresh basil
• ¼ cup extra-virgin olive oil or avocado oil
• ¼ cup grated Parmesan cheese
• ¼ cup roasted, salted walnuts (omit for nut-free)
• 3 cloves garlic, peeled
• 1 tablespoon lemon juice
• ½ teaspoon fine sea salt
• ¼ teaspoon ground black pepper
• 2 recipes Perfect Zoodles (here), warm, for serving

Directions:
1. Spray the air fryer basket with avocado oil. Preheat the air fryer to 400°F.
2. In a large bowl, whisk together the eggs, garlic, 1 teaspoon of the dried basil, the salt, and the pepper. In a separate small bowl, mix together the remaining teaspoon of dried basil and the Parmesan cheese.
3. Place the shrimp in the bowl with the egg mixture and use your hands to coat the shrimp. Roll one shrimp in the Parmesan mixture and press the coating onto the shrimp with your hands. Place the coated shrimp in the air fryer basket. Repeat with the remaining shrimp, leaving space between them in the air fryer basket. (If you're using a smaller air fryer, work in batches if necessary.)
4. Cook the shrimp in the air fryer for 7 minutes, or until cooked through and no longer translucent, flipping after 4 minutes.

5. While the shrimp cook, make the pesto: Place all the ingredients for the pesto in a food processor and pulse until smooth, with a few rough pieces of basil.
6. Just before serving, toss the warm zoodles with the pesto and place the shrimp on top.
7. Store leftover shrimp and pesto zoodles in separate airtight containers in the refrigerator for up to 3 days or in the freezer for up to a month. Reheat the shrimp in a preheated 400°F air fryer for 5 minutes, or until warmed through. To reheat the pesto zoodles, place them in a casserole dish that will fit in your air fryer and cook at 350°F for 2 minutes, or until heated through.

Nutrition:
• (per serving)   calories 397 | fat 26g | protein 31g | total carbs 10g | fiber 3g

Herbed Halibut Steaks With Vermouth

Servings: 4 | Cooking Time: 10 Minutes

Ingredients:
• 1 pound (454 g) halibut steaks
• Salt and pepper, to your liking
• 1 teaspoon dried basil
• 2 tablespoons honey
• ¼ cup vegetable oil
• 2 ½ tablespoons Worcester sauce
• 1 tablespoon freshly squeezed lemon juice
• 2 tablespoons vermouth
• 1 tablespoon fresh parsley leaves, coarsely chopped

Directions:
1. Place all the ingredients in a large-sized mixing dish. Gently stir to coat the fish evenly.
2. Set your Air Fryer to cook at 390°F, roast for 5 minutes. Pause the machine and flip the fish over.
3. Then, cook for another 5 minutes, check for doneness and cook for a few more minutes as needed. Bon appétit!

Nutrition:
• (per serving) calories 304 | fat 21 | protein 22 | total carbs 9 | fiber 8

Golden Cod With Mayo

Servings: 4 | Cooking Time: 9 Minutes

Ingredients:
• 1 pound (454 g) cod fillets
• 1½ cups finely ground blanched almond flour
• 2 teaspoons Old Bay seasoning
• ½ teaspoon paprika
• Sea salt, freshly ground black pepper, to taste
• ¼ cup sugar-free mayonnaise
• 1 large egg, beaten
• Avocado oil spray
• Elevated Tartar Sauce, for serving

Directions:
1. Cut the fish into ¾-inch-wide strips.
2. In a shallow bowl, stir together the almond flour, Old Bay seasoning, paprika, and salt and pepper to taste. In another shallow bowl, whisk together the mayonnaise and egg.
3. Dip the cod strips in the egg mixture, then the almond flour, gently pressing with your fingers to help adhere the coating.
4. Place the coated fish on a parchment paper–lined baking sheet and freeze for 30 minutes.
5. Spray the air fryer basket with oil. Set the air fryer to 400°F

(205ºC). Place the fish in the basket in a single layer, and spray each piece with oil.

6. Cook for 5 minutes. Flip and spray with more oil. Cook for 4 minutes or more, until the internal temperature reaches 140ºF (60ºC). Serve with the tartar sauce.

Nutrition:
- (per serving) calories 439 | fat 33 | protein 31 | total carbs 9 | fiber 4

Lemony Salmon Steak

Servings: 2 | Cooking Time: 12 Minutes

Ingredients:
- 2 salmon steaks
- Coarse sea salt, to taste
- ¼ teaspoon freshly ground black pepper, or more to taste
- 1 tablespoon sesame oil
- Zest of 1 lemon
- 1 tablespoon fresh lemon juice
- 1 teaspoon garlic, minced
- ½ teaspoon smoked cayenne pepper
- ½ teaspoon dried dill

Directions:
1. Preheat your Air Fryer to 380ºF (193ºC). Pat dry the salmon steaks with a kitchen towel.
2. In a ceramic dish, combine the remaining ingredients until everything is well whisked.
3. Add the salmon steaks to the ceramic dish and let them sit in the refrigerator for 1 hour. Now, place the salmon steaks in the cooking basket. Reserve the marinade.
4. Cook for 12 minutes, flipping halfway through the cooking time.
5. Meanwhile, cook the marinade in a small sauté pan over a moderate flame. Cook until the sauce has thickened.
6. Pour the sauce over the steaks and serve. Bon appétit!

Nutrition:
- (per serving) calories 476 | fat 16 | protein 47 | total carbs 3 | fiber 2

White Fish Fillets With Parmesan

Servings: 4 | Cooking Time: 12 Minutes

Ingredients:
- 1 cup Parmesan, grated
- 1 teaspoon garlic powder
- ½ teaspoon shallot powder
- 1 egg, well whisked
- 4 white fish fillets
- Salt and ground black pepper, to taste
- Fresh Italian parsley, to serve

Directions:
1. Place the Parmesan cheese in a shallow bowl.
2. In another bowl, combine the garlic powder, shallot powder, and the beaten egg.
3. Generously season the fish fillets with salt and pepper. Dip each fillet into the beaten egg.
4. Then, roll the fillets over the Parmesan mixture. Set your Air Fryer to cook at 370ºF. Air-fry for 10 to 12 minutes.
5. Serve garnished with fresh parsley and enjoy!

Nutrition:
- (per serving) calories 297 | fat 8 | protein 38 | total carbs 5 | fiber 4

Crab Cake

Servings: 4 | Cooking Time: 14 Minutes

Ingredients:
- Avocado oil spray
- ⅓ cup red onion, diced
- ¼ cup red bell pepper, diced
- 8 ounces (227 g) lump crab meat, picked over for shells
- 3 tablespoons finely ground blanched almond flour
- 1 large egg, beaten
- 1 tablespoon sugar-free mayonnaise
- 2 teaspoons Dijon mustard
- ⅛ teaspoon cayenne pepper
- Sea salt, freshly ground black pepper, to taste
- Elevated Tartar Sauce, for serving
- Lemon wedges, for serving

Directions:
1. Spray an air fryer–friendly baking pan with oil. Put the onion and red bell pepper in the pan and give them a quick spray with oil. Place the pan in the air fryer basket. Set the air fryer to 400ºF (205ºC) and cook the vegetables for 7 minutes, until tender.
2. Transfer the vegetables to a large bowl. Add the crab meat, almond flour, egg, mayonnaise, mustard, and cayenne pepper and season with salt and pepper. Stir until the mixture is well combined.
3. Form the mixture into four 1-inch-thick cakes. Cover with plastic wrap and refrigerate for 1 hour.
4. Place the crab cakes in a single layer in the air fryer basket and spray them with oil.
5. Cook for 4 minutes. Flip the crab cakes and spray with more oil. Cook for 3 minutes or more, until the internal temperature of the crab cakes reaches 155ºF (68ºC).
6. Serve with tartar sauce and a squeeze of fresh lemon juice.

Nutrition:
- (per serving) calories 121 | fat 8 | protein 11 | total carbs 3 | fiber 2

Tuna Patties With Cheese Sauce

Servings: 4 | Cooking Time: 20 Minutes

Ingredients:
- 1 pound (454 g) canned tuna, drained
- 1 egg, whisked
- 1 garlic clove, minced
- 2 tablespoons shallots, minced
- 1 cup Romano cheese, grated
- Sea salt and ground black pepper, to taste
- 1 tablespoon sesame oil
- Cheese Sauce:
- 1 tablespoon butter
- 1 cup beer
- 2 tablespoons Colby cheese, grated

Directions:
1. In a mixing bowl, thoroughly combine the tuna, egg, garlic, shallots, Romano cheese, salt, and black pepper. Shape the tuna mixture into four patties and place in your refrigerator for 2 hours.
2. Brush the patties with sesame oil on both sides. Cook in the preheated Air Fryer at 360ºF for 14 minutes.
3. In the meantime, melt the butter in a pan over a moderate heat. Add the beer and whisk until it starts bubbling.
4. Now, stir in the grated cheese and cook for 3 to 4 minutes longer or until the cheese has melted. Spoon the sauce over the fish

cake burgers and serve immediately.

Nutrition:
• (per serving) calories 309 | fat 15 | protein 31 | total carbs 8 | fiber 7

Crispy Flounder

Servings: 2 | Cooking Time: 12 Minutes

Ingredients:
• 2 flounder fillets
• 1 egg
• ½ teaspoon Worcestershire sauce
• ¼ cup coconut flour
• ¼ cup almond flour
• ½ teaspoon lemon pepper
• ½ teaspoon coarse sea salt
• ¼ teaspoon chili powder

Directions:
1. Rinse and pat dry the flounder fillets.
2. Whisk the egg and Worcestershire sauce in a shallow bowl. In a separate bowl, mix the coconut flour, almond flour, lemon pepper, salt, and chili powder.
3. Then, dip the fillets into the egg mixture. Lastly, coat the fish fillets with the coconut flour mixture until they are coated on all sides.
4. Spritz with cooking spray and transfer to the Air Fryer basket. Cook at 390ºfor 7 minutes.
5. Turn them over, spritz with cooking spray on the other side, and cook another 5 minutes. Bon appétit!

Nutrition:
• (per serving) calories 325 | fat 18.3 | protein 6.1 | total carbs 34.4 | fiber 2.2

Snapper With Shallot And Tomato

Servings: 2 | Cooking Time: 15 Minutes

Ingredients:
• 2 snapper fillets
• 1 shallot, peeled and sliced
• 2 garlic cloves, halved
• 1 bell pepper, sliced
• 1 small-sized serrano pepper, sliced
• 1 tomato, sliced
• 1 tablespoon olive oil
• ¼ teaspoon freshly ground black pepper
• ½ teaspoon paprika
• Sea salt, to taste
• 2 bay leaves

Directions:
1. Place two parchment sheets on a working surface. Place the fish in the center of one side of the parchment paper.
2. Top with the shallot, garlic, peppers, and tomato. Drizzle olive oil over the fish and vegetables. Season with black pepper, paprika, and salt. Add the bay leaves.
3. Fold over the other half of the parchment. Now, fold the paper around the edges tightly and create a half moon shape, sealing the fish inside.
4. Cook in the preheated Air Fryer at 390ºF (199ºC) for 15 minutes. Serve warm.

Nutrition:
• (per serving) calories 329 | fat 9 | protein 47 | total carbs 13 | fiber 12

Tilapia With Fennel Seeds

Servings: 4 | Cooking Time: 10 Minutes

Ingredients:
• 2-pound (907-g) tilapia fillet
• 1 teaspoon fennel seeds
• 1 tablespoon avocado oil
• ½ teaspoon lime zest, grated
• 1 tablespoon coconut aminos

Directions:
1. In the shallow bowl, mix fennel seeds with avocado oil, lime zest, and coconut aminos.
2. Then brush the tilapia fillet with fennel seeds and put in the air fryer.
3. Cook the fish at 380F (193ºC) for 10 minutes.

Nutrition:
• (per serving) calories 194 | fat 2 | protein 42 | total carbs 1 | fiber 0

Sardines Fritas

Servings: 4 | Cooking Time: 13 Minutes

Ingredients:
• 1½ pounds (680 g) sardines, cleaned and rinsed
• Salt and ground black pepper, to savor
• 1 tablespoon Italian seasoning mix
• 1 tablespoon lemon juice
• 1 tablespoon soy sauce
• 2 tablespoons olive oil

Directions:
1. Firstly, pat the sardines dry with a kitchen towel. Add salt, black pepper, Italian seasoning mix, lemon juice, soy sauce, and olive oil, marinate them for 30 minutes.
2. Air-fry the sardines at 350ºF for approximately 5 minutes. Increase the temperature to 385ºF and air-fry them for further 7 to 8 minutes.
3. Then, place the sardines in a nice serving platter. Bon appétit!

Nutrition:
• (per serving) calories 437 | fat 26 | protein 43 | total carbs 4 | fiber 3

Salmon Fritters With Zucchini

Servings: 4 | Cooking Time: 12 Minutes

Ingredients:
• 2 tablespoons almond flour
• 1 zucchini, grated
• 1 egg, beaten
• 6 ounces (170 g) salmon fillet, diced
• 1 teaspoon avocado oil
• ½ teaspoon ground black pepper

Directions:
1. Mix almond flour with zucchini, egg, salmon, and ground black pepper.
2. Then make the fritters from the salmon mixture.
3. Sprinkle the air fryer basket with avocado oil and put the fritters inside.
4. Cook the fritters at 375F (190ºC) for 6 minutes per side.

Nutrition:
• (per serving) calories 103 | fat 5 | protein 11 | total carbs 3 | fiber 2

Pecan-crusted Catfish

Servings:4 | Cooking Time: 12 Minutes

Ingredients:
- ½ cup pecan meal
- 1 teaspoon fine sea salt
- ¼ teaspoon ground black pepper
- 4 (4-ounce) catfish fillets
- FOR GARNISH (OPTIONAL):
- Fresh oregano
- Pecan halves

Directions:
1. Spray the air fryer basket with avocado oil. Preheat the air fryer to 375°F.
2. In a large bowl, mix the pecan meal, salt, and pepper. One at a time, dredge the catfish fillets in the mixture, coating them well. Use your hands to press the pecan meal into the fillets. Spray the fish with avocado oil and place them in the air fryer basket.
3. Cook the coated catfish for 12 minutes, or until it flakes easily and is no longer translucent in the center, flipping halfway through.
4. Garnish with oregano sprigs and pecan halves, if desired.
5. Store leftovers in an airtight container in the fridge for up to 3 days. Reheat in a preheated 350°F air fryer for 4 minutes, or until heated through.

Nutrition:
- (per serving)   calories 162 | fat 11g | protein 17g | total carbs 1g | fiber 1g

Cod Fillet With Turmeric

Servings: 2 | Cooking Time: 7 Minutes

Ingredients:
- 12 ounces (340 g) cod fillet
- 1 teaspoon ground turmeric
- 1 teaspoon chili flakes
- 1 tablespoon coconut oil, melted
- ½ teaspoon salt

Directions:
1. Mix coconut oil with ground turmeric, chili flakes, and salt.
2. Then mix cod fillet with ground turmeric and put in the air fryer basket.
3. Cook the cod at 385F (196°C) for 7 minutes.

Nutrition:
- (per serving) calories 199 | fat 8 | protein 30 | total carbs 2 | fiber 1

Simple Scallops

Servings:2 | Cooking Time: 4 Minutes

Ingredients:
- 12 medium sea scallops
- 1 teaspoon fine sea salt
- ¾ teaspoon ground black pepper, plus more for garnish if desired
- Fresh thyme leaves, for garnish (optional)

Directions:
1. Spray the air fryer basket with avocado oil. Preheat the air fryer to 390°F.
2. Rinse the scallops and pat completely dry. Spray avocado oil on the scallops and season them with the salt and pepper. Place them in the air fryer basket, spacing them apart (if you're using a smaller air fryer, work in batches if necessary). Cook for 2 minutes, then flip the scallops and cook for another 2 minutes, or until cooked through and no longer translucent. Garnish with ground black pepper and thyme leaves, if desired.
3. Best served fresh. Store leftovers in an airtight container in the fridge for up to 3 days. Reheat in a preheated 350°F air fryer for 2 minutes, or until heated through.

Nutrition:
- (per serving)   calories 106 | fat 2g | protein 18g | total carbs 3g | fiber 0.2g

Piri Piri King Prawns

Servings: 2 | Cooking Time: 8 Minutes

Ingredients:
- 12 king prawns, rinsed
- 1 tablespoon coconut oil
- ½ teaspoon piri piri powder
- Salt and ground black pepper, to taste
- 1 teaspoon garlic paste
- 1 teaspoon onion powder
- ½ teaspoon cumin powder
- 1 teaspoon curry powder

Directions:
1. In a mixing bowl, toss all ingredient until the prawns are well coated on all sides.
2. Cook in the preheated Air Fryer at 360ºF for 4 minutes. Shake the basket and cook for 4 minutes or more.
3. Serve over hot rice if desired. Bon appétit!

Nutrition:
- (per serving) calories 220 | fat 10 | protein 18 | total carbs 15 | fiber 14

Chapter 6 Poultry Recipes

Chicken Breast With Cilantro And Lime

Servings: 4 | Cooking Time: 15 Minutes

Ingredients:
- For the Chicken:
- 1 teaspoon turmeric
- 1 diced large onion
- 1 tablespoon avocado oil
- 1 teaspoon garam masala
- 1 teaspoon smoked paprika
- 1 teaspoon ground fennel seeds
- 1-pound (454-g) chicken breast, boneless & skinless
- 2 teaspoons minced ginger
- 2 teaspoons minced garlic cloves
- nonstick cooking oil spray
- salt & cayenne pepper, to taste
- To Top:
- ¼ cup chopped cilantro
- 2 teaspoons juiced lime

Directions:
1. Make slight piercing all over the chicken breast then set aside.
2. Using a large mixing bowl add in all the remaining ingredients and combine together.
3. Add the pierced chicken breast into the bowl then set aside for an hour to marinate.
4. Transfer the marinated chicken and veggies into the fryer basket then coat with the cooking oil spray.
5. Cook for 15 minutes at 360°F (182°C) then serve and enjoy with a garnish of cilantro topped with the juiced lime.

Nutrition:
- (per serving) calories 305 | fat 23 | protein 19 | total carbs 6 | fiber 5

Chicken Bacon Salad With Avocado-lime Dressing

Servings: 4 | Cooking Time: 8 Minutes

Ingredients:
- 8 slices reduced-sodium bacon
- 8 chicken breast tenders (about 1½ pounds / 680g)
- 8 cups chopped romaine lettuce
- 1 cup cherry tomatoes, halved
- ¼ red onion, thinly sliced
- 2 hard-boiled eggs, peeled and sliced
- Avocado-Lime Dressing:
- ½ cup plain Greek yogurt
- ¼ cup milk
- ½ avocado
- Juice of ½ lime
- 3 scallions, coarsely chopped
- 1 clove garlic
- 2 tablespoons fresh cilantro
- ⅛ teaspoon ground cumin
- Salt and freshly ground black pepper

Directions:
1. Preheat the air fryer to 400°F (205°C).
2. Wrap a piece of bacon around each piece of chicken and secure with a toothpick. Working in batches if necessary, arrange the bacon-wrapped chicken in a single layer in the air fryer basket. Air fry for 8 minutes until the bacon is browned and a thermometer inserted into the thickest piece of chicken register 165°F (74°C). Let it cool for a few minutes, then slice into bite-size pieces.
3. To make the dressing: In a blender or food processor, combine the yogurt, milk, avocado, lime juice, scallions, garlic, cilantro, and cumin. purée until smooth. Season to taste with salt and freshly ground pepper.
4. To assemble the salad, in a large bowl, combine the lettuce, tomatoes, and onion. Drizzle the dressing over the vegetables and toss gently until thoroughly combined. Arrange the chicken and eggs on top just before serving.

Nutrition:
- (per serving) calories 425 | fat 18 | protein 52 | total carbs 11 | fiber 7

Chicken-wrapped Bacon And Spinach

Servings: 4 | Cooking Time: 20 Minutes

Ingredients:
- 3 tablespoons pine nuts
- ¾ cup frozen spinach, thawed and squeezed dry
- ⅓ cup ricotta cheese
- 2 tablespoons grated Parmesan cheese
- 3 cloves garlic, minced
- Salt and freshly ground black pepper
- 4 small boneless, skinless chicken breast halves (about 1½ pounds / 680g)
- 8 slices bacon

Directions:
1. Place the pine nuts in a small pan and set in the air fryer basket. Set the air fryer to 400°F (205°C) and air fry for 2 to 3 minutes until toasted. Remove the pine nuts to a mixing bowl and continue preheating the air fryer.
2. In a large bowl, combine the spinach, ricotta, Parmesan, and garlic. Season to taste with salt and pepper and stir well until thoroughly combined.
3. Using a sharp knife, cut into the chicken breasts, slicing them across and opening them up like a book, but be careful not to cut them all the way through. Sprinkle the chicken with salt and pepper.
4. Spoon equal amounts of the spinach mixture into the chicken, then fold the top of the chicken breast back over the top of the stuffing. Wrap each chicken breast with 2 slices of bacon.
5. Working in batches if necessary, air fry the chicken for 18 to 20 minutes until the bacon is crisp and a thermometer inserted into the thickest part of the chicken registers 165°F (74°C).

Nutrition:
- (per serving) calories 440 | fat 20 | protein 63 | total carbs 4 | fiber 3

Chicken With Peanuts

Servings: 4 | Cooking Time: 15 Minutes

Ingredients:
- 1½ pounds (680 g) chicken tenderloins
- 2 tablespoons peanut oil
- ½ cup Parmesan cheese, grated
- Sea salt and ground black pepper, to taste
- ½ teaspoon garlic powder
- 1 teaspoon red pepper flakes
- 2 tablespoons peanuts, roasted and roughly chopped

Directions:
1. Start by preheating your Air Fryer to 360°F.
2. Brush the chicken tenderloins with peanut oil on all sides.
3. In a mixing bowl, thoroughly combine grated Parmesan cheese, salt, black pepper, garlic powder, and red pepper flakes. Dredge the chicken in the breading, shaking off any residual coating.
4. Lay the chicken tenderloins into the cooking basket. Cook for 12 to 13 minutes or until it is no longer pink in the center. Work in batches, an instant-read thermometer should read at least 165°F.
5. Serve garnished with roasted peanuts. Bon appétit!

Nutrition:
- (per serving) calories 280 | fat 19 | protein 3 | total carbs 22 | fiber 21

Herbed Turkey Breasts With Mustard

Servings: 4 | Cooking Time: 53 Minutes

Ingredients:
- ½ teaspoon dried thyme
- 1½ pounds (680g) turkey breasts
- ½ teaspoon dried sage
- 3 whole star anise
- 1½ tablespoons olive oil
- 1½ tablespoons hot mustard
- 1 teaspoon smoked cayenne pepper
- 1 teaspoon fine sea salt

Directions:
1. Set your Air Fryer to cook at 365°F (185°C).
2. Brush the turkey breast with olive oil and sprinkle with seasonings.
3. Cook at 365°F (185°C) for 45 minutes, turning twice. Now, pause the machine and spread the cooked breast with the hot mustard.
4. Air-fry for 6 to 8 more minutes. Let it rest before slicing and serving. Bon appétit!

Nutrition:
- (per serving) calories 321 | fat 17 | protein 3 | total carbs 21 | fiber 20

General Tso's Chicken

Servings:4 | Cooking Time: 20 Minutes

Ingredients:
- 1 pound boneless, skinless chicken breasts or thighs, cut into 1-inch cubes
- Fine sea salt and ground black pepper
- GENERAL TSO'S SAUCE:
- ½ cup chicken broth
- ⅓ cup Swerve confectioners'-style sweetener or equivalent amount of liquid or powdered sweetener (see here)
- ¼ cup coconut vinegar or unseasoned rice vinegar
- ¼ cup thinly sliced green onions, plus more for garnish if desired
- 1 tablespoon plus 1¼ teaspoons wheat-free tamari, or ¼ cup coconut aminos
- 3 small dried red chiles, chopped
- 1 clove garlic, minced
- 1½ teaspoons grated fresh ginger
- 1 teaspoon toasted sesame oil
- ¼ teaspoon guar gum (optional; see Tips)
- FOR SERVING (OPTIONAL):
- Fried Cauliflower Rice (here)
- Sautéed broccoli rabe
- FOR GARNISH (OPTIONAL):
- Diced red chiles
- Red pepper flakes
- Sesame seeds

Directions:
1. Preheat the air fryer to 400°F.
2. Very lightly season the chicken on all sides with salt and pepper (the sauce will add seasoning). Place the chicken in a single layer in a pie pan that fits in the air fryer and cook for 5 minutes.
3. While the chicken cooks, make the sauce: In a small bowl, stir together all the sauce ingredients except the guar gum until well combined. Sift in the guar gum (if using) and whisk until well combined.
4. Pour the sauce over the chicken and, stirring every 5 minutes, cook for another 12 to 15 minutes, until the sauce is bubbly and thick and the chicken is cooked through and the internal temperature reaches 165°F.
5. If you want the sauce to be even thicker and more flavorful, remove the chicken and return the sauce to the air fryer to cook for an additional 5 to 10 minutes.
6. Transfer the chicken to a large bowl. Serve with fried cauliflower rice and sautéed broccoli rabe, if desired, and garnish with diced red chiles, sliced green onions, red pepper flakes, and sesame seeds, if desired.
7. Store leftovers in an airtight container in the refrigerator for up to 4 days. Reheat in a preheated 375°F air fryer for 5 minutes, or until heated through.

Nutrition:
- (per serving) calories 254 | fat 10g | protein 34g | total carbs 5g | fiber 1g

Garlicky Hen With Fish Sauce

Servings: 4 | Cooking Time: 20 Minutes

Ingredients:
- ¼ cup fish sauce
- 1 teaspoon turmeric
- 1 tablespoon coconut aminos
- 1 chopped jalapeño peppers
- 1 cup chopped cilantro leaves
- 2 tablespoons stevia
- 2 teaspoons ground coriander
- 2 tablespoons lemongrass paste
- 2 halved whole cornish game hens, with the giblets removed
- 8 minced garlic cloves
- Salt and black pepper, to taste

Directions:
1. Using a high speed blender, add in the turmeric, salt, coriander, pepper, lemongrass paste, sugar, garlic, cilantro, fish sauce

and incorporate together.

2. Add in the broiler chicken and toss together until fully coated with the mixture then set aside to marinate for an hour.

3. Transfer the marinated broiler into the fryer basket and air fry for 10 minutes at 400°F (205°C).

4. Flip the broiler over then cook for an extra 10 minutes.

5. Serve and enjoy as desired.

Nutrition:
- (per serving) calories 222 | fat 9 | protein 14 | total carbs 4 | fiber 3

Porchetta-style Chicken Breasts

Servings:4 | Cooking Time: 15 Minutes

Ingredients:
- ½ cup fresh parsley leaves
- ¼ cup roughly chopped fresh chives
- 4 cloves garlic, peeled
- 2 tablespoons lemon juice
- 3 teaspoons fine sea salt
- 1 teaspoon dried rubbed sage
- 1 teaspoon fresh rosemary leaves
- 1 teaspoon ground fennel
- ½ teaspoon red pepper flakes
- 4 (4-ounce) boneless, skinless chicken breasts, pounded to ¼ inch thick (see Tip)
- 8 slices bacon
- Sprigs of fresh rosemary, for garnish (optional)

Directions:
1. Spray the air fryer basket with avocado oil. Preheat the air fryer to 340°F.

2. Place the parsley, chives, garlic, lemon juice, salt, sage, rosemary, fennel, and red pepper flakes in a food processor and puree until a smooth paste forms.

3. Place the chicken breasts on a cutting board and rub the paste all over the tops. With a short end facing you, roll each breast up like a jelly roll to make a log and secure it with toothpicks.

4. Wrap 2 slices of bacon around each chicken breast log to cover the entire breast. Secure the bacon with toothpicks.

5. Place the chicken breast logs in the air fryer basket and cook for 5 minutes, flip the logs over, and cook for another 5 minutes. Increase the heat to 390°F and cook until the bacon is crisp, about 5 minutes more.

6. Remove the toothpicks and garnish with fresh rosemary sprigs, if desired, before serving. Store leftovers in an airtight container in the refrigerator for up, to 4 days or in the freezer for up to a month. Reheat in a preheated 350°F air fryer for 5 minutes, then increase the heat to 390°F and cook for 2 minutes to crisp the bacon.

Nutrition:
- (per serving)   calories 468 | fat 25g | protein 56g | total carbs 3g | fiber 1g

Turkey Sausage With Cauliflower

Servings: 4 | Cooking Time: 28 Minutes

Ingredients:
- 1 pound (454 g) ground turkey
- 1 teaspoon garlic pepper
- 1 teaspoon garlic powder
- ⅓ teaspoon dried oregano
- ½ teaspoon salt
- ⅓ cup onions, chopped
- ½ head cauliflower, broken into florets
- ⅓ teaspoon dried basil
- ½ teaspoon dried thyme, chopped

Directions:
1. In a mixing bowl, thoroughly combine the ground turkey, garlic pepper, garlic powder, oregano, salt, and onion, stir well to combine. Spritz a nonstick skillet with pan spray, form the mixture into 4 sausages.

2. Then, cook the sausage over medium heat until they are no longer pink, for approximately 12 minutes.

3. Arrange the cauliflower florets at the bottom of a baking dish. Sprinkle with thyme and basil, spritz with pan spray. Top with the turkey sausages.

4. Roast for 28 minutes at 375°F (190°C), turning once halfway through. Eat warm.

Nutrition:
- (per serving) calories 289 | fat 25 | protein 11 | total carbs 3 | fiber 2

Lemon Chicken

Servings: 4 | Cooking Time: 7 To 10 Minutes

Ingredients:
- 1 pound (454 g) boneless, skinless chicken breasts or thighs
- 2 tablespoons avocado oil
- 1 tablespoon freshly squeezed lemon juice
- 1 teaspoon chopped fresh oregano
- ½ teaspoon garlic powder
- Sea salt
- Freshly ground black pepper

Directions:
1. Place the chicken in a zip-top bag or between two pieces of plastic wrap. Using a meat mallet or a heavy skillet, pound the chicken until it is very thin, about ¼ -inch thick.

2. In a small bowl, combine the avocado oil, lemon juice, oregano, garlic powder, salt, and pepper. Place the chicken in a shallow dish and pour the marinade over it. Toss to coat all the chicken, and let it rest at room temperature for 10 to 15 minutes.

3. Set the air fryer to 400°F (205°C). Place the chicken in a single layer in the air fryer basket and cook for 5 minutes. Flip and cook for another 2 to 5 minutes, until an instant-read thermometer reads 160°F (71°C). Allow it to rest for 5 minutes before serving.

Nutrition:
- (per serving) calories 178 | fat 10 | protein 23 | total carbs 2 | fiber 1

Bacon Lovers' Stuffed Chicken

Servings:4 | Cooking Time: 20 Minutes

Ingredients:
- 4 (5-ounce) boneless, skinless chicken breasts, pounded to ¼ inch thick (see Tip, here)
- 2 (5.2-ounce) packages Boursin cheese (or Kite Hill brand chive cream cheese style spread, softened, for dairy-free) (see Tip)
- 8 slices thin-cut bacon or beef bacon
- Sprig of fresh cilantro, for garnish (optional)

Directions:
1. Spray the air fryer basket with avocado oil. Preheat the air fryer to 400°F.

2. Place one of the chicken breasts on a cutting board. With a

sharp knife held parallel to the cutting board, make a 1-inch-wide incision at the top of the breast. Carefully cut into the breast to form a large pocket, leaving a ½-inch border along the sides and bottom. Repeat with the other 3 chicken breasts.

3. Snip the corner of a large resealable plastic bag to form a ¾-inch hole. Place the Boursin cheese in the bag and pipe the cheese into the pockets in the chicken breasts, dividing the cheese evenly among them.

4. Wrap 2 slices of bacon around each chicken breast and secure the ends with toothpicks. Place the bacon-wrapped chicken in the air fryer basket and cook until the bacon is crisp and the chicken's internal temperature reaches 165°F, about 18 to 20 minutes, flipping after 10 minutes. Garnish with a sprig of cilantro before serving, if desired.

5. Store leftovers in an airtight container in the refrigerator for up to 4 days. Reheat in a preheated 400°F air fryer for 5 minutes, or until warmed through.

Nutrition:
• (per serving) calories 686 | fat 51g | protein 52g | total carbs 2g | fiber 0g

Chicken Wing With Piri Piri Sauce

Servings: 6 | Cooking Time: 30 Minutes

Ingredients:
• 12 chicken wings
• 1½ ounces (43 g) butter, melted
• 1 teaspoon onion powder
• ½ teaspoon cumin powder
• 1 teaspoon garlic paste
• For the Sauce:
• 2 ounces (57 g) piri piri peppers, stemmed and chopped
• 1 tablespoon pimiento, seeded and minced
• 1 garlic clove, chopped
• 2 tablespoons fresh lemon juice
• ⅓ teaspoon sea salt
• ½ teaspoon tarragon

Directions:
1. Steam the chicken wings using a steamer basket that is placed over a saucepan with boiling water, reduce the heat.
2. Now, steam the wings for 10 minutes over a moderate heat. Toss the wings with butter, onion powder, cumin powder, and garlic paste.
3. Let the chicken wings cool to room temperature. Then, refrigerate them for 45 to 50 minutes.
4. Roast in the preheated Air Fryer at 330ºF (166ºC) for 25 to 30 minutes, make sure to flip them halfway through.
5. While the chicken wings are cooking, prepare the sauce by mixing all of the sauce ingredients in a food processor. Toss the wings with prepared piri piri Sauce and serve.

Nutrition:
• (per serving) calories 517 | fat 21 | protein 4 | total carbs 12 | fiber 11

Chicken Thighs With Creamy Rosemary Sauce

Servings: 4 | Cooking Time: 18 Minutes

Ingredients:
• ½ cup full-fat sour cream
• 1 teaspoon ground cinnamon
• ½ teaspoon whole grain mustard
• 1½ tablespoons mayonnaise
• 1 pound (454 g) chicken thighs, boneless, skinless, and cut into pieces
• 1½ tablespoons olive oil
• 2 heaping tablespoons fresh rosemary, minced
• ½ cup white wine
• 3 cloves garlic, minced
• ½ teaspoon smoked paprika
• Salt and freshly cracked black pepper, to taste

Directions:
1. Firstly, in a mixing dish, combine chicken thighs with olive oil and white wine, stir to coat.
2. After that, throw in the garlic, smoked paprika, ground cinnamon, salt, and black pepper, cover and refrigerate for 1 to 3 hours.
3. Set the Air Fryer to cook at 375ºF. Roast the chicken thighs for 18 minutes, turning halfway through and working in batches.
4. To make the sauce, combine the sour cream, whole grain mustard, mayonnaise and rosemary. Serve the turkey with the mustard/rosemary sauce and enjoy!

Nutrition:
• (per serving) calories 362 | fat 28 | protein 8 | total carbs 17 | fiber 16

Thai Tacos With Peanut Sauce

Servings:4 | Cooking Time: 6 Minutes

Ingredients:
• 1 pound ground chicken
• ¼ cup diced onions (about 1 small onion)
• 2 cloves garlic, minced
• ¼ teaspoon fine sea salt
• SAUCE:
• ¼ cup creamy peanut butter, room temperature
• 2 tablespoons chicken broth, plus more if needed
• 2 tablespoons lime juice
• 2 tablespoons grated fresh ginger
• 2 tablespoons wheat-free tamari or coconut aminos
• 1½ teaspoons hot sauce
• 5 drops liquid stevia (optional)
• FOR SERVING:
• 2 small heads butter lettuce, leaves separated
• Lime slices (optional)
• FOR GARNISH (OPTIONAL):
• Cilantro leaves
• Shredded purple cabbage
• Sliced green onions

Directions:
1. Preheat the air fryer to 350°F.
2. Place the ground chicken, onions, garlic, and salt in a 6-inch pie pan or a dish that will fit in your air fryer. Break up the chicken with a spatula. Place in the air fryer and cook for 5 minutes, or until the chicken is browned and cooked through. Break up the chicken again into small crumbles.
3. Make the sauce: In a medium-sized bowl, stir together the pea-

nut butter, broth, lime juice, ginger, tamari, hot sauce, and stevia (if using) until well combined. If the sauce is too thick, add another tablespoon or two of broth. Taste and add more hot sauce if desired.

4. Add half of the sauce to the pan with the chicken. Cook for another minute, until heated through, and stir well to combine.

5. Assemble the tacos: Place several lettuce leaves on a serving plate. Place a few tablespoons of the chicken mixture in each lettuce leaf and garnish with cilantro leaves, purple cabbage, and sliced green onions, if desired. Serve the remaining sauce on the side. Serve with lime slices, if desired.

6. Store leftover meat mixture in an airtight container in the refrigerator for up to 4 days; store leftover sauce, lettuce leaves, and garnishes separately. Reheat the meat mixture in a lightly greased pie pan in a preheated 350°F air fryer for 3 minutes, or until heated through.

Nutrition:
- (per serving)   calories 350 | fat 17g | protein 39g | total carbs 11g | fiber 3g

Traditional Kung Pao Chicken

Servings: 4 | Cooking Time: 20 Minutes

Ingredients:
- 1½ pounds (680 g) chicken breast, halved
- 1 tablespoon lemon juice
- 2 tablespoons mirin
- ¼ cup milk
- 2 tablespoons soy sauce
- 1 tablespoon olive oil
- 1 teaspoon ginger, peeled and grated
- 2 garlic cloves, minced
- ½ teaspoon salt
- ½ teaspoon Szechuan pepper
- ½ teaspoon xanthan gum

Directions:
1. In a large ceramic dish, place the chicken, lemon juice, mirin, milk, soy sauce, olive oil, ginger, and garlic. Let it marinate for 30 minutes in your refrigerator.
2. Spritz the sides and bottom of the cooking basket with a nonstick cooking spray. Arrange the chicken in the cooking basket and cook at 370°F for 10 minutes.
3. Turn over the chicken, baste with the reserved marinade and cook for 4 minutes longer. Taste for doneness, season with salt and pepper, and reserve.
4. Add the marinade to the preheated skillet over medium heat, add in xanthan gum. Let it cook for 5 to 6 minutes until the sauce thickens.
5. Spoon the sauce over the reserved chicken and serve immediately.

Nutrition:
- (per serving) calories 358 | fat 21 | protein 37 | total carbs 4 | fiber 3

Duck With Candy Onion

Servings: 4 | Cooking Time: 25 Minutes

Ingredients:
- 1½ pounds (680 g) duck breasts, skin removed
- 1 teaspoon kosher salt
- ½ teaspoon cayenne pepper
- ⅓ teaspoon black pepper

- ½ teaspoon smoked paprika
- 1 tablespoon Thai red curry paste
- 1 cup candy onions, halved
- ¼ small pack coriander, chopped

Directions:
1. Place the duck breasts between 2 sheets of foil, then, use a rolling pin to bash the duck until they are 1-inch thick.
2. Preheat your Air Fryer to 395°F.
3. Rub the duck breasts with salt, cayenne pepper, black pepper, paprika, and red curry paste. Place the duck breast in the cooking basket.
4. Cook for 11 to 12 minutes. Top with candy onions and cook for another 10 to 11 minutes.
5. Serve garnished with coriander and enjoy!

Nutrition:
- (per serving) calories 362 | fat 19 | protein 2 | total carbs 24 | fiber 21

Crispy Taco Chicken

Servings:4 | Cooking Time: 23 Minutes

Ingredients:
- 2 large eggs
- 1 tablespoon water
- Fine sea salt and ground black pepper
- 1 cup pork dust (see here)
- 1 teaspoon ground cumin
- 1 teaspoon smoked paprika
- 4 (5-ounce) boneless, skinless chicken breasts or thighs, pounded to ¼ inch thick (see Note; see Tip, here)
- 1 cup salsa
- 1 cup shredded Monterey Jack cheese (about 4 ounces) (omit for dairy-free)
- Sprig of fresh cilantro, for garnish (optional)

Directions:
1. Spray the air fryer basket with avocado oil. Preheat the air fryer to 400°F.
2. Crack the eggs into a shallow baking dish, add the water and a pinch each of salt and pepper, and whisk to combine. In another shallow baking dish, stir together the pork dust, cumin, and paprika until well combined.
3. Season the chicken breasts well on both sides with salt and pepper. Dip 1 chicken breast in the eggs and let any excess drip off, then dredge both sides of the chicken breast in the pork dust mixture. Spray the breast with avocado oil and place it in the air fryer basket. Repeat with the remaining 3 chicken breasts.
4. Cook the chicken in the air fryer for 20 minutes, or until the internal temperature reaches 165°F and the breading is golden brown, flipping halfway through.
5. Dollop each chicken breast with ¼ cup of the salsa and top with ¼ cup of the cheese. Return the breasts to the air fryer and cook for 3 minutes, or until the cheese is melted. Garnish with cilantro before serving, if desired.
6. Store leftovers in an airtight container in the refrigerator for up to 4 days. Reheat in a preheated 400°F air fryer for 5 minutes, or until warmed through.

Nutrition:
- (per serving, with breasts)   calories 486 | fat 29g | protein 54g | total carbs 3g | fiber 0.2g

Herbed Chicken Leg

Servings: 6 | Cooking Time: 23 To 27 Minutes

Ingredients:
- ½ cup avocado oil
- 2 teaspoons smoked paprika
- 1 teaspoon sea salt
- 1 teaspoon garlic powder
- ½ teaspoon dried rosemary
- ½ teaspoon dried thyme
- ½ teaspoon freshly ground black pepper
- 2 pounds (907 g) bone-in, skin-on chicken leg quarters

Directions:
1. In a blender or small bowl, combine the avocado oil, smoked paprika, salt, garlic powder, rosemary, thyme, and black pepper.
2. Place the chicken in a shallow dish or large zip-top bag. Pour the marinade over the chicken, making sure all the legs are coated. Cover and marinate for at least 2 hours or overnight.
3. Place the chicken in a single layer in the air fryer basket, working in batches if necessary. Set the air fryer to 400°F (205°C) and cook for 15 minutes. Flip the chicken legs, then reduce the temperature to 350°F (180°C). Cook for 8 to 12 minutes or more, until an instant-read thermometer reads 160°F (71°C) when inserted into the thickest piece of chicken.
4. Allow them to rest for 5 to 10 minutes before serving.

Nutrition:
- (per serving) calories 569 | fat 53 | protein 23 | total carbs 2 | fiber 1

Turkey And Bacon Burgers

Servings: 4 | Cooking Time: 26 Minutes

Ingredients:
- 2 tablespoons vermouth
- 2 strips Canadian bacon, sliced
- 1 pound (454 g) ground turkey
- ½ shallot, minced
- 2 garlic cloves, minced
- 2 tablespoons fish sauce
- Sea salt and ground black pepper, to taste
- 1 teaspoon red pepper flakes
- 4 tablespoons tomato ketchup
- 4 tablespoons mayonnaise
- 4 (1-ounce / 28-g) slices Cheddar cheese
- 4 lettuce leaves

Directions:
1. Start by preheating your Air Fryer to 400°F. Brush the Canadian bacon with the vermouth.
2. Cook for 3 minutes. Flip the bacon over and cook for an additional 3 minutes.
3. Then, thoroughly combine the ground turkey, shallots, garlic, fish sauce, salt, black pepper, and red pepper. Form the meat mixture into 4 burger patties.
4. Bake in the preheated Air Fryer at 370°F for 10 minutes. Flip them over and cook another for 10 minutes.
5. Serve turkey burgers with the ketchup, mayonnaise, bacon, cheese and lettuce, serve immediately.

Nutrition:
- (per serving) calories 308 | fat 16 | protein 4 | total carbs 17 | fiber 16

Chicken With Asiago Cheese

Servings: 4 | Cooking Time: 10 Minutes

Ingredients:
- 2 ounces (57 g) Asiago cheese, cut into sticks
- ⅓ cup keto tomato paste
- ½ teaspoon garlic paste
- 2 chicken breasts, cut in half lengthwise
- ½ cup green onions, chopped
- 1 tablespoon chili sauce
- ½ cup roasted vegetable stock
- 1 tablespoon sesame oil
- 1 teaspoon salt
- 2 teaspoons unsweetened cocoa
- ½ teaspoon sweet paprika, or more to taste

Directions:
1. Sprinkle chicken breasts with the salt and sweet paprika, drizzle with chili sauce. Now, place a stick of Asiago cheese in the middle of each chicken breast.
2. Then, tie the whole thing using a kitchen string, give a drizzle of sesame oil.
3. Transfer the stuffed chicken to the cooking basket. Add the other ingredients and toss to coat the chicken.
4. Afterward, cook for about 11 minutes at 395°F (202°C). Serve the chicken on two serving plates, garnish with fresh or pickled salad and serve immediately. Bon appétit!

Nutrition:
- (per serving) calories 390 | fat 12 | protein 2 | total carbs 8 | fiber 7

Rosemary Turkey Roast

Servings: 6 | Cooking Time: 45 Minutes

Ingredients:
- 2½ pounds (1.1kg) turkey breasts
- 1 tablespoon fresh rosemary, chopped
- 1 teaspoon sea salt
- ½ teaspoon ground black pepper
- 1 onion, chopped
- 1 celery stalk, chopped

Directions:
1. Start by preheating your Air Fryer to 360°F (182°C). Spritz the sides and bottom of the cooking basket with a nonstick cooking spray.
2. Place the turkey in the cooking basket. Add the rosemary, salt, and black pepper. Cook for 30 minutes in the preheated Air Fryer.
3. Add the onion and celery and cook for an additional 15 minutes. Bon appétit!

Nutrition:
- (per serving) calories 316 | fat 14 | protein 41 | total carbs 2 | fiber 1

Chicken With Secret Spice Rub

Servings: 4 | Cooking Time: 30 Minutes

Ingredients:
- 1 (4-pound / 1.8 kg) chicken, giblets removed
- ½ onion, quartered
- 1 tablespoon olive oil
- Secret Spice Rub:
- 2 teaspoons salt
- 1 teaspoon paprika

- ½ teaspoon onion powder
- ½ teaspoon garlic powder
- ½ teaspoon dried thyme
- ½ teaspoon freshly ground black pepper
- ¼ teaspoon cayenne

Directions:

1. Preheat the air fryer to 350°F (180°C).
2. Use paper towels to blot the chicken dry. Stuff the chicken with the onion. Rub the chicken with the oil.
3. To make the spice rub: In a small bowl, combine the salt, paprika, onion powder, garlic powder, thyme, black pepper, and cayenne, stir until thoroughly combined. Sprinkle the chicken with the spice rub until thoroughly coated.
4. Place the chicken breast side down in the air fryer basket. Air fry the chicken for 30 minutes. Use tongs to carefully flip the chicken over and air fry for an additional 30 minutes, or until the temperature of a thermometer inserted into the thickest part of the chicken registers 165°F (74°C).
5. Let the chicken rest for 10 minutes. Discard the onion and serve.

Nutrition:

- (per serving) calories 500 | fat 27 | protein 61 | total carbs 2 | fiber 0

Easy Turkey Drumsticks

Servings: 2 | Cooking Time: 23 Minutes

Ingredients:

- 1 tablespoon red curry paste
- ½ teaspoon cayenne pepper
- 1½ tablespoons minced ginger
- 2 turkey drumsticks
- ¼ cup coconut milk
- 1 teaspoon kosher salt, or more to taste
- ⅓ teaspoon ground pepper, to more to taste

Directions:

1. First of all, place turkey drumsticks with all ingredients in your refrigerator, let it marinate overnight.
2. Cook turkey drumsticks at 380°F (193°C) for 23 minutes, make sure to flip them over at half-time. Serve with the salad on the side.

Nutrition:

- (per serving) calories 298 | fat 16 | protein 12 | total carbs 25 | fiber 22

Chicken With Cauliflower And Italian Parsley

Servings: 6 | Cooking Time: 28 Minutes

Ingredients:

- 2 handful fresh Italian parsley, roughly chopped
- ½ cup fresh chopped chives
- 2 sprigs thyme
- 6 chicken drumsticks
- 1½ small-sized heads cauliflower, broken into large-sized florets
- 2 teaspoons mustard powder
- ⅓ teaspoon porcini powder
- 1 ½ teaspoons berbere spice
- ⅓ teaspoon sweet paprika
- ½ teaspoon shallot powder

- 1 teaspoon granulated garlic
- 1 teaspoon freshly cracked pink peppercorns
- ½ teaspoon sea salt

Directions:

1. Simply combine all items for the berbere spice rub mix. After that, coat the chicken drumsticks with this rub mix on all sides. Transfer them to the baking dish.
2. Now, lower the cauliflower onto the chicken drumsticks. Add thyme, chives and Italian parsley and spritz everything with a pan spray. Transfer the baking dish to the preheated Air Fryer.
3. Next step, set the timer for 28 minutes, roast at 355°F (181°C), turning occasionally. Bon appétit!

Nutrition:

- (per serving) calories 234 | fat 12 | protein 2 | total carbs 9 | fiber 7

Chicken Kiev

Servings:4 | Cooking Time: 25 Minutes

Ingredients:

- 1 cup (2 sticks) unsalted butter, softened (or butter-flavored coconut oil for dairy-free)
- 2 tablespoons lemon juice
- 2 tablespoons plus 1 teaspoon chopped fresh parsley leaves, divided, plus more for garnish
- 2 tablespoons chopped fresh tarragon leaves
- 3 cloves garlic, minced
- 1 teaspoon fine sea salt, divided
- 4 (4-ounce) boneless, skinless chicken breasts
- 2 large eggs
- 2 cups pork dust (see here)
- 1 teaspoon ground black pepper
- Sprig of fresh parsley, for garnish
- Lemon slices, for serving

Directions:

1. Spray the air fryer basket with avocado oil. Preheat the air fryer to 350°F.
2. In a medium-sized bowl, combine the butter, lemon juice, 2 tablespoons of the parsley, the tarragon, garlic, and ¼ teaspoon of the salt. Cover and place in the fridge to harden for 7 minutes.
3. While the butter mixture chills, place one of the chicken breasts on a cutting board. With a sharp knife held parallel to the cutting board, make a 1-inch-wide incision at the top of the breast. Carefully cut into the breast to form a large pocket, leaving a ½-inch border along the sides and bottom. Repeat with the other 3 breasts.
4. Stuff one-quarter of the butter mixture into each chicken breast and secure the openings with toothpicks.
5. Beat the eggs in a small shallow dish. In another shallow dish, combine the pork dust, the remaining 1 teaspoon of parsley, the remaining ¾ teaspoon of salt, and the pepper.
6. One at a time, dip the chicken breasts in the egg, shake off the excess egg, and dredge the breasts in the pork dust mixture. Use your hands to press the pork dust onto each breast to form a nice crust. If you desire a thicker coating, dip it again in the egg and pork dust. As you finish, spray each coated chicken breast with avocado oil and place it in the air fryer basket.
7. Cook the chicken in the air fryer for 15 minutes, flip the breasts, and cook for another 10 minutes, or until the internal temperature of the chicken is 165°F and the crust is golden brown.
8. Serve garnished with chopped fresh parsley and a parsley sprig, with lemon slices on the side.

9. Store leftovers in an airtight container in the refrigerator for up to 4 days or in the freezer for up to a month. Reheat in a preheated 350°F air fryer for 5 minutes, or until heated through.

Nutrition:
- (per serving)   calories 801 | fat 64g | protein 51g | total carbs 3g | fiber 1g

Spiced Chicken Thighs

Servings: 6 | Cooking Time: 20 Minutes

Ingredients:
- 2 teaspoons ground coriander
- 1 teaspoon ground allspice
- 1 teaspoon cayenne pepper
- 1 teaspoon ground ginger
- 1 teaspoon salt
- 1 teaspoon dried thyme
- ½ teaspoon ground cinnamon
- ½ teaspoon ground nutmeg
- 2 pounds (907 g) boneless chicken thighs, skin on
- 2 tablespoons olive oil

Directions:
1. In a small bowl, combine the coriander, allspice, cayenne, ginger, salt, thyme, cinnamon, and nutmeg. Stir until thoroughly combined.
2. Place the chicken in a 9 × 13-inch baking dish and use paper towels to pat dry. Thoroughly coat both sides of the chicken with the spice mixture. Cover and refrigerate for at least 2 hours, preferably overnight.
3. Preheat the air fryer to 360°F (182ºC).
4. Working in batches if necessary, arrange the chicken in a single layer in the air fryer basket and lightly coat with the olive oil. Pausing halfway through the cooking time to flip the chicken, air fry for 15 to 20 minutes, until a thermometer inserted into the thickest part registers 165°F (74ºC).

Nutrition:
- (per serving) calories 223 | fat 11 | protein 30 | total carbs 1 | fiber 1

Aromatic Chicken Thighs

Servings: 4 | Cooking Time: 15 Minutes

Ingredients:
- ¼ cup full-fat Greek yogurt
- ½ teaspoon cayenne pepper
- ½ teaspoon ground cinnamon
- ½ teaspoon ground black pepper
- 1 teaspoon kosher salt
- 1 teaspoon ground cumin
- 1 tablespoon juiced lime
- 1 tablespoon avocado oil
- 1 teaspoon smoked paprika
- 1 tablespoon keto tomato paste
- 1 tablespoon minced garlic
- 1-pound (454 g) chicken thighs, boneless & skinless

Directions:
1. Using a large mixing bowl, add in the tomato paste, garlic, oil, juiced lime, cumin, salt, black pepper, cinnamon, paprika, cayenne pepper, yogurt and mix until combined.
2. Add the chicken pieces into the mixing bowl and toss until combined, then set aside to marinate for an hour.
3. Arrange the marinated chicken in the fryer basket then cook

for 10 minutes at 370°F (188ºC).
4. Flip the chicken over and cook for an additional 5 minutes.
5. Serve and enjoy as desired.

Nutrition:
- (per serving) calories 298 | fat 23 | protein 20 | total carbs 4 | fiber 3

Duo-cheese Chicken With Jalapeños

Servings: 8 | Cooking Time: 14 To 17 Minutes

Ingredients:
- 2 pounds (907 g) boneless, skinless chicken breasts or thighs
- Sea salt
- Freshly ground black pepper
- 8 ounces (227 g) cream cheese, at room temperature
- 4 ounces (113 g) Cheddar cheese, shredded
- 2 jalapeños, seeded and diced
- 1 teaspoon minced garlic
- Avocado oil spray

Directions:
1. Place the chicken in a large zip-top bag or between two pieces of plastic wrap. Using a meat mallet or heavy skillet, pound the chicken until it is about ¼-inch thick. Season both sides of the chicken with salt and pepper.
2. In a medium bowl, combine the cream cheese, Cheddar cheese, jalapeños, and garlic. Divide the mixture among the chicken pieces. Roll up each piece from the long side, tucking in the ends as you go. Secure with toothpicks.
3. Set the air fryer to 350°F (180ºC). Spray the outside of the chicken with oil. Place the chicken in a single layer in the air fryer basket, working in batches if necessary, and cook for 7 minutes. Flip the chicken and cook for another 7 to 10 minutes, until an instant-read thermometer reads 160°F (71ºC).

Nutrition:
- (per serving) calories 264 | fat 17 | protein 28 | total carbs 2 | fiber 1

Turkey Meatballs With Pecorino Romano

Servings: 6 | Cooking Time: 7 Minutes

Ingredients:
- 1 pound (454 g) ground turkey
- 1 tablespoon fresh mint leaves, finely chopped
- 1 teaspoon onion powder
- 1½ teaspoons garlic paste
- 1 teaspoon crushed red pepper flakes
- ¼ cup melted butter
- ¾ teaspoon fine sea salt
- ¼ cup grated Pecorino Romano

Directions:
1. Simply place all of the above ingredients into the mixing dish, mix until everything is well incorporated.
2. Use an ice cream scoop to shape the meat into golf ball sized meatballs.
3. Air fry the meatballs at 380ºF for approximately 7 minutes, work in batches, shaking them to ensure evenness of cooking.
4. Serve with a simple tomato sauce garnished with fresh basil leaves. Bon appétit!

Nutrition:
- (per serving) calories 241 | fat 18 | protein 8 | total carbs 21 | fiber 20

Chicken Breasts With Lime

Servings: 4 | Cooking Time: 26 Minutes

Ingredients:
- ½ teaspoon stone-ground mustard
- ½ teaspoon minced fresh oregano
- ⅓ cup freshly squeezed lime juice
- 2 small-sized chicken breasts, skin-on
- 1 teaspoon kosher salt
- 1teaspoon freshly cracked mixed peppercorns

Directions:
1. Preheat your Air Fryer to 345ºF.
2. Toss all of the above ingredients in a medium-sized mixing dish, allow it to marinate overnight.
3. Cook in the preheated Air Fryer for 26 minutes. Bon appétit!

Nutrition:
- (per serving) calories 255 | fat 14 | protein 8 | total carbs 12 | fiber 11

Zucchini And Sausage Casserole

Servings: 4 | Cooking Time: 16 Minutes

Ingredients:
- 8 ounces (227 g) zucchini, spiralized
- 1 pound (454 g) smoked chicken sausage, sliced
- 1 tomato, puréed
- ½ cup Asiago cheese, shredded
- 1 tablespoon Italian seasoning mix
- 3 tablespoons Romano cheese, grated
- 1 tablespoon fresh basil leaves, chiffonade

Directions:
1. Salt the zucchini and let it stand for 30 minutes, pat it dry with kitchen towels.
2. Then, spritz a baking pan with cooking spray, add the zucchini to the pan. Stir in the chicken sausage, tomato purée, Asiago cheese, and Italian seasoning mix.
3. Bake in the preheated Air Fryer at 325ºF (163ºC) for 11 minutes.
4. Top with the grated Romano cheese. Turn the temperature to 390ºF (199ºC) and cook for an additional 5 minutes or until everything is thoroughly heated and the cheese is melted.
5. Garnish with fresh basil leaves. Bon appétit!

Nutrition:
- (per serving) calories 300 | fat 17 | protein 5 | total carbs 9 | fiber 7

Lemony Chicken Thighs With Greek Yogurt

Servings: 6 | Cooking Time: 20 Minutes

Ingredients:
- ¼ cup plain Greek yogurt
- 2 cloves garlic, minced
- 1 tablespoon grated fresh ginger
- ½ teaspoon ground cayenne
- ½ teaspoon ground turmeric
- ½ teaspoon garam masala
- 1 teaspoon ground cumin
- 1 teaspoon salt
- 2 pounds (907 g) boneless chicken thighs, skin on
- 2 tablespoons chopped fresh cilantro
- 1 lemon, cut into 6 wedges
- ½ sweet onion, sliced

Directions:
1. In a small bowl, combine the yogurt, garlic, ginger, cayenne, turmeric, garam masala, cumin, and salt. Whisk until thoroughly combined.
2. Transfer the yogurt mixture to a large resealable bag. Add the chicken, seal the bag, and massage the bag to ensure chicken is evenly coated. Refrigerate for 1 hour (or up to 8 hours).
3. Preheat the air fryer to 360°F (182ºC).
4. Remove the chicken from the marinade (discard the marinade) and arrange in a single layer in the air fryer basket. Pausing halfway through the cooking time to flip the chicken, air fry for 15 to 20 minutes, until a thermometer inserted into the thickest part registers 165°F (74ºC).
5. Transfer the chicken to a serving platter. Top with the cilantro and serve with the lemon wedges and sliced onion.

Nutrition:
- (per serving) calories 350 | fat 22 | protein 35 | total carbs 1 | fiber 1

Simple Turkey Breast

Servings: 10 | Cooking Time: 45 To 55 Minutes

Ingredients:
- 1 tablespoon sea salt
- 1 teaspoon paprika
- 1 teaspoon onion powder
- 1 teaspoon garlic powder
- ½ teaspoon freshly ground black pepper
- 4 pounds (1.8 kg) bone-in, skin-on turkey breast
- 2 tablespoons unsalted butter, melted

Directions:
1. In a small bowl, combine the salt, paprika, onion powder, garlic powder, and pepper.
2. Sprinkle the seasonings all over the turkey. Brush the turkey with some of the melted butter.
3. Set the air fryer to 350°F (180ºC). Place the turkey in the air fryer basket, skin-side down, and cook for 25 minutes.
4. Flip the turkey and brush it with the remaining butter. Continue cooking for another 20 to 30 minutes, until an instant-read thermometer reads 160°F.
5. Remove the turkey breast from the air fryer. Tent a piece of aluminum foil over the turkey, and allow it to rest for about 5 minutes before serving.

Nutrition:
- (per serving) calories 278 | fat 14 | protein 34 | total carbs 2 | fiber 1

Chicken Paillard

Servings:2 | Cooking Time: 10 Minutes

Ingredients:
- 2 large eggs, room temperature
- 1 tablespoon water
- ½ cup powdered Parmesan cheese (about 1½ ounces; see here) or pork dust (see here)
- 2 teaspoons dried thyme leaves
- 1 teaspoon ground black pepper
- 2 (5-ounce) boneless, skinless chicken breasts, pounded to ½ inch thick (see Tip, here)
- LEMON BUTTER SAUCE:
- 2 tablespoons unsalted butter, melted
- 2 teaspoons lemon juice

- ¼ teaspoon finely chopped fresh thyme leaves, plus more for garnish
- ⅛ teaspoon fine sea salt
- Lemon slices, for serving

Directions:

1. Spray the air fryer basket with avocado oil. Preheat the air fryer to 390°F.
2. Beat the eggs in a shallow dish, then add the water and stir well.
3. In a separate shallow dish, mix together the Parmesan, thyme, and pepper until well combined.
4. One at a time, dip the chicken breasts in the eggs and let any excess drip off, then dredge both sides of the chicken in the Parmesan mixture. As you finish, set the coated chicken in the air fryer basket.
5. Cook the chicken in the air fryer for 5 minutes, then flip the chicken and cook for another 5 minutes, or until cooked through and the internal temperature reaches 165°F.
6. While the chicken cooks, make the lemon butter sauce: In a small bowl, mix together all the sauce ingredients until well combined.
7. Plate the chicken and pour the sauce over it. Garnish with chopped fresh thyme and serve with lemon slices.
8. Store leftovers in an airtight container in the refrigerator for up to 4 days. Reheat in a preheated 390°F air fryer for 5 minutes, or until heated through.

Nutrition:
- (per serving)   calories 526 | fat 33g | protein 53g | total carbs 3g | fiber 1g

Bacon-wrapped Turkey With Asiago

Servings: 12 | Cooking Time: 13 Minutes

Ingredients:
- 1½ small-sized turkey breast, chop into 12 pieces
- 12 thin slices Asiago cheese
- Paprika, to taste
- Fine sea salt and ground black pepper, to taste
- 12 rashers bacon

Directions:

1. Lay out the bacon rashers, place 1 slice of Asiago cheese on each bacon piece.
2. Top with turkey, season with paprika, salt, and pepper, and roll them up, secure with a cocktail stick.
3. Air-fry at 365°F (185°C) for 13 minutes. Bon appétit!

Nutrition:
- (per serving) calories 568 | fat 34 | protein 5 | total carbs 30 | fiber 29

Chili Chicken Sliders With Scallions

Servings: 4 | Cooking Time: 18 Minutes

Ingredients:
- ⅓ teaspoon paprika
- ⅓ cup scallions, peeled and chopped
- 3 cloves garlic, peeled and minced
- 1 teaspoon ground black pepper, or to taste
- ½ teaspoon fresh basil, minced
- 1½ cups chicken, minced
- 1½ tablespoons coconut aminos
- ½ teaspoon grated fresh ginger
- ½ tablespoon chili sauce

- 1 teaspoon salt

Directions:

1. Thoroughly combine all ingredients in a mixing dish. Then, form into 4 patties.
2. Cook in the preheated Air Fryer for 18 minutes at 355°F.
3. Garnish with toppings of choice. Bon appétit!

Nutrition:
- (per serving) calories 366 | fat 10 | protein 12 | total carbs 35 | fiber 34

Turkey Wings Marinated With White Wine

Servings: 4 | Cooking Time: 28 Minutes

Ingredients:
- 1 teaspoon freshly cracked pink peppercorns
- 1½ pounds (680 g) turkey wings, cut into smaller pieces
- 2 teaspoons garlic powder
- ⅓ cup white wine
- ½ teaspoon garlic salt
- ½ tablespoon coriander, ground

Directions:

1. Toss all of the above ingredients in a mixing dish. Let it marinate for at least 3 hours.
2. Air-fry turkey wings for 28 minutes at 355°F. Bon appétit!

Nutrition:
- (per serving) calories 346 | fat 20 | protein 35 | total carbs 2 | fiber 1.9

Turkey Drumsticks With Hoisin Sauce

Servings: 4 | Cooking Time: 40 Minutes

Ingredients:
- 2 pounds (907 g) turkey drumsticks
- 2 tablespoons balsamic vinegar
- 2 tablespoons dry white wine
- 1 tablespoon sesame oil
- 1 sprig rosemary, chopped
- Salt and ground black pepper, to your liking
- 2 ½ tablespoons butter, melted
- For the Hoisin Sauce:
- 2 tablespoons hoisin sauce
- 1 tablespoon mustard

Directions:

1. Add the turkey drumsticks to a mixing dish, add the vinegar, wine, sesame oil, and rosemary. Let them marinate for 3 hours.
2. Then, preheat the Air Fryer to 350°F.
3. Season the turkey drumsticks with salt and black pepper, spread the melted butter over the surface of drumsticks.
4. Cook turkey drumsticks at 350°F for 30 to 35 minutes, working in batches. Turn the drumsticks over a few times during the cooking.
5. While the turkey drumsticks are roasting, prepare the Hoisin sauce by mixing the ingredients. After that, drizzle the turkey with the sauce mixture, roast for a further 5 minutes.
6. Let it rest for about 10 minutes before carving and serving. Bon appétit!

Nutrition:
- (per serving) calories 469 | fat 26 | protein 10 | total carbs 20 | fiber 19

Turkey With Gravy

Servings: 6 | Cooking Time: 20 Minutes

Ingredients:
- 2 teaspoons butter, softened
- 1 teaspoon dried sage
- 2 sprigs rosemary, chopped
- 1 teaspoon salt
- ¼ teaspoon freshly ground black pepper, or more to taste
- 1 whole turkey breast
- 2 tablespoons turkey broth
- 2 tablespoons whole-grain mustard
- 1 tablespoon butter

Directions:
1. Start by preheating your Air Fryer to 360ºF (182ºC).
2. To make the rub, combine 2 tablespoons of butter, sage, rosemary, salt, and pepper, mix well to combine and spread it evenly over the surface of the turkey breast.
3. Roast for 20 minutes in an Air Fryer cooking basket. Flip the turkey breast over and cook for a further 15 to 16 minutes. Now, flip it back over and roast for 12 minutes or more.
4. While the turkey is roasting, whisk the other ingredients in a saucepan. After that, spread the gravy all over the turkey breast.
5. Let the turkey rest for a few minutes before carving. Bon appétit!

Nutrition:
- (per serving) calories 384 | fat 8 | protein 131 | total carbs 2 | fiber 1

Nutty Turkey Breast

Servings: 2 | Cooking Time: 28 Minutes

Ingredients:
- 1½ tablespoons coconut aminos
- ½ tablespoon xanthan gum
- 2 bay leaves
- ⅓ cup dry sherry
- 1½ tablespoons chopped walnuts
- 1 teaspoon shallot powder
- 1 pound (454 g) turkey breasts, sliced
- 1 teaspoon garlic powder
- 2 teaspoons olive oil
- ½ teaspoon onion salt
- ½ teaspoon red pepper flakes, crushed
- 1 teaspoon ground black pepper

Directions:
1. Begin by preheating your Air Fryer to 395ºF. Place all ingredients, minus chopped walnuts, in a mixing bowl and let them marinate for at least 1 hour.
2. After that, cook the marinated turkey breast for approximately 23 minutes or until heated through.
3. Pause the machine, scatter chopped walnuts over the top and air-fry for an additional 5 minutes. Bon appétit!

Nutrition:
- (per serving) calories 395 | fat 20 | protein 12 | total carbs 31 | fiber 30

Turkey With Tabasco Sauce

Servings: 6 | Cooking Time: 22 Minutes

Ingredients:
- 1½ pounds (680g) ground turkey
- 6 whole eggs, well beaten
- ⅓ teaspoon smoked paprika
- 2 egg whites, beaten
- Tabasco sauce, for drizzling
- 2 tablespoons sesame oil
- 2 leeks, chopped
- 3 cloves garlic, finely minced
- 1 teaspoon ground black pepper
- ½ teaspoon sea salt

Directions:
1. Warm the oil in a pan over moderate heat, then, sweat the leeks and garlic until tender, stir periodically.
2. Next, grease 6 oven safe ramekins with pan spray. Divide the sautéed mixture among six ramekins.
3. In a bowl, beat the eggs and egg whites using a wire whisk. Stir in the smoked paprika, salt and black pepper, whisk until everything is thoroughly combined. Divide the egg mixture among the ramekins.
4. Air-fry approximately 22 minutes at 345ºF (174ºC). Drizzle Tabasco sauce over each portion and serve.

Nutrition:
- (per serving) calories 298 | fat 15 | protein 6 | total carbs 25 | fiber 24

Turkey Sliders With Chive Mayonnaise

Servings: 6 | Cooking Time: 15 Minutes

Ingredients:
- For the Turkey Sliders:
- ¾ pound (340 g) turkey mince
- ¼ cup pickled jalapeno, chopped
- 1 tablespoon oyster sauce
- 1-2 cloves garlic, minced
- 1 tablespoon chopped fresh cilantro
- 2 tablespoons chopped scallions
- Sea salt and ground black pepper, to savor
- For the Chive Mayo:
- 1 cup mayonnaise
- 1 tablespoon chives
- 1 teaspoon salt
- Zest of 1 lime

Directions:
1. In a mixing bowl, thoroughly combine all ingredients for the turkey patties.
2. Mold the mixture into 6 even-sized slider patties. Then, air-fry them at 365ºF for 15 minutes.
3. Meanwhile, make the Chive Mayonnaise by mixing the rest of the above ingredients. Serve warm.

Nutrition:
- (per serving) calories 252 | fat 16 | protein 7 | total carbs 30 | fiber 29

Glazed Turkey Tenderloins With Pickles

Servings: 4 | Cooking Time: 50 Minutes

Ingredients:
- 1 pound (454 g) turkey tenderloins
- 1 tablespoon Dijon-style mustard
- 1 tablespoon olive oil
- Sea salt and ground black pepper, to taste
- 1 teaspoon Italian seasoning mix
- 1 cup turkey stock
- ½ teaspoon xanthan gum
- 4 tablespoons tomato ketchup
- 4 tablespoons mayonnaise
- 4 pickles, sliced

Directions:
1. Rub the turkey tenderloins with the mustard and olive oil. Season with salt, black pepper, and Italian seasoning mix.
2. Cook the turkey tenderloins at 350ºF for 30 minutes, flipping them over halfway through. Let them rest for 5 to 7 minutes before slicing.
3. For the gravy, in a saucepan, place the drippings from the roasted turkey. Add in turkey stock and bring to a boil.
4. Stir in xanthan gum and whisk to combine. Let it simmer another 5 to 10 minutes until starting to thicken. Gravy will thicken more as it cools.
5. Serve turkey tenderloins with gravy, tomato ketchup, mayonnaise, and pickles. Serve and enjoy!

Nutrition:
- (per serving) calories 276 | fat 16 | protein 3 | total carbs 15 | fiber 13

Sesame Turkey Balls In Lettuce Cups

Servings:6 | Cooking Time: 15 Minutes

Ingredients:
- MEATBALLS:
- 2 pounds ground turkey
- 2 large eggs, beaten
- ¾ cup finely chopped button mushrooms
- ¼ cup finely chopped green onions, plus more for garnish if desired
- 2 tablespoons Swerve confectioners'-style sweetener or equivalent amount of liquid or powdered sweetener (see here)
- 2 teaspoons peeled and grated fresh ginger
- 2 teaspoons toasted sesame oil
- 1½ teaspoons wheat-free tamari, or 2 tablespoons coconut aminos
- 1 clove garlic, smashed to a paste
- SAUCE:
- ½ cup chicken broth
- ⅓ cup Swerve confectioners'-style sweetener or equivalent amount of liquid or powdered sweetener (see here)
- 2 tablespoons toasted sesame oil
- 2 tablespoons tomato sauce
- 2 tablespoons wheat-free tamari, or ½ cup coconut aminos
- 1 tablespoon lime juice
- ¼ teaspoon peeled and grated fresh ginger
- 1 clove garlic, smashed to a paste
- Boston lettuce leaves, for serving
- Sliced red chiles, for garnish (optional)
- Toasted sesame seeds, for garnish (optional)

Directions:

1. Preheat the air fryer to 350°F.
2. Place all the ingredients for the meatballs in a large bowl and, using your hands, mix them together until well combined. Shape the mixture into about twelve 1½-inch meatballs and place them in a pie pan that will fit in the air fryer, leaving space between them.
3. Make the sauce: In a medium-sized bowl, stir together all the sauce ingredients until well combined. Pour the sauce over the meatballs.
4. Place the pan in the air fryer and cook for 15 minutes, or until the internal temperature of the meatballs reaches 165°F, flipping after 6 minutes.
5. To serve, lay several lettuce leaves on a serving plate and place several meatballs on top. Garnish with sliced red chiles, green onions, and/or sesame seeds, if desired.
6. Store leftovers in an airtight container in the refrigerator for up to 4 days or in the freezer for up to a month. Reheat in a preheated 350°F air fryer for 5 minutes, or until warmed through.

Nutrition:
- (per serving) calories 322 | fat 19g | protein 32g | total carbs 2g | fiber 0.3g

Chicken Pesto Parmigiana

Servings:4 | Cooking Time: 23 Minutes

Ingredients:
- 2 large eggs
- 1 tablespoon water
- Fine sea salt and ground black pepper
- 1 cup powdered Parmesan cheese (about 3 ounces) (see here)
- 2 teaspoons Italian seasoning
- 4 (5-ounce) boneless, skinless chicken breasts or thighs, pounded to ¼ inch thick (see Note; see Tip, here)
- 1 cup pesto (here)
- 1 cup shredded mozzarella cheese (about 4 ounces)
- Finely chopped fresh basil, for garnish (optional)
- Grape tomatoes, halved, for serving (optional)

Directions:
1. Spray the air fryer basket with avocado oil. Preheat the air fryer to 400°F.
2. Crack the eggs into a shallow baking dish, add the water and a pinch each of salt and pepper, and whisk to combine. In another shallow baking dish, stir together the Parmesan and Italian seasoning until well combined.
3. Season the chicken breasts well on both sides with salt and pepper. Dip one chicken breast in the eggs and let any excess drip off, then dredge both sides of the breast in the Parmesan mixture. Spray the breast with avocado oil and place it in the air fryer basket. Repeat with the remaining 3 chicken breasts.
4. Cook the chicken in the air fryer for 20 minutes, or until the internal temperature reaches 165°F and the breading is golden brown, flipping halfway through.
5. Dollop each chicken breast with ¼ cup of the pesto and top with the mozzarella. Return the breasts to the air fryer and cook for 3 minutes, or until the cheese is melted. Garnish with basil and serve with halved grape tomatoes on the side, if desired.
6. Store leftovers in an airtight container in the refrigerator for up to 4 days. Reheat in a preheated 400°F air fryer for 5 minutes, or until warmed through.

Nutrition:
- (per serving, with breasts) calories 558 | fat 43g | protein 40g | total carbs 4g | fiber 1g

Chicken Croquettes With Creole Sauce

Servings: 4 | Cooking Time: 10 Minutes

Ingredients:
- 2 cups shredded cooked chicken
- ½ cup shredded Cheddar cheese
- 2 eggs
- ¼ cup finely chopped onion
- ¼ cup almond meal
- 1 tablespoon poultry seasoning
- Olive oil
- Creole Sauce:
- ¼ cup mayonnaise
- ¼ cup sour cream
- 1½ teaspoons Dijon mustard
- 1½ teaspoons fresh lemon juice
- ½ teaspoon garlic powder
- ½ teaspoon Creole seasoning

Directions:
1. In a large bowl, combine the chicken, Cheddar, eggs, onion, almond meal, and poultry seasoning. Stir gently until thoroughly combined. Cover and refrigerate for 30 minutes.
2. Meanwhile, to make the Creole sauce: In a small bowl, whisk together the mayonnaise, sour cream, Dijon mustard, lemon juice, garlic powder, and Creole seasoning until thoroughly combined. Cover and refrigerate until ready to serve.
3. Preheat the air fryer to 400°F (205°C). Divide the chicken mixture into 8 portions and shape into patties.
4. Working in batches if necessary, arrange the patties in a single layer in the air fryer basket and coat both sides lightly with olive oil. Pausing halfway through the cooking time to flip the patties, air fry for 10 minutes, or until lightly browned and the cheese is melted. Serve with the Creole sauce.

Nutrition:
- (per serving) calories 380 | fat 28 | protein 29 | total carbs 4 | fiber 4

Lemon-crusted Turkey

Servings: 4 | Cooking Time: 58 Minutes

Ingredients:
- 2 tablespoons olive oil
- 2 pounds (907 g) turkey breasts, bone-in skin-on
- Coarse sea salt and ground black pepper, to taste
- 1 teaspoon fresh basil leaves, chopped
- 2 tablespoons lemon zest, grated

Directions:
1. Rub olive oil on all sides of the turkey breasts, sprinkle with salt, pepper, basil, and lemon zest.
2. Place the turkey breasts skin side up on a parchment-lined cooking basket.
3. Cook in the preheated Air Fryer at 330ºF (166ºC) for 30 minutes. Now, turn them over and cook for an additional 28 minutes.
4. Serve with lemon wedges, if desired. Bon appétit!

Nutrition:
- (per serving) calories 416 | fat 22 | protein 49 | total carbs 0 | fiber 0

Roasted Chicken Leg With Leeks

Servings: 6 | Cooking Time: 18 Minutes

Ingredients:
- 2 leeks, sliced
- 2 large-sized tomatoes, chopped
- 3 cloves garlic, minced
- ½ teaspoon dried oregano
- 6 chicken legs, boneless and skinless
- ½ teaspoon smoked cayenne pepper
- 2 tablespoons olive oil
- A freshly ground nutmeg

Directions:
1. In a mixing dish, thoroughly combine all ingredients, minus the leeks. Place in the refrigerator and let it marinate overnight.
2. Lay the leeks onto the bottom of an Air Fryer cooking basket. Top with the chicken legs.
3. Roast chicken legs at 375ºF (190ºC) for 18 minutes, turning halfway through. Serve with hoisin sauce.

Nutrition:
- (per serving) calories 390 | fat 15 | protein 12 | total carbs 7 | fiber 6

Ham Chicken With Cheese

Servings: 4 | Cooking Time: 25 Minutes

Ingredients:
- ¼ cup unsalted butter, softened
- 4 ounces (113 g) cream cheese, softened
- 1½ teaspoons Dijon mustard
- 2 tablespoons white wine vinegar
- ¼ cup water
- 2 cups shredded cooked chicken
- ¼ pound (113 g) ham, chopped
- 4 ounces (113 g) sliced Swiss or Provolone cheese

Directions:
1. Preheat the air fryer to 380°F (193ºC). Lightly coat a 6-cup casserole dish that will fit in the air fryer, such as an 8-inch round pan, with olive oil and set aside.
2. In a large bowl and using an electric mixer, combine the butter, cream cheese, Dijon mustard, and vinegar. With the motor running on low speed, slowly add the water and beat until smooth. Set aside.
3. Arrange an even layer of chicken in the bottom of the prepared pan, followed by the ham. Spread the butter and cream cheese mixture on top of the ham, followed by the cheese slices on the top layer. Air fry for 20 to 25 minutes until warmed through and the cheese has browned.

Nutrition:
- (per serving) calories 480 | fat 36 | protein 34 | total carbs 4 | fiber 4

Chicken Strips With Satay Sauce

Servings:4 | Cooking Time: 10 Minutes

Ingredients:
- 4 (6-ounce) boneless, skinless chicken breasts, sliced into 16 (1-inch) strips
- 1 teaspoon fine sea salt
- 1 teaspoon paprika
- SAUCE:
- ¼ cup creamy almond butter (or sunflower seed butter for nut-free)
- 2 tablespoons chicken broth
- 1½ tablespoons coconut vinegar or unseasoned rice vinegar
- 1 clove garlic, minced
- 1 teaspoon peeled and minced fresh ginger
- ½ teaspoon hot sauce
- ⅛ teaspoon stevia glycerite, or 2 to 3 drops liquid stevia
- FOR GARNISH/SERVING (OPTIONAL):
- ¼ cup chopped cilantro leaves
- Red pepper flakes
- Sea salt flakes
- Thinly sliced red, orange, and yellow bell peppers
- special equipment:
- 16 wooden or bamboo skewers, soaked in water for 15 minutes

Directions:
1. Spray the air fryer basket with avocado oil. Preheat the air fryer to 400°F.
2. Thread the chicken strips onto the skewers. Season on all sides with the salt and paprika. Place the chicken skewers in the air fryer basket and cook for 5 minutes, flip, and cook for another 5 minutes, until the chicken is cooked through and the internal temperature reaches 165°F.
3. While the chicken skewers cook, make the sauce: In a medium-sized bowl, stir together all the sauce ingredients until well combined. Taste and adjust the sweetness and heat to your liking.
4. Garnish the chicken with cilantro, red pepper flakes, and salt flakes, if desired, and serve with sliced bell peppers, if desired. Serve the sauce on the side.
5. Store leftovers in an airtight container in the fridge for up to 4 days or in the freezer for up to a month. Reheat in a preheated 350°F air fryer for 3 minutes per side, or until heated through.

Nutrition:
- (per serving) calories 359 | fat 16g | protein 49g | total carbs 2g | fiber 1g

Chicken Thighs With Montreal Chicken Seasoning

Servings: 4 | Cooking Time: 25 Minutes

Ingredients:
- 1 tablespoon olive oil
- Juice of ½ lime
- 1 tablespoon coconut aminos
- 1½ teaspoons Montreal chicken seasoning
- 8 bone-in chicken thighs, skin on
- 2 tablespoons chopped fresh cilantro

Directions:
1. In a gallon-size resealable bag, combine the olive oil, lime juice, coconut aminos, and chicken seasoning. Add the chicken thighs, seal the bag, and massage the bag to ensure the chicken is thoroughly coated. Refrigerate for at least 2 hours, preferably overnight.

2. Preheat the air fryer to 400°F (205°C).
3. Remove the chicken from the marinade (discard the marinade) and arrange in a single layer in the air fryer basket. Pausing halfway through the cooking time to flip the chicken, air fry for 20 to 25 minutes, until a thermometer inserted into the thickest part registers 165°F (74ºC).
4. Transfer the chicken to a serving platter and top with the cilantro before serving.

Nutrition:
- (per serving) calories 335 | fat 22 | protein 31 | total carbs 0 | fiber 0

Chicken Cordon Bleu Meatballs

Servings:4 | Cooking Time: 15 Minutes

Ingredients:
- MEATBALLS:
- ½ pound ground chicken
- ½ pound ham, diced
- ½ cup finely grated Swiss cheese (about 2 ounces)
- ¼ cup chopped onions
- 3 cloves garlic, minced
- 1½ teaspoons fine sea salt
- 1 teaspoon ground black pepper, plus more for garnish if desired
- 1 large egg, beaten
- DIJON SAUCE:
- ¼ cup chicken broth, hot
- 3 tablespoons Dijon mustard
- 2 tablespoons lemon juice
- ¾ teaspoon fine sea salt
- ¼ teaspoon ground black pepper
- Chopped fresh thyme leaves, for garnish (optional)

Directions:
1. Spray the air fryer basket with avocado oil. Preheat the air fryer to 390°F.
2. In a large bowl, mix all the ingredients for the meatballs with your hands until well combined. Shape the meat mixture into about twelve 1½-inch balls. Place the meatballs in the air fryer basket, leaving space between them, and cook for 15 minutes, or until cooked through and the internal temperature reaches 165°F.
3. While the meatballs cook, make the sauce: In a small mixing bowl, stir together all the sauce ingredients until well combined.
4. Pour the sauce into a serving dish and place the meatballs on top. Garnish with ground black pepper and fresh thyme leaves, if desired.
5. Store leftover meatballs in an airtight container in the refrigerator for up to 5 days or in the freezer for up to a month. Reheat in a preheated 350°F air fryer for 4 minutes, or until heated through.

Nutrition:
- (per serving) calories 288 | fat 15g | protein 31g | total carbs 5g | fiber 0.5g

Cheesy And Spicy Turkey Meatloaf

Servings: 6 | Cooking Time: 50 Minutes

Ingredients:
- 2 pounds (907 g) turkey breasts, ground
- ½ pound (227 g) Cheddar cheese, cubed
- ½ cup turkey stock
- ⅓ teaspoon hot paprika
- 3 eggs, lightly beaten

- 1½ tablespoon olive oil
- 2 cloves garlic, pressed
- 1½ teaspoons dried rosemary
- ½ cup yellow onion, chopped
- ⅓ cup ground almonds
- ½ teaspoon black pepper
- A few dashes of Tabasco sauce
- 1 teaspoon seasoned salt
- ½ cup tomato sauce

Directions:
1. Heat the olive oil in a medium-sized saucepan that is placed over a moderate flame, now, sauté the onions, garlic, and dried rosemary until just tender, or for about 3 to 4 minutes.
2. In the meantime, set the Air Fryer to cook at 385ºF.
3. Place all the ingredients, minus the tomato sauce, in a mixing dish together with the sautéed mixture, thoroughly mix to combine.
4. Shape into meatloaf and top with the tomato sauce. Air-fry for 47 minutes. Bon appétit!

Nutrition:
- (per serving) calories 455 | fat 26 | protein 46 | total carbs 8 | fiber 7

Almond Chicken With Marinara Sauce

Servings: 4 | Cooking Time: 20 Minutes

Ingredients:
- 2 large skinless chicken breasts (about 1¼ pounds / 567g)
- Salt and freshly ground black pepper
- ½ cup almond meal
- ½ cup grated Parmesan cheese
- 2 teaspoons Italian seasoning
- 1 egg, lightly beaten
- 1 tablespoon olive oil
- 1 cup no-sugar-added marinara sauce
- 4 slices Mozzarella cheese or ½ cup shredded Mozzarella

Directions:
1. Preheat the air fryer to 360°F (182ºC).
2. Slice the chicken breasts in half horizontally to create 4 thinner chicken breasts. Working with one piece at a time, place the chicken between two pieces of parchment paper and pound with a meat mallet or rolling pin to flatten to an even thickness. Season both sides with salt and freshly ground black pepper.
3. In a large shallow bowl, combine the almond meal, Parmesan, and Italian seasoning, stir until thoroughly combined. Place the egg in another large shallow bowl.
4. Dip the chicken in the egg, followed by the almond meal mixture, pressing the mixture firmly into the chicken to create an even coating.
5. Working in batches if necessary, arrange the chicken breasts in a single layer in the air fryer basket and coat both sides lightly with olive oil. Pausing halfway through the cooking time to flip the chicken, air fry for 15 minutes, or until a thermometer inserted into the thickest part registers 165°F (74ºC).
6. Spoon the marinara sauce over each piece of chicken and top with the Mozzarella cheese. Air fry for an additional 3 to 5 minutes until the cheese is melted.

Nutrition:
- (per serving) calories 460 | fat 16 | protein 65 | total carbs 11 | fiber 9

Parmesan Turkey Meatball With Pepper

Servings: 4 | Cooking Time: 10 Minutes

Ingredients:
- 1 red bell pepper, seeded and coarsely chopped
- 2 cloves garlic, coarsely chopped
- ¼ cup chopped fresh parsley
- 1½ pounds (680g) 85% lean ground turkey
- 1 egg, lightly beaten
- ½ cup grated Parmesan cheese
- 1 teaspoon salt
- ½ teaspoon freshly ground black pepper

Directions:
1. Preheat the air fryer to 400°F (205ºC).
2. In a food processor fitted with a metal blade, combine the bell pepper, garlic, and parsley. Pulse until finely chopped. Transfer the vegetables to a large mixing bowl.
3. Add the turkey, egg, Parmesan, salt, and black pepper. Mix gently until thoroughly combined. Shape the mixture into 1¼-inch meatballs.
4. Working in batches if necessary, arrange the meatballs in a single layer in the air fryer basket, coat lightly with olive oil spray. Pausing halfway through the cooking time to shake the basket, air fry for 7 to 10 minutes, until lightly browned and a thermometer inserted into the center of a meatball registers 165°F (74ºC).

Nutrition:
- (per serving) calories 410 | fat 27 | protein 38 | total carbs 4 | fiber 3

Chicken With Lettuce

Servings: 4 | Cooking Time: 14 Minutes

Ingredients:
- 1 pound (454 g) chicken breast tenders, chopped into bite-size pieces
- ½ onion, thinly sliced
- ½ red bell pepper, seeded and thinly sliced
- ½ green bell pepper, seeded and thinly sliced
- 1 tablespoon olive oil
- 1 tablespoon fajita seasoning
- 1 teaspoon kosher salt
- Juice of ½ lime
- 8 large lettuce leaves
- 1 cup prepared guacamole

Directions:
1. Preheat the air fryer to 400°F (205ºC).
2. In a large bowl, combine the chicken, onion, and peppers. Drizzle with the olive oil and toss until thoroughly coated. Add the fajita seasoning and salt and toss again.
3. Working in batches if necessary, arrange the chicken and vegetables in a single layer in the air fryer basket. Pausing halfway through the cooking time to shake the basket, air fry for 14 minutes, or until the vegetables are tender and a thermometer inserted into the thickest piece of chicken registers 165°F (74ºC).
4. Transfer the mixture to a serving platter and drizzle with the fresh lime juice. Serve with the lettuce leaves and top with the guacamole.

Nutrition:
- (per serving) calories 330 | fat 22 | protein 25 | total carbs 8 | fiber 3

Chicken Legs With Turnip

Servings: 3 | Cooking Time: 25 Minutes

Ingredients:
- 1 pound (454 g) chicken legs
- 1 teaspoon Himalayan salt
- 1 teaspoon paprika
- ½ teaspoon ground black pepper
- 1 teaspoon butter, melted
- 1 turnip, trimmed and sliced

Directions:
1. Spritz the sides and bottom of the cooking basket with a non-stick cooking spray.
2. Season the chicken legs with salt, paprika, and ground black pepper.
3. Cook at 370ºF (188ºC) for 10 minutes. Increase the temperature to 380ºF (193ºC).
4. Drizzle turnip slices with melted butter and transfer them to the cooking basket with the chicken. Cook the turnips and chicken for 15 minutes or more, flipping them halfway through the cooking time.
5. As for the chicken, an instant-read thermometer should read at least 165ºF (74ºC).
6. Serve and enjoy!

Nutrition:
- (per serving) calories 207 | fat 7 | protein 29 | total carbs 3 | fiber 2

Chicken Kebabs

Servings: 5 | Cooking Time: 20 Minutes

Ingredients:
- ¼ diced red onion
- ½ diced zucchini
- ½ diced red pepper
- ½ diced green pepper
- ½ diced yellow pepper
- 1 teaspoon BBQ seasoning
- 1 tablespoon chicken seasoning
- 2 tablespoons coconut aminos
- 5 grape tomatoes
- 16 ounces (454 g) 1-inch cubed chicken breasts
- Salt & pepper, to taste
- Nonstick cooking oil spray

Directions:
1. Pat dry the chicken breasts then combine the BBQ seasoning, chicken seasoning, salt, pepper and coconut aminos together.
2. Generously coat the chicken cubes with the mixture then set aside to marinate for about an hour.
3. Sew the marinated chicken cubes onto the wooden skewers.
4. Alternatively layer the chicken cubes with onions, zucchini, pepper and top each skewer with a grape tomato.
5. Spray the layered skewers with the cooking oil then line the fryer basket with parchment paper and fit in a small grill rack.
6. Place the skewers on the grill rack then air fry at 350°F (180ºC) for 10 minutes.
7. Flip the skewers over and fry for an additional 10 minutes.
8. Allow the chicken to cool for a bit then serve and enjoy with any sauce of choice.

Nutrition:
- (per serving) calories 255 | fat 12 | protein 25 | total carbs 6 | fiber 5

Turkey Thighs With Lush Vegetables

Servings: 4 | Cooking Time: 45 Minutes

Ingredients:
- 1 red onion, cut into wedges
- 1 carrot, trimmed and sliced
- 1 celery stalk, trimmed and sliced
- 1 cup Brussels sprouts, trimmed and halved
- 1 cup roasted vegetable broth
- 1 tablespoon apple cider vinegar
- 4 turkey thighs
- ½ teaspoon mixed peppercorns, freshly cracked
- 1 teaspoon fine sea salt
- 1 teaspoon cayenne pepper
- 1 teaspoon onion powder
- ½ teaspoon garlic powder
- ⅓ teaspoon mustard seeds

Directions:
1. Take a baking dish that easily fits into your device, place the vegetables on the bottom of the baking dish and pour in roasted vegetable broth.
2. In a large-sized mixing dish, place the remaining ingredients, let them marinate for about 30 minutes. Lay them on the top of the vegetables.
3. Roast at 330ºF for 40 to 45 minutes. Bon appétit!

Nutrition:
- (per serving) calories 393 | fat 21 | protein 16 | total carbs 36 | fiber 35

Chicken Sausage With Nestled Eggs And Pepper

Servings: 6 | Cooking Time: 17 Minutes

Ingredients:
- 6 eggs
- 2 bell peppers, seeded and sliced
- 1 teaspoon dried oregano
- 1 teaspoon hot paprika
- 1 teaspoon freshly cracked black pepper
- 6 chicken sausages
- 1 teaspoon sea salt
- 1½ shallots, cut into wedges
- 1 teaspoon dried basil

Directions:
1. Take four ramekins and divide chicken sausages, shallot, and bell pepper among those ramekins. Cook at 315ºF for about 12 minutes.
2. Now, crack an egg into each ramekin. Sprinkle the eggs with hot paprika, basil, oregano, salt, and cracked black pepper. Cook for 5 more minutes at 405ºF.
3. Bon appétit!

Nutrition:
- (per serving) calories 211 | fat 15 | protein 15 | total carbs 26 | fiber 25

Turkey With Mustard Sauce

Servings: 4 | Cooking Time: 18 Minutes

Ingredients:
- ½ teaspoon cumin powder
- 2 pounds (907 g) turkey breasts, quartered
- 2 cloves garlic, smashed
- ½ teaspoon hot paprika
- 2 tablespoons melted butter
- 1 teaspoon fine sea salt
- Freshly cracked mixed peppercorns, to taste
- Fresh juice of 1 lemon
- For the Mustard Sauce:
- 1½ tablespoons mayonnaise
- 1½ cups Greek yogurt
- ½ tablespoon yellow mustard

Directions:
1. Grab a medium-sized mixing dish and combine together the garlic and melted butter, rub this mixture evenly over the surface of the turkey.
2. Add the cumin powder, followed by paprika, salt, peppercorns, and lemon juice. Place in your refrigerator for at least 55 minutes.
3. Set your Air Fryer to cook at 375°F (190°C). Roast the turkey for 18 minutes, turning halfway through, roast in batches.
4. In the meantime, make the mustard sauce by mixing all ingredients for the sauce. Serve warm roasted turkey with the mustard sauce. Bon appétit!

Nutrition:
- (per serving) calories 471 | fat 23 | protein 16 | total carbs 34 | fiber 33

Mayo-dijon Chicken

Servings: 6 | Cooking Time: 13 To 16 Minutes

Ingredients:
- ½ cup sugar-free mayonnaise
- 1 tablespoon Dijon mustard
- 1 tablespoon freshly squeezed lemon juice (optional)
- 1 tablespoon coconut aminos
- 1 teaspoon Italian seasoning
- 1 teaspoon sea salt
- ½ teaspoon freshly ground black pepper
- ¼ teaspoon cayenne pepper
- 1½ pounds (680g) boneless, skinless chicken breasts or thighs

Directions:
1. In a small bowl, combine the mayonnaise, mustard, lemon juice (if using), coconut aminos, Italian seasoning, salt, black pepper, and cayenne pepper.
2. Place the chicken in a shallow dish or large zip-top plastic bag. Add the marinade, making sure all the pieces are coated. Cover and refrigerate for at least 30 minutes or up to 4 hours.
3. Set the air fryer to 400°F (205°C). Arrange the chicken in a single layer in the air fryer basket, working in batches if necessary. Cook for 7 minutes. Flip the chicken and continue cooking for 6 to 9 minutes or more, until an instant-read thermometer reads 160°F (71°C).

Nutrition:
- (per serving) calories 236 | fat 17 | protein 23 | total carbs 2 | fiber 1

Chapter 7 Side Dishes Recipes

Chapter 7 Side Dishes Recipes

Kohlrabi Fritters

Servings: 5 | Cooking Time: 7 Minutes

Ingredients:
- 8 oz. kohlrabi
- 1 egg
- 1 tablespoon almond flour
- ½ teaspoon salt
- 1 teaspoon olive oil
- 1 teaspoon ground black pepper
- 1 tablespoon dried parsley
- ¼ teaspoon chili pepper

Directions:
1. Peel the kohlrabi and grate it.
2. Combine the grated kohlrabi with salt, ground black pepper, dried parsley, and chili pepper.
3. Crack the egg into the mixture and whisk it.
4. Make medium fritters from the mixture.
5. Preheat the air fryer to 380 F.
6. Grease the air fryer basket tray with olive oil and place the fritters inside.
7. Cook the fritters for 4 minutes.
8. Turn the fritters and cook for 3 minutes more.
9. Allow to cool slightly before serving.

Nutrition:
- (per serving) calories 66 | fat 4.7 | protein 3.2 | total carbs 4.4 | fiber 2.4

Cabbage Steaks

Servings: 4 | Cooking Time: 5 Minutes

Ingredients:
- 9 oz. white cabbage, sliced
- 1 teaspoon salt
- 1 teaspoon butter
- 1 teaspoon olive oil
- 1 teaspoon paprika
- ½ teaspoon ground black pepper

Directions:
1. Combine the olive oil and paprika together.
2. Melt the butter and add it to the olive oil mixture.
3. Add the ground black pepper and combine.
4. Rub the sliced white cabbage with the spice mixture.
5. Sprinkle the cabbage slices with the salt.
6. Preheat the air fryer to 400 F.
7. Put the cabbage slices in the air fryer rack and cook the dish for 3 minutes.
8. Turn the cabbage over.
9. Serve.

Nutrition:
- (per serving) calories 37 | fat 2.3 | protein 0.9 | total carbs 4.2 | fiber 1.9

Cauliflower Rice With Parmesan And Pesto

Servings: 7 | Cooking Time: 13 Minutes

Ingredients:
- 1-pound cauliflower head
- 2 tablespoon pesto sauce
- 6 oz. Parmesan, shredded
- 1 teaspoon salt
- 1 teaspoon olive oil
- ½ cup heavy cream
- 1 tablespoon butter
- 1 tablespoon dried dill
- 1 teaspoon dried parsley
- 1 teaspoon chili flakes

Directions:
1. Wash the cauliflower head and chop roughly.
2. Place the chopped cauliflower in a blender and blend well until you get rice.
3. Transfer the cauliflower to the air fryer and coat it with salt, olive oil, butter, dried dill, dried parsley, and chili flakes.
4. Mix the rice carefully with a wooden spatula.
5. Add the heavy cream and cook the dish at 370 F for 10 minutes.
6. Add shredded Parmesan and pesto sauce.
7. Mix well and cook for 3 minutes more at the same temperature.
8. Serve immediately.

Nutrition:
- (per serving) calories 165 | fat 12.6 | protein 9.8 | total carbs 5.1 | fiber 1.8

Zucchini Salad

Servings: 4 | Cooking Time: 7 Minutes

Ingredients:
- 2 medium zucchini, thinly sliced
- 5 tablespoons olive oil, divided
- ¼ cup chopped fresh parsley
- 2 tablespoons chopped fresh mint
- Zest and juice of ½ lemon
- 1 clove garlic, minced
- ¼ cup crumbled feta cheese
- Freshly ground black pepper

Directions:
1. Preheat the air fryer to 400°F (205ºC).
2. In a large bowl, toss the zucchini slices with 1 tablespoon of the olive oil.
3. Working in batches if necessary, arrange the zucchini slices in an even layer in the air fryer basket. Pausing halfway through the cooking time to shake the basket, air fry for 5 to 7 minutes until soft and lightly browned on each side.
4. Meanwhile, in a small bowl, combine the remaining 4 tablespoons olive oil, parsley, mint, lemon zest, lemon juice, and garlic.
5. Arrange the zucchini on a plate and drizzle with the dressing. Sprinkle the feta and black pepper on top. Serve warm or at room temperature.

Nutrition:
- (per serving) calories 195 | fat 19 | protein 3 | total carbs 5 | fiber 4

Sriracha Broccoli

Servings: 5 | Cooking Time: 6 Minutes

Ingredients:
- 1 teaspoon sriracha
- 1 tablespoon olive oil
- 1 teaspoon flax seeds
- 1 teaspoon ground white pepper
- 1 teaspoon kosher salt
- 1-pound broccoli
- 4 tablespoons chicken stock

Directions:
1. Wash the broccoli and separate into florets.
2. Then combine the chicken stock, ground white pepper, flax seeds, and sriracha.
3. Add the olive oil and whisk the mixture.
4. Preheat the air fryer to 400 F.
5. Put the broccoli florets in the air fryer basket rack and coat with the sriracha mixture,
6. Cook the broccoli for 6 minutes.
7. Shake the broccoli gently and transfer a serving plate.

Nutrition:
- (per serving) calories 61 | fat 3.3 | protein 2.7 | total carbs 6.7 | fiber 2.6

Air Fryer Bok Choy

Servings: 6 | Cooking Time: 10 Minutes

Ingredients:
- 4 oz chive stems
- 1-pound bok choy
- 1 teaspoon minced garlic
- 1 tablespoon mustard
- 1 teaspoon ground ginger
- 2 tablespoon apple cider vinegar
- 2 teaspoons olive oil
- 1 tablespoon butter

Directions:
1. Wash the bok choy and chop it.
2. Place the chopped bok choy in the air fryer basket tray.
3. Coat the chopped bok choy with minced garlic, sliced chives, mustard, ground ginger, apple cider vinegar, olive oil, and butter.
4. Preheat the air fryer to 360 F.
5. Cook the bok choy for 10 minutes.
6. Stir gently before serving.

Nutrition:
- (per serving) calories 59 | fat 4.2 | protein 1.9 | total carbs 4.4 | fiber 1.5

Butter Mashed Cauliflower

Servings: 5 | Cooking Time: 13 Minutes

Ingredients:
- 2 tablespoon butter
- 4 tablespoons heavy cream
- 1-pound cauliflower
- 1 teaspoon garlic powder
- ½ teaspoon salt
- 1 teaspoon ground chili pepper
- 1 teaspoon olive oil

Directions:
1. Preheat the air fryer to 360 F.
2. Chop the cauliflower roughly and place it in the air fryer basket tray.
3. Coat the cauliflower with garlic powder, salt, ground chili pepper, and olive oil.
4. Cook the cauliflower for 10 minutes.
5. Stir the cauliflower gently, add the heavy cream, and cook it for 3 minutes more at 390 F.
6. Transfer the cooked cauliflower to a blender.
7. Blend well until you get a soft and smooth texture.
8. Add the butter and stir carefully.
9. Serve the mashed cauliflower hot or warm.

Nutrition:
- (per serving) calories 115 | fat 10.1 | protein 2.2 | total carbs 5.6 | fiber 2.3

Zucchini Boats With Cheese

Servings: 4 | Cooking Time: 12 Minutes

Ingredients:
- 1 medium zucchini
- 3 oz bok choy
- 1 garlic clove, sliced
- 6 oz. Cheddar cheese
- 4 tablespoons heavy cream
- 1 tablespoon coconut flour
- ¼ teaspoon salt
- ½ teaspoon ground black pepper
- 1 teaspoon paprika
- 1 teaspoon olive oil

Directions:
1. Cut the zucchini into 2 halves crosswise.
2. Remove the flesh from the zucchini halves.
3. Blend the zucchini flesh and combine it with the sliced garlic clove.
4. Sprinkle the zucchini flesh with salt, ground black pepper, and paprika.
5. Mix well.
6. Combine the heavy cream and coconut flour then whisk.
7. Fill the zucchini halves with the zucchini flesh mixture.
8. Grind the bok choy and coat it with the heavy cream mixture.
9. Shred the Cheddar cheese.
10. Add the bok choy mixture to the zucchini halves.
11. Drizzle the zucchini with olive oil.
12. Preheat the air fryer to 400 F.
13. Put the zucchini halves in the air fryer and cook them for 10 minutes.
14. Sprinkle the zucchini boats with the shredded cheese and cook for 2 minutes.
15. Transfer the cooked zucchini boats to a plate.
16. Cut every zucchini half into 2 pieces.

Nutrition:
- (per serving) calories 255 | fat 21.2 | protein 12.2 | total carbs 5 | fiber 1.8

Cauliflower Rice Balls

Servings: 4 | Cooking Time: 8 Minutes

Ingredients:
- 1 (10-ounce / 283-g) steamer bag cauliflower rice, cooked according to package instructions
- ½ cup shredded Mozzarella cheese
- 1 large egg
- 2 ounces (57 g) plain pork rinds, finely crushed
- ¼ teaspoon salt
- ½ teaspoon Italian seasoning

Directions:
1. Place cauliflower into a large bowl and mix with Mozzarella.
2. Whisk egg in a separate medium bowl. Place pork rinds into another large bowl with salt and Italian seasoning.
3. Separate cauliflower mixture into four equal sections and form each into a ball. Carefully dip a ball into whisked egg, then roll in pork rinds. Repeat with remaining balls.
4. Place cauliflower balls into ungreased air fryer basket. Adjust the temperature to 400°F (205°C) and set the timer for 8 minutes. Rice balls will be golden when done.
5. Use a spatula to carefully move cauliflower balls to a large dish for serving. Serve warm.

Nutrition:
- (per serving) calories 158 | fat 9 | protein 15 | total carbs 4 | fiber 2

Spiced Asparagus

Servings: 6 | Cooking Time: 6 Minutes

Ingredients:
- 1-pound asparagus
- 1 teaspoon salt
- 1 teaspoon chili flakes
- ½ teaspoon ground white pepper
- 1 tablespoon sesame oil
- 1 tablespoon flax seeds

Directions:
1. Combine the sesame oil with the salt, chili flakes, and ground white pepper.
2. Preheat the air fryer to 400 F.
3. Place the asparagus in the air fryer basket tray and coat it with the sesame oil-spice mixture.
4. Cook the asparagus for 6 minutes.

Nutrition:
- (per serving) calories 42 | fat 2.7 | protein 1.9 | total carbs 3.4 | fiber 2

Butter Sliced Mushrooms With Chives

Servings: 2 | Cooking Time: 10 Minutes

Ingredients:
- 1 cup white mushrooms
- 4 oz chive stems
- 1 tablespoon butter
- 1 teaspoon olive oil
- 1 teaspoon dried rosemary
- 1/3 teaspoon salt
- ¼ teaspoon ground nutmeg

Directions:
1. Preheat the air fryer to 400 F.
2. Pour the olive oil and butter in the air fryer basket tray.

3. Add dried rosemary, salt, and ground nutmeg.
4. Stir gently.
5. Dice the chives.
6. Add the diced chives in the air fryer basket tray.
7. Cook for 5 minutes.
8. Meanwhile, chop the white mushrooms.
9. Add the mushrooms.
10. Stir the mixture and cook it for a further 5 minutes at the same temperature.
11. Stir then serve.

Nutrition:
- (per serving) calories 104 | fat 8.4 | protein 1.8 | total carbs 6.8 | fiber 1.9

Zucchini Gratin

Servings: 6 | Cooking Time: 13 Minutes

Ingredients:
- 2 zucchinis
- 1 tablespoon dried parsley
- 1 tablespoon coconut flour
- 5 oz. Parmesan cheese, shredded
- 1 teaspoon butter
- 1 teaspoon ground black pepper

Directions:
1. Combine the dried parsley, coconut flour, ground black pepper, and shredded cheese in a large bowl.
2. Shake well to combine.
3. Wash the zucchini and slice them.
4. Cut the zucchini to make squares.
5. Grease the air fryer basket tray with butter and place the zucchini squares inside.
6. Preheat the air fryer to 400 F.
7. Coat the zucchini squares with the dried parsley mixture.
8. Cook the zucchini gratin for 13 minutes or until golden brown.

Nutrition:
- (per serving) calories 98 | fat 6 | protein 8.6 | total carbs 4.2 | fiber 1.3

Curried Cauliflower

Servings: 4 | Cooking Time: 20 Minutes

Ingredients:
- ¼ cup olive oil
- 2 teaspoons curry powder
- ½ teaspoon salt
- ¼ teaspoon freshly ground black pepper
- 1 head cauliflower, cut into bite-size florets
- ½ red onion, sliced
- 2 tablespoons freshly chopped parsley, for garnish (optional)

Directions:
1. Preheat the air fryer to 400°F (205°C).
2. In a large bowl, combine the olive oil, curry powder, salt, and pepper. Add the cauliflower and onion. Toss gently until the vegetables are completely coated with the oil mixture. Transfer the vegetables to the basket of the air fryer.
3. Pausing about halfway through the cooking time to shake the basket, air fry for 20 minutes until the cauliflower is tender and beginning to brown. Top with the parsley, if desired, before serving.

Nutrition:
- (per serving) calories 165 | fat 14 | protein 3 | total carbs 10 | fiber 6

Winter Squash Spaghetti

Servings: 8 | Cooking Time: 10 Minutes

Ingredients:
- 4 tablespoons heavy cream
- 1 cup chicken stock
- 1-pound winter spaghetti squash
- 1 teaspoon salt
- 1 teaspoon ground black pepper
- 1 teaspoon butter

Directions:
1. Peel the winter squash and grate it to get spaghetti.
2. Preheat the air fryer to 400 F.
3. Put the squash spaghetti in the air fryer basket tray.
4. Coat it with the chicken stock and salt.
5. Add the ground black pepper and cook for 10 minutes.
6. Strain the excess liquid from the squash.
7. Add the butter and heavy cream and stir it.
8. Serve the side dish immediately.

Nutrition:
- (per serving) calories 55 | fat 3.4 | protein 0.7 | total carbs 6.4 | fiber 0.9

Shirataki Noodles

Servings: 4 | Cooking Time: 3 Minutes

Ingredients:
- 2 cups water
- 1 teaspoon salt
- 1 tablespoon Italian seasoning
- 8 oz shirataki noodles

Directions:
1. Preheat the air fryer to 365 F.
2. Pour the water in the air fryer basket tray and preheat for 3 minutes.
3. Add the shirataki noodles, salt, and Italian seasoning.
4. Cook the shirataki noodles for 1 minute at the same temperature.
5. Strain the noodles and cook them for 2 minutes more at 360 F.
6. Allow to cool for 1-2 minutes.
7. Stir the noodles gently before serving.

Nutrition:
- (per serving) calories 16 | fat 1 | protein 0 | total carbs 1.4 | fiber 0

Eggplant Stew

Servings: 9 | Cooking Time: 13 Minutes

Ingredients:
- 1 eggplant
- 1 zucchini
- 4 oz chive stems
- 1 green pepper
- 2 garlic cloves, peeled
- 1 teaspoon turmeric
- 1 teaspoon paprika
- 1 teaspoon dried dill
- 1 teaspoon dried parsley
- 1 cup chicken stock
- ½ cup heavy cream
- 1 teaspoon kosher salt

Directions:

1. Cut the zucchini and eggplant into cubes.
2. Coat the vegetables with the dried parsley, dried dill, paprika, and turmeric.
3. Chop the garlic cloves.
4. Chop the chives and green pepper.
5. Preheat the air fryer to 390 F.
6. Pour the chicken stock into the air fryer and add the eggplant.
7. Cook the eggplant for 2 minutes.
8. Add the chopped chives and green pepper.
9. Add the chopped garlic cloves and heavy cream.
10. Cook the stew for 11 minutes at the same temperature.
11. Serve hot.

Nutrition:
- (per serving) calories 49 | fat 2.6 | protein 1.2 | total carbs 6.1 | fiber 2.5

Kohlrabi Fries

Servings: 4 | Cooking Time: 30 Minutes

Ingredients:
- 2 pounds (907 g) kohlrabi, peeled and cut into ¼–½-inch fries
- 2 tablespoons olive oil
- Salt and freshly ground black pepper

Directions:
1. Preheat the air fryer to 400°F (205ºC).
2. In a large bowl, combine the kohlrabi and olive oil. Season to taste with salt and black pepper. Toss gently until thoroughly coated.
3. Working in batches if necessary, spread the kohlrabi in a single layer in the air fryer basket. Pausing halfway through the cooking time to shake the basket, air fry for 20 to 30 minutes until the fries are lightly browned and crunchy.

Nutrition:
- (per serving) calories 120 | fat 7 | protein 4 | total carbs 14 | fiber 12

Sesame Broccoli Florets

Servings: 3 | Cooking Time: 6 Minutes

Ingredients:
- 1 pound (454 g) broccoli florets
- 2 tablespoons sesame oil
- ½ teaspoon shallot powder
- ½ teaspoon porcini powder
- 1 teaspoon garlic powder
- Sea salt and ground black pepper, to taste
- ½ teaspoon cumin powder
- ¼ teaspoon paprika
- 2 tablespoons sesame seeds

Directions:
1. Start by preheating the Air Fryer to 400ºF.
2. Blanch the broccoli in salted boiling water until al dente, for about 3 to 4 minutes. Drain well and transfer to the lightly greased Air Fryer basket.
3. Add the sesame oil, shallot powder, porcini powder, garlic powder, salt, black pepper, cumin powder, paprika, and sesame seeds.
4. Cook for 6 minutes, tossing halfway through the cooking time. Bon appétit!

Nutrition:
- (per serving) calories 160 | fat 13.2 | protein 9.7 | total carbs 3.5 | fiber 1.4

Creamed Spinach

Servings: 6 | Cooking Time: 11 Minutes

Ingredients:
- 2 cups spinach
- 1 cup cream
- 2 tablespoon butter
- ¼ cup coconut milk
- 1 oz. walnuts, crushed
- 5 oz. Cheddar cheese, shredded
- 1 teaspoon salt

Directions:
1. Wash the spinach and chop it.
2. Sprinkle the spinach with salt and mix well.
3. Preheat the air fryer to 380 F.
4. Put the spinach in the air fryer basket tray.
5. Add coconut milk, crushed walnuts, butter, and cream.
6. Cook the spinach for 8 minutes.
7. Stir the spinach using a wooden spatula.
8. Add the shredded cheese and cook for 3 minutes.
9. Mix the melted cheese and spinach carefully before serving.

Nutrition:
- (per serving) calories 209 | fat 19.1 | protein 7.9 | total carbs 2.9 | fiber 0.8

Bok Choy With Chili-garlic Sauce

Servings: 4 | Cooking Time: 10 Minutes

Ingredients:
- 2 tablespoons olive oil
- 2 tablespoons coconut aminos
- 2 teaspoons sesame oil
- 2 teaspoons chili-garlic sauce
- 2 cloves garlic, minced
- 1 head (about 1 pound / 454 g) bok choy, sliced lengthwise into quarters
- 2 teaspoons black sesame seeds

Directions:
1. Preheat the air fryer to 400°F (205°C).
2. In a large bowl, combine the olive oil, coconut aminos, sesame oil, chili-garlic sauce, and garlic. Add the bok choy and toss, massaging the leaves with your hands if necessary, until thoroughly coated.
3. Arrange the bok choy in the basket of the air fryer. Pausing about halfway through the cooking time to shake the basket, air fry for 7 to 10 minutes until the bok choy is tender and the tips of the leaves begin to crisp. Remove from the basket and let it cool for a few minutes before coarsely chopping. Serve sprinkled with the sesame seeds.

Nutrition:
- (per serving) calories 100 | fat 8 | protein 2 | total carbs 4 | fiber 3

Bell Peppers With Sriracha Mayonnaise

Servings: 2 | Cooking Time: 14 Minutes

Ingredients:
- 4 bell peppers, seeded and sliced (1-inch pieces)
- 1 onion, sliced (1-inch pieces)
- 1 tablespoon olive oil
- ½ teaspoon dried rosemary
- ½ teaspoon dried basil
- Kosher salt, to taste
- ¼ teaspoon ground black pepper
- ⅓ cup mayonnaise
- ⅓ teaspoon Sriracha

Directions:
1. Toss the bell peppers and onions with the olive oil, rosemary, basil, salt, and black pepper.
2. Place the peppers and onions on an even layer in the cooking basket. Cook at 400ºF for 12 to 14 minutes.
3. Meanwhile, make the sauce by whisking the mayonnaise and Sriracha. Serve immediately.

Nutrition:
- (per serving) calories 346 | fat 34.1 | protein 9.5 | total carbs 2.3 | fiber 0.9

Brussels Sprouts With Bacon

Servings: 4 | Cooking Time: 12 Minutes

Ingredients:
- 2 cups trimmed and halved fresh Brussels sprouts
- 2 tablespoons olive oil
- ¼ teaspoon salt
- ¼ teaspoon ground black pepper
- 2 tablespoons balsamic vinegar
- 2 slices cooked sugar-free bacon, crumbled

Directions:
1. In a large bowl, toss Brussels sprouts in olive oil, then sprinkle with salt and pepper. Place into ungreased air fryer basket. Adjust the temperature to 375°F (190°C) and set the timer for 12 minutes, shaking the basket halfway through cooking. Brussels sprouts will be tender and browned when done.
2. Place sprouts in a large serving dish and drizzle with balsamic vinegar. Sprinkle bacon over top. Serve warm.

Nutrition:
- (per serving) calories 112 | fat 9 | protein 3 | total carbs 5 | fiber 3

Shredded Brussels Sprouts

Servings: 6 | Cooking Time: 15 Minutes

Ingredients:
- 17 oz. Brussels sprouts
- 1 oz. butter
- 1 tablespoon olive oil
- 1 teaspoon ground white pepper
- 1 teaspoon salt
- 1 tablespoon apple cider vinegar

Directions:
1. Place the Brussels sprouts in a blender to shred them.
2. Preheat the air fryer to 380 F.
3. Put the shredded Brussel sprouts in the air fryer basket tray.
4. Add butter, olive oil, ground white pepper, salt, and apple cider vinegar.
5. Mix the shredded Brussel sprouts carefully using a spoon.
6. Cook in the preheated air fryer for 15 minutes.
7. Stir before serving.

Nutrition:
- (per serving) calories 90 | fat 6.4 | protein 2.8 | total carbs 7.6 | fiber 3.1

Simple Zoodles

Servings: 2 | Cooking Time: 8 Minutes

Ingredients:
- 1 (12-inch) zucchini
- Special Equipment:
- Spiral slicer

Directions:
1. Spray the air fryer basket with avocado oil. Preheat the air fryer to 400°F.
2. Cut the ends off the zucchini to create nice even edges. If you desire completely white noodles, peel the zucchini. Using a spiral slicer, cut the zucchini into long, thin noodles.
3. Spread out the zucchini noodles in the air fryer basket in a single layer and cook for 8 minutes, or until soft. Remove from the air fryer and serve immediately.
4. Store leftovers in an airtight container for 4 days. Reheat in a single layer in the air fryer for 3 minutes, or until heated through.

Nutrition:
- (per serving) calories 29 | fat 0 | protein 2 | total carbs 6 | fiber 2

Easy Air Fried Mushroom

Servings: 4 | Cooking Time: 10 Minutes

Ingredients:
- 8 ounces (227 g) cremini mushrooms, halved
- 2 tablespoons salted butter, melted
- ¼ teaspoon salt
- ¼ teaspoon ground black pepper

Directions:
1. In a medium bowl, toss mushrooms with butter, then sprinkle with salt and pepper. Place into ungreased air fryer basket. Adjust the temperature to 400°F (205ºC) and set the timer for 10 minutes, shaking the basket halfway through cooking. Mushrooms will be tender when done. Serve warm.

Nutrition:
- (per serving) calories 63 | fat 5 | protein 1 | total carbs 3 | fiber 3

Fennel Quiche

Servings: 5 | Cooking Time: 18 Minutes

Ingredients:
- 10 oz. fennel, chopped
- 1 cup spinach
- 5 eggs
- ½ cup almond flour
- 1 teaspoon olive oil
- 1 tablespoon butter
- 1 teaspoon salt
- ¼ cup heavy cream
- 1 teaspoon ground black pepper

Directions:
1. Chop the spinach and combine it with the chopped fennel in a large bowl.
2. Crack the egg in a separate bowl and whisk.
3. Combine the whisked eggs with the almond flour, butter, salt, heavy cream, and ground black pepper.
4. Whisk together to mix.
5. Preheat the air fryer to 360 F.
6. Grease the air fryer basket tray with the olive oil.
7. Add both mixtures.
8. Cook the quiche for 18 minutes.

9. Let the quiche cool.
10. Remove it from the air fryer and slice into servings.

Nutrition:
- (per serving) calories 209 | fat 16.1 | protein 8.3 | total carbs 7.4 | fiber 3

Cauliflower Head

Servings: 6 | Cooking Time: 15 Minutes

Ingredients:
- 1-pound cauliflower head
- 1 teaspoon onion powder
- ½ cup heavy cream
- 5 oz. Parmesan, grated
- 1 teaspoon garlic powder
- 1 teaspoon salt

Directions:
1. Combine the heavy cream, onion powder, garlic powder, salt, and grated Parmesan in a large bowl.
2. Mix well.
3. Place the cauliflower in the heavy cream mixture.
4. Coat the cauliflower with the heavy cream using your hands.
5. Preheat the air fryer to 360 F.
6. Put the cauliflower head in the air fryer basket and cook for 12 minutes.
7. Increase the temperature to 390 F and cook the cauliflower head for 3 minutes.

Nutrition:
- (per serving) calories 132 | fat 8.8 | protein 9.4 | total carbs 5.8 | fiber 2

Cabbage With Dijon Mustard

Servings: 4 | Cooking Time: 10 Minutes

Ingredients:
- 1 small head cabbage, cored and sliced into 1-inch-thick slices
- 2 tablespoons olive oil, divided
- ½ teaspoon salt
- 1 tablespoon Dijon mustard
- 1 teaspoon apple cider vinegar
- 1 teaspoon granular erythritol

Directions:
1. Drizzle each cabbage slice with 1 tablespoon olive oil, then sprinkle with salt. Place slices into ungreased air fryer basket, working in batches if needed. Adjust the temperature to 350°F (180ºC) and set the timer for 10 minutes. Cabbage will be tender and edges will begin to brown when done.
2. In a small bowl, whisk remaining olive oil with mustard, vinegar, and erythritol. Drizzle over cabbage in a large serving dish. Serve warm.

Nutrition:
- (per serving) calories 111 | fat 7 | protein 3 | total carbs 12 | fiber 8

Mexican Zucchini

Servings: 8 | Cooking Time: 12 Minutes

Ingredients:
- 3 zucchini
- 1 tablespoon olive oil
- ½ teaspoon chili powder
- 1 teaspoon garlic powder
- 6 oz. Cheddar cheese, shredded

Directions:
1. Cut the zucchini into cubes.
2. Coat the zucchini cubes with chili powder, garlic powder, and olive oil.
3. Preheat the air fryer to 400 F.
4. Place the zucchini cubes in the air fryer and cook for 10 minutes.
5. Sprinkle the zucchini with the shredded cheese.
6. Cook for 2 minutes.
7. When the zucchini is cooked –transfer the dish to the serving plates.

Nutrition:
- (per serving) calories 115 | fat 9 | protein 6.3 | total carbs 3.1 | fiber 0.9

Creamed Eggs

Servings: 2 | Cooking Time: 18 Minutes

Ingredients:
- 1 teaspoon garlic paste
- 1½ tablespoons olive oil
- ½ cup crème fraîche
- ⅓ teaspoon ground black pepper, to your liking
- ⅓ cup Swiss cheese, crumbled
- 1 teaspoon cayenne pepper
- ⅓ cup Swiss chard, torn into pieces
- 5 eggs
- ¼ cup yellow onions, chopped
- 1 teaspoon fine sea salt

Directions:
1. Crack your eggs into a mixing dish, then, add the crème fraîche, salt, ground black pepper, and cayenne pepper.
2. Next, coat the inside of a baking dish with olive oil and tilt it to spread evenly. Scrape the egg/cream mixture into the baking dish. Add the other ingredients, mix to combine well.
3. Bake for 18 minutes at 292°F. Serve immediately.

Nutrition:
- (per serving) calories 388 | fat 27 | protein 6 | total carbs 29 | fiber 0.6

Pork Onion Rings

Servings: 8 | Cooking Time: 5 Minutes

Ingredients:
- 1 large egg
- ¼ cup coconut flour
- 2 ounces (57 g) plain pork rinds, finely crushed
- 1 large white onion, peeled and sliced into 8 (¼-inch) rings

Directions:
1. Whisk egg in a medium bowl. Place coconut flour and pork rinds in two separate medium bowls. Dip each onion ring into egg, then coat in coconut flour. Dip coated onion ring in egg once more, then press gently into pork rinds to cover all sides.

2. Place rings into ungreased air fryer basket. Adjust the temperature to 400°F (205ºC) and set the timer for 5 minutes, turning the onion rings halfway through cooking. Onion rings will be golden and crispy when done. Serve warm.

Nutrition:
- (per serving) calories 79 | fat 3 | protein 6 | total carbs 6 | fiber 4

Celery Croquettes With Chive Mayo

Servings: 4 | Cooking Time: 6 Minutes

Ingredients:
- 2 medium-sized celery stalks, trimmed and grated
- ½ cup of leek, finely chopped
- 1 tablespoon garlic paste
- ¼ teaspoon freshly cracked black pepper
- 1 teaspoon fine sea salt
- 1 tablespoon fresh dill, finely chopped
- 1 egg, lightly whisked
- ¼ cup almond flour
- ½ cup parmesan cheese, freshly grated
- ¼ teaspoon baking powder
- 2 tablespoons fresh chives, chopped
- 4 tablespoons mayonnaise

Directions:
1. Place the celery on a paper towel and squeeze them to remove excess liquid.
2. Combine the vegetables with the other ingredients, except the chives and mayo. Shape the balls using 1 tablespoon of the vegetable mixture.
3. Then, gently flatten each ball with your palm or a wide spatula. Spritz the croquettes with a non - stick cooking oil.
4. Air-fry the vegetable croquettes in a single layer for 6 minutes at 360ºF.
5. Meanwhile, mix fresh chives and mayonnaise. Serve warm croquettes with chive mayo. Bon appétit!

Nutrition:
- (per serving) calories 214 | fat 18 | protein 7 | total carbs 6.8 | fiber 5.2

Tomato Salad With Arugula

Servings: 4 | Cooking Time: 10 Minutes

Ingredients:
- 4 green tomatoes
- ½ teaspoon salt
- 1 large egg, lightly beaten
- ½ cup peanut flour
- 1 tablespoon Creole seasoning
- 1 (5-ounce / 142-g) bag arugula
- Buttermilk Dressing
- 1 cup mayonnaise
- ½ cup sour cream
- 2 teaspoons fresh lemon juice
- 2 tablespoons finely chopped fresh parsley
- 1 teaspoon dried dill
- 1 teaspoon dried chives
- ½ teaspoon salt
- ½ teaspoon garlic powder
- ½ teaspoon onion powder

Directions:
1. Preheat the air fryer to 400°F (205ºC).
2. Slice the tomatoes into ½-inch slices and sprinkle with the salt.

Let them sit for 5 to 10 minutes.

3. Place the egg in a small shallow bowl. In another small shallow bowl, combine the peanut flour and Creole seasoning. Dip each tomato slice into the egg wash, then dip into the peanut flour mixture, turning to coat evenly.

4. Working in batches if necessary, arrange the tomato slices in a single layer in the air fryer basket and spray both sides lightly with olive oil. Air fry until browned and crisp, for 8 to 10 minutes.

5. To make the buttermilk dressing: In a small bowl, whisk together the mayonnaise, sour cream, lemon juice, parsley, dill, chives, salt, garlic powder, and onion powder.

6. Serve the tomato slices on top of a bed of the arugula with the dressing on the side.

Nutrition:
• (per serving) calories 560 | fat 54 | protein 9 | total carbs 16 | fiber 13

Bacon-wrapped Asparagus

Servings: 4 | Cooking Time: 10 Minutes

Ingredients:
• 8 slices reduced-sodium bacon, cut in half
• 16 thick (about 1 pound / 454 g) asparagus spears, trimmed of woody ends

Directions:
1. Preheat the air fryer to 350°F (180°C).
2. Wrap a half piece of bacon around the center of each stalk of asparagus.
3. Working in batches, if necessary, arrange seam-side down in a single layer in the air fryer basket. Cook for 10 minutes until the bacon is crisp and the stalks are tender.

Nutrition:
• (per serving) calories 110 | fat 7 | protein 8 | total carbs 5 | fiber 3

Cauliflower Mash

Servings: 6 | Cooking Time: 15 Minutes

Ingredients:
• 1 (12-ounce / 340-g) steamer bag cauliflower florets, cooked according to package instructions
• 2 tablespoons salted butter, softened
• 2 ounces (57 g) cream cheese, softened
• ½ cup shredded sharp Cheddar cheese
• ¼ cup pickled jalapeños
• ½ teaspoon salt
• ¼ teaspoon ground black pepper

Directions:
1. Place cooked cauliflower into a food processor with remaining ingredients. Pulse twenty times until cauliflower is smooth and all ingredients are combined.
2. Spoon mash into an ungreased 6-inch round nonstick baking dish. Place dish into air fryer basket. Adjust the temperature to 380°F (193°C) and set the timer for 15 minutes. The top will be golden brown when done. Serve warm.

Nutrition:
• (per serving) calories 117 | fat 9 | protein 4 | total carbs 3 | fiber 2

Garlic Green Peppers

Servings: 4 | Cooking Time: 15 Minutes

Ingredients:
• 1 teaspoon minced garlic
• 1-pound green pepper
• 1 teaspoon salt
• 1 tablespoon olive oil

Directions:
1. Wash the green peppers carefully and remove the seeds.
2. Cut the green peppers into medium squares.
3. Preheat the air fryer to 320 F.
4. Place the squares in a large mixing bowl.
5. Coat the peppers with olive oil, salt, and minced garlic.
6. Mix well.
7. Place the prepared green peppers in the air fryer basket tray.
8. Cook the dish for 15 minutes, stirring halfway through.

Nutrition:
• (per serving) calories 54 | fat 0.6 | protein 1 | total carbs 5.5 | fiber 1.9

Spinach Poppers

Servings:16 | Cooking Time: 8 Minutes

Ingredients:
• 4 ounces (113 g) cream cheese, softened
• 1 cup chopped fresh spinach leaves
• ½ teaspoon garlic powder
• 8 mini sweet bell peppers, tops removed, seeded, and halved lengthwise

Directions:
1. In a medium bowl, mix cream cheese, spinach, and garlic powder. Place 1 tablespoon mixture into each sweet pepper half and press down to smooth.
2. Place poppers into ungreased air fryer basket. Adjust the temperature to 400°F (205°C) and set the timer for 8 minutes. Poppers will be done when cheese is browned on top and peppers are tender-crisp. Serve warm.

Nutrition:
• (per serving) calories 116 | fat 8 | protein 3 | total carbs 5 | fiber 4

Chinese Greens

Servings: 5 | Cooking Time: 10 Minutes

Ingredients:
• 1 tablespoon chives
• 1 teaspoon sesame seeds
• 1 tablespoon apple cider vinegar
• 2 tablespoon butter
• 1 tablespoon olive oil
• ½ teaspoon salt
• 8 oz bok choy
• 1 tablespoon garlic, sliced
• ½ teaspoon stevia extract

Directions:
1. Preheat the air fryer to 360 F.
2. Slice the bok choy and place it in the air fryer basket tray.
3. Cover the bok choy with salt and butter.
4. Cook for 10 minutes.
5. When the bok choy is cooked let it chill slightly and transfer to a serving bowl.

6. Combine the chives, sesame seeds, apple cider vinegar, olive oil, and stevia extract in a shallow bowl.
7. Add the sliced garlic and mix.
8. Drizzle the cooked bok choy with the prepared garlic mixture.
9. Stir and serve.

Nutrition:
- (per serving) calories 78 | fat 7.8 | protein 1 | total carbs 1.8 | fiber 0.6

Eggplant Salad With White Mushrooms

Servings: 6 | Cooking Time: 23 Minutes

Ingredients:
- 1 cup water
- 1 eggplant
- 6 oz. white mushrooms
- 1 garlic clove, sliced
- 2 tablespoon apple cider vinegar
- 1 tablespoon olive oil
- 1 teaspoon olive oil
- ½ tablespoon flax seeds
- 1 teaspoon ground black pepper
- 1 teaspoon salt

Directions:
1. Peel the eggplant and cut it into medium cubes.
2. Sprinkle the eggplant cubes with ½ teaspoon of salt.
3. Stir the eggplant cubes gently and leave them for 5 minutes.
4. Meanwhile, chop the white mushrooms.
5. Preheat the air fryer to 400 F.
6. Pour water in the air fryer basket tray.
7. Add the chopped mushrooms, ½ teaspoon salt, and cook them for 8 minutes.
8. Strain water from the mushrooms and chill them.
9. Place the eggplant cubes in the air fryer and sprinkle them with the olive oil.
10. Cook the eggplant for 15 minutes at 400 F stirring halfway through.
11. Combine the eggplant with the chopped mushrooms in a salad bowl.
12. Sprinkle the dish with flax seeds, olive oil, sliced garlic clove, and ground black pepper.
13. Add the apple cider vinegar and stir.
14. Let the salad rest for 5 minutes before serving.

Nutrition:
- (per serving) calories 62 | fat 3.5 | protein 2 | total carbs 6.9 | fiber 3.8

Warm Broccoli Salad

Servings: 4 | Cooking Time: 6 Minutes

Ingredients:
- 12 oz. broccoli
- 4 oz. bacon, chopped, cooked
- 1 tablespoon chives
- 1 tablespoon apple cider vinegar
- 1 teaspoon stevia extract
- 1 teaspoon flax seeds
- 1 tablespoon olive oil

Directions:
1. Preheat the air fryer to 400 F.
2. Separate the broccoli into small florets and place them in the air fryer.

3. Drizzle the broccoli florets with olive oil and cook for 6 minutes.
4. Meanwhile, drizzle the chopped bacon with apple cider vinegar.
5. Place the bacon in a salad bowl.
6. Add chives, flax seeds, and stevia extract.
7. Shake the mixture gently.
8. When the broccoli florets are cooked transfer them to the salad bowl and stir the salad carefully.
9. Serve immediately.

Nutrition:
- (per serving) calories 217 | fat 15.8 | protein 13 | total carbs 6.3 | fiber 2.4

Tomato And Zucchini Boats

Servings: 4 | Cooking Time: 10 Minutes

Ingredients:
- 1 large zucchini, ends removed, halved lengthwise
- 6 grape tomatoes, quartered
- ¼ teaspoon salt
- ¼ cup feta cheese
- 1 tablespoon balsamic vinegar
- 1 tablespoon olive oil

Directions:
1. Use a spoon to scoop out 2 tablespoons from center of each zucchini half, making just enough space to fill with tomatoes and feta.
2. Place tomatoes evenly in centers of zucchini halves and sprinkle with salt. Place into ungreased air fryer basket. Adjust the temperature to 350°F (180°C) and set the timer for 10 minutes. When done, zucchini will be tender.
3. Transfer boats to a serving tray and sprinkle with feta, then drizzle with vinegar and olive oil. Serve warm.

Nutrition:
- (per serving) calories 74 | fat 5 | protein 2 | total carbs 4 | fiber 3

Tomato Provençal

Servings: 4 | Cooking Time: 15 Minutes

Ingredients:
- 4 small ripe tomatoes connected on the vine
- ¼ teaspoon fine sea salt
- ¼ teaspoon ground black pepper
- ½ cup powdered Parmesan cheese
- 2 tablespoons chopped fresh parsley
- ¼ cup minced onions
- 2 cloves garlic, minced
- ½ teaspoon chopped fresh thyme leaves
- For Garnish:
- Fresh parsley leaves
- Ground black pepper
- Sprig of fresh basil

Directions:
1. Spray the air fryer basket with avocado oil. Preheat the air fryer to 350°F.
2. Slice the tops off the tomatoes without removing them from the vine. Do not discard the tops. Use a large spoon to scoop the seeds out of the tomatoes. Sprinkle the insides of the tomatoes with the salt and pepper.
3. In a medium-sized bowl, combine the cheese, parsley, onions, garlic, and thyme. Stir to combine well. Divide the mixture even-

ly among the tomatoes.

4. Spray avocado oil on the tomatoes and place them in the air fryer basket. Place the tomato tops in the air fryer basket next to, not on top of, the filled tomatoes. Cook for 15 minutes, or until the filling is golden and the tomatoes are soft yet still holding their shape.

5. Garnish with fresh parsley, ground black pepper, and a sprig of basil. Serve warm, with the tomato tops on the vine.

6. Store leftovers in an airtight container in the refrigerator for up to 4 days. Reheat in a preheated 350°F air fryer for about 3 minutes, until heated through.

Nutrition:
• (per serving) calories 68 | fat 3 | protein 5 | total carbs 6 | fiber 1

Air Fryer Garlic Bulbs

Servings: 18 | Cooking Time: 10 Minutes

Ingredients:
• 1-pound garlic heads
• 2 tablespoons olive oil
• 1 teaspoon dried oregano
• 1 teaspoon dried basil
• 1 teaspoon ground coriander
• ¼ teaspoon ground ginger

Directions:
1. Cut the ends of the garlic bulbs.
2. Place each bulb on foil.
3. Coat them with olive oil, dried oregano, dried basil, ground coriander, and ground ginger.
4. Preheat the air fryer to 400 F.
5. Wrap the garlic in foil and place in the air fryer.
6. Cook for 10 minutes until soft.
7. Let them cool for at least 10 minutes before serving.

Nutrition:
• (per serving) calories 57 | fat 1.4 | protein 8.2 | total carbs 6 | fiber 0

Bean Mushroom Casserole

Servings: 4 | Cooking Time: 12 Minutes

Ingredients:
• 1 pound (454 g) fresh green beans, ends trimmed, strings removed, and chopped into 2-inch pieces
• 1 (8-ounce / 227-g) package sliced brown mushrooms
• ½ onion, sliced
• 1 clove garlic, minced
• 1 tablespoon olive oil
• ½ teaspoon salt
• ¼ teaspoon freshly ground black pepper
• 4 ounces (113 g) cream cheese
• ½ cup chicken stock
• ¼ teaspoon ground nutmeg
• ½ cup grated Cheddar cheese

Directions:
1. Preheat the air fryer to 400°F (205°C). Coat a 6-cup casserole dish with olive oil and set aside.
2. In a large bowl, combine the green beans, mushrooms, onion, garlic, olive oil, salt, and pepper. Toss until the vegetables are thoroughly coated with the oil and seasonings.
3. Transfer the mixture to the air fryer basket. Pausing halfway through the cooking time to shake the basket, air fry for 10 minutes until tender.

4. While the vegetables are cooking, in a 2-cup glass measuring cup, warm the cream cheese and chicken stock in the microwave on high for 1 to 2 minutes until the cream cheese is melted. Add the nutmeg and whisk until smooth.

5. Transfer the vegetables to the prepared casserole dish and pour the cream cheese mixture over the top. Top with the Cheddar cheese. Air fry for another 10 minutes until the cheese is melted and beginning to brown.

Nutrition:
• (per serving) calories 250 | fat 19 | protein 10 | total carbs 14 | fiber 10

Taco Salad

Servings: 8 | Cooking Time: 12 Minutes

Ingredients:
• 12 oz. ground beef
• 1 teaspoon salt
• 1 teaspoon paprika
• 1 teaspoon turmeric
• 1 teaspoon chili pepper
• ½ teaspoon chili flakes
• 1 teaspoon ground black pepper
• 8 oz. Cheddar cheese
• 1 tablespoon sesame oil
• 1 tomato
• ¼ cup heavy cream
• 1 cup lettuce

Directions:
1. Combine the ground beef with the salt, paprika, turmeric, chili pepper, chili flakes, and ground black pepper.
2. Stir the mixture with a fork.
3. Coat the ground beef mixture with the sesame oil and place it in the air fryer basket tray.
4. Cook at 365 F for 12 minutes. Stir once during the cooking.
5. Meanwhile, chop the tomato roughly and tear the lettuce.
6. Place the vegetables in a large salad bowl.
7. Cut the Cheddar cheese into cubes and add them to the lettuce mixture.
8. Allow the beef to cool to room temperature.
9. Add the ground beef to the lettuce salad.
10. Sprinkle the dish with the heavy cream and stir using two wooden spatulas.

Nutrition:
• (per serving) calories 160 | fat 13 | protein 9.5 | total carbs 1.5 | fiber 0.4

Sausage-stuffed Mushroom Caps

Servings: 2 | Cooking Time: 8 Minutes

Ingredients:
• 6 large portobello mushroom caps
• ½ pound (227g) Italian sausage
• ¼ cup chopped onion
• 2 tablespoons blanched finely ground almond flour
• ¼ cup grated Parmesan cheese
• 1 teaspoon minced fresh garlic

Directions:
1. Use a spoon to hollow out each mushroom cap, reserving scrapings.
2. In a medium skillet over medium heat, brown the sausage for about 10 minutes or until fully cooked and no pink remains. Drain

and then add reserved mushroom scrapings, onion, almond flour, Parmesan, and garlic. Gently fold ingredients together and continue cooking for an additional minute, then remove from heat.

3. Evenly spoon the mixture into mushroom caps and place the caps into a 6-inch round pan. Place pan into the air fryer basket.

4. Adjust the temperature to 375°F (190ºC) and set the timer for 8 minutes.

5. When finished cooking, the tops will be browned and bubbling. Serve warm.

Nutrition:
• (per serving) calories 404 | fat 25 | protein 24 | total carbs 18 | fiber 14

Bamboo Shoots

Servings: 2 | Cooking Time: 4 Minutes

Ingredients:
• 8 oz. bamboo shoots
• 2 garlic cloves, sliced
• 1 tablespoon olive oil
• ½ teaspoon chili flakes
• 2 tablespoon chives
• ½ teaspoon salt
• 3 tablespoons fish stock

Directions:
1. Preheat the air fryer to 400 F.
2. Cut the bamboo shoots into strips.
3. Combine the sliced garlic cloves, olive oil, chili flakes, salt, and fish stock in the air fryer basket tray.
4. Cook for 1 minute.
5. Stir the mixture gently.
6. Add the bamboo strips and chives.
7. Stir the dish carefully and cook for 3 minutes more.
8. Stir again before serving.

Nutrition:
• (per serving) calories 100 | fat 7.6 | protein 3.7 | total carbs 7 | fiber 2.6

Creamy Snow Peas

Servings: 5 | Cooking Time: 5 Minutes

Ingredients:
• ½ cup heavy cream
• 1 teaspoon butter
• 1 teaspoon salt
• 1 teaspoon paprika
• 1-pound snow peas
• ¼ teaspoon nutmeg

Directions:
1. Preheat the air fryer to 400 F.
2. Wash the snow peas carefully and place them in the air fryer basket tray.
3. Then sprinkle the snow peas with the butter, salt, paprika, nutmeg, and heavy cream.
4. Cook the snow peas for 5 minutes.
5. When the time is over – shake the snow peas gently and transfer them to the serving plates.
6. Enjoy!

Nutrition:
• (per serving) calories 98 | fat 5.9 | protein 3.5 | total carbs 6.9 | fiber 2.4

Parsley Butter Mushrooms

Servings: 5 | Cooking Time: 7 Minutes

Ingredients:
• 10 oz. white mushrooms
• 4 oz chive stems, sliced
• 1 teaspoon olive oil
• 1/3 teaspoon garlic powder
• 3 tablespoon butter
• ½ cup heavy cream
• 2 tablespoon dried parsley
• ½ teaspoon salt

Directions:
1. Slice the mushrooms and sprinkle them with the garlic powder and salt.
2. Preheat the air fryer to 400 F.
3. Put the sliced mushrooms in the air fryer basket tray.
4. Drizzle the mushrooms with olive oil. Add chives.
5. Cook the mushrooms for 2 minutes.
6. Stir the sliced mushrooms carefully.
7. Add the butter and heavy cream.
8. Sprinkle the mushrooms with the dried parsley.
9. Stir the mushrooms carefully and cook them for 5 minutes more.
10. Stir before serving.

Nutrition:
• (per serving) calories 133 | fat 12.5 | protein 2.4 | total carbs 4.5 | fiber 1.1

Caramelized Broccoli

Servings: 4 | Cooking Time: 8 Minutes

Ingredients:
• 4 cups broccoli florets
• 3 tablespoons melted ghee or butter-flavored coconut oil
• 1½ teaspoons fine sea salt or smoked salt
• Mayonnaise, for serving (optional, omit for egg-free)

Directions:
1. Spray the air fryer basket with avocado oil. Preheat the air fryer to 400°F.
2. Place the broccoli in a large bowl. Drizzle it with the ghee, toss to coat, and sprinkle it with the salt. Transfer the broccoli to the air fryer basket and cook for 8 minutes, or until tender and crisp on the edges.
3. Store leftovers in an airtight container in the fridge for up to 4 days or in the freezer for up to a month. Reheat in a preheated 400°F air fryer for 5 minutes, or until crisp.

Nutrition:
• (per serving) calories 107 | fat 9 | protein 3 | total carbs 6 | fiber 2

Celery Sticks

Servings: 4 | Cooking Time: 15 Minutes

Ingredients:
• 1 pound (454 g) celery, cut into matchsticks
• 2 tablespoons peanut oil
• 1 jalapeño, seeded and minced
• ¼ teaspoon dill
• ½ teaspoon basil
• Salt and white pepper to taste

Directions:

1. Start by preheating your Air Fryer to 380ºF.
2. Toss all ingredients together and place them in the Air Fryer basket.
3. Cook for 15 minutes, shaking the basket halfway through the cooking time. Transfer to a serving platter and enjoy!

Nutrition:
- (per serving) calories 450 | fat 25.6 | protein 3.4 | total carbs 50.8 | fiber 0.3

Parmesan Flan

Servings: 4 | Cooking Time: 25 Minutes

Ingredients:
- ½ cup grated Parmesan cheese
- 1 cup heavy cream, very warm
- ⅛ teaspoon fine sea salt
- ⅛ teaspoon ground white pepper
- 1 large egg
- 1 large egg yolk
- For Serving/Garnish (Optional):
- 2 cups arugula
- 1 cup heirloom cherry tomatoes, halved
- 4 slices Italian cured beef (omit for vegetarian)
- Ground black pepper

Directions:
1. Preheat the air fryer to 350°F. Grease four 4-ounce (113-g) ramekins well.
2. Place the Parmesan in a medium-sized bowl and pour in the warm cream. Stir well to combine and add the salt and pepper.
3. In a separate medium-sized bowl, beat the egg and yolk until well combined. Gradually stir in the warm Parmesan mixture.
4. Pour the egg-and-cheese mixture into the prepared ramekins, cover the ramekins with foil, and place them in a casserole dish that will fit in your air fryer.
5. Pour boiling water into the casserole dish until the water reaches halfway up the sides of the ramekins. Place the casserole dish in the air fryer and bake until the flan is just set (the mixture will jiggle slightly when moved), for about 25 minutes. Check after 20 minutes.
6. Let the flan rest for 15 minutes. Serve with arugula, halved cherry tomatoes, and slices of Italian cured beef, if desired. Garnish with ground black pepper, if desired.
7. Store leftovers in an airtight container in the fridge for up to 5 days. Reheat the flan in a ramekin in a preheated 350°F air fryer for 5 minutes, or until heated through.

Nutrition:
- (per serving) calories 345 | fat 32 | protein 14 | total carbs 2 | fiber 0.2

Stewed Celery Stalk

Servings: 6 | Cooking Time: 8 Minutes

Ingredients:
- 1-pound celery stalk
- 1 tablespoon butter
- 3 oz chive stems, diced
- 1 cup chicken stock
- 2 tablespoons heavy cream
- 1 teaspoon salt
- 1 tablespoon paprika

Directions:
1. Chop the celery stalk roughly.

2. Pour the chicken stock into the air fryer basket tray and add the diced chives.
3. Preheat the air fryer to 400 F.
4. Cook the chives for 4 minutes.
5. Reduce the heat to 365 F.
6. Add the chopped celery stalk, butter, salt, paprika, and heavy cream.
7. Stir the vegetable mixture.
8. Cook the celery for 8 minutes more or until the celery is soft.

Nutrition:
- (per serving) calories 59 | fat 4.2 | protein 1.1 | total carbs 4.9 | fiber 2

Cauliflower With Lime Juice

Servings: 4 | Cooking Time: 7 Minutes

Ingredients:
- 2 cups chopped cauliflower florets
- 2 tablespoons coconut oil, melted
- 2 teaspoons chili powder
- ½ teaspoon garlic powder
- 1 medium lime
- 2 tablespoons chopped cilantro

Directions:
1. In a large bowl, toss cauliflower with coconut oil. Sprinkle with chili powder and garlic powder. Place seasoned cauliflower into the air fryer basket.
2. Adjust the temperature to 350°F (180ºC) and set the timer for 7 minutes.
3. Cauliflower will be tender and begin to turn golden at the edges. Place into serving bowl.
4. Cut the lime into quarters and squeeze juice over cauliflower. Garnish with cilantro.

Nutrition:
- (per serving) calories 73 | fat 6 | protein 1 | total carbs 3 | fiber 2

Zucchini Noodles

Servings: 4 | Cooking Time: 5 Minutes

Ingredients:
- 1 green zucchini
- 1 cup chicken stock
- 1 teaspoon butter
- ½ teaspoon salt
- ½ teaspoon ground white pepper

Directions:
1. Preheat the air fryer to 400 F.
2. Make the zucchini noodles using a spiralizer.
3. Pour the chicken stock into the air fryer basket tray.
4. Add salt and ground white pepper.
5. Cook the zucchini stock for 2 minutes.
6. Add the zucchini noodles and cook them for 3 minutes.
7. Strain the chicken stock and add butter.
8. Mix the zucchini noodles gently.

Nutrition:
- (per serving) calories 19 | fat 1.2 | protein 0.8 | total carbs 2 | fiber 0.6

Pecan-crusted Brussels Sprouts

Servings: 4 | Cooking Time: 30 Minutes

Ingredients:
- ½ cup pecans
- 1½ pounds (680g) fresh Brussels sprouts, trimmed and quartered
- 2 tablespoons olive oil
- Salt and freshly ground black pepper
- ¼ cup crumbled Gorgonzola cheese

Directions:
1. Spread the pecans in a single layer of the air fryer and set the heat to 350°F (180°C). Air fry for 3 to 5 minutes until the pecans are lightly browned and fragrant. Transfer the pecans to a plate and continue preheating the air fryer, increasing the heat to 400°F (205°C).
2. In a large bowl, toss the Brussels sprouts with the olive oil and season with salt and black pepper to taste.
3. Working in batches if necessary, arrange the Brussels sprouts in a single layer in the air fryer basket. Pausing halfway through the baking time to shake the basket, air fry for 20 to 25 minutes until the sprouts are tender and starting to brown on the edges.
4. Transfer the sprouts to a serving bowl and top with the toasted pecans and Gorgonzola. Serve warm or at room temperature.

Nutrition:
- (per serving) calories 250 | fat 19 | protein 9 | total carbs 17 | fiber 9

Fennel Wedges

Servings: 5 | Cooking Time: 6 Minutes

Ingredients:
- 1 teaspoon stevia extract
- ½ teaspoon fresh thyme
- ½ teaspoon salt
- 1 teaspoon olive oil
- 14 oz. fennel
- 1 teaspoon butter
- 1 teaspoon dried oregano
- ½ teaspoon chili flakes

Directions:
1. Slice the fennel into wedges.
2. Melt the butter.
3. Combine the butter, olive oil, dried oregano, and chili flakes in a bowl.
4. Combine well.
5. Add salt, fresh thyme, and stevia extract.
6. Whisk gently.
7. Brush the fennel wedges with the mixture.
8. Preheat the air fryer to 370 F.
9. Place the fennel wedges in the air fryer rack.
10. Cook the fennel wedges for 3 minutes on each side.

Nutrition:
- (per serving) calories 41 | fat 1.9 | protein 1 | total carbs 6.1 | fiber 2.6

Crispy Green Beans

Servings: 4 | Cooking Time: 8 Minutes

Ingredients:
- 2 teaspoons olive oil
- ½ pound (227g) fresh green beans, ends trimmed
- ¼ teaspoon salt
- ¼ teaspoon ground black pepper

Directions:
1. In a large bowl, drizzle olive oil over green beans and sprinkle with salt and pepper.
2. Place green beans into ungreased air fryer basket. Adjust the temperature to 350°F (180°C) and set the timer for 8 minutes, shaking the basket two times during cooking. Green beans will be dark golden and crispy at the edges when done. Serve warm.

Nutrition:
- (per serving) calories 37 | fat 2 | protein 1 | total carbs 4 | fiber 2

Keto Summer Vegetables

Servings: 8 | Cooking Time: 15 Minutes

Ingredients:
- 1 eggplant
- 1 tomato
- 1 zucchini
- 3 oz chive stems
- 2 green peppers
- 1 teaspoon paprika
- 1 tablespoon olive oil
- ½ teaspoon ground nutmeg
- ½ teaspoon ground thyme
- 1 teaspoon salt

Directions:
1. Preheat the air fryer to 390 F.
2. Wash the eggplant, tomato, and zucchini carefully.
3. Chop all the vegetables roughly.
4. Place the chopped vegetables in the air fryer basket tray.
5. Coat the vegetables with the paprika, olive oil, ground nutmeg, ground thyme, and salt.
6. Stir the vegetables using two spatulas.
7. Cut the green peppers into squares.
8. Add the squares into the vegetable mixture. Stir gently.
9. Cook for 15 minutes, stirring after 10 minutes then serve.

Nutrition:
- (per serving) calories 48 | fat 2.1 | protein 1.4 | total carbs 7.4 | fiber 3.3

Turmeric Cauliflower Rice

Servings: 6 | Cooking Time: 10 Minutes

Ingredients:
- 4 oz chive stems
- 3 tablespoon butter
- 1 teaspoon salt
- 1-pound cauliflower
- 1 teaspoon turmeric
- 1 teaspoon minced garlic
- 1 teaspoon ground ginger
- 1 cup chicken stock

Directions:
1. Wash the cauliflower and chop it roughly.
2. Place the chopped cauliflower in a blender and blend until you have a rice texture.
3. Transfer the cauliflower rice to a mixing bowl.
4. Add the diced chives.
5. Coat the cauliflower with the salt, turmeric, minced garlic, and ground ginger.
6. Mix well.
7. Preheat the air fryer to 370 F.
8. Place the cauliflower inside.
9. Add the butter and chicken stock.
10. Cook for 10 minutes.
11. Remove the cauliflower rice from the air fryer and strain the excess liquid before serving.

Nutrition:
- (per serving) calories 82 | fat 6 | protein 2 | total carbs 6.5 | fiber 2.4

Cripsy Broccoli With Bacon

Servings: 2 | Cooking Time: 10 Minutes

Ingredients:
- 3 cups fresh broccoli florets
- 1 tablespoon coconut oil
- ½ cup shredded sharp Cheddar cheese
- ¼ cup full-fat sour cream
- 4 slices sugar-free bacon, cooked and crumbled
- 1 scallion, sliced on the bias

Directions:
1. Place broccoli into the air fryer basket and drizzle it with coconut oil.
2. Adjust the temperature to 350°F (180ºC) and set the timer for 10 minutes.
3. Toss the basket two or three times during cooking to avoid burned spots.
4. When broccoli begins to crisp at ends, remove from fryer. Top with shredded cheese, sour cream, and crumbled bacon and garnish with scallion slices.

Nutrition:
- (per serving) calories 361 | fat 25 | protein 18 | total carbs 11 | fiber 7

Parmesan-crusted Brussels Sprouts

Servings: 4 | Cooking Time: 8 Minutes

Ingredients:
- 2 cups Brussels sprouts, trimmed and halved
- 3 tablespoons ghee or coconut oil, melted
- 1 teaspoon fine sea salt or smoked salt
- Dash of lime or lemon juice
- Thinly sliced Parmesan cheese, for serving (optional, omit for dairy-free)
- Lemon slices, for serving (optional)

Directions:
1. Spray the air fryer basket with avocado oil. Preheat the air fryer to 400°F.
2. In a large bowl, toss together the Brussels sprouts, ghee, and salt. Add the lime or lemon juice.
3. Place the Brussels sprouts in the air fryer basket and cook for 8 minutes, or until crispy, shaking the basket after 5 minutes. Serve with thinly sliced Parmesan and lemon slices, if desired.
4. Best served fresh. Store leftovers in an airtight container in the fridge for up to 5 days. Reheat in a preheated 390°F air fryer for 3 minutes, or until heated through.

Nutrition:
- (per serving) calories 149 | fat 12 | protein 4 | total carbs 10 | fiber 4

Chapter 8 Main, Sides And Vegetarian Recipes

Chapter 8 Main, Sides And Vegetarian Recipes

Rosemary Whole Chicken

Servings: 12 | Cooking Time: 75 Minutes

Ingredients:
- 6-pound whole chicken
- 1 teaspoon kosher salt
- 1 teaspoon ground black pepper
- 1 teaspoon ground paprika
- 1 tablespoon minced garlic
- 3 tablespoon butter
- 1 teaspoon olive oil
- ¼ cup water
- 3 oz chive stems

Directions:
1. Rub the whole chicken with the kosher salt and ground black pepper inside and outside.
2. Sprinkle it with the ground paprika and minced garlic.
3. Dice the chives.
4. Put the diced chives inside the whole chicken.
5. Then add the butter.
6. Rub the chicken with olive oil.
7. Preheat the air fryer to 360 F and pour water in the air fryer basket.
8. Place the chicken on the rack inside the air fryer.
9. Cook the chicken for 75 minutes.
10. When the chicken is cooked it should have slightly crunchy skin.
11. Cut the cooked chicken into the servings.

Nutrition:
- (per serving) calories 464 | fat 20.1 | protein 65.8 | total carbs 0.9 | fiber 0.2

Fried Cauliflower Rice With Green Onions

Servings: 4 | Cooking Time: 8 Minutes

Ingredients:
- 2 cups cauliflower florets
- ⅓ cup sliced green onions, plus more for garnish
- 3 tablespoons wheat-free tamari or coconut aminos
- 1 clove garlic, smashed to a paste or minced
- 1 teaspoon grated fresh ginger
- 1 teaspoon fish sauce or fine sea salt
- 1 teaspoon lime juice
- ⅛ teaspoon ground black pepper

Directions:
1. Preheat the air fryer to 375°F.
2. Place the cauliflower in a food processor and pulse until it resembles grains of rice.
3. Place all the ingredients, including the riced cauliflower, in a large bowl and stir well to combine.
4. Transfer the cauliflower mixture to a 6-inch pie pan or a casserole dish that will fit in your air fryer. Cook for 8 minutes, or until soft, shaking halfway through. Garnish with sliced green onions before serving.
5. Store leftovers in an airtight container in the fridge for up to 4 days. Reheat in a preheated 375°F air fryer for 4 minutes, or until heated through.

Nutrition:
- (per serving) calories 30 | fat 0 | protein 3 | total carbs 4 | fiber 1

Beef Jerky

Servings: 6 | Cooking Time: 2.5 Hours

Ingredients:
- 14 oz. beef flank steak
- 1 teaspoon chili pepper
- 3 tablespoon apple cider vinegar
- 1 teaspoon ground black pepper
- 1 teaspoon onion powder
- 1 teaspoon garlic powder
- ¼ teaspoon liquid smoke

Directions:
1. Slice the beefsteak into the medium strips and then tenderize each piece.
2. Take a bowl and combine the apple cider vinegar, ground black pepper, onion powder, garlic powder, and liquid smoke.
3. Whisk gently with a fork.
4. Then transfer the beef pieces in the prepared mixture and stir well.
5. Leave the meat to marinade for up to 8 hours.
6. Put the marinated beef pieces in the air fryer rack.
7. Cook the beef jerky for 2.5 hours at 150 F.

Nutrition:
- (per serving) calories 129 | fat 4.1 | protein 20.2 | total carbs 1.1 | fiber 0.2

Stuffed Bell Peppers

Servings: 2 | Cooking Time: 15 Minutes

Ingredients:
- 2 bell peppers, tops and seeds removed
- Salt and pepper, to taste
- ⅔ cup cream cheese
- 2 tablespoons mayonnaise
- 1 tablespoon fresh celery stalks, chopped

Directions:
1. Arrange the peppers in the lightly greased cooking basket. Cook in the preheated Air Fryer at 400°F for 15 minutes, turning them over halfway through the cooking time.
2. Season with salt and pepper.
3. Then, in a mixing bowl, combine the cream cheese with the mayonnaise and chopped celery. Stuff the pepper with the cream cheese mixture and serve.

Nutrition:
- (per serving) calories 378 | fat 38 | protein 2.5 | total carbs 17.6 | fiber 2.6

Balsamic Green Beans

Servings: 4 | Cooking Time: 10 Minutes

Ingredients:
- ¾ pound (340 g) green beans, cleaned
- 1 tablespoon balsamic vinegar
- ¼ teaspoon kosher salt
- ½ teaspoon mixed peppercorns, freshly cracked
- 1 tablespoon butter
- 2 tablespoons toasted sesame seeds, to serve

Directions:
1. Set your Air Fryer to cook at 390ºF.
2. Mix the green beans with all of the above ingredients, apart from the sesame seeds. Set the timer for 10 minutes.
3. Meanwhile, toast the sesame seeds in a small-sized nonstick skillet, make sure to stir continuously.
4. Serve sautéed green beans on a nice serving platter sprinkled with toasted sesame seeds. Bon appétit!

Nutrition:
- (per serving) calories 73 | fat 3.0 | protein 1.6 | total carbs 6.1 | fiber 2.1

Crunchy-top Personal Mac 'n' Cheese

Servings:4 | Cooking Time: 15 Minutes

Ingredients:
- 2 cups frozen chopped cauliflower, thawed
- 2 ounces cream cheese (¼ cup), softened
- ¼ cup shredded Gruyère or Swiss cheese
- ¼ cup shredded sharp cheddar cheese
- 2 tablespoons finely diced onions
- 3 tablespoons beef broth
- ¼ teaspoon fine sea salt
- TOPPING:
- ¼ cup pork dust (see here)
- ¼ cup unsalted butter, melted, plus more for greasing ramekins
- 4 slices bacon, finely diced
- FOR GARNISH (OPTIONAL):
- Chopped fresh thyme or chives

Directions:
1. Preheat the air fryer to 375°F.
2. Place the cauliflower on a paper towel and pat dry. Cut any large pieces of cauliflower into ½-inch pieces.
3. In a medium-sized bowl, stir together the cream cheese, Gruyère, cheddar, and onions. Slowly stir in the broth and combine well. Add the salt and stir to combine. Add the cauliflower and stir gently to mix the cauliflower into the cheese sauce.
4. Grease four 4-ounce ramekins with butter. Divide the cauliflower mixture among the ramekins, filling each three-quarters full.
5. Make the topping: In a small bowl, stir together the pork dust, butter, and bacon until well combined. Divide the topping among the ramekins.
6. Place the ramekins in the air fryer (if you're using a smaller air fryer, work in batches if necessary) and cook for 15 minutes, or until the topping is browned and the bacon is crispy.
7. Garnish with fresh thyme or chives, if desired.
8. Store leftovers in the ramekins covered with foil. Reheat in a preheated 375°F air fryer for 6 minutes, or until the cauliflower is heated through and the top is crispy.

Nutrition:
- (per serving) calories 305 | fat 26g | protein 12g | total carbs 6g

| fiber 3g

Sweet Fauxtato Casserole

Servings:6 | Cooking Time: 55 Minutes

Ingredients:
- 2 cups cauliflower florets (see Tip)
- 1 cup chicken broth or water
- 1 cup canned pumpkin puree
- ⅓ cup unsalted butter, melted (or coconut oil for dairy-free), plus more for the pan
- ¼ cup Swerve confectioners'-style sweetener or equivalent amount of liquid or powdered sweetener (see here)
- ¼ cup unsweetened, unflavored almond milk or heavy cream
- 2 large eggs, beaten
- 1 teaspoon fine sea salt
- 1 teaspoon vanilla extract
- TOPPING:
- 1 cup chopped pecans
- ½ cup blanched almond flour or pecan meal
- ½ cup Swerve confectioners'-style sweetener or equivalent amount of powdered sweetener (see here)
- ⅓ cup unsalted butter, melted (or coconut oil for dairy-free)
- Chopped fresh parsley leaves, for garnish (optional)

Directions:
1. Preheat the air fryer to 350°F.
2. Place the cauliflower florets in a 6-inch pie pan or a casserole dish that will fit in your air fryer. Add the broth to the pie pan. Cook in the air fryer for 20 minutes, or until the cauliflower is very tender.
3. Drain the cauliflower and transfer it to a food processor. Set the pie pan aside; you'll use it in the next step. Blend the cauliflower until very smooth. Add the pumpkin, butter, sweetener, almond milk, eggs, salt, and vanilla and puree until smooth.
4. Grease the pie pan that you cooked the cauliflower in with butter. Pour the cauliflower-pumpkin mixture into the pan. Set aside.
5. Make the topping: In a large bowl, mix together all the ingredients for the topping until well combined. Crumble the topping over the cauliflower-pumpkin mixture.
6. Cook in the air fryer for 30 to 35 minutes, until cooked through and golden brown on top. Garnish with fresh parsley before serving, if desired.
7. Store leftovers in an airtight container in the fridge for up to 4 days or in the freezer for up to a month. Reheat in a preheated 350°F air fryer for 6 minutes, or until heated through.

Nutrition:
- (per serving) calories 421 | fat 40g | protein 8g | total carbs 10g | fiber 5g

Zucchini With Spinach

Servings: 6 | Cooking Time: 7 Minutes

Ingredients:
- 4 eggs, slightly beaten
- ½ cup almond flour
- ½ cup goat cheese, crumbled
- 1 teaspoon fine sea salt
- 4 garlic cloves, minced
- 1 cup baby spinach
- ½ cup Parmesan cheese grated
- ⅓ teaspoon red pepper flakes
- 1 pound (454 g) zucchini, peeled and grated

- ⅓ teaspoon dried dill weed

Directions:
1. Thoroughly combine all ingredients in a bowl. Now, roll the mixture to form small croquettes.
2. Air fry at 335ºF (168ºC) for 7 minutes or until golden. Tate, adjust for seasonings and serve warm.

Nutrition:
- (per serving) calories 171 | fat 10.8 | protein 3.1 | total carbs 15.9 | fiber 14.9

Spinach Artichoke Tart

Servings:6 | Cooking Time: 40 Minutes

Ingredients:
- CRUST:
- 1 cup blanched almond flour
- 1 cup grated Parmesan cheese (about 3 ounces)
- 1 large egg
- FILLING:
- 4 ounces cream cheese (½ cup), softened
- 1 (8-ounce) package frozen chopped spinach, thawed and drained
- ½ cup artichoke hearts, drained and chopped
- ⅓ cup shredded Parmesan cheese, plus more for topping
- 1 large egg
- 1 clove garlic, minced
- ¼ teaspoon fine sea salt

Directions:
1. Preheat the air fryer to 350°F.
2. Make the crust: Place the almond flour and cheese in a large bowl and mix until well combined. Add the egg and mix until the dough is well combined and stiff.
3. Press the dough into a 6-inch pie pan. Bake for 8 to 10 minutes, until it starts to brown lightly.
4. Meanwhile, make the filling: Place the cream cheese in a large bowl and stir to break it up. Add the spinach, artichoke hearts, cheese, egg, garlic, and salt. Stir well to combine.
5. Pour the spinach mixture into the prebaked crust and sprinkle with additional Parmesan. Place in the air fryer and cook for 25 to 30 minutes, until cooked through.
6. Store leftovers in an airtight container in the fridge for up to 4 days or in the freezer for up to a month. Reheat in a preheated 350°F air fryer for 5 minutes, or until heated through.

Nutrition:
- (per serving)   calories 228 | fat 7g | protein 14g | total carbs 6g | fiber 2g

Tempura Bowl

Servings: 3 | Cooking Time: 10 Minutes

Ingredients:
- 7 tablespoons whey protein isolate
- 1 teaspoon baking powder
- Kosher salt and ground black pepper, to taste
- ½ teaspoon paprika
- 1 teaspoon dashi granules
- 2 eggs
- 1 tablespoon mirin
- 3 tablespoons soda water
- 1 cup Parmesan cheese, grated
- 1 onion, cut into rings
- 1 bell pepper

- 1 zucchini, cut into slices
- 3 asparagus spears
- 2 tablespoons olive oil

Directions:
1. In a shallow bowl, mix the whey protein isolate, baking powder, salt, black pepper, paprika, dashi granules, eggs, mirin, and soda water.
2. In another shallow bowl, place grated Parmesan cheese.
3. Dip the vegetables in tempura batter, lastly, roll over Parmesan cheese to coat evenly. Drizzle each piece with olive oil.
4. Cook in the preheated Air Fryer at 400ºF for 10 minutes, shaking the basket halfway through the cooking time. Work in batches until the vegetables are crispy and golden brown. Bon appétit!

Nutrition:
- (per serving) calories 324 | fat 19.2 | protein 11.6 | total carbs 19.5 | fiber 2

Garlic Butter Breadsticks

Servings:6 | Cooking Time: 12 Minutes

Ingredients:
- DOUGH:
- 1¾ cups shredded mozzarella cheese (about 7 ounces)
- 2 tablespoons unsalted butter
- 1 large egg, beaten
- ¾ cup blanched almond flour
- ⅛ teaspoon fine sea salt
- GARLIC BUTTER:
- 3 tablespoons unsalted butter, softened
- 2 cloves garlic, minced
- TOPPING:
- ½ cup shredded Parmesan cheese (about 2 ounces)
- 1 teaspoon dried basil leaves
- 1 teaspoon dried oregano leaves
- FOR SERVING (OPTIONAL):
- ½ cup marinara sauce

Directions:
1. Preheat the air fryer to 400°F. Place a piece of parchment paper in a 6-inch square casserole dish and spray it with avocado oil.
2. Make the dough: Place the mozzarella cheese and butter in a microwave-safe bowl and microwave for 1 to 2 minutes, until the cheese is entirely melted. Stir well. Add the egg and, using a hand mixer on low speed, combine well. Add the almond flour and salt and combine well with the hand mixer.
3. Lay a piece of parchment paper on the countertop and place the dough on it. Knead it for about 3 minutes; the dough should be thick yet pliable. (Note: If the dough is too sticky, chill it in the refrigerator for an hour or overnight.) Place the dough in the prepared casserole dish and use your hands to spread it out to fill the bottom of the casserole dish.
4. Make the garlic butter: In a small dish, stir together the butter and garlic until well combined.
5. Spread the garlic butter on top of the dough. Top with the Parmesan, basil, and oregano. Place in the air fryer and cook for 10 minutes, or until golden brown and cooked through.
6. Cut into 1-inch-wide breadsticks and serve with marinara sauce, if desired. Best served fresh, but leftovers can be stored in an airtight container in the fridge for up to 3 days. Reheat in a preheated 400°F air fryer for 3 minutes, or until the cheese is hot and bubbly.

Nutrition:

- (per serving) calories 301 | fat 26g | protein 14g | total carbs 6g | fiber 2g

Beef Strips With Zucchini Spirals

Servings: 8 | Cooking Time: 13 Minutes

Ingredients:
- 1-pound beef brisket
- 1 teaspoon ground black pepper
- 1 tomato
- 1 teaspoon salt
- 1 zucchini
- 1 teaspoon olive oil
- 1 teaspoon Italian spices
- 4 tablespoon water

Directions:
1. Cut the beef brisket into strips.
2. Sprinkle the beef strips with the ground black pepper and salt.
3. Chop the tomato roughly and transfer it to a blender.
4. Blend well until you get a smooth puree.
5. Grease the air fryer basket tray with the olive oil and put the beef strips inside.
6. Cook the beef strips for 9 minutes at 365 F.
7. Stir the beef strips carefully after 4 minutes of cooking.
8. Meanwhile, wash the zucchini carefully and make spirals using a spiralizer.
9. When meat is cooked – add the zucchini spirals over the meat.
10. Sprinkle with the tomato puree, water, and Italian spices.
11. Cook the dish for 4 minutes more at 360 F.
12. Stir with a wooden spatula before serving.

Nutrition:
- (per serving) calories 226 | fat 5.3 | protein 12 | total carbs 35.25 | fiber 8

Cayenne Pepper Rib Eye Steak

Servings: 2 | Cooking Time: 13 Minutes

Ingredients:
- 1-pound rib eye steak
- 1 teaspoon salt
- 1 teaspoon cayenne pepper
- ½ teaspoon chili flakes
- 3 tablespoon cream
- 1 teaspoon olive oil
- 1 teaspoon lemongrass
- 1 tablespoon butter
- 1 teaspoon garlic powder

Directions:
1. Preheat the air fryer to 360 F.
2. Take a shallow bowl and combine the cayenne pepper, salt, chili flakes, lemongrass, and garlic powder together.
3. Mix the spices gently.
4. Sprinkle the rib eye steak with the spice mixture.
5. Melt the butter and combine it with cream and olive oil.
6. Churn the mixture.
7. Pour the churned mixture into the air fryer basket tray.
8. Add the rib eye steak.
9. Cook the steak for 13 minutes. Do not stir the steak during the cooking.
10. When the steak is cooked transfer it to a paper towel to soak all the excess fat.
11. Serve the steak. You can slice the steak if desired.

Nutrition:
- (per serving) calories 708 | fat 59 | protein 40.4 | total carbs 2.3 | fiber 0.4

Pork Meatballs Stuffed With Cheddar Cheese

Servings: 6 | Cooking Time: 8 Minutes

Ingredients:
- 1-pound ground pork
- 5 oz. Cheddar cheese
- 1 tablespoon dried oregano
- 1 large egg
- ½ teaspoon salt
- 1 teaspoon paprika
- 1 tablespoon butter
- ½ teaspoon nutmeg
- 1 teaspoon minced garlic
- ½ teaspoon ground ginger

Directions:
1. Crack the egg into a bowl and whisk it.
2. Add salt, paprika, nutmeg, and ground ginger to the bowl.
3. Stir gently and add the ground pork.
4. Add dried oregano and minced garlic.
5. Mix well using a spoon until well combined and make 6 medium balls.
6. Cut the Cheddar cheese into 6 medium cubes.
7. Fill the pork meatballs with the cheese cubes.
8. Preheat the air fryer to 365 F.
9. Toss the butter in the air fryer basket tray and melt it.
10. Add the pork meatballs and cook them for 8 minutes, stirring halfway through.

Nutrition:
- (per serving) calories 295 | fat 20.6 | protein 23 | total carbs 3 | fiber 0

Spinach Cheese Casserole

Servings: 4 | Cooking Time: 15 Minutes

Ingredients:
- 1 tablespoon salted butter, melted
- ¼ cup diced yellow onion
- 8 ounces (227 g) full-fat cream cheese, softened
- ⅓ cup full-fat mayonnaise
- ⅓ cup full-fat sour cream
- ¼ cup chopped pickled jalapeños
- 2 cups fresh spinach, chopped
- 2 cups cauliflower florets, chopped
- 1 cup artichoke hearts, chopped

Directions:
1. In a large bowl, mix butter, onion, cream cheese, mayonnaise, and sour cream. Fold in jalapeños, spinach, cauliflower, and artichokes.
2. Pour the mixture into a 4-cup round baking dish. Cover with foil and place into the air fryer basket.
3. Adjust the temperature to 370°F (188°C) and set the timer for 15 minutes.
4. In the last 2 minutes of cooking, remove the foil to brown the top. Serve warm.

Nutrition:
- (per serving) calories 423 | fat 36.3 | protein 6.7 | total carbs 12.1 | fiber 6.8

Turkey Meatballs With Dried Dill

Servings: 9 | Cooking Time: 11 Minutes

Ingredients:
- 1-pound ground turkey
- 1 teaspoon chili flakes
- ¼ cup chicken stock
- 2 tablespoon dried dill
- 1 egg
- 1 teaspoon salt
- 1 teaspoon paprika
- 1 tablespoon coconut flour
- 2 tablespoons heavy cream
- 1 teaspoon olive oil

Directions:
1. Crack the egg in a bowl and whisk it with a fork.
2. Add the ground turkey and chili flakes.
3. Sprinkle the mixture with dried dill, salt, paprika, coconut flour, and mix it up.
4. Make the meatballs from the ground turkey mixture.
5. Preheat the air fryer to 360 F.
6. Grease the air fryer basket tray with the olive oil.
7. Then put the meatballs inside.
8. Cook the meatballs for 6 minutes – for 3 minutes on each side.
9. Sprinkle the meatballs with the heavy cream.
10. Cook the meatballs for 5 minutes more.
11. When the turkey meatballs are cooked – let them rest for 2-3 minutes.

Nutrition:
- (per serving) calories 124 | fat 7.9 | protein 14.8 | total carbs 1.2 | fiber 0.5

Riced Cauliflower With Eggs

Servings: 4 | Cooking Time: 12 Minutes

Ingredients:
- 2 cups cauliflower, food-processed into rice-like particles
- 2 tablespoons peanut oil
- ½ cup scallions, chopped
- 2 bell peppers, chopped
- 4 eggs, beaten
- Sea salt and ground black pepper, to taste
- ½ teaspoon granulated garlic

Directions:
1. Grease a baking pan with nonstick cooking spray.
2. Add the cauliflower rice and the other ingredients to the baking pan.
3. Cook at 400ºF for 12 minutes, checking occasionally to ensure even cooking. Enjoy!

Nutrition:
- (per serving) calories 149 | fat 11 | protein 6.1 | total carbs 2.4 | fiber 0.6

Garlic Lamb Shank

Servings: 5 | Cooking Time: 24 Minutes

Ingredients:
- 17 oz. lamb shanks
- 2 tablespoon garlic, peeled
- 1 teaspoon kosher salt
- 1 tablespoon dried parsley
- 4 oz chive stems, chopped
- ½ cup chicken stock
- 1 teaspoon butter
- 1 teaspoon dried rosemary
- 1 teaspoon nutmeg
- ½ teaspoon ground black pepper

Directions:
1. Chop the garlic roughly.
2. Make cuts in the lamb shank and fill with the chopped garlic.
3. Coat the lamb shank with the kosher salt, dried parsley, dried rosemary, nutmeg, and ground black pepper.
4. Stir the spices on the lamb shank gently.
5. Put the butter and chicken stock in the air fryer basket tray.
6. Preheat the air fryer to 380 F.
7. Put the chives in the air fryer basket tray.
8. Add the lamb shank and cook the meat for 24 minutes.
9. When the lamb shank is cooked, transfer it to a serving plate and sprinkle with the remaining liquid from the cooked meat.

Nutrition:
- (per serving) calories 205 | fat 8.2 | protein 27.2 | total carbs 3.8 | fiber 0.8

Chicken Poppers

Servings: 6 | Cooking Time: 10 Minutes

Ingredients:
- ½ cup coconut flour
- 1 teaspoon chili flakes
- 1 teaspoon ground black pepper
- 1 teaspoon garlic powder
- 11 oz. chicken breast, boneless, skinless
- 1 tablespoon olive oil

Directions:
1. Cut the chicken breast into medium cubes and put them in a large bowl.
2. Sprinkle the chicken cubes with the chili flakes, ground black pepper, garlic powder, and stir them well using your hands.
3. After this, sprinkle the chicken cubes with the almond flour.
4. Shake the bowl with the chicken cubes gently to coat the meat.
5. Preheat the air fryer to 365 F.
6. Grease the air fryer basket tray with the olive oil.
7. Place the chicken cubes inside.
8. Cook the chicken poppers for 10 minutes.
9. Turn the chicken poppers over after 5 minutes of cooking.
10. Allow the cooked chicken poppers to cool before serving.

Nutrition:
- (per serving) calories 123 | fat 4.6 | protein 13.2 | total carbs 6.9 | fiber 3.9

Swedish Meatballs

Servings: 6 | Cooking Time: 11 Minutes

Ingredients:
- 1 tablespoon almond flour
- 1-pound ground beef
- 1 teaspoon dried parsley
- 1 teaspoon dried dill
- ½ teaspoon ground nutmeg
- 1 oz chive stems
- 1 teaspoon garlic powder
- 1 teaspoon salt
- ½ cup heavy cream
- ¼ cup chicken stock

- 1 teaspoon mustard
- 1 teaspoon ground black pepper
- 1 tablespoon butter

Directions:
1. Combine the ground beef and almond flour together in the bowl.
2. Add the dried dill, dried parsley, ground nutmeg, garlic powder, chopped chives, salt, ground black pepper, and mustard.
3. Mix well to combine.
4. Make the meatballs from the mixture.
5. Preheat the air fryer to 380 F.
6. Put the meatballs in the air fryer basket tray.
7. Add the butter and cook the dish for 5 minutes.
8. Turn the meatballs over.
9. Coat the meatballs with the heavy cream and chicken stock.
10. Cook for 6 minutes more.
11. Serve immediately with the cream gravy.

Nutrition:
- (per serving) calories 227 | fat 12.9 | protein 24.6 | total carbs 2.7 | fiber 0.9

Fried Mushrooms With Parmesan

Servings: 4 | Cooking Time: 6 Minutes

Ingredients:
- 1 pound (454 g) button mushrooms
- 1½ cups pork rinds
- 1 cup Parmesan cheese, grated
- 2 eggs, whisked
- ½ teaspoon salt
- 2 tablespoons fresh parsley leaves, roughly chopped

Directions:
1. Pat the mushrooms dry with a paper towel.
2. To begin, set up your "breading" station. Mix the pork rinds and Parmesan cheese in a shallow dish. In a separate dish, whisk the eggs.
3. Start by dipping the mushrooms into the eggs. Press your mushrooms into the parm/pork rind mixture, coating evenly.
4. Spritz the Air Fryer basket with cooking oil. Add the mushrooms and cook at 400°F for 6 minutes, flipping them halfway through the cooking time.
5. Sprinkle with the salt. Serve garnished with fresh parsley leaves. Bon appétit!

Nutrition:
- (per serving) calories 338 | fat 22.3 | protein 2.1 | total carbs 8 | fiber 1.2

Lemon Duck Legs

Servings: 6 | Cooking Time: 25 Minutes

Ingredients:
- 1 lemon
- 2-pound duck legs
- 1 teaspoon ground coriander
- 1 teaspoon ground nutmeg
- 1 teaspoon kosher salt
- ½ teaspoon dried rosemary
- 1 tablespoon olive oil
- 1 teaspoon stevia extract
- ¼ teaspoon sage

Directions:
1. Squeeze the juice from the lemon and grate the zest.

2. Combine the lemon juice and lemon zest together in a large mixing bowl.
3. Add the ground coriander, ground nutmeg, kosher salt, dried rosemary, and sage.
4. Add the olive oil and stevia extract.
5. Whisk carefully and add the duck legs.
6. Stir the duck legs and leave them for 15 minutes to marinade.
7. Preheat the air fryer to 380 F.
8. Put the marinated duck legs in the air fryer and cook for 25 minutes, turning after 15 minutes.
9. Allow the duck to rest before serving.

Nutrition:
- (per serving) calories 296 | fat 11.5 | protein 44.2 | total carbs 1.6 | fiber 0.5

Zucchini Cheese Tart

Servings: 6 | Cooking Time: 50 Minutes

Ingredients:
- ½ cup grated Parmesan cheese, divided
- 1½ cups almond flour
- 1 tablespoon coconut flour
- ½ teaspoon garlic powder
- ¾ teaspoon salt, divided
- ¼ cup unsalted butter, melted
- 1 zucchini, thinly sliced (about 2 cups)
- 1 cup ricotta cheese
- 3 eggs
- 2 tablespoons heavy cream
- 2 cloves garlic, minced
- ½ teaspoon dried tarragon

Directions:
1. Preheat the air fryer to 330°F (166°C). Coat a round 6-cup pan with olive oil and set aside.
2. In a large bowl, whisk ¼ cup of the Parmesan with the almond flour, coconut flour, garlic powder, and ¼ teaspoon of the salt. Stir in the melted butter until the dough resembles coarse crumbs. Press the dough firmly into the bottom and up the sides of the prepared pan. Air fry for 12 to 15 minutes until the crust begins to brown. Let it cool to room temperature.
3. Meanwhile, place the zucchini in a colander and sprinkle with the remaining ½ teaspoon salt. Toss gently to distribute the salt and let it sit for 30 minutes. Use paper towels to pat the zucchini dry.
4. In a large bowl, whisk together the ricotta, eggs, heavy cream, garlic, and tarragon. Gently stir in the zucchini slices. Pour the cheese mixture into the cooled crust and sprinkle with the remaining ¼ cup Parmesan.
5. Increase the air fryer to 350°F (180°C). Place the pan in the air fryer basket and air fry for 45 to 50 minutes, or until set and a tester inserted into the center of the tart comes out clean. Serve warm or at room temperature.

Nutrition:
- (per serving) calories 390 | fat 30 | protein 19 | total carbs 14 | fiber 12

Roast Eggplant And Zucchini Bites

Servings: 8 | Cooking Time: 30 Minutes

Ingredients:
- 2 teaspoons fresh mint leaves, chopped
- 1½ teaspoons red pepper chili flakes
- 2 tablespoons melted butter
- 1 pound (454 g) eggplant, peeled and cubed
- 1 pound (454 g) zucchini, peeled and cubed
- 3 tablespoons olive oil

Directions:
1. Toss all of the above ingredients in a large-sized mixing dish.
2. Roast the eggplant and zucchini bites for 30 minutes at 325ºF (163ºC) in your Air Fryer, turning once or twice.
3. Serve with a homemade dipping sauce.

Nutrition:
- (per serving) calories 110 | fat 8.3 | protein 2.6 | total carbs 8.8 | fiber 6.3

Pandan Chicken

Servings: 4 | Cooking Time: 10 Minutes

Ingredients:
- 15oz. chicken
- 1 pandan leaf
- 3 oz chive stems, diced
- 1 teaspoon minced garlic
- 1 teaspoon chili flakes
- 1 teaspoon stevia
- 1 teaspoon ground black pepper
- 1 teaspoon turmeric
- 1 tablespoon butter
- ¼ cup coconut milk
- 1 tablespoon chives powder

Directions:
1. Cut the chicken into 4 big cubes.
2. Put the chicken cubes in a large bowl.
3. Sprinkle the chicken with the minced garlic, diced chives, chili flakes, stevia, ground black pepper, chives powder, and turmeric.
4. Mix the meat up using your hands.
5. Cut the pandan leaf into 4 parts.
6. Wrap the chicken cubes into the pandan leaf.
7. Pour the coconut milk into a bowl with the wrapped chicken and leave it for 10 minutes.
8. Preheat the air fryer to 380 F.
9. Put the pandan chicken in the air fryer basket and cook for 10 minutes.
10. When the chicken is cooked – transfer to serving plates and let it chill for at least 2-3 minutes.

Nutrition:
- (per serving) calories 250 | fat 12.6 | protein 29.9 | total carbs 3.1 | fiber 0.9

Pork Bites

Servings: 6 | Cooking Time: 14 Minutes

Ingredients:
- 1-pound pork tenderloin
- 2 eggs
- 1 teaspoon butter
- ¼ cup almond flour
- 1 teaspoon kosher salt
- 1 teaspoon paprika
- 1 teaspoon ground coriander
- ½ teaspoon lemon zest

Directions:
1. Chop the pork tenderloin into the large cubes.
2. Sprinkle the pork cubes with the kosher salt, paprika, ground coriander, and lemon zest.
3. Mix the meat gently.
4. Crack the egg into a bowl and whisk it.
5. Coat the meat cubes with the egg mixture and then the almond flour.
6. Preheat the air fryer to 365 F.
7. Put the butter in the air fryer basket tray and then place the pork bites inside.
8. Cook the pork bites for 14 minutes.
9. Turn the pork bites over after 7 minutes of cooking.
10. When the pork bites are cooked – serve them hot.

Nutrition:
- (per serving) calories 142 | fat 5.4 | protein 21.9 | total carbs 0.6 | fiber 0.3

Marinated Turmeric Cauliflower Steaks

Servings:4 | Cooking Time: 15 Minutes

Ingredients:
- ¼ cup avocado oil
- ¼ cup lemon juice
- 2 cloves garlic, minced
- 1 teaspoon grated fresh ginger
- 1 tablespoon turmeric powder
- 1 teaspoon fine sea salt
- 1 medium head cauliflower
- Full-fat sour cream (or Kite Hill brand almond milk yogurt for dairy-free), for serving (optional)
- Extra-virgin olive oil, for serving (optional)
- Chopped fresh cilantro leaves, for garnish (optional)

Directions:
1. Preheat the air fryer to 400°F.
2. In a large shallow dish, combine the avocado oil, lemon juice, garlic, ginger, turmeric, and salt. Slice the cauliflower into ½-inch steaks and place them in the marinade. Cover and refrigerate for 20 minutes or overnight.
3. Remove the cauliflower steaks from the marinade and place them in the air fryer basket. Cook for 15 minutes, or until tender and slightly charred on the edges.
4. Serve with sour cream and a drizzle of olive oil, and sprinkle with chopped cilantro leaves if desired.
5. Store leftovers in an airtight container in the fridge for up to 4 days or in the freezer for up to a month. Reheat in a preheated 400°F air fryer for 5 minutes, or until warm.

Nutrition:
- (per serving)   calories 69 | fat 4g | protein 4g | total carbs 8g | fiber 4g

Ground Beef Mash

Servings: 4 | Cooking Time: 15 Minutes

Ingredients:
- 1-pound ground beef
- 3 oz chive stems
- 1 teaspoon garlic, sliced
- 1 teaspoon ground white pepper
- ¼ cup cream
- 1 teaspoon olive oil
- 2 green peppers
- 1 teaspoon dried dill
- 1 teaspoon cayenne pepper
- 2 teaspoon chicken stock

Directions:
1. Dice the chive stems.
2. Combine the chives with the sliced garlic.
3. Combine the mixture carefully with a teaspoon.
4. Sprinkle the ground beef with the ground white pepper.
5. Add dried dill and cayenne pepper.
6. Grease the air fryer basket tray with the olive oil.
7. Preheat the air fryer to 365 F.
8. Put the spiced ground beef in the air fryer basket tray.
9. Cook the beef mixture for 3 minutes.
10. Stir it carefully.
11. Add the chives mixture and chicken stock.
12. Mix it gently and cook at the same temperature for 2 minutes more.
13. Meanwhile, chop the green peppers into the small pieces.
14. Add the chopped green peppers in the air fryer.
15. Add the cream and stir it until well combined.
16. Cook the ground beef mixture for 10 minutes more.
17. Mix the ground beef mixture with a hand blender.
18. Serve hot.

Nutrition:
- (per serving) calories 258 | fat 9.3 | protein 35.5 | total carbs 6.8 | fiber 1.9

Garlic Chicken

Servings: 4 | Cooking Time: 16 Minutes

Ingredients:
- 3 oz. fresh coriander root
- 1 teaspoon olive oil
- 3 tablespoon minced garlic
- ¼ lemon, sliced
- ½ teaspoon salt
- 1 teaspoon ground black pepper
- ½ teaspoon chili flakes
- 1 tablespoon dried parsley
- 1-pound chicken thighs

Directions:
1. Peel the fresh coriander and grate it.
2. Then combine the olive oil with the minced garlic, salt, ground black pepper, chili flakes, and dried parsley.
3. Combine the mixture and sprinkle over the chicken tights.
4. Add the sliced lemon and grated coriander root.
5. Mix the chicken thighs carefully and leave them to marinate for 10 minutes in the fridge.
6. Meanwhile, preheat the air fryer to 365 F.
7. Put the chicken in the air fryer basket tray.
8. Add all the remaining liquid from the chicken and cook for 15 minutes.
9. Turn the chicken over and cook it for 1 minute more.
10. Serve hot.

Nutrition:
- (per serving) calories 187 | fat 11.4 | protein 20 | total carbs 3.6 | fiber 1

Fried Yellow Beans

Servings: 3 | Cooking Time: 8 Minutes

Ingredients:
- ¾ pound (340 g) wax yellow beans, cleaned
- 2 tablespoons peanut oil
- 4 tablespoons Romano cheese, grated
- Sea salt and ground black pepper, to taste
- ½ teaspoon red pepper flakes, crushed
- 2 tablespoons pecans, sliced
- ⅓ cup blue cheese, crumbled

Directions:
1. Toss the wax beans with the peanut oil, Romano cheese, salt, black pepper, and red pepper.
2. Place the wax beans in the lightly greased cooking basket.
3. Cook in the preheated Air Fryer at 400°F for 5 minutes. Shake the basket once or twice.
4. Add the pecans and cook for 3 minutes or more or until lightly toasted. Serve topped with blue cheese and enjoy!

Nutrition:
- (per serving) calories 236 | fat 21 | protein 2.5 | total carbs 7.9 | fiber 0.6

Korean Beef Bowl

Servings: 4 | Cooking Time: 18 Minutes

Ingredients:
- 1 tablespoon minced garlic
- 1 teaspoon ground ginger
- 4 oz chive stems, chopped
- 2 tablespoon apple cider vinegar
- 1 teaspoon stevia extract
- 1 tablespoon flax seeds
- 1 teaspoon olive oil
- 1 teaspoon olive oil
- 1-pound ground beef
- 4 tablespoon chicken stock

Directions:
1. Coat the ground beef with the apple cider vinegar and stir the meat with a spoon.
2. Add the ground ginger, minced garlic, and olive oil.
3. Mix well.
4. Preheat the air fryer to 370 F.
5. Put the ground beef in the air fryer basket tray and cook for 8 minutes.
6. Stir the ground beef carefully and sprinkle with the chopped chives, flax seeds, olive oil, and chicken stock.
7. Mix well and cook for 10 minutes more.
8. Stir and serve hot.

Nutrition:
- (per serving) calories 258 | fat 10.1 | protein 35.3 | total carbs 4.2 | fiber 1.2

Cheese Chicken Drumsticks

Servings: 4 | Cooking Time: 13 Minutes

Ingredients:
- 1-pound chicken drumstick
- 6 oz. Cheddar cheese, sliced
- 1 teaspoon dried rosemary
- 1 teaspoon dried oregano
- ½ teaspoon salt
- ½ teaspoon chili flakes

Directions:
1. Sprinkle the chicken drumsticks with dried rosemary, dried oregano, salt, and chili flakes.
2. Massage the drumsticks carefully and leave for 5 minutes to marinade.
3. Preheat the air fryer to 370 F.
4. Place the marinated chicken drumsticks in the air fryer tray and cook them for 10 minutes.
5. Turn the chicken drumsticks over and cover them with a layer of the sliced cheese.
6. Cook the chicken for 3 minutes more at the same temperature.
7. Then transfer the chicken drumsticks onto a large serving plate.
8. Serve the dish hot – the cheese should be melted.

Nutrition:
- (per serving) calories 226 | fat 9.8 | protein 16.4 | total carbs 1 | fiber 0.3

Cheese Stuffed Zucchini

Servings: 4 | Cooking Time: 8 Minutes

Ingredients:
- 1 large zucchini, cut into four pieces
- 2 tablespoons olive oil
- 1 cup Ricotta cheese, room temperature
- 2 tablespoons scallions, chopped
- 1 heaping tablespoon fresh parsley, roughly chopped
- 1 heaping tablespoon coriander, minced
- 2 ounces (57 g) Cheddar cheese, preferably freshly grated
- 1 teaspoon celery seeds
- ½ teaspoon salt
- ½ teaspoon garlic pepper

Directions:
1. Cook your zucchini in the Air Fryer cooking basket for approximately 10 minutes at 350°F (180°C). Check for doneness and cook for 2-3 minutes longer if needed.
2. Meanwhile, make the stuffing by mixing the other items.
3. When your zucchini is thoroughly cooked, open them up. Divide the stuffing among all zucchini pieces and bake for an additional 5 minutes.

Nutrition:
- (per serving) calories 199 | fat 16.4 | protein 9.2 | total carbs 4.5 | fiber 4

Liver Burgers

Servings: 7 | Cooking Time: 10 Minutes

Ingredients:
- ½ teaspoon turmeric
- ½ teaspoon ground coriander
- 1 teaspoon ground thyme
- ½ teaspoon salt
- 2 teaspoon butter
- 1 tablespoon almond flour
- 1 tablespoon coconut flour
- 1 teaspoon chili flakes
- 1-pound chicken liver
- 1 egg

Directions:
1. Grind the chicken liver.
2. Put the ground chicken in a mixing bowl.
3. Crack the egg in a separate bowl and whisk it.
4. Add the turmeric, ground coriander, ground thyme, and salt in the whisked egg mixture.
5. Add the whisked egg mixture to the ground liver.
6. Add the coconut flour and almond flour.
7. Mix with a spoon. You should get a non-sticky liver mixture. Add more almond flour if desired.
8. Preheat the air fryer to 360 F.
9. Then melt the butter and grease the air fryer basket tray with the melted butter.
10. Make medium liver burgers and put them in the prepared air fryer basket tray.
11. Cook the burgers for 5 minutes on each side. The burger should be a little bit crunchy.
12. When the liver burgers are cooked – let them chill a little before serving.

Nutrition:
- (per serving) calories 155 | fat 8.1 | protein 17.7 | total carbs 2.4 | fiber 0.9

Family Meatloaf

Servings: 12 | Cooking Time: 25 Minutes

Ingredients:
- 3 tablespoon butter
- 10 oz. ground turkey
- 7 oz. ground chicken
- 1 teaspoon dried dill
- ½ teaspoon ground coriander
- 2 tablespoons almond flour
- 1 tablespoon minced garlic
- 3 oz. fresh spinach
- 1 teaspoon salt
- 1 egg
- ½ tablespoon paprika
- 1 teaspoon sesame oil

Directions:
1. Put the ground turkey and ground chicken in a large bowl.
2. Sprinkle the meat with dried dill, ground coriander, almond flour, minced garlic, salt, and paprika.
3. Then chop the fresh spinach and add it to the ground poultry mixture.
4. Crack the egg into the meat mixture and mix well until you get a smooth texture.
5. Great the air fryer basket tray with the olive oil.
6. Preheat the air fryer to 350 F.
7. Roll the ground meat mixture gently to make the flat layer.
8. Put the butter in the center of the meat layer.
9. Make the shape of the meatloaf from the ground meat mixture. Use your fingertips for this step.
10. Place the prepared meatloaf in the air fryer basket tray.
11. Cook for 25 minutes.
12. When the meatloaf is cooked allow it to rest before serving.

Nutrition:
- (per serving) calories 142 | fat 9.8 | protein 13 | total carbs 1.7 | fiber 0.8

Corn Beef

Servings: 3 | Cooking Time: 19 Minutes

Ingredients:
- 3 oz chive stems
- 1 teaspoon black pepper
- ¼ teaspoon cayenne pepper
- 1 cup water
- 1-pound minced beef
- 1 teaspoon butter
- ½ teaspoon ground paprika

Directions:
1. Dice the chives finely.
2. Pour water into the pizza tray and place the diced chives.
3. Sprinkle the chives with the black pepper, cayenne pepper, and ground paprika.
4. Add water and mix the chives up carefully.
5. Preheat the air fryer to 400 F and put the tray into the air fryer basket.
6. Cook the chives for 4 minutes.
7. Remove the tray from the air fryer and add the minced garlic.
8. Combine the chives-meat mixture carefully and return it back in the air fryer.
9. Cook the beef mixture for 7 minutes at the same temperature.
10. Mix the meat mixture carefully with the help of a fork and cook for 8 minutes more.
11. Remove the cooked beef from the air fryer and mix it gently with a fork.
12. Transfer the cooked beef to serving plates.

Nutrition:
- (per serving) calories 310 | fat 10.8 | protein 46.4 | total carbs 4.2 | fiber 1.2

Mushroom With Artichoke And Spinach

Servings: 4 | Cooking Time: 14 Minutes

Ingredients:
- 2 tablespoons olive oil
- 4 large portobello mushrooms, stems removed and gills scraped out
- ½ teaspoon salt
- ¼ teaspoon freshly ground pepper
- 4 ounces (113 g) goat cheese, crumbled
- ½ cup chopped marinated artichoke hearts
- 1 cup frozen spinach, thawed and squeezed dry
- ½ cup grated Parmesan cheese
- 2 tablespoons chopped fresh parsley

Directions:
1. Preheat the air fryer to 400°F (205°C).
2. Rub the olive oil over the portobello mushrooms until thoroughly coated. Sprinkle both sides with the salt and black pepper. Place top-side down on a clean work surface.
3. In a small bowl, combine the goat cheese, artichoke hearts, and spinach. Mash with the back of a fork until thoroughly combined. Divide the cheese mixture among the mushrooms and sprinkle with the Parmesan cheese.
4. Air fry for 10 to 14 minutes until the mushrooms are tender and the cheese has begun to brown. Top with the fresh parsley

just before serving.

Nutrition:
- (per serving) calories 270 | fat 23 | protein 8 | total carbs 11 | fiber 7

Air Fryer Beef Tongue

Servings: 6 | Cooking Time: 20 Minutes

Ingredients:
- 1-pound beef tongue
- 1 teaspoon salt
- 1 teaspoon ground black pepper
- 1 teaspoon paprika
- 1 tablespoon butter
- 4 cup water

Directions:
1. Preheat the air fryer to 365 F.
2. Put the beef tongue in the air fryer basket tray and add water.
3. Sprinkle the mixture with salt, ground black pepper, and paprika.
4. Cook the beef tongue for 15 minutes.
5. Strain the water from the beef tongue.
6. Cut the beef tongue into strips.
7. Toss the butter in the air fryer basket tray and add the beef strips.
8. Cook the strips for 5 minutes at 360 F.
9. When the beef tongue is cooked transfer to a serving plate.

Nutrition:
- (per serving) calories 234 | fat 18.8 | protein 14.7 | total carbs 0.4 | fiber 0.2

Stuffed Beef Heart

Servings: 4 | Cooking Time: 20 Minutes

Ingredients:
- 1-pound beef heart
- 5 oz chive stems
- ½ cup fresh spinach
- 1 teaspoon salt
- 1 teaspoon ground black pepper
- 3 cups chicken stock
- 1 teaspoon butter

Directions:
1. Remove all the fat from the beef heart.
2. Dice the chives.
3. Chop the fresh spinach.
4. Combine the diced chives, fresh spinach, and butter together. Stir it.
5. Make a cut in the beef heart and fill it with the spinach-chives mixture.
6. Preheat the air fryer to 400 F.
7. Pour the chicken stock into the air fryer basket tray.
8. Sprinkle the prepared stuffed beef heart with the salt and ground black pepper.
9. Put the beef heart in the air fryer and cook it for 20 minutes.
10. Remove the cooked heart from the air fryer and slice it.
11. Sprinkle the slices with the remaining liquid from the air fryer.

Nutrition:
- (per serving) calories 216 | fat 6.8 | protein 33.3 | total carbs 3.8 | fiber 0.8

Meatball Casserole

Servings: 7 | Cooking Time: 21 Minutes

Ingredients:
- 1 eggplants
- 10 oz. ground chicken
- 8 oz. ground beef
- 1 teaspoon minced garlic
- 1 teaspoon ground white pepper
- 1 tomato
- 1 egg
- 1 tablespoon coconut flour
- 8 oz. Parmesan, shredded
- 2 tablespoon butter
- 1/3 cup cream

Directions:
1. Combine the ground chicken and ground beef in a large bowl.
2. Add the minced garlic and ground white pepper.
3. Crack the egg into the bowl with the ground meat mixture and stir it carefully until well combined.
4. Then add the coconut flour and mix.
5. Make small meatballs from the ground meat.
6. Preheat the air fryer to 360 F.
7. Sprinkle the air fryer basket tray with the butter and pour the cream.
8. Peel the eggplant and chop it.
9. Put the meatballs over the cream and sprinkle them with the chopped eggplant.
10. Slice the tomato and place it over the eggplant.
11. Make a layer of shredded cheese over the sliced tomato.
12. Put the casserole in the air fryer and cook it for 21 minutes.
13. Let the casserole cool to room temperature before serving.

Nutrition:
- (per serving) calories 314 | fat 16.8 | protein 33.9 | total carbs 7.5 | fiber 3.4

Bacon Pork Bites

Servings: 6 | Cooking Time: 14 Minutes

Ingredients:
- 1-pound pork brisket
- 6 oz. bacon, sliced
- 1 teaspoon salt
- 1 teaspoon turmeric
- ½ teaspoon red pepper
- 1 teaspoon olive oil
- 1 tablespoon apple cider vinegar

Directions:
1. Cut the pork brisket into medium bites.
2. Put the pork bites in the big mixing bowl.
3. Sprinkle the meat with the turmeric, salt, red pepper, and apple cider vinegar.
4. Mix the pork bites carefully and leave them for 10 minutes to marinade.
5. Wrap the pork bites in the sliced bacon.
6. Secure the pork bites with the toothpicks.
7. Preheat the air fryer to 370 F.
8. Put the prepared bacon pork bites on the air fryer tray.
9. Cook the pork bites for 8 minutes.
10. Turn the pork over.
11. Cook the dish for 6 minutes more.

Nutrition:

- (per serving) calories 239 | fat 13.7 | protein 26.8 | total carbs 2.8 | fiber 0.2

Asparagus With Broccoli

Servings: 4 | Cooking Time: 22 Minutes

Ingredients:
- ½ pound (227g) asparagus, cut into 1 ½-inch pieces
- ½ pound (227g) broccoli, cut into 1 ½-inch pieces
- 2 tablespoons olive oil
- Some salt and white pepper, to taste
- ½ cup vegetable broth
- 2 tablespoons apple cider vinegar

Directions:
1. Place the vegetables in a single layer in the lightly greased cooking basket. Drizzle the olive oil over the vegetables.
2. Sprinkle with salt and white pepper.
3. Cook at 380ºF (193ºC) for 15 minutes, shaking the basket halfway through the cooking time.
4. Add ½ cup of vegetable broth to a saucepan, bring to a rapid boil and add the vinegar. Cook for 5 to 7 minutes or until the sauce has reduced by half.
5. Spoon the sauce over the warm vegetables and serve immediately. Bon appétit!

Nutrition:
- (per serving) calories 181 | fat 7 | protein 3 | total carbs 4 | fiber 1

Garlic Thyme Mushrooms

Servings:4 | Cooking Time: 10 Minutes

Ingredients:
- 3 tablespoons unsalted butter (or butter-flavored coconut oil for dairy-free), melted
- 1 (8-ounce) package button mushrooms, sliced
- 2 cloves garlic, minced
- 3 sprigs fresh thyme leaves, plus more for garnish
- ½ teaspoon fine sea salt

Directions:
1. Spray the air fryer basket with avocado oil. Preheat the air fryer to 400°F.
2. Place all the ingredients in a medium-sized bowl. Use a spoon or your hands to coat the mushroom slices.
3. Place the mushrooms in the air fryer basket in one layer; work in batches if necessary. Cook for 10 minutes, or until slightly crispy and brown. Garnish with thyme sprigs before serving.
4. Store leftovers in an airtight container in the fridge for up to 5 days or in the freezer for up to a month. Reheat in a preheated 350°F air fryer for 5 minutes, or until heated through.

Nutrition:
- (per serving)   calories 82 | fat 9g | protein 1g | total carbs 1g | fiber 0.2g

Cauliflower With Cheese

Servings: 4 | Cooking Time: 30 Minutes

Ingredients:
- 5 cups cauliflower florets
- ⅔ cup almond flour
- ½ teaspoon salt
- ¼ cup unsalted butter, melted
- ¼ cup grated Parmesan cheese

Directions:

1. In a food processor fitted with a metal blade, pulse the cauliflower until finely chopped. Transfer the cauliflower to a large microwave-safe bowl and cover it with a paper towel. Microwave for 5 minutes. Spread the cauliflower on a towel to cool.
2. When cool enough to handle, draw up the sides of the towel and squeeze tightly over a sink to remove the excess moisture. Return the cauliflower to the food processor and whirl until creamy. Sprinkle the flour and salt and pulse until a sticky dough comes together.
3. Transfer the dough to a workspace lightly floured with almond flour. Shape the dough into a ball and divide into 4 equal sections. Roll each section into a rope 1-inch thick. Slice the dough into squares with a sharp knife.
4. Preheat the air fryer to 400°F (205ºC).
5. Working in batches if necessary, place the gnocchi in a single layer in the basket of the air fryer and spray generously with olive oil. Pausing halfway through the cooking time to turn the gnocchi, air fry for 25 to 30 minutes until golden brown and crispy on the edges. Transfer to a large bowl and toss with the melted butter and Parmesan cheese.

Nutrition:
• (per serving) calories 360 | fat 20 | protein 9 | total carbs 14 | fiber 10

Shepherd's Pie

Servings: 5 | Cooking Time: 25 Minutes

Ingredients:
• 2 tablespoons olive oil
• 2 bell peppers, seeded and sliced
• 1 celery, chopped
• 1 onion, chopped
• 2 garlic cloves, minced
• 1 cup cooked bacon, diced
• 1½ cups beef bone broth
• 5 ounces (142 g) green beans, drained
• Sea salt and freshly ground black pepper, to taste
• 8 ounces (227 g) cauliflower pulsed in a food processor to a fine-crumb like consistency
• ½ cup milk
• 2 tablespoons butter, melted

Directions:

1. Heat the olive oil in a saucepan over medium-high heat. Now, cook the peppers, celery, onion, and garlic until they have softened, for about 7 minutes
2. Add the bacon and broth. Bring to a boil and cook for 2 minutes or more. Stir in green beans, salt and black pepper, continue to cook until everything is heated through.
3. Transfer the mixture to the lightly greased baking pan.
4. Microwave cauliflower rice for 5 minutes.
5. In a small bowl, combine the cauliflower, milk, and melted butter. Stir until well mixed and spoon evenly over the vegetable mixture. Smooth it with a spatula and transfer to the Air Fryer cooking basket.
6. Bake in the preheated Air Fryer at 400ºF for 12 minutes. Place on a wire rack to cool slightly before slicing and serving. Bon appétit!

Nutrition:
• (per serving) calories 214 | fat 18.5 | protein 8.5 | total carbs 4.4 | fiber 0.9

Zucchini And Bell Pepper Kabobs

Servings: 4 | Cooking Time: 15 Minutes

Ingredients:
• 1 medium-sized zucchini, cut into 1-inch pieces
• 2 red bell peppers, cut into 1-inch pieces
• 1 green bell pepper, cut into 1-inch pieces
• 1 red onion, cut into 1-inch pieces
• 2 tablespoons olive oil
• Sea salt, to taste
• ½ teaspoon black pepper, preferably freshly cracked
• ½ teaspoon red pepper flakes

Directions:

1. Soak the wooden skewers in water for 15 minutes.
2. Thread the vegetables on skewers, drizzle olive oil all over the vegetable skewers, sprinkle with spices.
3. Cook in the preheated Air Fryer at 400ºF for 13 minutes. Serve warm and enjoy!

Nutrition:
• (per serving) calories 86 | fat 6.9 | protein 1.1 | total carbs 5.9 | fiber 1.1

Cauliflower And Mushroom With Yogurt Tahini Sauce

Servings: 4 | Cooking Time: 16 Minutes

Ingredients:
• 1 pound (454 g) cauliflower florets
• 1 pound (454 g) button mushrooms
• 2 tablespoons olive oil
• ½ teaspoon white pepper
• ½ teaspoon dried dill weed
• ½ teaspoon cayenne pepper
• ½ teaspoon celery seeds
• ½ teaspoon mustard seeds
• Salt, to taste
• Yogurt Tahini Sauce:
• 1 cup plain yogurt
• 2 heaping tablespoons tahini paste
• 1 tablespoon lemon juice
• 1 tablespoon extra-virgin olive oil
• ½ teaspoon Aleppo pepper, minced

Directions:

1. Toss the cauliflower and mushrooms with olive oil and spices. Preheat your Air Fryer to 380ºF.
2. Add the cauliflower to the cooking basket and cook for 10 minutes.
3. Add the mushrooms, turn the temperature to 390ºand cook for 6 minutes or more.
4. While the vegetables are cooking, make the sauce by whisking all ingredients. Serve the warm vegetables with the sauce on the side. Bon appétit!

Nutrition:
• (per serving) calories 185 | fat 14.8 | protein 3.9 | total carbs 9.2 | fiber 3.1

Keto Beef Stew

Servings: 6 | Cooking Time: 23 Minutes

Ingredients:
- 10 oz. beef short ribs
- 1 cup chicken stock
- 1 garlic clove
- 3 oz chive stems
- 4 oz. green peas
- ¼ teaspoon salt
- 1 teaspoon turmeric
- 1 green pepper
- 2 teaspoon butter
- ½ teaspoon chili flakes
- 4 oz. kale

Directions:
1. Preheat the air fryer to 360 F.
2. Place the butter in the air fryer basket tray.
3. Add the beef short ribs.
4. Sprinkle the beef short ribs with the salt, turmeric, and chili flakes.
5. Cook the beef short ribs for 15 minutes.
6. Meanwhile, remove the seeds from the green pepper and chop it.
7. Chop the kale and dice the chives.
8. When the time is over – pour the chicken stock in the beef short ribs.
9. Add the chopped green pepper and diced chives.
10. After this, sprinkle the mixture with the green peas.
11. Peel the garlic clove and add it to the mixture too.
12. Mix it up using the wooden spatula.
13. Then chop the kale and add it to the stew mixture.
14. Stir the stew mixture one more time and cook it at 360 F for 8 minutes more.
15. When the stew is cooked – let it rest little.
16. Then mix the stew up and transfer to the serving plates.
17. Enjoy!

Nutrition:
- (per serving) calories 144 | fat 5.8 | protein 15.7 | total carbs 7 | fiber 1.9

Broccoli Croquettes

Servings: 4 | Cooking Time: 10 Minutes

Ingredients:
- ½ pound (227 g) broccoli florets
- 1 tablespoon ground flaxseeds
- 1 yellow onion, finely chopped
- 1 bell pepper, seeded and chopped
- 2 garlic cloves, pressed
- 1 teaspoon turmeric powder
- ½ teaspoon ground cumin
- ½ cup almond flour
- ½ cup Parmesan cheese
- 2 eggs, whisked
- Salt and ground black pepper, to taste
- 2 tablespoons olive oil

Directions:
1. Blanch the broccoli in salted boiling water until al-dente, for about 3 to 4 minutes. Drain well and transfer to a mixing bowl, mash the broccoli florets with the remaining ingredients.
2. Form the mixture into patties and place them in the lightly greased Air Fryer basket.
3. Cook at 400°F for 6 minutes, turning them over halfway through the cooking time, work in batches.
4. Serve warm with mayonnaise. Enjoy!

Nutrition:
- (per serving) calories 219 | fat 16.6 | protein 6.5 | total carbs 10 | fiber 1

Mushroom Soufflés

Servings: 4 | Cooking Time: 12 Minutes

Ingredients:
- 3 large eggs, whites and yolks separated
- ½ cup sharp white Cheddar cheese
- 3 ounces (85 g) cream cheese, softened
- ¼ teaspoon cream of tartar
- ¼ teaspoon salt
- ¼ teaspoon ground black pepper
- ½ cup cremini mushrooms, sliced

Directions:
1. In a large bowl, whip egg whites until stiff peaks form, for about 2 minutes. In a separate large bowl, beat Cheddar, egg yolks, cream cheese, cream of tartar, salt, and pepper together until combined.
2. Fold egg whites into cheese mixture, being careful not to stir. Fold in mushrooms, then pour mixture evenly into four ungreased 4-inch ramekins.
3. Place ramekins into air fryer basket. Adjust the temperature to 350°F (180ºC) and set the timer for 12 minutes. Eggs will be browned on the top and firm in the center when done. Serve warm.

Nutrition:
- (per serving) calories 185 | fat 14 | protein 10 | total carbs 2 | fiber 2

Fried Cauliflower Rice

Servings:4 | Cooking Time: 8 Minutes

Ingredients:
- 2 cups cauliflower florets
- ⅓ cup sliced green onions, plus more for garnish
- 3 tablespoons wheat-free tamari or coconut aminos
- 1 clove garlic, smashed to a paste or minced
- 1 teaspoon grated fresh ginger
- 1 teaspoon fish sauce or fine sea salt (see Note)
- 1 teaspoon lime juice
- ⅛ teaspoon ground black pepper

Directions:
1. Preheat the air fryer to 375°F.
2. Place the cauliflower in a food processor and pulse until it resembles grains of rice.
3. Place all the ingredients, including the riced cauliflower, in a large bowl and stir well to combine.
4. Transfer the cauliflower mixture to a 6-inch pie pan or a casserole dish that will fit in your air fryer. Cook for 8 minutes, or until soft, shaking halfway through. Garnish with sliced green onions before serving.
5. Store leftovers in an airtight container in the fridge for up to 4 days. Reheat in a preheated 375°F air fryer for 4 minutes, or until heated through.

Nutrition:
- (per serving)   calories 30 | fat 0g | protein 3g | total carbs 4g | fiber 1g

Eggplant With Tomato And Cheese

Servings: 4 | Cooking Time: 5 Minutes

Ingredients:
- 1 eggplant, peeled and sliced
- 2 bell peppers, seeded and sliced
- 1 red onion, sliced
- 1 teaspoon fresh garlic, minced
- 4 tablespoons olive oil
- 1 teaspoon mustard
- 1 teaspoon dried oregano
- 1 teaspoon smoked paprika
- Salt and ground black pepper, to taste
- 1 tomato, sliced
- 6 ounces (170 g) halloumi cheese, sliced lengthways

Directions:
1. Start by preheating your Air Fryer to 370ºF (188ºC). Spritz a baking pan with nonstick cooking spray.
2. Place the eggplant, peppers, onion, and garlic on the bottom of the baking pan. Add the olive oil, mustard, and spices. Transfer to the cooking basket and cook for 14 minutes.
3. Top with the tomatoes and cheese, increase the temperature to 390ºF (199ºC) and cook for 5 minutes or more until bubbling. Let it sit on a cooling rack for 10 minutes before serving.
4. Bon appétit!

Nutrition:
- (per serving) calories 306 | fat 16.1 | protein 39.6 | total carbs 8.8 | fiber 7

Baked Rainbow Vegetables

Servings: 4 | Cooking Time: 50 Minutes

Ingredients:
- 1 pound (454 g) cauliflower, chopped into small florets
- 2 tablespoons olive oil
- ½ teaspoon red pepper flakes, crushed
- ½ teaspoon freshly ground black pepper
- Salt, to taste
- 3 bell peppers, thinly sliced
- 1 serrano pepper, thinly sliced
- 2 medium-sized tomatoes, sliced
- 1 leek, thinly sliced
- 2 garlic cloves, minced
- 1 cup Monterey cheese, shredded

Directions:
1. Start by preheating your Air Fryer to 350ºF. Spritz a casserole dish with cooking oil.
2. Place the cauliflower in the casserole dish in an even layer, drizzle 1 tablespoon of olive oil over the top. Then, add the red pepper, black pepper, and salt.
3. Add 2 bell peppers and ½ of the leeks. Add the tomatoes and the remaining 1 tablespoon of olive oil.
4. Add the remaining peppers, leeks, and minced garlic. Top with the cheese.
5. Cover the casserole with foil and bake for 32 minutes. Remove the foil and increase the temperature to 400ºF, bake an additional 16 minutes. Bon appétit!

Nutrition:
- (per serving) calories 233 | fat 17.2 | protein 1.1 | total carbs 9.7 | fiber 3.2

Succulent Beef Steak

Servings: 4 | Cooking Time: 12 Minutes

Ingredients:
- 1 tablespoon butter
- 2 tablespoons fresh orange juice
- 1 teaspoon lime zest
- 1-pound beef steak
- 1 teaspoon ground ginger
- 1 teaspoon dried oregano
- 1 tablespoon cream
- ½ teaspoon minced garlic

Directions:
1. Combine the fresh orange juice, butter, lime zest, ground ginger, dried oregano, cream, and minced garlic together.
2. Combine the mixture well.
3. Then tenderize the steak gently.
4. Brush the beefsteak with the combined spice mix carefully and leave the steak for 7 minutes to marinade.
5. Preheat the air fryer to 360 F.
6. Put the marinated beef steak in the air fryer basket and cook the meat for 12 minutes. The beef should be well done.

Nutrition:
- (per serving) calories 245 | fat 10.2 | protein 34.6 | total carbs 1.7 | fiber 0.3

Double-cheese Cauliflower Croquettes

Servings: 4 | Cooking Time: 16 Minutes

Ingredients:
- 1 pound (454 g) cauliflower florets
- 2 eggs
- 1 tablespoon olive oil
- 2 tablespoons scallions, chopped
- 1 garlic clove, minced
- 1 cup Colby cheese, shredded
- ½ cup Parmesan cheese, grated
- Sea salt and ground black pepper, to taste
- ¼ teaspoon dried dill weed
- 1 teaspoon paprika

Directions:
1. Blanch the cauliflower in salted boiling water for about 3 to 4 minutes until al dente. Drain well and pulse in a food processor.
2. Add the remaining ingredients, mix to combine well. Shape the cauliflower mixture into bite-sized tots.
3. Spritz the Air Fryer basket with cooking spray.
4. Cook in the preheated Air Fryer at 375ºF for 16 minutes, shaking halfway through the cooking time. Serve with your favorite sauce for dipping. Bon appétit!

Nutrition:
- (per serving) calories 274 | fat 19 | protein 6.4 | total carbs 18.8 | fiber 2.7

Burrata-stuffed Tomatoes

Servings:4 | Cooking Time: 5 Minutes

Ingredients:
- 4 medium tomatoes
- ½ teaspoon fine sea salt
- 4 (2-ounce) Burrata balls
- Fresh basil leaves, for garnish
- Extra-virgin olive oil, for drizzling

Directions:
1. Preheat the air fryer to 300°F.
2. Core the tomatoes and scoop out the seeds and membranes using a melon baller or spoon. Sprinkle the insides of the tomatoes with the salt.
3. Stuff each tomato with a ball of Burrata. Place in the air fryer and cook for 5 minutes, or until the cheese has softened.
4. Garnish with basil leaves and drizzle with olive oil. Serve warm.
5. Store leftovers in an airtight container in the refrigerator for up to 4 days. Reheat in a preheated 300°F air fryer for about 3 minutes, until heated through.

Nutrition:
- (per serving) calories 108 | fat 7g | protein 6g | total carbs 5g | fiber 2g

Balsamic Cauliflower And Mushroom

Servings: 3 | Cooking Time: 12 Minutes

Ingredients:
- ½ pound (227 g) cauliflower florets
- ½ pound (227 g) button mushrooms, whole
- 1 cup pearl onions, whole
- Pink Himalayan salt and ground black pepper, to taste
- ¼ teaspoon smoked paprika
- 1 teaspoon garlic powder
- ½ teaspoon dried thyme
- ½ teaspoon dried marjoram
- 3 tablespoons olive oil
- 2 tablespoons balsamic vinegar

Directions:
1. Toss all ingredients in a large mixing dish.
2. Roast in the preheated Air Fryer at 400ºF for 5 minutes. Shake the basket and cook for 7 minutes or more.
3. Serve with some extra fresh herbs if desired. Bon appétit!

Nutrition:
- (per serving) calories 170 | fat 14 | protein 4.2 | total carbs 9.7 | fiber 2.9

Goulash

Servings: 6 | Cooking Time: 17 Minutes

Ingredients:
- 4 oz chive stems
- 2 green peppers, chopped
- 1 teaspoon olive oil
- 14 oz. ground chicken
- 2 tomatoes
- ½ cup chicken stock
- 2 garlic cloves, sliced
- 1 teaspoon salt
- 1 teaspoon ground black pepper
- 1 teaspoon mustard

Directions:
1. Chop chives roughly.
2. Spray the air fryer basket tray with the olive oil.
3. Preheat the air fryer to 365 F.
4. Put the chopped chives in the air fryer basket tray.
5. Add the chopped green pepper and cook the vegetables for 5 minutes.
6. Add the ground chicken.
7. Chop the tomatoes into the small cubes and add them in the air fryer mixture too.
8. Cook the mixture for 6 minutes more.
9. Add the chicken stock, sliced garlic cloves, salt, ground black pepper, and mustard.
10. Mix well to combine.
11. Cook the goulash for 6 minutes more.

Nutrition:
- (per serving) calories 161 | fat 6.1 | protein 20.3 | total carbs 6 | fiber 1.7

Crispy Brussels Sprouts

Servings:4 | Cooking Time: 8 Minutes

Ingredients:
- 2 cups Brussels sprouts, trimmed and halved
- 3 tablespoons ghee or coconut oil, melted
- 1 teaspoon fine sea salt or smoked salt
- Dash of lime or lemon juice
- Thinly sliced Parmesan cheese, for serving (optional; omit for dairy-free)
- Lemon slices, for serving (optional)

Directions:
1. Spray the air fryer basket with avocado oil. Preheat the air fryer to 400°F.
2. In a large bowl, toss together the Brussels sprouts, ghee, and salt. Add the lime or lemon juice.
3. Place the Brussels sprouts in the air fryer basket and cook for 8 minutes, or until crispy, shaking the basket after 5 minutes. Serve with thinly sliced Parmesan and lemon slices, if desired.
4. Best served fresh. Store leftovers in an airtight container in the fridge for up to 5 days. Reheat in a preheated 390°F air fryer for 3 minutes, or until heated through.

Nutrition:
- (per serving) calories 149 | fat 12g | protein 4g | total carbs 10g | fiber 4g

Bruschetta

Servings:12 | Cooking Time: 8 Minutes

Ingredients:
- 1 small tomato, diced
- 2 tablespoons chopped fresh basil leaves
- 1 teaspoon dried oregano leaves
- ¼ teaspoon fine sea salt
- 3 tablespoons unsalted butter, softened (or olive oil for dairy-free)
- 1 clove garlic, minced
- 1 recipe Hot Dog Buns (here), cut into twelve ½-inch-thick slices
- ¼ cup plus 2 tablespoons shredded Parmesan cheese

Directions:
1. Spray the air fryer basket with avocado oil. Preheat the air fryer to 360°F.
2. In a small bowl, stir together the tomato, basil, oregano, and salt until well combined. Set aside.
3. In another small bowl, mix together the butter and garlic. Spread the garlic butter on one side of each hot dog bun slice.
4. Place the slices in the air fryer basket buttered side down, spaced about ⅛ inch apart. Cook for 4 minutes. Remove the slices from the air fryer, flip them so that the buttered side is up, and top each slice with 1½ tablespoons of Parmesan and a dollop of the tomato mixture.
5. Increase the air fryer temperature to 390°F and return the slices to the air fryer basket. Cook for another 2 to 4 minutes, until the bread is crispy and the cheese is melted.
6. Serve immediately. Alternatively, stop after step 3 and store the slices of bread and the tomato mixture in separate airtight containers in the fridge for up to 5 days. When you're ready to eat, cook as instructed in steps 4 and 5.

Nutrition:
- (per serving)   calories 268 | fat 22g | protein 10g | total carbs 14g | fiber 10g

Herbed Broccoli And Celery Root

Servings: 2 | Cooking Time: 15 Minutes

Ingredients:
- ½ pound (227 g) broccoli florets
- 1 celery root, peeled and cut into 1-inch pieces
- 1 onion, cut into wedges
- 2 tablespoons unsalted butter, melted
- ½ cup chicken broth
- ¼ cup tomato sauce
- 1 teaspoon parsley
- 1 teaspoon rosemary
- 1 teaspoon thyme

Directions:
1. Start by preheating your Air Fryer to 380°F. Place all ingredients in a lightly greased casserole dish. Stir to combine well.
2. Bake in the preheated Air Fryer for 10 minutes. Gently stir the vegetables with a large spoon and cook for 5 minutes or more.
3. Serve in individual bowls with a few drizzles of lemon juice. Bon appétit!

Nutrition:
- (per serving) calories 141 | fat 11.3 | protein 2.5 | total carbs 8.1 | fiber 2.6

Chili Pepper Lamb Chops

Servings: 6 | Cooking Time: 10 Minutes

Ingredients:
- 21 oz. lamb chops
- 1 teaspoon chili pepper
- ½ teaspoon chili flakes
- 1 teaspoon onion powder
- 1 teaspoon garlic powder
- 1 teaspoon cayenne pepper
- 1 tablespoon olive oil
- 1 tablespoon butter
- ½ teaspoon lime zest

Directions:
1. Melt the butter and combine it with the olive oil.
2. Whisk then add chili pepper, chili flakes, onion powder, garlic powder, cayenne pepper, and lime zest.
3. Mix well.
4. Coat the lamb chops with the marinade.
5. Leave the meat for at least 5 minutes in the fridge.
6. Preheat the air fryer to 400 F.
7. Place the marinated lamb chops in the air fryer and cook them for 5 minutes.
8. Turn the chops over.
9. Cook the lamb chops for 5 minutes more.

Nutrition:
- (per serving) calories 227 | fat 11.6 | protein 28.1 | total carbs 1 | fiber 0.2

Chapter 9 Desserts Recipes

Keto Sweet Mini Rolls

Servings: 10 | Cooking Time: 15 Minutes

Ingredients:
- 1 tablespoon ground cinnamon
- 3 tablespoon Erythritol
- 1 teaspoon baking powder
- 1 teaspoon fresh lemon juice
- 1 teaspoon lemon zest
- 1 cup almond flour
- 1 tablespoon coconut flakes
- 1 egg
- 1 pinch salt
- 1/3 cup heavy cream

Directions:
1. Combine the ground cinnamon and Erythritol in a bowl.
2. Then combine the baking powder, fresh lemon juice, lemon zest, and almond flour.
3. Add coconut flakes, salt, and heavy cream.
4. Crack the egg in a separate bowl and whisk it.
5. Then add the whisked egg in the almond flour mixture.
6. Mix well to combine.
7. Roll the dough with a rolling pin.
8. Then sprinkle the surface of the dough with the ground cinnamon mixture.
9. Roll it.
10. Cut the roll into 6 parts.
11. Preheat the air fryer to 350 F.
12. Place the rolls in the air fryer and cook them for 15 minutes.
13. Check they are cooked through with a toothpick.
14. Allow to cool before serving.

Nutrition:
- (per serving) calories 107 | fat 8.4 | protein 3.8 | total carbs 7.4 | fiber 1.2

Crusted Mini Cheesecake

Servings: 8 | Cooking Time: 18 Minutes

Ingredients:
- For the Crust:
- ⅓ teaspoon grated nutmeg
- 1½ tablespoons erythritol
- 1½ cups almond meal
- 8 tablespoons melted butter
- 1 teaspoon ground cinnamon
- A pinch of kosher salt, to taste
- For the Cheesecake:
- 2 eggs
- ½ cups unsweetened chocolate chips
- 1½ tablespoons sour cream
- 4 ounces (113 g) soft cheese
- ½ cup Swerve
- ½ teaspoon vanilla essence

Directions:
1. Firstly, line eight cups of mini muffin pan with paper liners.
2. To make the crust, mix the almond meal together with erythritol, cinnamon, nutmeg, and kosher salt.

3. Now, add melted butter and stir well to moisten the crumb mixture.
4. Divide the crust mixture among the muffin cups and press gently to make even layers.
5. In another bowl, whip together the soft cheese, sour cream and Swerve until uniform and smooth. Fold in the eggs and the vanilla essence.
6. Then, divide chocolate chips among the prepared muffin cups. Then, add the cheese mix to each muffin cup.
7. Bake for about 18 minutes at 345ºF (174ºC). Bake in batches if needed. To finish, transfer the mini cheesecakes to a cooling rack, store in the fridge.

Nutrition:
- (per serving) calories 314 | fat 29 | protein 7 | total carbs 7 | fiber 4

Poppy Seed Muffin

Servings: 5 | Cooking Time: 10 Minutes

Ingredients:
- 5 tablespoons coconut oil, softened
- 1 egg, beaten
- 1 teaspoon vanilla extract
- 1 tablespoon poppy seeds
- 1 teaspoon baking powder
- 2 tablespoons erythritol
- 1 cup coconut flour

Directions:
1. In the mixing bowl, mix coconut oil with egg, vanilla extract, poppy seeds, baking powder, erythritol, and coconut flour.
2. When the mixture is homogenous, pour it in the muffin molds and transfer it in the air fryer basket.
3. Cook the muffins for 10 minutes at 365F (185ºC).

Nutrition:
- (per serving) calories 239 | fat 17 | protein 5 | total carbs 17 | fiber 7

Chocolate Chip Cookies

Servings: 5 | Cooking Time: 15 Minutes

Ingredients:
- 1 cup almond flour
- 3 tablespoon macadamia nuts, crushed
- 1 egg
- 3 tablespoon butter, unsalted
- 2 tablespoon dark chocolate chips
- ¼ teaspoon salt
- ¼ teaspoon baking powder
- ½ teaspoon vanilla extract
- 1 teaspoon stevia extract

Directions:
1. Crack the egg into a mixing bowl and whisk using a hand whisker.
2. Add butter and almond flour.
3. Add salt, baking powder, vanilla extract, and stevia extract.
4. Sprinkle the mixture with the crushed macadamia nuts and dark chocolate chips.

5. Knead the dough until smooth.
6. Then make 5 balls from the dough and flatten a little.
7. Preheat the air fryer to 360 F.
8. Put the cookies in the air fryer and cook for 15 minutes.
9. Allow the cookies to cool before serving.

Nutrition:
- (per serving) calories 157 | fat 15.2 | protein 3 | total carbs 4.2 | fiber 1

Rhubarb Bars

Servings: 14 | Cooking Time: 8 Minutes

Ingredients:
- ½ cup rhubarb
- ¼ cup Erythritol
- ¼ teaspoon ground ginger
- ½ cup coconut flour
- 3 tablespoon heavy cream
- 1 teaspoon vanilla extract
- 1 tablespoon butter

Directions:
1. Blend the rhubarb and combine it with Erythritol and ground ginger.
2. Add coconut flour and heavy cream.
3. Add vanilla extract and butter.
4. Knead the dough.
5. Roll the dough and cut it into 6 squares.
6. Preheat the air fryer to 350 F.
7. Place the rhubarb squares in the air fryer and cook for 8 minutes.
8. Allow to cool before serving.

Nutrition:
- (per serving) calories 43 | fat 1.5 | protein 0.7 | total carbs 6.8 | fiber 2

Cashew Thin Pie

Servings: 16 | Cooking Time: 18 Minutes

Ingredients:
- 1 egg
- 1 cup coconut flour
- 2 oz. cashews, crushed
- 1 oz. dark chocolate, melted
- 1/3 cup heavy cream
- ½ teaspoon baking soda
- 1 teaspoon apple cider vinegar
- 1 tablespoon butter

Directions:
1. Crack the egg in a blender and add coconut flour.
2. Add melted chocolate, heavy cream, baking soda, apple cider vinegar, and butter.
3. Blend well.
4. Transfer the dough to a bowl and sprinkle it with the crushed cashews.
5. Knead the dough.
6. Preheat the air fryer to 350 F.
7. Place the dough in the air fryer dish and flatten into the shape of a pie.
8. Cook the pie for 18 minutes.
9. Allow to cool before removing from the dish.
10. Cut it into servings.

Nutrition:

- (per serving) calories 79 | fat 4.8 | protein 2.1 | total carbs 7.3 | fiber 3.1

Poppy Seed Balls

Servings: 14 | Cooking Time: 8 Minutes

Ingredients:
- ½ cup heavy cream
- 1 cup coconut flour
- ¼ teaspoon salt
- ½ teaspoon ground cinnamon
- 4 tablespoon poppy seeds
- ¼ teaspoon ground ginger
- 1 teaspoon butter
- ½ teaspoon baking powder
- ½ teaspoon apple cider vinegar
- 3 tablespoon stevia extract

Directions:
1. Mix the coconut flour, salt, ground cinnamon, poppy seeds, ground ginger, and baking powder together in a bowl.
2. Melt the butter gently and add to the dried mixture.
3. Add apple cider vinegar and stevia extract.
4. Add heavy cream and knead to a soft dough.
5. Make the log from the dough and cut into 11 balls.
6. Preheat the air fryer to 365 F.
7. Put the poppy seed balls in the air fryer basket.
8. Cook the balls for 3 minutes.
9. Shake them a little and cook for 5 minutes more.
10. Check if the balls are cooked using a toothpick.
11. Cool before serving.

Nutrition:
- (per serving) calories 63 | fat 4.2 | protein 1.7 | total carbs 7.4 | fiber 4.1

Lime Bar

Servings: 10 | Cooking Time: 35 Minutes

Ingredients:
- 3 tablespoons coconut oil, melted
- 3 tablespoons Splenda
- 1½ cup coconut flour
- 3 eggs, beaten
- 1 teaspoon lime zest, grated
- 3 tablespoons lime juice

Directions:
1. Cover the air fryer basket bottom with baking paper.
2. Then in the mixing bowl, mix Splenda with coconut flour, eggs, lime zest, and lime juice.
3. Pour the mixture in the air fryer basket and flatten gently.
4. Cook the meal at 350F (180ºC) for 35 minutes.
5. Then cool the cooked meal little and cut into bars.

Nutrition:
- (per serving) calories 144 | fat 7 | protein 4 | total carbs 16 | fiber 8

Keto Chocolate Spread

Servings: 6 | Cooking Time: 3 Minutes

Ingredients:
- 1 oz. dark chocolate
- 3 oz. hazelnuts, crushed
- 4 tablespoon butter
- ¼ cup almond milk
- ½ teaspoon vanilla extract
- 1 teaspoon stevia

Directions:
1. Preheat the air fryer to 360 F.
2. Put the dark chocolate, crushed hazelnuts, butter, almond milk, vanilla extract, and stevia in the air fryer basket.
3. Mix well and cook for 2 minutes.
4. Mix again with a hand mixer.
5. Cook the mixture for 1 minute.
6. Stir the mixture again and pour it into a glass vessel.
7. Put the mixture in the fridge and let it cool until it is solid.

Nutrition:
- (per serving) calories 206 | fat 20.1 | protein 2.8 | total carbs 5.8 | fiber 1.8

Strawberry Grated Pie

Servings: 12 | Cooking Time: 25 Minutes

Ingredients:
- ½ cup strawberry, chopped
- 1 cup almond flour
- 1 tablespoon coconut flour
- 1 pinch salt
- 4 tablespoon Erythritol
- ½ teaspoon baking soda
- 1 teaspoon apple cider vinegar
- 1/3 cup butter
- ¼ teaspoon ground nutmeg

Directions:
1. Combine the almond flour, coconut flour, salt, Erythritol, baking soda, apple cider vinegar, butter, and ground nutmeg in a mixing bowl.
2. Knead until well combined.
3. Place the dough in the fridge for 10 minutes.
4. Preheat the air fryer to 350 F.
5. Grate the dough.
6. Separate the grated dough into 2 parts.
7. Then place the first part of the grated dough in the air fryer dish.
8. Sprinkle it with the chopped strawberry.
9. Then cover it with the second part of the grated dough.
10. Put the pie in the air fryer and cook for 25 minutes.
11. Allow to cool.
12. Remove the pie from the air fryer and slice into servings.

Nutrition:
- (per serving) calories 114 | fat 11.5 | protein 2.5 | total carbs 8.1 | fiber 1.4

Chia Seed Crackers

Servings: 10 | Cooking Time: 4 Minutes

Ingredients:
- 5 tablespoon chia seeds
- 2 oz. Cheddar cheese, shredded
- ½ cup water
- 1 oz. psyllium husk powder
- 1 teaspoon olive oil
- 1 teaspoon onion powder
- 1 teaspoon paprika
- ½ teaspoon dried rosemary
- ½ teaspoon ground ginger

Directions:
1. Combine the chia seeds with water, husk powder, and onion powder.
2. Add paprika, dried rosemary, and ground ginger.
3. Shred Cheddar cheese and add it to the mixture.
4. Mix well and make a smooth dough. The dough should be very elastic.
5. Then roll the dough and make medium crackers with a cutter. The crackers should be thin.
6. Preheat the air fryer to 360 F.
7. Put the crackers in the air fryer tray.
8. Cook for 4 minutes.
9. Cool and serve.

Nutrition:
- (per serving) calories 89 | fat 5.8 | protein 3.1 | total carbs 7 | fiber 6.2

Vanilla-cinnamon Cookies

Servings: 14 | Cooking Time: 10 Minutes

Ingredients:
- 1 egg
- 1 tablespoon ground cinnamon
- 1 teaspoon vanilla extract
- 2 teaspoon swerve
- 1 scoop stevia powder
- 1 teaspoon baking soda
- 1 teaspoon apple cider vinegar
- 2 tablespoon coconut flour
- 1 cup almond flour
- 2 tablespoon heavy cream
- ¼ teaspoon salt
- 3 tablespoon butter

Directions:
1. Crack the egg in a blender and blend.
2. Then add ground cinnamon, vanilla extract, swerve, stevia powder, baking soda, and apple cider vinegar.
3. Blend the mixture for 30 seconds.
4. Add coconut flour, almond flour, heavy cream, salt, and butter.
5. Blend the mixture for 2 minutes.
6. You should get a soft and elastic dough.
7. Roll the dough and make the cookies using a cookie cutter.
8. Preheat the air fryer to 355 F.
9. Cover the air fryer dish with parchment paper and place the cookies.
10. Cook for 10 minutes.
11. Let the cookies cool before serving.

Nutrition:
- (per serving) calories 89 | fat 7.5 | protein 2.3 | total carbs 3.2 | fiber 1.6

Baked Cheesecake

Servings: 6 | Cooking Time: 35 Minutes

Ingredients:
- ½ cup almond flour
- 1½ tablespoons unsalted butter, melted
- 2 tablespoons erythritol
- 1 (8-ounce / 227-g) package cream cheese, softened
- ¼ cup powdered erythritol
- ½ teaspoon vanilla paste
- 1 egg, at room temperature
- Topping:
- 1½ cups sour cream
- 3 tablespoons powdered erythritol
- 1 teaspoon vanilla extract

Directions:
1. Thoroughly combine the almond flour, butter, and 2 tablespoons of erythritol in a mixing bowl. Press the mixture into the bottom of lightly greased custard cups.
2. Then, mix the cream cheese, ¼ cup of powdered erythritol, vanilla, and egg using an electric mixer on low speed. Pour the batter into the pan, covering the crust.
3. Bake in the preheated Air Fryer at 330ºF (166ºC) for 35 minutes until edges are puffed and the surface is firm.
4. Mix the sour cream, 3 tablespoons of powdered erythritol, and vanilla for the topping, spread over the crust and allow it to cool to room temperature.
5. Transfer to your refrigerator for 6 to 8 hours. Serve well chilled.

Nutrition:
- (per serving) calories 306 | fat 27 | protein 8 | total carbs 9 | fiber 7

Sweet Fat Bombs

Servings: 15 | Cooking Time: 7 Minutes

Ingredients:
- 5 tablespoon swerve
- 6 tablespoon peanut butter
- ½ teaspoon vanilla extract
- ¼ teaspoon salt
- 6 tablespoon Erythritol
- 1 teaspoon stevia extract
- 8 tablespoon fresh lemon juice
- 3 eggs
- 1 teaspoon lime zest
- 2 tablespoon coconut oil

Directions:
1. Melt the peanut butter and combine it with the swerve.
2. Add vanilla extract, salt, and Erythritol.
3. Whisk the mixture.
4. Take the truffle molds and fill with the peanut butter mixture.
5. Freeze mixture.
6. Preheat the air fryer to 350 F.
7. Combine the stevia extract, fresh lemon juice, lime zest, and coconut oil in a bowl.
8. Whisk well.
9. Pour the fresh lemon mixture in the air fryer basket and cook for 5 minutes.
10. Stir every 2 minutes.
11. Crack the eggs in the lemon mixture and blend with a hand mixer.

12. When the mixture is smooth cook at 365 F for 2 minutes more.
13. Remove the cooked curd mixture and allow to cool.
14. Place the cooked curd mixture in a pastry bag.
15. Remove the truffle from the freezer.
16. Fill the truffles with the curd mixture and keep the bomb in a cool place.

Nutrition:
- (per serving) calories 201 | fat 19.3 | protein 3 | total carbs 7.8 | fiber 0.4

Keto Donuts

Servings: 8 | Cooking Time: 4 Minutes

Ingredients:
- 2 eggs
- ½ cup almond flour
- ¼ teaspoon salt
- ¼ teaspoon baking powder
- ½ teaspoon vanilla extract
- ¼ teaspoon ground ginger
- 1 tablespoon butter
- 2 tablespoon Erythritol
- 4 teaspoon heavy cream

Directions:
1. Crack the eggs in a blender and blend them.
2. Add salt, baking powder, vanilla extract, and ground ginger.
3. Blend again well.
4. Then transfer the blended egg mixture into a mixing bowl.
5. Add the almond flour, butter, Erythritol, and heavy cream.
6. Knead the dough until well combined. If it is sticky add more almond flour.
7. Roll the dough with a rolling pin.
8. Use a cutter to make the donuts.
9. Preheat the air fryer to 350 F.
10. Put the donuts in the air fryer basket.
11. Cook for 4 minutes.
12. Transfer to a serving plate.

Nutrition:
- (per serving) calories 80 | fat 6.8 | protein 3 | total carbs 5.6 | fiber 0.8

Poppy Seed Swirls

Servings: 10 | Cooking Time: 17 Minutes

Ingredients:
- 5 tablespoon poppy seeds
- 1 teaspoon baking soda
- 1 teaspoon fresh lemon juice
- 2 cup almond flour
- ½ cup heavy cream
- 1 tablespoon butter
- ¼ cup Erythritol
- ¼ teaspoon ground nutmeg

Directions:
1. Pour heavy cream into a bowl.
2. Add almond flour and baking soda.
3. Combine the mixture with fresh lemon juice, butter, Erythritol, and ground nutmeg.
4. Knead the dough and let it rest for 10 minutes.
5. Then roll the dough.
6. Sprinkle with the poppy seeds generously.

7. Roll the dough and cut it into 10 swirls.
8. Preheat the air fryer to 350 F.
9. Put the poppy seeds swirls in the air fryer basket.
10. Cook the swirls for 17 minutes.
11. Check if the swirls are cooked and remove them from the air fryer.

Nutrition:
• (per serving) calories 189 | fat 16 | protein 5.7 | total carbs 12.1 | fiber 2.9

Almond Fruit Cookie

Servings: 8 | Cooking Time: 13 Minutes

Ingredients:
• ½ cup slivered almonds
• 1 stick butter, room temperature
• 4 ounces (113 g) monk fruit
• ⅔ cup blanched almond flour
• ⅓ cup coconut flour
• ⅓ teaspoon ground cloves
• 1 tablespoon ginger powder
• ¾ teaspoon pure vanilla extract

Directions:
1. In a mixing dish, beat the monk fruit, butter, vanilla extract, ground cloves, and ginger until light and fluffy. Then, throw in the coconut flour, almond flour, and slivered almonds.
2. Continue mixing until it forms a soft dough. Cover and place in the refrigerator for 35 minutes. Meanwhile, preheat the Air Fryer to 315ºF (157ºC).
3. Roll dough into small cookies and place them on the Air Fryer cake pan, gently press each cookie using the back of a spoon.
4. Bake these butter cookies for 13 minutes. Bon appétit!

Nutrition:
• (per serving) calories 199 | fat 19 | protein 3 | total carbs 4 | fiber 2

Keto Fudge

Servings: 3 | Cooking Time: 1 Minute

Ingredients:
• ½ cup heavy cream
• ½ cup butter
• 1 teaspoon ground cinnamon
• 15 drops liquid stevia
• 1 pinch salt

Directions:
1. Melt the butter and combine it with ground cinnamon.
2. Add the heavy cream and liquid stevia.
3. Add salt and mix using a hand mixer.
4. Preheat the air fryer to 360 F.
5. Pour the whisked mixture into the air fryer and cook for 1 minute.
6. Pour the mixture into a bowl and allow to cool for 10 minutes.
7. Whisk for 1 minute and place in the fridge until solid.

Nutrition:
• (per serving) calories 299 | fat 32.9 | protein 0.7 | total carbs 1.9 | fiber 0.4

Cheesecake Mousse

Servings: 12 | Cooking Time: 4 Minutes

Ingredients:
• ¼ cup heavy cream
• 1 egg
• ½ cup cream cheese
• 1/3 cup Erythritol
• ¼ teaspoon lime zest
• 2 scoop stevia

Directions:
1. Crack the egg into a mixer bowl and whisk.
2. Add the heavy cream and keep whisking until the mixture is fluffy.
3. Then add cream cheese, lime zest, stevia, and Erythritol.
4. Whisk well.
5. Preheat the air fryer to 310 F.
6. Pour the cheesecake mixture into the air fryer tray and cook for 14 minutes, stirring every 4 minutes.
7. Whisk carefully using a hand whisker.
8. Cool before serving.

Nutrition:
• (per serving) calories 43 | fat 4.8 | protein 1.3 | total carbs 7.1 | fiber 0

Cream Pie With Lemon

Servings: 8 | Cooking Time: 21 Minutes

Ingredients:
• 1 lemon
• 1cup heavy cream
• 2 eggs
• 3 tablespoon butter
• 1 teaspoon baking soda
• 3 tablespoon coconut flour
• 1 ½ cup almond flour
• 2 teaspoon swerve
• 1 scoop stevia
• ¼ teaspoon salt

Directions:
1. Wash the lemon and slice it into thin rings.
2. Crack the eggs into a blender.
3. Add heavy cream, butter, and baking soda.
4. Blend well on the maximum speed for 2 minutes.
5. Add coconut flour, almond flour, swerve, and salt.
6. Blend the mixture for 3 minutes.
7. The blended dough should be smooth but non-sticky.
8. Preheat the air fryer to 300 F.
9. Place parchment paper in the air fryer dish.
10. Roll the dough with a rolling pin and transfer to the air fryer dish.
11. Then place the sliced lemon over the piecrust.
12. Sprinkle the pie with stevia.
13. Cook for 21 minutes.
14. Chill the pie to room temperature.
15. Cut into servings.

Nutrition:
• (per serving) calories 247 | fat 21.3 | protein 6.7 | total carbs 8.4 | fiber 3.7

Golden Cheese Cookie

Servings: 6 | Cooking Time: 7 Minutes

Ingredients:
- ½ cup blanched finely ground almond flour
- ½ cup powdered erythritol, divided
- 2 tablespoons butter, softened
- 1 large egg
- ½ teaspoon unflavored gelatin
- ½ teaspoon baking powder
- ½ teaspoon vanilla extract
- ½ teaspoon pumpkin pie spice
- 2 tablespoons pure pumpkin purée
- ½ teaspoon ground cinnamon, divided
- ¼ cup low-carb, sugar-free chocolate chips
- 3 ounces (85 g) full-fat cream cheese, softened

Directions:
1. In a large bowl, mix almond flour and ¼ cup erythritol. Stir in butter, egg, and gelatin until combined.
2. Stir in baking powder, vanilla, pumpkin pie spice, pumpkin purée, and ¼ teaspoon cinnamon, then fold in chocolate chips.
3. Pour batter into 6-inch round baking pan. Place pan into the air fryer basket.
4. Adjust the temperature to 300°F (150°C) and set the timer for 7 minutes.
5. When fully cooked, the top will be golden brown and a toothpick inserted in center will come out clean. Let it cool at least 20 minutes.
6. To make the frosting: mix cream cheese, remaining ¼ teaspoon cinnamon, and remaining ¼ cup erythritol in a large bowl. Using an electric mixer, beat until it becomes fluffy. Spread onto the cooled cookie. Garnish with additional cinnamon if desired.

Nutrition:
- (per serving) calories 199 | fat 16 | protein 5 | total carbs 22 | fiber 20

Avocado Muffins

Servings: 7 | Cooking Time: 12 Minutes

Ingredients:
- 1 oz. dark chocolate, melted
- 1 cup almond flour
- ½ cup avocado, pitted
- ½ teaspoon baking soda
- 4 tablespoon butter
- 1 teaspoon apple cider vinegar
- 3 scoop stevia powder
- 1 egg

Directions:
1. Put the almond flour in a bowl.
2. Add baking soda and apple cider vinegar.
3. Add melted chocolate and stevia powder.
4. Crack the egg into a separate bowl and whisk it.
5. Add whisked egg in the almond flour mixture.
6. Add butter.
7. Then peel the avocado and mash it.
8. Add the mashed avocado in the almond flour mixture.
9. Use a hand mixer to make the almond flour mixture smooth and well combined.
10. Preheat the air fryer to 355 F.
11. Pour the almond flour mixture in the muffin molds. Fill ½ part of every muffin mold.
12. Put the muffins in the air fryer and cook for 9 minutes.
13. Reduce the temperature to 340 F and cook the muffins for 3 minutes more.
14. Chill before serving.

Nutrition:
- (per serving) calories 133 | fat 12.4 | protein 2.2 | total carbs 4.2 | fiber 1.3

Coconut Tart With Walnuts

Servings: 6 | Cooking Time: 13 Minutes

Ingredients:
- 1 cup coconut milk
- 2 eggs
- ½ stick butter, at room temperature
- 1 teaspoon vanilla essence
- ¼ teaspoon ground cardamom
- ¼ teaspoon ground cloves
- ½ cup walnuts, ground
- ½ cup swerve
- ½ cup almond flour

Directions:
1. Begin by preheating your Air Fryer to 360°F. Spritz the sides and bottom of a baking pan with nonstick cooking spray.
2. Mix all ingredients until well combined. Scrape the batter into the prepared baking pan.
3. Bake approximately 13 minutes, use a toothpick to test for doneness. Bon appétit!

Nutrition:
- (per serving) calories 227 | fat 20.4 | protein 5 | total carbs 7.1 | fiber 0.9

Pistachio Cookies

Servings: 9 | Cooking Time: 9 Minutes

Ingredients:
- 1/3 cup pistachios, crushed
- ½ cup almond flour
- 1 egg
- 5 tablespoon heavy cream
- 1 pinch salt
- 3 tablespoon Erythritol
- ½ teaspoon baking soda
- 1 teaspoon apple cider vinegar
- 2 tablespoon butter
- 1 teaspoon cream cheese

Directions:
1. Combine crushed pistachio and almond flour in a bowl.
2. Add salt and baking soda. Stir and add Erythritol.
3. Combine apple cider vinegar and butter in a separate bowl.
4. Add cream cheese and heavy cream to the apple cider vinegar.
5. Crack the egg in the cream cheese mixture and whisk.
6. Then combine the dried mixture and cream mixture together.
7. Knead the dough. Add more flour if desired.
8. Roll the dough.
9. Cut the cookies with a cutter.
10. Preheat the air fryer to 360 F,
11. Put the cookies in the air fryer and cook for 9 minutes until crunchy.

Nutrition:
- (per serving) calories 109 | fat 10.3 | protein 2.6 | total carbs 7.2 | fiber 0.9

Toasted Coconut Flakes

Servings: 4 | Cooking Time: 3 Minutes

Ingredients:
- 1 cup unsweetened coconut flakes
- 2 teaspoons coconut oil
- ¼ cup granular erythritol
- ⅛ teaspoon salt

Directions:
1. Toss coconut flakes and oil in a large bowl until coated. Sprinkle with erythritol and salt.
2. Place coconut flakes into the air fryer basket.
3. Adjust the temperature to 300°F (150°C) and set the timer for 3 minutes.
4. Toss the flakes when 1 minute remains. Add an extra minute if you would like a more golden coconut flake.
5. Store in an airtight container up to 3 days.

Nutrition:
- (per serving) calories 165 | fat 15 | protein 1 | total carbs 20 | fiber 17

Nuts Fudge

Servings: 10 | Cooking Time: 3 Minutes

Ingredients:
- ½ cup peanut butter
- ½ cup macadamia nuts
- ¼ cup cream cheese
- 1 teaspoon vanilla extract
- 3 tablespoon Erythritol

Directions:
1. Preheat the air fryer to 360 F.
2. Place the peanut butter in the air fryer dish.
3. Add vanilla extract and Erythritol. Stir.
4. Cook for 3 minutes.
5. Remove the peanut butter mixture from the air fryer and stir it for 3 minutes.
6. Add cream cheese and whisk.
7. Place the prepared fudge mixture on the tray and flatten it.
8. Freeze until solid.
9. Then cut the fudge into 8 parts.

Nutrition:
- (per serving) calories 162 | fat 15 | protein 4.8 | total carbs 8.2 | fiber 1.5

Macadamia Nut Brownies

Servings: 16 | Cooking Time: 25 Minutes

Ingredients:
- 2 eggs
- 1/3 cup macadamia nuts, crushed
- 3 tablespoon butter, melted
- 1 cup coconut flour
- ½ teaspoon baking powder
- 1 teaspoon fresh lemon juice
- 4 oz. dark chocolate, melted
- 3 tablespoon swerve

Directions:
1. Crack the eggs into a mixer bowl and mix.
2. Add melted butter and keep mixing for 2 minutes.
3. Add coconut flour, baking powder, fresh lemon juice, melted dark chocolate, and swerve.
4. Mix using a silicon spatula.
5. Add the crushed macadamia nuts and stir carefully.
6. Preheat the air fryer to 355 F.
7. Pour the brownie dough into the air fryer basket tray and cook for 25 minutes.
8. Cooked brownies should be soft but well cooked.
9. Slice the brownies into 12 pieces.

Nutrition:
- (per serving) calories 112 | fat 7.6 | protein 2.4 | total carbs 7.5 | fiber 3.4

Avocado Pudding With Almond Flakes

Servings: 6 | Cooking Time: 4 Minutes

Ingredients:
- ½ cup almond milk
- 2 avocado, pitted
- 1 teaspoon vanilla extract
- 7 drops liquid stevia
- 1 egg
- 3 tablespoon almond flakes
- 2 tablespoon butter
- ¼ teaspoon ground cinnamon

Directions:
1. Peel the avocado and chop it.
2. Put the chopped avocado in a blender and blend until you get a soft texture.
3. Then crack the egg in a bowl and pour the almond milk.
4. Add vanilla extract, liquid stevia, butter, and ground cinnamon.
5. Mix well with a hand mixer.
6. Preheat the air fryer to 250 F.
7. Pour the almond milk mixture and cook for 4 minutes. Stir the liquid every minute.
8. Allow the liquid to chill.
9. Pour the almond milk liquid into the blender with the smooth avocado.
10. Blend for 1 minute on a medium speed.
11. Then pour the pudding into glass vessels.
12. Sprinkle the pudding with almond flakes and keep in the fridge.

Nutrition:
- (per serving) calories 247 | fat 23.9 | protein 3.3 | total carbs 7.7 | fiber 5.4

Pumpkin Air Cookies

Servings: 8 | Cooking Time: 8 Minutes

Ingredients:
- ½ cup pumpkin puree
- ¼ cup almond flour
- 1 tablespoon coconut flakes
- ½ teaspoon baking soda
- 3 tablespoon Erythritol
- 1 pinch salt
- 1 teaspoon ground cinnamon

Directions:
1. Combine the pumpkin puree with the almond flour.
2. Then sprinkle the mixture with the coconut flakes, baking soda, Erythritol, salt, and ground cinnamon.
3. Knead the dough.
4. If the dough is not smooth enough add more almond flour.
5. Roll the dough and use a cutter to make the cookies into 8 and

roll the balls.
6. Flatten the balls into the shape of cookies.
7. Preheat the air fryer to 360 F.
8. Put the cookies in the air fryer and cook for 8 minutes.

Nutrition:
- (per serving) calories 29 | fat 1.9 | protein 1 | total carbs 8 | fiber 1

Chocolate Chip Cookie

Servings: 8 | Cooking Time: 11 Minutes

Ingredients:
- 1 stick butter, at room temperature
- 1¼ cups Swerve
- ¼ cup chunky peanut butter
- 1 teaspoon vanilla paste
- 1 fine almond flour
- ⅔ cup coconut flour
- ⅓ cup cocoa powder, unsweetened
- 1 ½ teaspoons baking powder
- ¼ teaspoon ground cinnamon
- ¼ teaspoon ginger
- ½ cup chocolate chips, unsweetened

Directions:
1. In a mixing dish, beat the butter and Swerve until creamy and uniform. Stir in the peanut butter and vanilla.
2. In another mixing dish, thoroughly combine the flour, cocoa powder, baking powder, cinnamon, and ginger.
3. Add the flour mixture to the peanut butter mixture, mix to combine well. Afterwards, fold in the chocolate chips.
4. Drop by large spoonfuls onto a parchment-lined Air Fryer basket. Bake at 365ºF (185ºC) for 11 minutes or until golden brown on the top. Bon appétit!

Nutrition:
- (per serving) calories 303 | fat 28 | protein 6 | total carbs 10 | fiber 5

Blackberry Muffins

Servings: 8 | Cooking Time: 12 Minutes

Ingredients:
- 1½ cups almond flour
- ½ teaspoon baking soda
- 1 teaspoon baking powder
- ¼ teaspoon kosher salt
- ½ cup swerve
- 2 eggs, whisked
- ½ cup milk
- ¼ cup coconut oil, melted
- ½ teaspoon vanilla paste
- ½ cup fresh blackberries

Directions:
1. In a mixing bowl, combine the almond flour, baking soda, baking powder, swerve, and salt. Whisk to combine well.
2. In another mixing bowl, mix the eggs, milk, coconut oil, and vanilla.
3. Now, add the wet egg mixture to dry the flour mixture. Then, carefully fold in the fresh blackberries, gently stir to combine.
4. Scrape the batter mixture into the muffin cups. Bake your muffins at 350ºF for 12 minutes or until the tops are golden brown.
5. Sprinkle some extra icing sugar over the top of each muffin if desired. Serve and enjoy!

Nutrition:
- (per serving) calories 192 | fat 17.3 | protein 5.5 | total carbs 5.7 | fiber 1

Pecan And Mixed Berries Streusel

Servings: 3 | Cooking Time: 17 Minutes

Ingredients:
- 3 tablespoons pecans, chopped
- 3 tablespoons almonds, slivered
- 2 tablespoons walnuts, chopped
- 3 tablespoons granulated swerve
- ½ teaspoon ground cinnamon
- 1 egg
- 2 tablespoons cold salted butter, cut into pieces
- ½ cup mixed berries

Directions:
1. Mix your nuts, swerve, cinnamon, egg, and butter until well combined.
2. Place mixed berries on the bottom of a lightly greased Air Fryer-safe dish. Top with the prepared topping.
3. Bake at 340ºF for 17 minutes. Serve at room temperature. Bon appétit!

Nutrition:
- (per serving) calories 255 | fat 22.8 | protein 9.1 | total carbs 7.3 | fiber 0.6

Coconut Muffin

Servings: 5 | Cooking Time: 25 Minutes

Ingredients:
- ½ cup coconut flour
- 2 tablespoons cocoa powder
- 3 tablespoons erythritol
- 1 teaspoon baking powder
- 2 tablespoons coconut oil
- 2 eggs, beaten
- ½ cup coconut shred

Directions:
1. In the mixing bowl, mix all ingredients.
2. Then pour the mixture in the molds of the muffin and transfer in the air fryer basket.
3. Cook the muffins at 350F (180ºC) for 25 minutes.

Nutrition:
- (per serving) calories 206 | fat 16 | protein 4 | total carbs 13 | fiber 6

Vanilla Roll

Servings: 20 | Cooking Time: 20 Minutes

Ingredients:
- 5 eggs
- ½ cup Erythritol
- 1 cup almond flour
- 1 tablespoon vanilla extract
- 1 pinch salt
- 1 cup heavy cream
- 2 scoop liquid stevia

Directions:
1. Crack the eggs and separate the egg yolks and egg whites.
2. Then whisk the egg yolk with Erythritol.
3. After this, combine the egg yolk mixture with the salt and al-

mond flour.
4. Stir.
5. Whisk the egg whites until you have strong peaks.
6. Add the egg whites to the egg yolk mixture.
7. Add the vanilla extract.
8. Stir carefully.
9. Preheat the air fryer to 290 F.
10. Pour the dough in the air fryer dish and flatten it with a spatula.
11. Cook for 20 minutes.
12. Place the pie in a wet towel.
13. Whisk the heavy cream with the liquid stevia until thickened.
14. Spread the cooked dough with the whisked cream.
15. Roll it using the wet towel.
16. Let the roll rest for 10 minutes.
17. Cut into servings.

Nutrition:
• (per serving) calories 70 | fat 6 | protein 2.7 | total carbs 7.5 | fiber 0.6

Keto Vanilla Mousse

Servings: 4 | Cooking Time: 6 Minutes

Ingredients:
• 1 teaspoon vanilla extract
• ½ cup cream cheese
• ½ cup almond milk
• ¼ cup blackberries
• 2 teaspoon stevia extract
• 2 tablespoon butter
• ¼ teaspoon cinnamon

Directions:
1. Preheat the air fryer to 320 F.
2. Combine butter, vanilla extract, and almond milk and transfer the mixture to the air fryer.
3. Cook the mixture for 6 minutes or well combined.
4. Then stir it carefully and chill to room temperature.
5. Crush the blackberries.
6. Whisk the cream cheese using a hand whisker for 2 minutes.
7. Add the crushed blackberries and whisk for 1 minute more.
8. Add cinnamon and stevia extract.
9. Stir gently.
10. Combine the almond butter liquid and cream cheese mixture together.
11. Mix using a hand mixer.
12. When well mixed pour into a glass vessel.
13. Place it in the fridge and cool.

Nutrition:
• (per serving) calories 228 | fat 23.1 | protein 3.1 | total carbs 3.5 | fiber 1.2

Macadamia Bar

Servings: 10 | Cooking Time: 30 Minutes

Ingredients:
• 3 tablespoons butter, softened
• 1 teaspoon baking powder
• 1 teaspoon apple cider vinegar
• 1.5 cups coconut flour
• 3 tablespoons Swerve
• 1 teaspoon vanilla extract
• 2 eggs, beaten

• 2 ounces macadamia nuts, chopped
• Cooking spray

Directions:
1. Spray the air fryer basket with cooking spray.
2. Then mix all remaining ingredients in the mixing bowl and stir until you get a homogenous mixture.
3. Pour the mixture in the air fryer basket and cook at 345F (174ºC) for 30 minutes.
4. When the mixture is cooked, cut it into bars and transfer in the serving plates.

Nutrition:
• (per serving) calories 158 | fat 10 | protein 4 | total carbs 13 | fiber 5

Almond And Chocolate Cookies

Servings: 10 | Cooking Time: 15 Minutes

Ingredients:
• 2 cups almond flour
• ½ cup coconut flour
• 5 ounces (142 g) swerve
• 5 ounces (142 g) butter, softened
• 1 egg, beaten
• 1 teaspoon vanilla essence
• 4 ounces (113 g) double cream
• 3 ounces (85 g) bakers' chocolate, unsweetened
• 1 teaspoon cardamom seeds, finely crushed

Directions:
1. Start by preheating your Air Fryer to 350ºF.
2. In a mixing bowl, thoroughly combine the flour, swerve, and butter. Mix until your mixture resembles breadcrumbs.
3. Gradually, add the egg and vanilla essence. Shape your dough into small balls and place in the parchment-lined Air Fryer basket.
4. Bake in the preheated Air Fryer for 10 minutes. Rotate the pan and bake for another 5 minutes. Transfer the freshly baked cookies to a cooling rack.
5. As the biscuits are cooling, melt the double cream and bakers' chocolate in the Air Fryer safe bowl at 350ºF. Add the cardamom seeds and stir well.
6. Spread the filling over the cooled biscuits and sandwich together. Bon appétit!

Nutrition:
• (per serving) calories 303 | fat 29.6 | protein 8.5 | total carbs 6.5 | fiber 1.6

Cream Puffs

Servings:8 | Cooking Time: 6 Minutes

Ingredients:
• ½ cup blanched finely ground almond flour
• ½ cup low-carb vanilla protein powder
• ½ cup granular erythritol
• ½ teaspoon baking powder
• 1 large egg
• 5 tablespoons unsalted butter, melted
• 2 ounces (57 g) full-fat cream cheese
• ¼ cup powdered erythritol
• ¼ teaspoon ground cinnamon
• 2 tablespoons heavy whipping cream
• ½ teaspoon vanilla extract

Directions:
1. Mix almond flour, protein powder, granular erythritol, baking

powder, egg, and butter in a large bowl until a soft dough forms.
2. Place the dough in the freezer for 20 minutes. Wet your hands with water and roll the dough into eight balls.
3. Cut a piece of parchment to fit your air fryer basket. Working in batches as necessary, place the dough balls into the air fryer basket on top of parchment.
4. Adjust the temperature to 380°F (193ºC) and set the timer for 6 minutes.
5. Flip cream puffs halfway through the cooking time.
6. When the timer beeps, remove the puffs and allow them to cool.
7. In a medium bowl, beat the cream cheese, powdered erythritol, cinnamon, cream, and vanilla until fluffy.
8. Place the mixture into a pastry bag or a storage bag with the end snipped. Cut a small hole in the bottom of each puff and fill with some of the cream mixture.
9. Store in an airtight container up to 2 days in the refrigerator.

Nutrition:
• (per serving) calories 178 | fat 12 | protein 15 | total carbs 22 | fiber 21

Delightful Custard

Servings: 4 | Cooking Time: 28 Minutes

Ingredients:
• 5 eggs
• ½ cup cream cheese
• ½ cup water
• 1 teaspoon vanilla extract
• 2 tablespoon Erythritol

Directions:
1. Preheat the air fryer to 320 F.
2. Crack the eggs in a mixing bowl and whisk them.
3. Then add the cream cheese and water.
4. Whisk well for 2 minutes.
5. Add vanilla extract and Erythritol.
6. Stir it until well combined.
7. Pour the mixture into four ramekins and transfer to the air fryer.
8. Cook for 28 minutes.
9. Allow to cool before serving.

Nutrition:
• (per serving) calories 183 | fat 15.6 | protein 9.1 | total carbs 8.8 | fiber 0

Avocado Brownies

Servings: 6 | Cooking Time: 20 Minutes

Ingredients:
• 1 avocado, pitted
• 2 teaspoon Erythritol
• ¼ teaspoon vanilla extract
• 1 oz. dark chocolate
• 3 tablespoon almond flour
• ½ teaspoon stevia powder
• 1 egg
• 1 teaspoon coconut oil
• ¼ teaspoon baking powder
• ¼ teaspoon salt

Directions:
1. Peel the avocado and chop it roughly.
2. Put the avocado in a blender.

3. Melt the dark chocolate and add it to the blender.
4. Add vanilla extract and blend the mixture until smooth.
5. Add almond flour, stevia powder, coconut oil, baking powder, salt, and Erythritol.
6. Crack the egg in the mixture and blend until smooth.
7. Preheat the air fryer to 355 F.
8. Pour the avocado brownie mixture into the air fryer tray and flatten using a spatula.
9. Cook the brownie dough for 20 minutes.
10. Cut into 6 brownie bars and allow to cool.

Nutrition:
• (per serving) calories 131 | fat 11.2 | protein 2.7 | total carbs 8.3 | fiber 2.8

Zucchini Bread

Servings: 12 | Cooking Time: 40 Minutes

Ingredients:
• 2 cups coconut flour
• 2 teaspoons baking powder
• ¾ cup erythritol
• ½ cup coconut oil, melted
• 1 teaspoon apple cider vinegar
• 1 teaspoon vanilla extract
• 3 eggs, beaten
• 1 zucchini, grated
• 1 teaspoon ground cinnamon

Directions:
1. In the mixing bowl, mix coconut flour with baking powder, erythritol, coconut oil, apple cider vinegar, vanilla extract, eggs, zucchini, and ground cinnamon.
2. Transfer the mixture in the air fryer basket and flatten it in the shape of the bread.
3. Cook the bread at 350F (180ºC) for 40 minutes.

Nutrition:
• (per serving) calories 179 | fat 12 | protein 4 | total carbs 15 | fiber 7

Raspberry And Chocolate Cake

Servings: 4 | Cooking Time: 27 Minutes

Ingredients:
• ⅓ cup monk fruit
• ¼ cup unsalted butter, room temperature
• 1 egg plus 1 egg white, lightly whisked
• 3 ounces (85 g) almond flour
• 2 tablespoons Dutch-process cocoa powder
• ½ teaspoon ground cinnamon
• 1 tablespoon candied ginger
• ⅛ teaspoon table salt
• For the Filling:
• 2 ounces (57 g) fresh raspberries
• ⅓ cup monk fruit
• 1 teaspoon fresh lime juice

Directions:
1. Firstly, set your Air Fryer to cook at 315ºF. Then, spritz the inside of two cake pans with the butter-flavored cooking spray.
2. In a mixing bowl, beat the monk fruit and butter until creamy and uniform. Then, stir in the whisked eggs. Stir in the almond flour, cocoa powder, cinnamon, ginger and salt.
3. Press the batter into the cake pans, use a wide spatula to level the surface of the batter. Bake for 20 minutes or until a wooden

stick inserted in the center of the cake comes out completely dry.
4. While your cake is baking, stir together all of the ingredients for the filling in a medium saucepan. Cook over high heat, stirring frequently and mashing with the back of a spoon, bring to a boil and decrease the temperature.
5. Continue to cook, stirring until the mixture thickens, for another 7 minutes. Let the filling cool to room temperature.
6. Spread ½ of raspberry filling over the first crust. Top with another crust, spread remaining filling over top. Spread frosting over top and sides of your cake.
7. Enjoy!

Nutrition:
• (per serving) calories 217 | fat 18.8 | protein 8.6 | total carbs 7.5 | fiber 0.7

Chocolate Chip Cookie Cake

Servings: 8 | Cooking Time: 15 Minutes

Ingredients:
• 4 tablespoons salted butter, melted
• ⅓ cup granular brown erythritol
• 1 large egg
• ½ teaspoon vanilla extract
• 1 cup blanched finely ground almond flour
• ½ teaspoon baking powder
• ¼ cup low-carb chocolate chips

Directions:
1. In a large bowl, whisk together butter, erythritol, egg, and vanilla. Add flour and baking powder, and stir until combined.
2. Fold in chocolate chips, then spoon batter into an ungreased 6-inch round nonstick baking dish.
3. Place dish into air fryer basket. Adjust the temperature to 300°F (150°C) and set the timer for 15 minutes. When edges are browned, cookie cake will be done.
4. Slice and serve warm.

Nutrition:
• (per serving) calories 170 | fat 16 | protein 4 | total carbs 15 | fiber 11

Blackberry Pie

Servings: 8 | Cooking Time: 20 Minutes

Ingredients:
• 1 cup almond flour
• 2 tablespoon butter, unsalted
• 1 tablespoon baking powder
• 1 large egg
• ½ cup blackberries
• 1 scoop stevia extract

Directions:
1. Preheat the air fryer to 350 F.
2. Crack the egg in a bowl and whisk.
3. Add baking powder, stevia extract, and butter.
4. Mix well.
5. Leave 1 teaspoon of almond flour to one side.
6. Put all the remaining almond flour in the egg mixture.
7. Knead to a smooth and sticky dough.
8. Cover the air fryer tray with parchment paper.
9. Put the dough in the air fryer dish and flatten into the shape of a pie crust.
10. Place the blackberries over the piecrust.
11. Sprinkle the pie with the 1 teaspoon of almond flour.

12. Cook the pie for 20 minutes.
13. When the surface of the pie is golden brown it is cooked.
14. Cool before serving.

Nutrition:
• (per serving) calories 60 | fat 3.5 | protein 1.7 | total carbs 2.5 | fiber 0.9

Keto Cream Cheese Soufflé

Servings: 10 | Cooking Time: 16 Minutes

Ingredients:
• 5 eggs
• 1 cup cream cheese
• 4 tablespoon heavy cream
• 6 tablespoon almond flour
• 4 tablespoon Erythritol
• 1 teaspoon coconut flakes

Directions:
1. Separate the eggs into egg yolks and egg whites.
2. Mix the egg yolks with Erythritol carefully.
3. Add the cream cheese and almond flour.
4. Mix with a hand mixer for 2 minutes on maximum.
5. Then add heavy cream and mix for 1 minute more.
6. Whisk the egg whites until you have strong peaks.
7. Add the egg whites to the egg mixture slowly and stir all the time.
8. Combine the mixture with the coconut flakes.
9. Preheat the air fryer to 330 F.
10. Pour the cream cheese mixture into 7 ramekins.
11. Place the ramekins in the air fryer and cook for 16 minutes.
12. Chill to room temperature before serving.

Nutrition:
• (per serving) calories 172 | fat 16.8 | protein 6.4 | total carbs 8.3 | fiber 0.5

Chocolate Brownies

Servings: 8 | Cooking Time: 35 Minutes

Ingredients:
• 5 ounces (142 g) unsweetened chocolate, chopped into chunks
• 2 tablespoons instant espresso powder
• 1 tablespoon cocoa powder, unsweetened
• ½ cup almond butter
• ½ cup almond meal
• ¾ cup Swerve
• 1 teaspoon pure coffee extract
• ½ teaspoon lime peel zest
• ¼ cup coconut flour
• 2 eggs plus 1 egg yolk
• ½ teaspoon baking soda
• ½ teaspoon baking powder
• ½ teaspoon ground cinnamon
• ⅓ teaspoon ancho chile powder
• For the Chocolate Mascarpone Frosting:
• 4 ounces (113 g) mascarpone cheese, at room temperature
• 1½ ounces (43 g) unsweetened chocolate chips
• 1½ cups Swerve
• ¼ cup unsalted butter, at room temperature
• 1 teaspoon vanilla paste
• A pinch of fine sea salt

Directions:
1. First of all, microwave the chocolate and almond butter until

completely melted, allow the mixture to cool at room temperature.

2. Then, whisk the eggs, Swerve, cinnamon, espresso powder, coffee extract, ancho chile powder, and lime zest.

3. Next step, add the vanilla/egg mixture to the chocolate/butter mixture. Stir in the almond meal and coconut flour along with baking soda, baking powder and cocoa powder.

4. Finally, press the batter into a lightly buttered cake pan. Air-fry for 35 minutes at 345ºF (174ºC).

5. In the meantime, make the frosting. Beat the butter and mascarpone cheese until creamy. Add in the melted chocolate chips and vanilla paste.

6. Gradually, stir in the Swerve and salt, beat until everything's well combined. Lastly, frost the brownies and serve.

Nutrition:
• (per serving) calories 363 | fat 33 | protein 7 | total carbs 10 | fiber 5

Coconut And Chocolate Pudding

Servings: 10 | Cooking Time: 15 Minutes

Ingredients:
• 1 stick butter
• 1¼ cups bakers' chocolate, unsweetened
• 1 teaspoon liquid stevia
• 2 tablespoons full fat coconut milk
• 2 eggs, beaten
• ⅓ cup coconut, shredded

Directions:
1. Begin by preheating your Air Fryer to 330ºF.
2. In a microwave-safe bowl, melt the butter, chocolate, and stevia. Allow it to cool to room temperature.
3. Add the remaining ingredients to the chocolate mixture, stir to combine well. Scrape the batter into a lightly greased baking pan.
4. Bake in the preheated Air Fryer for 15 minutes or until a toothpick comes out dry and clean. Enjoy!

Nutrition:
• (per serving) calories 229 | fat 21.3 | protein 5.4 | total carbs 4.4 | fiber 0.5

Walnut Butter Cookie

Servings: 8 | Cooking Time: 15 Minutes

Ingredients:
• ½ cup walnuts, ground
• ½ cup coconut flour
• 1 cup almond flour
• ¾ cup Swerve
• 1 stick butter, room temperature
• 2 tablespoons rum
• ½ teaspoon pure vanilla extract
• ½ teaspoon pure almond extract

Directions:
1. In a mixing dish, beat the butter with Swerve, vanilla, and almond extract until light and fluffy. Then, throw in the flour and ground walnuts, add in rum.
2. Continue mixing until it forms a soft dough. Cover and place in the refrigerator for 20 minutes. In the meantime, preheat the Air Fryer to 330ºF (166ºC).
3. Roll the dough into small cookies and place them on the Air Fryer cake pan, gently press each cookie using a spoon.
4. Bake butter cookies for 15 minutes in the preheated Air Fryer.

Bon appétit!

Nutrition:
• (per serving) calories 228 | fat 22 | protein 4 | total carbs 4 | fiber 2

Pecan Chocolate Brownies

Servings: 6 | Cooking Time: 20 Minutes

Ingredients:
• ½ cup blanched finely ground almond flour
• ½ cup powdered erythritol
• 2 tablespoons unsweetened cocoa powder
• ½ teaspoon baking powder
• ¼ cup unsalted butter, softened
• 1 large egg
• ¼ cup chopped pecans
• ¼ cup low-carb, sugar-free chocolate chips

Directions:
1. In a large bowl, mix almond flour, erythritol, cocoa powder, and baking powder. Stir in butter and egg.
2. Fold in pecans and chocolate chips. Scoop mixture into 6 -inch round baking pan. Place pan into the air fryer basket.
3. Adjust the temperature to 300ºF (150ºC) and set the timer for 20 minutes.
4. When fully cooked a toothpick inserted in center will come out clean. Allow it to fully cool and firm up for 20 minutes.

Nutrition:
• (per serving) calories 215 | fat 18 | protein 4 | total carbs 22 | fiber 19

Hazelnut Cookies

Servings: 6 | Cooking Time: 10 Minutes

Ingredients:
• 1 cup almond flour
• ½ cup coconut flour
• 1 teaspoon baking soda
• 1 teaspoon fine sea salt
• 1 stick butter
• 1 cup Swerve
• 2 teaspoons vanilla
• 2 eggs, at room temperature
• 1 cup hazelnuts, coarsely chopped

Directions:
1. Begin by preheating your Air Fryer to 350ºF (180ºC).
2. Mix the flour with the baking soda, and sea salt.
3. In the bowl of an electric mixer, beat the butter, Swerve, and vanilla until creamy. Fold in the eggs, one at a time, and mix until well combined.
4. Slowly and gradually, stir in the flour mixture. Finally, fold in the coarsely chopped hazelnuts.
5. Divide the dough into small balls using a large cookie scoop, drop onto the prepared cookie sheets. Bake for 10 minutes or until golden brown, rotating the pan once or twice through the cooking time.
6. Work in batches and cool for a couple of minutes before removing to wire racks. Enjoy!

Nutrition:
• (per serving) calories 328 | fat 32 | protein 7 | total carbs 5 | fiber 3

Blueberry Cream Flan

Servings: 6 | Cooking Time: 25 Minutes

Ingredients:
- ¾ cup extra-fine almond flour
- 1 cup fresh blueberries
- ½ cup coconut cream
- ¾ cup coconut milk
- 3 eggs, whisked
- ½ cup Swerve
- ½ teaspoon baking soda
- ½ teaspoon baking powder
- ⅓ teaspoon ground cinnamon
- ½ teaspoon ginger
- ¼ teaspoon grated nutmeg

Directions:
1. Lightly grease 2 mini pie pans using a nonstick cooking spray. Lay the blueberries on the bottom of the pie pans.
2. In a saucepan that is preheated over a moderate flame, warm the cream along with coconut milk until thoroughly heated.
3. Remove the pan from the heat, mix in the flour along with baking soda and baking powder.
4. In a medium-sized mixing bowl, whip the eggs, Swerve, and spices, whip until the mixture is creamy.
5. Add the creamy milk mixture. Carefully spread this mixture over the fruits.
6. Bake at 320º(160ºC) for about 25 minutes. Serve.

Nutrition:
- (per serving) calories 250 | fat 22 | protein 7 | total carbs 9 | fiber 6

Golden Doughnut Holes

Servings:20 | Cooking Time: 6 Minutes

Ingredients:
- 1 cup blanched finely ground almond flour
- ½ cup low-carb vanilla protein powder
- ½ cup granular erythritol
- ¼ cup unsweetened cocoa powder
- ½ teaspoon baking powder
- 2 large eggs, whisked
- ½ teaspoon vanilla extract

Directions:
1. Mix all ingredients in a large bowl until a soft dough forms. Separate and roll dough into twenty balls, about 2 tablespoons each.
2. Cut a piece of parchment to fit your air fryer basket. Working in batches if needed, place doughnut holes into air fryer basket on ungreased parchment. Adjust the temperature to 380°F (193ºC) and set the timer for 6 minutes, flipping doughnut holes halfway through cooking. Doughnut holes will be golden and firm when done. Let it cool completely before serving, for about 10 minutes.

Nutrition:
- (per serving) calories 103 | fat 7 | protein 8 | total carbs 13 | fiber 11

Ricotta Mousse

Servings: 8 | Cooking Time: 6 Minutes

Ingredients:
- 2 eggs
- ½ cup heavy cream
- 1 cup ricotta
- 3 tablespoon Erythritol
- 1 oz. butter
- 1 teaspoon vanilla extract

Directions:
1. Crack the eggs in a bowl and mix them with a hand mixer.
2. Then combine the mixed eggs with the heavy cream.
3. Preheat the air fryer to 350 F.
4. Pour the heavy cream mixture into the air fryer.
5. Cook for 5 minutes.
6. Stir the liquid every minute.
7. Combine the heavy cream mixture with the vanilla extract and stir.
8. Cook the liquid for 1 minute more.
9. Pour the cooked heavy cream liquid in a bowl and whisk for 4 minutes.
10. When the liquid reaches room temperature add ricotta and butter.
11. Mix for 1 minute more.
12. Then place the cooked mousse in a glass vessel and keep in the fridge.

Nutrition:
- (per serving) calories 111 | fat 9.2 | protein 5.1 | total carbs 7.6 | fiber 0

Sunflower Cookies

Servings: 8 | Cooking Time: 10 Minutes

Ingredients:
- 5 oz. sunflower seed butter
- ½ teaspoon salt
- 1 tablespoon stevia extract
- 6 tablespoon coconut flour
- ¼ teaspoon salt
- ¼ teaspoon olive oil

Directions:
1. Combine the sunflower seed butter and coconut flour together.
2. Sprinkle the mixture with salt and stevia extract.
3. Add olive oil and mix well.
4. Mix until you have a well combined dough.
5. Separate the dough into 8 balls and flatten gently.
6. Preheat the air fryer to 365 F.
7. Put the flattened balls into the air fryer rack.
8. Cook for 10 minutes.
9. Allow to cool before serving.

Nutrition:
- (per serving) calories 126 | fat 9.2 | protein 4.2 | total carbs 8.6 | fiber 2.3

Pecan Butter Cookie

Servings: 12 | Cooking Time: 24 Minutes

Ingredients:
- 1 cup chopped pecans
- ½ cup salted butter, melted
- ½ cup coconut flour
- ¾ cup erythritol, divided
- 1 teaspoon vanilla extract

Directions:
1. In a food processor, blend together pecans, butter, flour, ½ cup erythritol, and vanilla for 1 minute until a dough forms.
2. Form dough into twelve individual cookie balls, about 1 tablespoon each.
3. Cut three pieces of parchment to fit air fryer basket. Place four cookies on each ungreased parchment and place one piece parchment with cookies into air fryer basket. Adjust air fryer temperature to 325°F (163ºC) and set the timer for 8 minutes. Repeat cooking with remaining batches.
4. When the timer goes off, allow cookies to cool for 5 minutes on a large serving plate until cool enough to handle. While still warm, dust cookies with remaining erythritol. Allow to cool completely, about for 15 minutes, before serving.

Nutrition:
- (per serving) calories 151 | fat 14 | protein 2 | total carbs 13 | fiber 10

Orange And Coconut Cake

Servings: 6 | Cooking Time: 17 Minutes

Ingredients:
- ¾ cup coconut flour
- ⅓ cup coconut milk
- 2 tablespoons orange jam, unsweetened
- 1 stick butter
- ¾ cup granulated swerve
- 2 eggs
- 1¼ cups almond flour
- ½ teaspoon baking powder
- ⅓ teaspoon grated nutmeg
- ¼ teaspoon salt

Directions:
1. Set the Air Fryer to cook at 355ºF. Spritz the inside of a cake pan with the cooking spray. Then, beat the butter with granulated swerve until fluffy.
2. Fold in the eggs, continue mixing until smooth. Throw in the coconut flour, salt, and nutmeg, then, slowly and carefully pour in the coconut milk.
3. Finally, add almond flour, baking powder and orange jam, mix thoroughly to create the cake batter.
4. Then, press the batter into the cake pan. Bake for 17 minutes and transfer your cake to a cooling rack. Frost the cake and serve chilled. Enjoy!

Nutrition:
- (per serving) calories 339 | fat 33.1 | protein 7.2 | total carbs 6.8 | fiber 0.4

Mint Pie

Servings: 2 | Cooking Time: 25 Minutes

Ingredients:
- 1 tablespoon instant coffee
- 2 tablespoons almond butter, softened
- 2 tablespoons erythritol
- 1 teaspoon dried mint
- 3 eggs, beaten
- 1 teaspoon spearmint, dried
- 4 teaspoons coconut flour
- Cooking spray

Directions:
1. Spray the air fryer basket with cooking spray.
2. Then mix all ingredients in the mixer bowl.
3. When you get a smooth mixture, transfer it in the air fryer basket. Flatten it gently.
4. Cook the pie at 365F (185ºC) for 25 minutes.

Nutrition:
- (per serving) calories 313 | fat 19 | protein 16 | total carbs 20 | fiber 8

Blackberry Tart

Servings: 16 | Cooking Time: 25 Minutes

Ingredients:
- ½ cup blackberry
- 1/3 cup Erythritol
- 1 cup almond flour
- 4 tablespoon butter
- 1 pinch salt
- 1 teaspoon vanilla extract
- 2 tablespoon coconut flour
- 1 egg

Directions:
1. Combine the blackberries with Erythritol. Stir the mixture carefully.
2. Crack the egg in a bowl and whisk.
3. Add almond flour and salt.
4. Combine the mixture with the butter, vanilla extract, and coconut flour.
5. Knead the dough.
6. Preheat the air fryer to 355 F.
7. Cover the air fryer dish with parchment paper.
8. Roll the dough with a rolling pin.
9. Place the rolled dough in the air fryer dish.
10. Place the blackberries over the dough.
11. Cook the tart for 25 minutes.
12. Allow to cool before cutting into serving.

Nutrition:
- (per serving) calories 78 | fat 6.6 | protein 2.1 | total carbs 7.6 | fiber 1.3

Peanut Butter Cookies

Servings: 12 | Cooking Time: 10 Minutes

Ingredients:
- 4 tablespoon Erythritol
- 8 tablespoon peanut butter
- 1 egg
- ¼ teaspoon salt

Directions:
1. Take a large bowl and add Erythritol.
2. Add peanut butter and salt.
3. Crack the egg into the bowl with the peanut butter.
4. Mix the dough until well combined.
5. Roll the dough with a rolling pin.
6. Make the cookie shapes with a cutter.
7. Make a cross with a fork in every cookie.
8. Preheat an air fryer to 360 F.
9. Put the cookies in the air fryer basket.
10. Cook for 10 minutes.
11. Allow to cool before serving.

Nutrition:
- (per serving) calories 72 | fat 6.6 | protein 3.8 | total carbs 8.3 | fiber 0.6

White Chocolate Cookies

Servings: 10 | Cooking Time: 11 Minutes

Ingredients:
- ¾ cup butter
- 1 ⅔ cups almond flour
- ½ cup coconut flour
- 2 tablespoons coconut oil
- ¾ cup granulated swerve
- ⅓ teaspoon ground anise star
- ⅓ teaspoon ground allspice
- ⅓ teaspoon grated nutmeg
- ¼ teaspoon fine sea salt
- 8 ounces (227 g) white chocolate, unsweetened
- 2 eggs, well beaten

Directions:
1. Put all of the above ingredients, minus 1 egg, into a mixing dish. Then, knead with hand until a soft dough is formed. Place in the refrigerator for 20 minutes.
2. Roll the chilled dough into small balls, flatten your balls and preheat the Air Fryer r to 350ºF.
3. Make an egg wash by using the remaining egg. Then, glaze the cookies with the egg wash, bake about 11 minutes. Bon appétit!

Nutrition:
- (per serving) calories 389 | fat 36.3 | protein 9.7 | total carbs 7 | fiber 1.1

Vanilla Scones

Servings: 6 | Cooking Time: 10 Minutes

Ingredients:
- 4 ounce coconut flour
- ½ teaspoon baking powder
- 1 teaspoon apple cider vinegar
- 2 teaspoons mascarpone
- ¼ cup heavy cream
- 1 teaspoon vanilla extract
- 1 tablespoon erythritol
- Cooking spray

Directions:
1. In the mixing bowl, mix coconut flour with baking powder, apple cider vinegar, mascarpone, heavy cream, vanilla extract, and erythritol.
2. Knead the dough and cut into scones.
3. Then put them in the air fryer basket and sprinkle with cooking spray.
4. Cook the vanilla scones at 365F (185ºC) for 10 minutes.

Nutrition:
- (per serving) calories 104 | fat 4 | protein 3 | total carbs 14 | fiber 6

Peanut Butter Cups With Coconut

Servings: 5 | Cooking Time: 4 Minutes

Ingredients:
- 1/3 cup coconut milk
- 2 tablespoon coconut flakes
- 2 tablespoon butter, melted
- 5 tablespoon peanut butter
- 3 tablespoon almond flour
- 1 pinch salt
- ½ teaspoon vanilla extract

Directions:
1. Combine the peanut butter and almond flour together.
2. Add salt and vanilla extract.
3. Cut the dough into 5 parts.
4. Place the dough into 5 ramekins in the shape of a pie crust.
5. Preheat the air fryer to 360 F and cook for 4 minutes.
6. Combine the coconut milk and coconut flakes.
7. Add butter and mix with a hand mixer.
8. Put the mixture in the freezer and chill for at least 10 minutes.
9. Remove the ramekins and allow to cool.
10. Pour the coconut milk mixture into the cooked pie crusts.
11. Serve or keep in the fridge.

Nutrition:
- (per serving) calories 205 | fat 19.1 | protein 5.4 | total carbs 5.3 | fiber 1.9

Made in United States
Troutdale, OR
12/02/2023

15230108R10084